Contents

The Burmese Labyrinth

A History of the Rohingya Tragedy

Carlos Sardiña Galache

VERSO
London • New York

First published by Verso 2020
© Carlos Sardiña Galache 2020

All rights reserved

The moral rights of the author have been asserted

The maps on pages vi and vii are reproduced with permission from *New Left Review*, where they first appeared in Mary Callahan's "Myanmar's Perpetual Junta."

1 3 5 7 9 10 8 6 4 2

Verso
UK: 6 Meard Street, London W1F 0EG
US: 20 Jay Street, Suite 1010, Brooklyn, NY 11201
versobooks.com

Verso is the imprint of New Left Books

ISBN-13: 978-1-78873-321-2
ISBN-13: 978-1-78873-320-5 (LIBRARY)
ISBN-13: 978-1-78873-322-9 (UK EBK)
ISBN-13: 978-1-78873-323-6 (US EBK)

British Library Cataloguing in Publication Data
A catalogue record for this book is available from the British Library

Library of Congress Cataloging-in-Publication Data
A catalog record for this book is available from the Library of Congress

Typeset in Minion Pro by Hewer Text UK Ltd, Edinburgh
Printed and bound by CPI Group (UK) Ltd, Croydon CR0 4YY

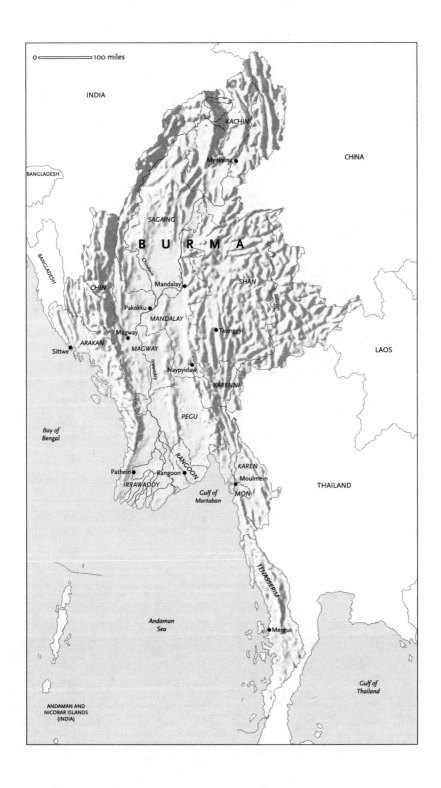

INDIA

BANGLADESH

CHINA

KACHIN

Myitkyina

SAGAING

B U R M A

Chindwin

CHIN

Mandalay

SHAN

Salween

Pakokku

MANDALAY

Magway

Taunggyi

Sittwe

ARAKAN

MAGWAY

Irrawaddy

Naypyidaw

LAOS

KARENNI

Bay of
Bengal

PEGU

KAREN

Pathein

RANGOON

Rangoon

Moulmein

THAILAND

IRRAWADDY

Gulf of
Martaban

MON

TENASSERIM

Andaman
Sea

Mergui

Gulf of
Thailand

ANDAMAN AND
NICOBAR ISLANDS
(INDIA)

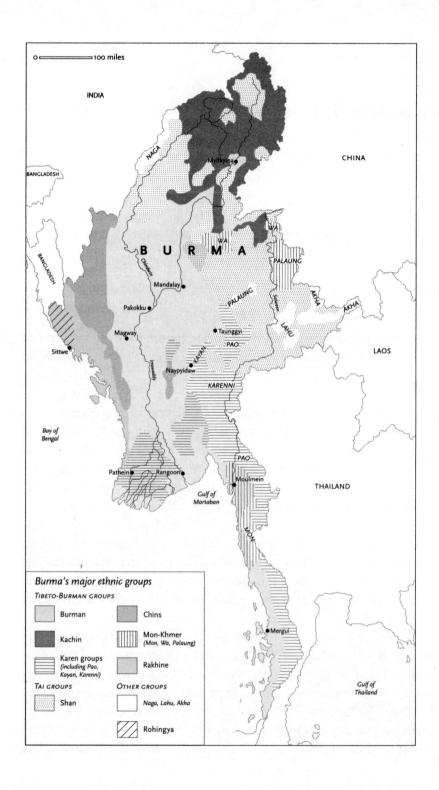

0 ⊏══════⊐ 100 miles

INDIA

BANGLADESH

CHINA

NAGA

Myitkyina

WA

WA

B U R M A

PALAUNG

BANGLADESH

Chindwin

Mandalay

PALAUNG

AKHA

AKHA

Pakokku

Magway

Taunggyi

PAO

LAHU

LAOS

Irrawaddy

Sittwe

KAYAN

Naypyidaw

Bay of
Bengal

KARENNI

Pathein

Rangoon

PAO

Moulmein

THAILAND

Gulf of
Martaban

MON

Mergui

Gulf of
Thailand

Burma's major ethnic groups

TIBETO-BURMAN GROUPS

- Burman
- Kachin
- Karen groups
  *(including Pao,
  Kayan, Karenni)*

TAI GROUPS

- Shan

- Chins
- Mon-Khmer
  (Mon, Wa, Palaung)
- Rakhine

OTHER GROUPS

- Naga, Lahu, Akha
- Rohingya

Note on Burmese Terms

In 1989, the military junta ruling Burma changed the official name of the country, and those of several regions and cities, returning them to their old names in the literary Burmese language. By the Adaptation of Expressions Law, both 'Burma' and 'Burmese' were changed to 'Myanmar'. The change only affected languages other than Burmese, as 'Myanmar' had been the official name of the country in the language of the Burman majority. One of the explanations was that 'Burma' had been imposed by the British colonial power. But that was not entirely true, since 'Burma' is just a transliteration of the less formal word for the country in Burmese, and not a new name imposed by the colonial over-lord – as is the case, for example, of 'the Philippines', a completely new name coined by the Spaniards in honour of the conquering King Philip II. In reality, 'Burma' and 'Myanmar' mean exactly the same, and asking speakers of other languages to use one instead of the other is the equivalent of asking non-German-speakers to use 'Deutschland' instead of 'Germany'.

The United Nations and some governments accepted the change, but many other countries and the international media continued to call the country 'Burma'. There was a time when choosing one term or the other had political connotations, as Aung San Suu Kyi had opposed the change. But 'Myanmar' has become internationally accepted since the transition in 2012. Throughout this book, I will use the name 'Burma', except when quoting other writers or public documents where

'Myanmar' is used. This is both a matter of personal preference and a function of the fact that, for most of the long period covered in the book, the country was known as Burma.

The name of the state of 'Arakan' was changed to 'Rakhine' in 1983, probably to please Rakhine nationalists. Throughout this book, I use 'Arakan' to refer to the state, and 'Rakhine' to refer to the majority ethnic group in Arakan, as I understand Arakan, the place, to have more inclusive connotations.

The majority group in the country is called 'Bamar' or 'Burman'. I have opted for 'Burman' because it is consistent with the use of Burma rather than Myanmar. 'Burmese' refers to any citizen of the country, regardless of ethnicity. But the Burmese language is that spoken by the Burman majority. In colonial times, it was the other way round: 'Burmese' was used for the ethnic group 'Burman'. I have noted this when necessary. It is also worth pointing out that many members of the ethnic minorities use 'Burmese' when referring to the 'Burmans'. This shows the extent of confusion about national identity and the failure to create a multi-ethnic Burmese nationalism.

In some press reports and books that adopt the 'Myanmar' terminology, some names are different to those used in this book. I show here the equivalent variants of the most important names for states and cities used throughout the book (others, such as Kachin, are the same in both terminologies):

Burma (country)/Burmese (citizens of, language)	Myanmar
Burman (ethnic group)	Bamar
Rangoon (city)	Yangon
Arakan (state)/Arakanese (ethnic group)	Rakhine
Irrawaddy (river and division)	Ayeyarwady
Karen (both state and ethnic group)	Kayin
Karenni (both state and ethnic group)	Kayah
Moulmein (city)	Mawlamyine
Tenasserim (division)	Tanintharyi

Members of ethnic groups like the Burman, Mon or Rakhine, do not have surnames, so their names are repeated in full every time they are mentioned – with the exception of Aung San Suu Kyi, who is often called simply 'Suu Kyi'. Other ethnic groups like the Kachin or Chin names do often include family or clan names, and sometimes individuals may be referred to only by their surnames.

The Burmese often use honorifics determined by the relative age or social status of the person addressing them. For instance, to refer to a mature woman, or one holding a senior position, the speaker would add 'Daw' (as in 'Daw Aung San Suu Kyi', used often in Burmese media). For senior men, either by age or position, 'U' is commonly added (as in 'U Nu'). Further examples of these honorifics include the following:

Daw	for mature women and/or women occupying senior positions (roughly equivalent to 'aunt' or 'Ms')
Ma	for young women or women of roughly the same age as the speaker (roughly equivalent to 'sister' or 'Ms')
U	for mature men and/or men occupying senior positions (roughly equivalent to 'uncle' or 'Mr')
Ko	for young men or men of roughly similar age to the speaker (roughly equivalent to 'brother')
Maung	for younger men, often part of the name
Saya	for teachers or older men with special status
Ashin	for monks
Sayadaw	for senior monks
Bo	for military commanders
Bogyoke	for military generals
Thakin	'master', used by the nationalists in the 1930s and 1940s to indicate that they were the masters of their own country

I have not used these honorifics except in cases when they are so closely associated with the name of the person that they are rarely omitted (as in the case of the first prime minister of independent Burma, U Nu), or when quoting others using them.

Introduction: Trapped in the Burmese Labyrinth

How can we understand the violence and turmoil in Burma during most of the last decade, particularly the brutal ethnic cleansing of the Rohingya, a Muslim minority living in the west of the country? This has been a period of profound political and social changes in the country. Since 2011, the military junta that had ruled for decades has dissolved itself, the army loosened its tight grip on power, and initiated a carefully managed transition to a pseudo-democratic system. As a consequence, while maintaining considerable control over the state apparatus, the military allowed a degree of opening that resulted in new freedoms that the Burmese had not enjoyed for decades.

I visited the country for the first time in late 2010, only a few months before the change of regime, and travelled there often as a journalist in subsequent years to cover the transformations brought by the transition. It was an exciting time to work on the country, and I was able to visit areas hitherto out of limits and interview people who had been virtually silent, or silenced, for decades. At times, reporting on such changes gave one a heady feeling of discovery, but this excitement was often tempered by the cold realities of a nation that continued to be in turmoil: war, murderous intercommunal conflict, and deep-seated hatreds being expressed openly, which were ultimately acted upon in the most brutal manner.

This was most starkly seen in 2012, when sectarian violence erupted in the impoverished state of Arakan, in the west of the country. The conflict was between the Rohingya community and the state's majority, the Buddhist Rakhine. Dozens, possibly hundreds, were killed as mobs from one community fell upon the other. Entire neighbourhoods were razed to the ground; tens of thousands lost their houses, seeking refuge in camps for internally displaced persons. The Rohingya, who had been severely oppressed by the military for decades, bore the brunt of the violence, and it soon emerged that the security forces had often sided with the Rakhine mobs attacking them.

The Rohingya were clearly the main victims, but that was not how they were seen by many in Burma. There is a widespread perception in the country that the Rohingya constitute a foreign threat to be contained at all costs. In the years following 2012, anti-Rohingya sentiment increased throughout the country, and the government dramatically ramped up the policies of exclusion and apartheid they had imposed for decades. In 2017, this culminated in the violent ethnic cleansing of more than three-fifths of the Rohingya population by the Burmese military.

A few weeks after the 2012 riots I visited Sittwe, Arakan state's capital, and interviewed several people from both communities. I saw how whole quarters had been destroyed, and witnessed the misery in the camps where most Rohingya from the city had been confined – and still are. At that time, the National League for Democracy (NLD) – the party led by Aung San Suu Kyi, the revered leader of the pro-democracy opposition during the dark years of dictatorship – had placed a few MPs in parliament in a by-election held a few months before, including Suu Kyi herself. The party had little weight in parliament, but everybody expected it to dominate following the next general election, as indeed it did. I had met and interviewed some members of the party, including its leader, and felt a deep sympathy and respect for their struggle. Admittedly, their politics were somewhat vague, the personality cult around Suu Kyi seemed excessive, and the party was lacking in internal democracy. But those were traits I and many others were willing to overlook or explain away as stemming from the tremendous challenges it faced in its fight against the military dictatorship. Nevertheless, the party's commitment to human rights and dignity seemed beyond doubt. It was, therefore, a shock when I enquired about the crisis in Arakan, and found almost invariably that NLD members shared the same assumptions about the Rohingya as Rakhine nationalists, government officials and, by all indications, large sections of Burmese society.

Understanding the roots of those prejudices became a sort of obsession for me, and for the next years it would be the main focus of my work. How could people who had made great sacrifices in the name of freedom, human rights and democracy harbour such hatred against a vulnerable and persecuted minority? Why had a beleaguered minority like the Rohingya come to be so reviled, and even feared, by so many people in the country? And, probably most centrally, how had national and ethnic identities come to be construed in the country?

The answers to these questions might explain how some of the horrors I had covered could possibly have happened. Of course, understanding violence and racial hatred does not mean condoning or justifying them. On the contrary, I believe that understanding the sources of such hatred and the barbarity to which it may lead is a moral endeavour and a precondition of fighting it. Sometimes the savagery to which those racial hatreds lead is impossible to comprehend. The cruelty many Rohingya have suffered defies language and logic, as it comes from the darkest depths of the human soul. But such hatred and savagery are only activated and made 'permissible' in a certain combination of circumstances. If we are to have any hope of understanding such behaviour, we need to investigate those circumstances – historical, social, political and psychological. To find answers to all those questions, it is necessary to look beyond Arakan, to other conflicts in Burma that at first sight might seem detached from what has happened there.

When the first wave of sectarian violence was sweeping Arakan in June 2012, I happened to be several hundreds of kilometres to the north-east, in the hills of Kachin state. I was in the territory along the Chinese border controlled by the Kachin Independence Army (KIA), an ethno-ationalist armed group that had been fighting the Burmese military (known as the Tatmadaw) intermittently for five decades in the cause of self-determination for the Kachin people, a mostly Christian ethnic group. One year before, a precarious ceasefire between the two armies that had lasted for seventeen years had been broken, and the state was at war again. I had travelled there to report on the protracted conflict, which had displaced tens of thousands from their homes. The Kachin were hospitable hosts, and they went to great lengths to explain why they wanted independence, or at least autonomy, for their Kachin land, and why they did not regard themselves as belonging to the same nation as the Burmans – the most numerous and dominant ethnic group in the country.

But the KIA was not the only ethno-nationalist group fighting the government. Throughout Burma's short history as an independent nation-state, many others had fought Burman domination. The Shan, the Karen, the Wa, the Mon, the Karenni, the Chin, the Rakhine and the Rohingya themselves – virtually every ethnic group in the country – have all at some point produced an armed insurgency, and some were still active during the transition. As a result, large areas of the country's borderlands are beyond the control of the central state. At the beginning of the transition, more than six decades after independence, the project of building a Burmese nation looked very much like a failure.

One year later, in 2013, a new wave of intercommunal violence erupted, this time in the plains of Central Burma. Angry Buddhist mobs attacked Muslim quarters in several towns and cities. The violence was not directed at the Rohingya – a group the overwhelming majority of Muslims outside Arakan do not belong to – but at Muslims in general, both for their religion and for not being regarded as Burmese. The violence had been partly incited by extremist Buddhist monks expounding a hateful brand of nationalism, who had spread a variety of paranoid theories about the threat of an Islamic conspiracy to take over the country. Those extremist monks were at the forefront of a succession of ultra-nationalist movements that came to play a prominent role in Burmese politics during the transition, largely dictating the terms of public debate.

These issues – the plight of Rohingya, the wars in the borderlands (especially involving the Kachin), and a sometimes deadly Buddhist ultranationalism deploying very narrow criteria about who belongs in the country – constitute the main threads traced in this book. These three problems have usually been analysed separately, or the anti-Muslim violence in central Burma has been understood as a mere extension of the anti-Rohingya violence in Arakan – and, while each has its own specific dynamic and history, the three phenomena cannot be completely separated. In many ways they are interconnected, often feeding each other. All of them pertain to notions of belonging and nationalism, and to the ways in which these forces have shaped a country perpetually at war with itself.

This is one of the reasons why this book devotes more space to the conflict in Arakan and to the Rohingya than to other issues in the country. The liminal case of the 'excluded' is symptomatic of how the Burmese define themselves; every nationalism is just as concerned with who belongs to the nation as it is with who does not. The conflict in Arakan and the exclusion of the Rohingya thus serve to throw light on conflicts elsewhere in Burma.

The structure of this book reproduces the way I have approached Burma over the years, as a journalist covering contemporary developments, but often diverted to a study of the past in an attempt to find clues to its present enigmas.

Part I covers the period between the beginning of the democratic opening in 2011 to the election in 2015, which the NLD won by a land-slide. The year 2011 was a dramatic turning point in the country's recent history, which in many ways seemed to be a new beginning for a country that had suffered several false starts since its independence in 1948. It was a period in which the speed of history seemed to have been accelerated after decades of apparent stagnation under the military dictatorship. It is during this period that the immediate causes of the ethnic cleansing of the Rohingya, as well as the resumption of the war in Kachin state or the emergence of Buddhist ultra-nationalism, are broadly to be found, though their historical roots are of course deeper.

In Part II I rely mostly on secondary sources. It is an attempt to explain the history of the territory that we know as Burma in order to illuminate how that past affects the present, as well as how it has been interpreted, and often manipulated, for present political purposes. I rely here almost exclusively on secondary sources.

Part III takes up the narrative pursued in Part I, covering the period from late 2015 to 2019. During this time, while Aung San Suu Kyi and the NLD were in power, the war continued in Kachin State and the Rohingya suffered a brutal campaign of ethnic cleansing at the hands of the military, pushing a majority of them into neighbouring Bangladesh.

I do not believe that Burma's past has determined its present in a mechanical, inflexible way. Many trends could have gone in other directions if chance and free human choices had been different. History is not characterized by an ineluctable fate beyond the control of its protagonists; but it does largely condition the sorts of choices available to them. As Karl Marx famously wrote: 'Men make their own history, but they do not make it as they please; they do not make it under self-selected circumstances, but under circumstances existing already, given and transmitted from the past. The tradition of all dead generations weighs like a nightmare on the brains of the living.'

The title of this book pays homage to *The Spanish Labyrinth*, written by the British author Gerald Brennan in the aftermath of the biggest tragedy that hit my country in the twentieth century: the civil war that ravaged Spain between 1936 and 1939, leading to four decades of National–Catholic dictatorship. Brennan wrote on the background of the war, attempting to make sense of how a country that fascinated him so much had sunk to such depths of savagery. The book became a classic of Spanish studies in my country and abroad, and its translation was widely, and clandestinely, circulated in Spain during the years of Francoist dictatorship. Like Brennan, I write about a country that is not mine, but that I have come to feel close to, in spite of the huge cultural differences it has from my own, and the sadness I may feel about its many tragedies.

It seems to me that Burma, like many other countries, is trapped in its own labyrinth – a labyrinth composed of wars, dangerous delusions, unaddressed grievances, furious hatreds and power structures that leave most of its inhabitants impoverished in virtually every sense. The Burmese people are trying to find their way out of that maze, and if they seem to be unable to find the exit, it is precisely because many of them are trapped inside and can see only its confining walls, and not its over-all shape. In this book, I try to offer both a sense of how different people see things from inside such a labyrinth, by giving voice to the people I have interviewed over the years, and a general vision of the historical, cultural, social and political forces that have shaped it.

Brennan was not Spanish, and I am not Burmese. When I read Brennan's book, I often felt that there were things he just did not under-stand – that only a Spaniard could possibly appreciate; some of his generalizations annoyed me at times. I can imagine that any Burmese reading this book may have similar feelings, and I can only apologise in advance, and assure them that I have tried my best to understand the country. But at his best moments, it was precisely Brennan's detachment that produced insights that only a foreigner, seeing things 'from outside', could offer. That is partly why his book remains readable seven decades after its publication. This book is written from a similar position of detachment – but one that does not represent any attempt to be 'neutral'. Most conflicts in Burma, particularly in Arakan, revolve around clashes of historical narratives, and my intention is not to present the versions of 'all sides' without critically examining them. Ultimately, the motivation of this book is the hope of adding something of value, however small, to the collective endeavour of mapping the Burmese labyrinth. My hope is that this endeavour might help *all* the people of Burma to cast off the dead weight of history.

PART I

'Discipline-Flourishing Democracy'

1

The Transition

The transition to a 'discipline-flourishing democracy' started with an election, held on 7 November 2010. The event hardly seemed promising at the time. Few thought that it would herald a period of deep change in the country. It seemed unthinkable that an extremely repressive and deeply entrenched military dictatorship might voluntarily relinquish its power, even partially. The election itself was a tightly controlled affair, and was conducted without any transparency. Few journalists covered the election from within the country, and most of those who did so travelled clandestinely, at a moment in which it was nearly impossible to obtain a media visa.

No international observers were present, and the election was widely condemned as a sham. The results were as unsurprising as they were unlikely: the Union Solidarity and Development Party (USDP), a proxy for the military, won 50.7 per cent of the votes, and the National Unity Party, an older proxy party of the military founded in 1988, came second, with 19.3 per cent. Both parties represented a regime widely despised by most of the population, and it was difficult to believe that they could possibly have come out on top in a free and fair election.

Few doubted that the National League for Democracy (NLD) would have emerged as the victor in any fair election. For many Burmese, it was the only party that could possibly represent their democratic aspirations. Over the past twenty-two years, millions of Burmans – the majority ethnic group in the country – had placed their faith in the NLD, or more accurately, in its leader, the charismatic Aung San Suu Kyi, as the saviour of the country. Daughter of Aung San, who led the country to independence from the British in the aftermath of World War II, Suu Kyi had established herself as the leader of the pro-democratic opposition to military rule in 1988, when a massive wave of urban protests had overthrown the dictatorship of General Ne Win, who was replaced by a no-less-dictatorial military junta. Her party won an election in 1990, yet the generals refused to acknowledge the results, and she was forced to spend most of the subsequent years under house arrest for her political opposition. During this period of seclusion her mystique as a human rights icon, both within Burma and abroad, only grew. In 1991 she was awarded the Nobel Peace Prize. At the time of the 2010 election, she was still locked in her house, a lakeside villa in Rangoon where she had spent a great part of her childhood.

The NLD was undoubtedly the most popular party in the country, at least among the Burman majority, but it had decided to boycott the election. In April, the NLD had issued a statement announcing its decision on the basis that 'the electoral laws issued by the [State Peace and Development Council] are unfair and unjust'. It also criticized the Constitution, stating that 'forcing parties to pledge to obey and abide [by] the 2008 Constitution is a violation of democracy and human rights'.[1] The electoral laws made the process of registering a party extremely cumbersome, and the decision to accept parties was made by an Election Commission controlled by the junta. It was also very expensive: the parties had to pay US$500 to register each candidate, meaning that they would have to pay the huge total of US$580,000 if they wished to compete for every available seat.[2] But the main objection was to the law that banned anyone with a criminal conviction from being a member of a registered party. Most of the party leaders were political prisoners or former political prisoners. The rules were clear: if the NLD wanted to register for the elections, it had to purge its most prominent members, including Suu Kyi herself.

If the electoral law was hardly democratic, the 2008 Constitution was no more so. The process of drafting it had taken decades, and the NLD had played no significant role in it. After the NLD electoral victory in 1990, nothing happened for three years. Finally, in 1993, when the junta allowed a National Convention to draft the new Constitution, its composition did not reflect the results of the election, as most of its members were appointed by the military. Eventually, in 1996, the party of Suu Kyi boycotted the drafting process, and the Convention was suspended for eight years. When it convened again in 2004, the NLD did not participate.

It took four years to draft the new Constitution, and it was approved in a popular referendum held in 2008. In the days ahead of the referendum, a devastating cyclone hit the southern coast of the country, killing at least 138,000 people in the Burma Delta. It was the biggest natural catastrophe in the nation's history, and the refusal of the military junta to accept any international aid for three weeks provoked a diplomatic uproar. In spite of the disaster, the junta went ahead with the referendum one week later, postponing it for three weeks in the most affected areas. The new constitution was approved by an improbable 92 per cent of the votes.

The Constitution was clearly designed to provide legal cover to the military's permanent control over the country. It reserves 25 per cent of seats in parliament to unelected military officers appointed by the commander-in-chief of the armed forces. This military bloc makes any constitutional change extremely difficult, and dependent on the authorization of the military, as any major amendment requires 'the prior approval of more than seventy-five per cent of all the representatives of the Pyidaungsu Hluttaw [both houses of parliament], after which in a nation-wide referendum only with the votes of more than half of those who are eligible to vote'.[3]

Moreover, the Tatmadaw (as the Burmese army is known locally) would retain a great measure of executive power through the appointment of the three most important ministers – those in the Ministry of Home Affairs, the Ministry of Defence and the Ministry of Border Affairs – headed by Defence Service personnel nominated by the commander-in-chief of the armed forces.[4] The three security ministries are under the control of the military, while the Ministry of Home Affairs also included the General Administration Department (GAD) – the ubiquitous and all-powerful government body that controls bureaucracy and administration at all levels.[5]

There was also a clause in the Constitution seemingly designed to prevent Suu Kyi from ever ruling the country. Article 59d of the Constitution asserts that the president 'shall he himself, one of the parents, the spouse, one of the legitimate children or their spouses not owe allegiance to a foreign power, not be subject of a foreign power or citizen of a foreign country'.[6] This immediately excluded Suu Kyi, as she was the widow of a British citizen and had two British sons.

If the generals had designed the Constitution to ensure that the military kept a great deal of power to the detriment of any civilian government, they had also designed it to preserve a highly centralized state and make only marginal concessions to the ethnic groups that had been demanding independence, or at least greater autonomy within a federal state, since the British had left Burma in 1948. Burma is home to enormous ethno-linguistic diversity. The Burmans are the majority in the central regions, but the country's border areas are rugged mountainous landscapes with a bewildering variety of ethno-linguistic groups, many of which have attempted to evade central government control since independence in 1948.

Since then, most of these ethnic groups have formed armed organizations to resist attempts by the Burman-dominated government to unify the state. Some continue to do so, making the armed conflicts in the borderlands of Burma among the longest running in the world. Conflicts of variable intensity have always been a crucial part of the lives of the inhabitants of some of those remote areas, isolated from the rest of the country by poor communications and infrastructure. Often the only Burmans those living in the rural border areas have met are soldiers, or the administrators of a repressive state who accompany them.

Consequently, many among the non-Burman groups bitterly resent the domination imposed by the Burmans after independence, and the new political order designed by the generals failed to address their grievances. The Constitution divided the country between seven Burman-majority 'regions' in Burma's heartland and seven 'states' in the periphery, named after the majority ethnic group inhabiting them; but the two types of territory enjoy similar status and autonomy. Neither regions nor states can enact their own constitution or laws, and the most senior authority in each of them, the chief minister, has to be appointed by the president of the country.[7] Moreover, the chief minister is not necessarily, in practice, the most powerful figure in a state or regional government, since the GAD and the security forces are constitutionally under the complete control of the Tatmadaw.

Before the election, the junta had been putting pressure on the ethnic armed organizations, some of which had maintained fragile ceasefires for years, to become border-guarding forces under the command of the military. The strongest and most important armed groups refused the order, insisting that their political demands had not been met. This created friction that included a small conflict between the army and a faction of a Karen rebel army on the border with Thailand, which sent more than 10,000 refugees to the neighbouring country the day after the election.[8] Nevertheless, the junta allowed some ethnic parties to run in the election, though it selected them carefully; some, like the Kachin people, would have no voice in parliament in the upcoming administration.

In other states, ethnic parties attained more than 25 per cent of the vote. One of the most successful was the Rakhine Nationalities Development Party (RNDP), a forerunner of the Arakan National Party (ANP), representing the Rakhine Buddhist community in Arakan. Arakan is a complex state, the second-poorest in the country, and is deeply fractured along ethno-religious lines. The rift between its two main communities, Rakhine Buddhists and Rohingya Muslims, has grown during the transition period, despite the fact that the two communities have lived side by side for generations. It is often overlooked that the Rakhine, despite closing ranks with the Burmese state and military when it comes to opposing the Rohingya, are fiercely against the domination of the Burmans, whom they regard as their oppressors. They have a strong argument for such resentment in relation, for instance, to the natural resources in their state – mainly the huge gas reserves off the coast, which the central government has exploited with the help of international companies, yielding little or no benefit to the local population.

Burmans and Rakhine share the Buddhist religion and a very similar language; but for most of its history Arakan was an independent kingdom, until the late eighteenth century, when it was conquered by the Burmans. Among all the ethnic groups in the country, the Rakhine are perhaps the most similar, linguistically and culturally, to the Burmans. But despite this, or perhaps because of it, they are among the groups most vociferously assertive of their differences and autonomist aspirations. Rakhine nationalists often say that they are sandwiched between the Burmese government and the Rohingya, whom they and many others in Burma often call 'Bengalis', indicating their purported foreign origins. The resentment against one feeds the resentment against the other, in what is in reality a triangular conflict pitting three groups against the other: Rakhine, Burman and Rohingya.

The Rohingya Muslims, who had been stripped of citizenship by the military junta, were allowed to vote in 2010. There were even two Rohingya parties, the National Democratic Party for Development (NDPD) and the National Development and Peace Party (NDPP), the latter widely assumed to be a proxy of the military. These parties campaigned mostly in the Rohingya-majority townships of Northern Arakan, along the border with Bangladesh. There were reports that the NDPD had come under pressure from state officials to prevent it from campaigning, and even that villagers were threatened with eviction if they voted for it.[9] Eventually, two Rohingya would sit in parliament – both members of the USDP. Paradoxically, during the subsequent period, in which the Rohingya community would suffer a rapid process of complete disenfranchisement, they also had representation in parliament for the first time in decades, and one of their MPs, Shwe Maung, would be a vocal critic of the government. It was widely assumed that the Rohingya were being allowed to vote in 2010 in order to prevent the Rakhine nationalists from attaining too much power; but it is also true that the Rohingya had been allowed to vote in every election or referendum held in Burma since independence. In any case, Rakhine nationalists resented that the Rohingya had a political voice at a crucial moment of transition in which the future of the country was at stake, and this may partly explain the role that Rakhine nationalists would play in the intercommunal riots two years later.

By late 2010, there remained little doubt that the new political order was scarcely conducive to fulfilling either the autonomist goals of the ethnic minorities or the democratic aspirations of the Burman majority. Nobody expected much from the new president, Thein Sein, a quiet man of the old regime who had been prime minister (a mostly ceremonial position) under the military junta. But in fact his government would introduce far-reaching political and economic reforms. During this period, the country changed at breakneck speed: hundreds of political prisoners were released; the opposition was allowed to conduct its activities more or less freely; freedom of speech was relatively respected, as the government relaxed restrictions on the media; mobile phones and access to the internet, both virtually nonexistent before 2012, spread throughout the country. Most crucially, the parliament turned out to be more open and assertive than had been thought possible. Burma, a pariah country shunned by the Western democracies for more than two decades, was now welcomed into the 'international community' with open arms. The United States and the European Union gradually lifted the sanctions they had imposed, and foreign investors began to flock to the country.

The transition came as a surprise that elicited much speculation over the motivations of the military. Some argued that it was due to geopolitical considerations, as Burma had come to rely too much on China as a consequence of Western sanctions and isolation.[10] Pro-democracy activists abroad claimed that the sanctions had pushed the generals to introduce reforms. Thein Sein has said that the move was necessary to lift the country from its economic backwardness.[11] The Burmese military is notoriously opaque, and the real causes of this period of rapid political change are difficult to know. There were probably many reasons to launch the reforms, but one thing is certain: the generals loosened their grip and allowed the transition to take place not from a position of weakness, but from the position of overwhelming strength they had achieved over many years.[12] By the time of the election in 2010, after decades of crushing the opposition and strengthening itself, the military was the only well-established institution in the country, so it could afford to cede some of its power in the confidence that it would retain a pre-eminent position.

As the transition progressed, it would become increasingly clear that it was irreversible – albeit within limits that, in moments of euphoria, were not quite visible. But the transition would also bring to light complexities and dark aspects of Burmese society to which very few had previously paid attention: the intercommunal violence in Arakan and beyond; the emergence of an extremely exclusionary brand of Burman ethno-nationalism that seemed to permeate every stratum of society; and the ambiguous, and sometimes explicitly racist, positions taken by the pro-democracy camp and long-time defenders of human rights. All of this contradicted what one author has termed the 'neat, if overly simplified, plotline of bad military versus good citizenry'[13] that many foreign journalists and external observers, including me, had long taken almost for granted.

Before the transition period, the most common narrative on Burma was that of a democratic opposition led by a courageous and graceful woman, heroically combating by nonviolent means a brutal and cruel regime led by a clique of thuggish generals. Admittedly, quite what the ideology of Aung San Suu Kyi and her party was had never been clear, and nor had her vision of the country's future, beyond some platitudes about human rights, democracy and freedom. But it was easy to believe that her heart was in the right place; and the sacrifices that she and many pro-democracy activists, who had endured years of jail, were clear proof of their courage and commitment.

The many conflicts with ethnic minorities in the country's periphery were seen either as some sort of subplot, subsumed within the central epic story of democracy versus dictatorship, or as part of the same struggle, on the assumption that Suu Kyi's NLD and the ethnic groups were on the same side. The plight of the Rohingya minority, in many respects unique, barely registered, or was seen as part of the wider struggle of the minorities for their rights. The communal cleavages that in the past had violently pitted Rakhine against Rohingya in Arakan, or Buddhists against Muslims in central Burma, were little understood, and were often explained away as mere manipulations by the military. At times they probably had been orchestrated by the military; but the military was exploiting deep divisions that pre-dated its rise to power, and – as would become clear during the transition – were more pervasive in Burmese society than most foreigners had realized.

Such distortions and simplifications, as well as the idealization of Suu Kyi and the pro-democracy camp, had to do with the fact that the country had been largely closed to foreigners, but also with the way many of us approached the issue. Orientalist fantasizing surely played its role, but the point of entry to Burma was equally important, if not more so. This was usually not Burma itself, but Mae Sot, a Thai town on the Burmese border where a sizable Burmese community has lived for decades. Most of the Burmese people living in Mae Sot are labourers working in garment factories, or refugees of all ethnicities living in a camp nearby. But our contacts were usually either Burman political exiles, many of whom had fled the country after spending years in Burma's prisons as political prisoners, or activists of ethnic minorities, mostly Karen, either belonging to or closely associated with the Karen National Union (KNU). In a sense, Mae Sot was a distorted microcosm of Burma. Karen and Burman activists lived alongside one another, often working and socialising together. It was not uncommon to share a drink with groups that would include, say, a former Karen guerrilla and a Burman ex-political prisoner, both of whom would share a loathing for the military regime, appear to share the same goals, and express similar admiration for Aung San Suu Kyi.

It was self-evident that the military dictatorship was the common enemy, and that would lead many of us to assume that the same goals were shared by the pro-democracy camp, mostly ethnic Burmans, and the Karen insurgents – and by extension other ethnic groups. At that time, few politically conscious members of the ethnic minorities had much reason to distrust Aung San Suu Kyi. While everybody knew that the NLD was a pre-eminently Burman party, it was fair to allow it the benefit of any doubt, given that it had never held power and had made vague promises of federalism.

As journalists, our next step usually included an incursion into the territories held in Burma by the Karen guerrillas – or by some other group, such as the Shan or Kachin – along the Thai or Chinese borders. These were trips on which the reporter would be embedded with armed groups keen to present a positive image of themselves. Moreover, in central Burma, travelling as undercover journalists with tourist visas, who could potentially expose anybody talking to us to danger, we would mostly interview NLD politicians or other pro-democracy activists loosely associated with the party. It is unlikely that those sources were willingly misleading us; most of them were probably sincerely committed to the causes they claimed to defend. But they offered us a very narrow picture of the country, and we often had only ourselves to blame. We rarely asked 'hard questions', or talked with government officials, who in our stories remained the faceless bad guys lurking in the shadows. Many of us had formed an idealized image of Burma, and most of our contacts and sources were happy to help us to confirm it again and again.

I was beholden to that image when I travelled to Rangoon for the first time, in November 2010. It was just a few weeks after the election, and Aung San Suu Kyi had recently been released from house arrest. The NLD headquarters was a ramshackle building not far from the iconic Shwedagon Pagoda, constantly watched by secret policemen sitting in a tea shop across the street. Most members of the party I interviewed in the headquarters were former political prisoners with harrowing stories about the harsh conditions they had endured in jail, generally narrated in an almost casual manner. It was difficult not to sympathize with their cause, even though the party had an excessive resemblance to a personality cult devoted to Aung San Suu Kyi, often described as 'our great leader'.

The first man I interviewed there was the legendary U Win Tin. Born in Central Burma in 1930, Win Tin had worked as a journalist for most of his life. He had been the editor-in-chief of a couple of newspapers, including one that was closed in 1978 for its critical coverage of the Ne Win regime. In 1988 he took an active role in the popular uprising that toppled Ne Win, and was one of the cofounders of the NLD. He was said to have been one of the key figures in convincing Aung San Suu Kyi to join the struggle for democracy. After that, he had spent almost nineteen years in jail, at times in solitary confinement in a dog cell. He was an affable man who would wear the blue shirt that all prisoners wear in Burma's jails as a gesture of solidarity until his death in 2014. If Suu Kyi was often described as the 'mother' of the pro-democracy camp in Burma, U Win Tin was surely its 'father'.

The NLD was in a very precarious position in those days. After it refused to register for the election, the government warned its members that they could not carry on with any political activity and were only allowed to do 'social work'. Even in the worst years of persecution by the military, the NLD had been recognized as a political party – though this had rarely implied the freedom to organize or campaign. But now, for the first time since its founding, it had been explicitly outlawed as a party, or at least put into a dangerous legal limbo. 'The government has told us that we can become an NGO or something like that, but we cannot do that: this is a political party, and the most popular in the country for that matter, as we won the last free elections with an overwhelming victory', U Win Tin told me, referring to the party's victory in 1990. 'For the moment we don't know if the government is allowing us to work because of the international support we enjoy or they are waiting for the right time to attack us. Maybe they are waiting to convene the parliament and form the new government to take action against us. We don't really know, we are waiting to see what happens. In any case, when Daw Aung San Suu Kyi was released it was clearly demonstrated that she enjoys the support of most of our country and the international community', he added.

A few months later, in August 2011, I had the chance to interview 'the Lady' – as Suu Kyi is widely known – in the same ramshackle building. With her aristocratic demeanour and unfailing politeness, Suu Kyi impressed a young journalist like me with a charisma that had been built over the years not only by her, but also by the adoration she inspired in many Burmese people, and the admiration with which the overwhelming majority of foreign journalists wrote about her. The uncertainty about where the transition was leading and the role that the NLD could play in it had not changed since my previous visit. Suu Kyi was vague about the plans for the party and its political philosophy, and I interpreted such vagueness as caution. 'I always say that I am cautiously optimistic. If one is engaged in the kind of work we do, surely we should do it with certain degree of optimism; one has to believe that the goals are not only necessary but also attainable. We believe we can change things, and that's only possible through negotiation and national reconciliation', she said. When I asked her to describe what kind of democracy she aspired to build, she replied vaguely that there is democracy 'when people's voices are heard', so I pushed her on the concept's ideological underpinnings. 'The universal declaration of human rights', she replied.

It was difficult to predict at that time, but that situation of uncertainty and legal precariousness did not last for long. A couple of weeks later, in August 2011, Aung San Suu Kyi met Thein Sein; this was the first of several meetings in successive months. The contents of those conversations remain a mystery, as well as the concessions that both sides would be willing to make. But the NLD was allowed to enter the political arena.

In a by-election held in April 2012, the NLD gained almost all of the disputed forty-five seats in parliament, including one for Suu Kyi herself. Western countries had based their policies towards Burma on indications made by Aung San Suu Kyi, or on how she was treated. Such policies had been mostly punitive, including sanctions and embargoes, at least since the late nineties. But the fact that she was now a member of parliament, and her party a legal political force, provided, in the eyes of the so-called 'international community', a veneer of legitimacy to the transition designed by the generals. She was even allowed to travel abroad, and foreign dignitaries also visited her and others in Burma during the period.

The main strategy of Suu Kyi over this period was to seek the reconciliation she had mentioned in our interview, and that meant primarily reconciliation between her party and the military. Two years after the beginning of the transition, something happened that would previously have been unthinkable: she attended a military parade on Armed Forces Day in the capital, Naypyidaw, surrounded by the generals of the same army that had kept her captive for almost fifteen years.[14] Her rapprochement with the military should not have come as a surprise. In her first major speech, during the heady days of the 1988 uprising, when she entered politics, she had said that she felt a 'strong attachment for the armed forces', as 'not only were they built up by my father, as a child I was cared for by his soldiers'.[15] The personal is often political when it comes to 'the Lady'.

A defining moment for the new Burma, and for Suu Kyi herself, came when she visited Salingyi Township, in Sagaing Division, in 2013. A typical township of the rural areas of central Burma, Salingyi was afflicted by a problem all too common throughout Burma: the eviction of farmers from their lands to make way for mega-projects or big business in the name of economic development. Suu Kyi played a role that would lead to a situation without precedent in the country: people in Salingyi would protest against her – and they would do so spontaneously, without being organized or coerced to do so by the military, as had happened on occasion in the past.

The inhabitants of the dusty villages of Salingyi have been mostly farmers for generations, but life in the township has been dominated in recent years by the gigantic Letpadaung copper mine, the biggest in the country. The mine was opened in 1978, but it was greatly expanded when it began to be operated by the Canadian company Ivanhoe in 1996. In 2010, Ivanhoe yielded to pressures from foreign activists denouncing the human rights violation of the military regime, and withdrew from the project. After that, Wanbao Mining Ltd, a subsidiary of Norinco, a Chinese arms manufacturer, stepped in.[16] Since then, the exploitation of the mine is a joint venture of Wanbao and the Union of Myanmar Economic Holdings Ltd (UMEHL), a vast conglomerate owned and run by the Tatmadaw. None of these deals were made in a transparent manner. Nobody had bothered to consult the local population, and the government had evicted hundreds of farmers from their lands in the mid 1990s using laws from the British colonial era. The situation had become even worse after Wanbao bought the project and continued to develop and expand the mine, evicting more farmers for little or no compensation.

In November 2012, many villagers, led by local Buddhist monks and activists, staged a series of protests against the project. The police repressed the protests with brutality, shooting protestors and even using white phosphorus, burning the skin of many of them. In the new Burma, where the media had freedom to report on such incidents, the brutality provoked a scandal.

Aung San Suu Kyi was now a member of parliament, after her party had won some seats in a by-election in April that year, and was invited by President Thein Sein to head a Commission to investigate the incident and the mine project. She accepted the role. The report issued by the Commission in March 2013 failed to demand accountability for the police brutality or the use of white phosphorus, simply recommended improvements in police training.[17] The Commission recognized that the mine was bringing little benefit to local villagers, but it argued for the continued expansion of the project, albeit recommending an increase in the compensation handed to the farmers and more thorough environmental assessments. The argument in defence of the project was that it was in Burma's national interest to continue operations in the mine, as halting them would discourage foreign investors from doing business in the country.[18] An abstract 'national interest' seemed to override the concrete interests of the very same individuals who were members of the nation.

After the Commission issued the report, Suu Kyi visited the area to talk with the villagers. She was received by the farmers with a hostility she appeared utterly unprepared to confront. She was heckled and shouted at by villagers who were unwilling to listen to her explanations of why a project that was damaging them so much should continue. At some point she took refuge in her car while angry villagers shouted at her. Looking from the window, she seemed completely puzzled. 'We had so much hope on her, but her report is like a death sentence', said a woman, crying. The villagers might have refused to understand an argument based on a 'national interest' that seemed to exclude them; or perhaps they understood it only too well – but it was clear that she had not understood their position. She had called for compensation for the farmers, but she appeared unable to grasp that they were fighting for their land, too – for an environment to which they felt deeply attached, and where their lives had a meaning for them. Reportedly, she asked in exasperation: 'Why do they want the mountain?'[19]

I visited the area a few months later to witness the impact of the mine for myself. The situation was tense, and during the day the police were ubiquitous in the area. But the farmers were protecting the activists organizing the protests, forming patrols and preventing the security forces from searching for them in their villages at night. The deleterious impact of the mine was visible even on the very skin of some of the people I met. Ma Myint Myint, a fragile forty-two-year-old woman, suffered painful open sores all over her body after taking showers with water polluted with acid. In a country with an abysmal public health system, she was too poor to afford treatment in a private hospital, so she had to endure the pain using only an ointment that barely alleviated it.

The area around the mine included a barren yellow landscape, on which farmers who had previously cultivated the land were now forced to eke out a living extracting and processing low-quality copper in small improvised mines. They were receiving the crumbs of a project that was worth millions of dollars. One of them was Ko Nyo, a forty-eight-year-old man living with his wife and two children. He used to make the equivalent of US$150 a month when he was a farmer, and had also been able to produce some food for his family. He had been evicted from his land a couple of years before, and making copper was providing him with the equivalent of only US$90 per month.

The compensation given to those who received it was completely insufficient, according to the young lawyer acting on behalf of the farmers, Saw Kyaw Min, as it was based on a valuation of the land made during the colonial period, more than seven decades before. Given this harsh reality, and the fact that Suu Kyi seemed to have sided with the companies and the military, all the farmers expressed deep disappointment with her. They felt they had been betrayed and were now alone in their struggle. The only person I talked to at the time who said he was not disappointed with Suu Kyi was Thein Aung, a fifty-three-year-old farmer who told me that he 'had never believed in her to feel any disappointment now'. These sentiments were far from universal among the Burman majority, but a crack had now been opened in Suu Kyi's hitherto untarnished image.

*　　*　　*

The transition was supposed to be a pact of three elites: the military, the pro-democracy opposition led by Suu Kyi, and the leaders of the ethnic minorities.[20] The pact between the first two would be surprisingly successful – but not so much the pact with the third. In any case, the terms of such a transition were dictated exclusively by the military, which had designed a bullet-proof constitution and still wielded great power. The reaction of Suu Kyi to such imbalance of power was to try her best to reassure the generals that she and her party posed no threat to them. Since her release from house arrest, Suu Kyi had mostly engaged in playing politics in the opaque corridors of power in Naypyidaw, making tours abroad that mostly served to legitimize the transition in the eyes of the Western powers, rather than listening to the grievances of the Burmese population, whose support she probably took for granted. Even the outspoken Win Tin criticized this aloofness from the public, and it became increasingly easier to find Burmese saying that she was not close enough to the people.[21] She went as far as to assure the 'cronies' (a handful of extremely rich businessmen who had amassed huge fortunes during the junta period through their contacts with the generals) that she would not threaten their position, merely asking them to 'act fairly' and 'work for others'.[22]

In the name of 'national reconciliation', Suu Kyi renounced two important weapons she had at her disposal to extract concessions from the generals – her popular support at home, and the influence she wielded on foreign powers like the United States, at a moment when the government was keen to develop closer relations with the West. Such a strategy reveals Suu Kyi's deep distrust of participatory politics. Recalling her attitude to the protests against the copper mine in Letpadaung, she reacted with indifference, and even veiled hostility, to the wishes of the people.

The only issue on which she campaigned strongly was the clause in the Constitution that prevented her from becoming president. Shortly after her release, she called for a multi-ethnic conference;[23] but the issue was mostly swept aside by the NLD during the Thein Sein years, leaving the initiative to the government. Moreover, the NLD was scarcely active for most of the period. Suu Kyi's strategy of winning the trust of the generals rendered the party politically impotent, reducing it to merely reacting to developments shaped by others. Moreover, as the transition proceeded, an ugly truth, previously obscured, became increasingly clear: on the most crucial issues afflicting the country, the NLD's vision for Burma was not so different from that of the military. Regarding the questions of citizenship, who belonged to the Burmese nation and who did not, and the political rights of the ethnic minorities resentful of Burman domination, the NLD failed to offer any alternative to the military. These were precisely the issues that would prove crucial during the transition.

2

The War in the 'Green Hell'

On the night of 9 June 2011, three months after Thein Sein assumed the presidency of Burma, a series of explosions woke up Labang Hkawn Tawng, a stout, widowed farmer in her sixties, and her grandson while they were sleeping in their house in Sang Gang, a tiny, remote village in the hills of Kachin State, the northernmost state in Burma. Still half-asleep, at first she did not know what was going on, but soon she realized: the Tatmadaw and the KIA were fighting around the village. Frightened and with no time to collect their belongings, she and her grandson fled to the forest with the rest of the villagers, all of them ethnic Kachin. After hiding for several days, they were found by a group of KIA soldiers who directed them to Nhkawng Pa, a camp for internally displaced people located in the very small territory that the KIO controls along the border with China, where I interviewed her one year later.

The war between the Tatmadaw and the KIA resumed that night around Sang Gang, after a ceasefire that had lasted for seventeen years. The resumption of hostilities disrupted the lives of hundreds of thousands of Kachin people, like Laban Hkawn Tawng. In the subsequent months and years, more than 100,000 Kachin people were displaced from their villages, many seeking refuge in KIO-controlled areas. An unknown number of soldiers on both sides, as well as civilians, perished in the beautiful but unforgivingly harsh mountainous rainforest in Kachin State, which the British and American soldiers who had fought against the Japanese in World War II called the 'Green Hell'. In the meantime, the government of Thein Sein launched a series of peace talks with the KIA and other armed groups, and even publicly ordered the army in mid 2012 'not to launch any offensive actions'.[1] The army did not respect the order, and even escalated its operations throughout the year, culminating in the bombing with jet fighters of Laiza, the town on the border with China where the headquarters of the KIO/KIA are located, over Christmas that year.[2]

The main stumbling block in the negotiations – as the chief of the KIO's negotiating team, Sumlut Gam, told me in his office in Laiza in 2012 – was that the Burmese government wanted to sign a ceasefire before engaging in any political dialogue about the status of Kachin State, while the KIO wanted the opposite: not to lay down its weapons until reaching a political agreement. The reluctance of the KIO to sign a new ceasefire was related to frustrations with the long ceasefire that had been ended one year before. Sumlut Gam believed that the government had cheated them in 1994, when they had accepted the ceasefire in the hope that it would lead to a political dialogue that never took place. 'At that time, they told us that the army did not have legitimacy to maintain that kind of dialogue', he said.

In this context, the war was inextricably linked with the negotiation process. Colonel Maran Zaw Tawng, one of the main military strategists of the KIA, believed that neither side could win an outright military victory. The Burmese army might be better equipped and superior in terms of manpower, but the Kachin soldiers of the KIA were better prepared to survive the extreme environment, having good knowledge of the difficult terrain. The Kachin fighters were also adept in the guerrilla tactics that had made them famous in World War II, when they fought against the Japanese alongside the British army. Given this military stalemate, Colonel Zaw Tawng told me, the objective of the KIA was to maintain an upper hand in the battlefield so as to improve their position at the negotiating table.

The immediate cause of the war was the decision of the Tatmadaw to send reinforcements to the site where the construction of a dam was planned in the Ta Ping River, near Sang Gang village. According to the KIO, the location was in their territory, and the reinforcement violated the ceasefire signed in 1994. But that was just the spark; tensions between the Tatmadaw and the KIA/KIO had been steadily mounting over the years ahead of the transfer of power.

An important contributing factor was the plan for another, much larger dam to be built about forty kilometres in the north of Myitkyina, the capital of Kachin State, at the confluence of the Mali and N'mai rivers, which forms the Irrawaddy River. In 2005, a bilateral agreement was signed between the Chinese state-owned China Power Investment Corporation, the Burmese Ministry of Electric Power and the huge Burmese conglomerate Asia World. This company had been founded by a man who had made his fortune as a drug lord in northern Shan State, and was currently chaired by his son, Steven Law. The Myitsone dam would be the biggest dam built by a Chinese company outside its borders, and would produce 6,000 MW; 90 per cent of the electricity it generated would be destined for the power grid of the Chinese province of Yunnan, and such energy would not be directed to Burma until fifty years after its completion. No Kachin organization was ever consulted on the project.

In preparation for the dam's construction, five villages were emptied, and around 2,000 people uprooted from their ancestral lands and relocated in new villages. Local activists had protested against the dam since 2009, seeing it as further proof of the Burman state encroachment onto their lands, and as part of a wider conspiracy to Burmanize their land.[3] Some Kachin I spoke with in 2012 feared that the dam could break at some point and flood Myitkyina, drowning its 300,000 inhabitants. The protests grew more vocal over the years, even when the government started to arrest some of the activists. Then, in March 2011, three months before the resumption of the war, the KIO chairman, Lanyaw Zawng Hra, sent a letter to the Chinese government warning that the project might spark a civil war in Kachin State[4] – a warning that went unheeded. But with the democratic opening and the change of regime, a new movement sprang up against the dam, this time led by Burman activists in Rangoon. To some extent, this was a movement of inter-ethnic solidarity; but it also represented Burmese nationalism, reflecting increasing anti-Chinese sentiment.

The 'Save the Irrawaddy' campaign rallied the support of pro-democracy forces in Rangoon, including Aung San Suu Kyi herself. The popular appeal of the movement was due in no small measure to the symbolic power that the Irrawaddy has in the Burmese national imagination as the 'bloodline' of the country. On 30 September 2011, President Thein Sein made the astonishing announcement that his government would suspend the construction of the Myitsone dam, 'to respect the people's will'.[5] It was the first time in decades that the Burmese government had yielded to a popular demand, and it was a stroke of political genius by which Thein Sein was able to kill two birds with one stone: on the one hand, he appeared to be responsive to popular demands, thus boosting his democratic and reformist credentials; on the other, his snub to China signalled his intentions to initiate his rapprochement with the Western powers that had isolated the Burmese regime diplomatically for more than two decades.

In fact, Thein Sein only suspended the Myitsone project for the duration of his mandate. The issue is still pending, with the Chinese demanding some sort of compensation. It is doubtful that the Chinese are ever going to build the dam as originally envisaged, as the political cost for any Burmese government would be far too high, and in recent years Yunnan has attained a surplus of electricity,[6] so the need for the electricity is not as pressing as it originally would have been. But the Burmese government will at some point have to offer some alternative project by which China can recoup its losses. In any case, the suspension was a victory, as the dam has never been built. But a victory for whom? Not for the 2,000 people evicted from their villages. When, in 2012, I visited one of the villages to which they have been relocated, people complained about the way they had been uprooted, unable to farm their original lands and sent to places without fertile soil, where they struggled to make ends meet. Many had left for other places in order to find jobs. It was virtually a ghost village, made up of wooden houses so badly built by the government that the cold wind entered through cracks in the walls during the winter.

For the Kachin people at large, it was a mixed victory. The protest was stirred up by Burman activists in Rangoon, not by them, and many of their underlying grievances remained unaddressed. As early as 2012, a Kachin activist in Rangoon complained to me that those activists and Aung San Suu Kyi had hijacked their protests. Moreover, the inter-ethnic solidarity with the Kachin was short-lived for many Burman activists and politicians, including Aung San Suu Kyi, soon to be replaced by an apparent indifference. Both Kachin and Burman activists had fought against the dam for nationalist reasons, but in the framework of two different nationalisms. In any case, the suspension was insufficient to stop the war that had begun three months before. In fact, nobody expected it to stop. The reasons for the war ran much deeper, and were as much economic as they were political.

The military junta that replaced the dictatorship of General Ne Win in 1988 ruled the country for a total of twenty-three years, but always portrayed itself as merely a 'provisional government' ruling in a permanent state of exception. Its purported raison d'être was to restore the order and stability necessary to establish a constitutional system – hence its original name, the State Law and Order Restoration Council (SLORC). In the meantime, it strengthened its position in restive border areas like Kachin State, both militarily and politically, and extended its control over state institutions including the bureaucracy and the judiciary.

After approving the Constitution by a referendum in 2008, the junta sent orders in April 2009 to the ethnic armed organizations to accept being placed under the command of the army as Border Guard Forces (BGF). This happened before the promised 'legitimate' government was in power, and without the offer of any political concessions in return. The KIA refused to obey.[7] The KIO supported the formation of the Kachin State Progressive Party (KSPP), with some former high-ranking KIO leaders at its helm, but the government did not allow it to register, presumably as punishment for the KIO's refusal of the order to transform itself into a BGF.[8] In short, as the change of regime approached, the KIO could see how any avenue of political representation in the new post-military order was closed.

The Kachin are one of the ethnic groups in Burma that have only the most tenuous cultural, linguistic or religious linkages with the Burman majority. Many Kachin, like many members of other ethnic minorities, have little reason to feel any attachment to the Burmese nation-state, which has been dominated by the Burmans throughout the country's recent history. In precolonial times, the writ of the Burmese kingdoms did not extend into the rugged mountains where the ancestors of the Kachin have lived for generations. More recently, like that of other ethnic minorities, the experience that many Kachin people have had of contact with the Burmese state – particularly those living in rural areas – is of soldiers and other security forces treating them as potential enemies, and often conscripting them to carry out gruesome forced labour, or even to use them as human landmine-sweepers.[9] The government has always accepted the Kachin as one of Burma's 'national races', formally enjoying equal rights; but they have often been treated as second-class citizens in the context of an implicit racial hierarchy in which the Burman majority, supposedly more civilized, sits at the apex, and 'hill tribes' like the Kachin, the Chin and the Karen occupy a lower place.

The Kachin nation comprises six or seven different ethno-linguistic groups, or 'tribes': Jinghpaw, Zaiwa, Lachid, Rawang, Lisu, Lawngwaw (or Maru) and Nung; but there is much controversy about the inclusion of some of these groups under the Kachin umbrella. This is particularly true of the Lisu and the Rawang, many of whom regard themselves as a distinct ethnic group. Kachin ethno-nationalism is a relatively new phenomenon, and is mostly dominated by the Jinghpaw.[10] These groups speak their own languages, the most dominant being the Jinghpaw, and are predominantly Christian (the majority are Baptist, but there is a significant Catholic minority, as well as some Anglicans). Kachin State is also home to other ethnic groups: a sizeable Shanni population, a group related to the Shan, and many Burman and Rakhine workers. In fact, the Kachin are in a minority in the state, albeit the largest one.

The Kachin community is not free from internal fissures, and the allegiance to Kachin nationhood varies between the different 'tribes', the Lisu and the Rawang scarcely identifying themselves as Kachin. But over time the Kachin have developed tight and complex kinship networks that make them a remarkably cohesive community in times of crisis.[11] The Kachin also have relatively strong social institutions independent of a government that provides little assistance to its citizens, and even less in the neglected areas of the periphery. In the territory controlled by the government, the Kachin Baptist Convention (KBC) is much more than a religious organization; it also plays a social role that includes education, development projects and rehabilitation centres for drug users, according to the church's ethos of 'holistic mission'.[12]

The struggle of the KIO/KIA also has some religious overtones, clearly expressed in its motto: 'God is our victory.' But it would be misleading to see the KIA as an army of crusaders. Religion is a rallying point that resonates powerfully in a deeply religious population, but the goals of the KIO are eminently political. Whether the final aim is full independence or autonomy within a federal Burma is more difficult to discern. Until the mid 1970s, the KIO officially demanded independence. It then switched to demanding autonomy, though some see it as a mere step towards independence. As I was told in 2012 by the late Reverend Maran Ja Gun, a Kachin historian, linguist and influential ideologue of the KIO, at his house in Laiza, 'Our ultimate goal will probably be full independence.'

Kachin nationalists see Burman domination as the main obstacle to the progress of their nation. Their nationalism is predicated on respect for Kachin traditions, and a certain idealization of the period when the Kachin *duwas* (tribal chiefs) governed without Burman interference,[13] but also on a project of modernization on Kachin terms that is currently hampered by the central government.[14] In that sense, the Kachin nationalist project is arguably more forward-looking than others in the country. The Kachin never had a state as such, and that makes it difficult to rely on nostalgia for a golden age of power and wealth as the basis for a future Kachin nation. However, this does not necessarily mean that Kachin nationalists are politically progressive.

The KIO/KIA has built a mini-state in its territory with its own police force, hospitals, schools and TV station, Laiza TV. The KIO also provides bases in its territory for other armed groups, such as the All Burma Student's Democratic Front (ABSDF – a mostly Burman guerrilla group born out of the protests against the military regime in 1988) and the Arakan Army (AA – a Rakhine ethno-nationalist armed group founded in 2009 that draws its recruits mainly from Rakhine workers in the jade mines of Hpakant). Politically, the KIO has become one of the most important armed groups in Burma – though the allied United Wa State Army (UWSA), whose force is estimated at between 20,000 and 30,000 soldiers, outnumbers the approximately 10,000 soldiers of the KIO.[15] The KIO and the UWSA are the most influential armed groups that refused to sign the Nationwide Ceasefire Agreement (NCA) proposed by the government, after seven other armed groups, including the Karen National Army (KNU) and the Restoration Council of Shan State (RCSS), signed it in October 2015.

The position of the KIO remained the same at the time of writing: no ceasefire until there is a meaningful political dialogue. But there has been increasing pressure on the organization to sign, not less, from what Swedish journalist Bertil Lintner has described as the 'peace-industrial complex':[16] dozens of foreign organizations and well-paid experts on 'conflict resolution', who have flocked to Burma since the transition started and who in many cases exert more pressure on the armed groups than on the government. But the KIO seems able to rely on the support of the Kachin people – though it is an open question how long such support will last if this inconclusive war of attrition continues indefinitely.

The military government used the ceasefire signed in 1994 to strengthen the army and increase not only its military presence in Kachin State but, more crucially, its economic stakes in that land rich in natural resources, most importantly timber and jade. The jewel in its crown is its vast complex of jadeite mines at Hpakant, in the west of the state, most of which were gradually snatched from the KIO by the government after the ceasefire. This reduced one of the Kachin guerrillas' main sources of revenue. The jade business was greatly expanded during the ceasefire years, and it is now in the hands of military-owned conglomerates; a few generals, including the family of the former junta supremo, senior General Than Shwe; a few cronies; and an assortment of drug lords associated with the latter.

The financial rewards of the jade business in Hpakant are astonishingly high. According to a report published in 2015 by Global Witness, the value of jade production may have amounted in 2014 to as much as US$31 billion, of which the Burmese state received only US$374 million in official revenues – less than 2 per cent of the total. To put things in perspective, the jade business amounted to 48 per cent of the country's official GDP and forty-six times the government's expenditure on healthcare.[17] It goes without saying that the wider Kachin population does not receive any benefit from this massive economic plunder, which is also resulting in enormous environmental devastation in Kachin State. The jade mines have also attracted many workers from all over the country, lured by the prospect of making a fortune – albeit unlikely. The big money is made by others. Instead, the workers are often given heroin or methamphetamine, at first to endure the harsh working conditions. Eventually, when they have become addicted, many of them are paid only with drugs.

It is the Kachin population that has suffered most acutely from the conflict. Since the war was reignited in 2011, the Burmese government has for most of the time blocked any access to humanitarian agencies to the tens of thousands of displaced people sheltered in KIO-controlled areas. The conditions in the camps for internally displaced persons (IDPs) in those areas are far from perfect, but the KIO and several Kachin civil society groups have been able to organize them with remarkable efficiency, all the more impressive given the harsh circumstances.

Knowing well that its survival depends on popular support, the KIO has made an effort to protect the IDPs in its territory, whereas those in government-controlled areas live in fear of the Burmese authorities. Since the resumption of the war, dozens of people have been accused of being members of the KIO or having links with the organization. Most have been charged with violating Article 17.1 of the Unlawful Association Act, which makes punishable any link with a clandestine organization. A prominent case has been that of Lahtaw Brang Shawng, a young farmer and father of two who was arrested in June 2012 by Military Affairs Security (MAS) agents and accused of being part of a KIO bomb plot. Brang Shawng and his family had escaped from the fighting around their village a few months before, and were IDPs living in a camp in Myitkyina.

A few weeks after Brang Shawng's arrest, I interviewed his wife, Ze Nyoi, and his lawyer, Mar Khar. Ze Nyoi, a soft-spoken woman whose sad expression bore the emotional scars of her ordeal, had led protests against the detention of her husband, of whose innocence she was convinced. 'They claim he holds a university degree, but that's not true. He's a very simple man who speaks very little Burmese and had to provide for all his family. He couldn't go anywhere and join the KIA, as they claim', she told me, pointing to the fact that many Kachin in rural areas do not speak the language of the majority. She had visited her husband three or four times when he was under detention – short visits of no more than five minutes, always in the presence of the police. 'He couldn't talk much, but I could see clearly he was injured, and they didn't provide any medical treatment for him, they only gave him paraceta-mol', she said. The authorities wanted to make an example for other IDPs, so one week after his detention they paraded a dishevelled Brang Shawng in the IDP camp, ostensibly to re-enact the crime, but most likely to intimidate the other displaced people in the camp.

It was so evident that Brang Shawng had been tortured to extract a confession that the first judge who heard his case asked him to remove his shirt, his lawyer told me. What he discovered, apart from bruises all over his torso, was an audio recorder taped to his chest by the police, to make sure he repeated the confession they had dictated to him. In a rare example of judicial independence, the judge refused to accept his confession; but he was quickly replaced by a more compliant judge. 'They didn't have any evidence against him, only his confession, extracted after weeks of torture', Mar Khar told me. Eventually, on July 2013, Brang Shawng was sentenced to three years in jail – but President Thein Sein pardoned him one week later with another dozen Kachin serving time for similar offences.

In 2014, I met Brang Shawng in the camp. He was a man broken by the torture he had suffered for months on end. Covered with scars, he was unable to move properly and work for his family, and he suffered constant headaches and memory loss as a consequence of the many blows he had received to his head.

In the Kachin war, as in many others, allegiances are complex affairs, and opportunities for profit often trump military or ideological considerations. The story of a man I met in Myitkyina on December 2017 is instructive about these grey zones and the economy of the war. Let us call him Hkun Lah; a Kachin man in his fifties, he was the son of a distinguished soldier who had fought in World War II with the US army, and then had joined the Burmese army after independence. When I met him, he was working in one of the camps for IDPs in the state's capital. He had joined the Burmese army in the mid 1980s, 'as it gave me the chance to play football', he explained half-jokingly. As a Kachin, he was always under suspicion in the military. He could join the army, but he had little chance of being promoted to a high-ranking position, and he was confined to administrative duties.

He had relatives in the KIO and secretly sympathized with them. For years, he passed secret documents and ammunition to the enemy, until he was caught in 2009. He was arrested and sentenced to seven years in jail, but he was released only two years later, in an amnesty ordered by the president. If the sentence was not very long, that was due to the fact that he was only charged with passing secret documents, not for giving ammunition to the KIA. He explained that the army simply did not want to dig into the issue too much, because investigating it would have led to uncovering the embarrassing fact that many in the Burmese military were involved in selling ammunition for a considerable profit to the KIA and other groups. 'Many people were involved [in] that, including high-ranking officers who were Burmans; it was better not to stir that', he explained.

The Tatmadaw is not the only enemy that the KIO and the Kachin are fighting. They are also waging a war against a faceless foe – drug addiction – that has been undermining communities throughout the state for years. Drugs are widely available in Burma, and the country is the second-largest producer of opium in the world after Afghanistan. According to the United Nations Office on Drugs and Crime, in 2015 there were around 55,500 hectares of opium poppy plantations in the country. Most were in Shan State, the southern neighbour of Kachin State, but around 4,200 were in Kachin.[18] Shan State is also the biggest source of methamphetamine in Southeast Asia. Many of these narcotics make their way into both government- and KIA-controlled areas.

To combat the use of drugs, the KIO established the Drug Eradication Committee in 2010. As well as dealing with drug users, the KIO is also waging a war on drug producers. When an opium poppy field is discovered in its territory, soldiers destroy the harvest and attempt to persuade the owners to plant different crops. If a farmer is discovered planting poppies again, he is sent to jail. In 2014, I interviewed the secretary of the Committee, Hpaudau Gam Ba, a burly man who had been a member of the KIO since 1988, and who also ran a rehabilitation centre in Laiza. Many Kachin believe that the drug scourge in his community is part of a well-planned conspiracy by the Tatmadaw to weaken the Kachin. This notion is so widely spread and accepted that it is virtually impossible to find any Kachin who does not subscribe to it.[19] 'Some people from the government even distribute the drugs themselves and then jail the Kachin addicts. This is part of their strategy to divide and rule', Gam Ba told me.

Nobody has conclusively demonstrated that there is a master plan to flood Kachin with drugs, and other explanations are perfectly plausible: since Kachin neighbours areas with high production of narcotics, it is natural that so many of them find their way there; law enforcement is often arbitrary not only in Kachin, but throughout Burma, and corrupt policemen, generals and civil servants are known to be involved on the drug-trade; and members of other ethnicities use drugs in Kachin and elsewhere in the country.

The theory surely gives too much credit to the leaders of the Tatmadaw, whose control of the country, and particularly the border areas, is far from complete. But the conspiracy, whether real or imagined, has a strong explanatory power for many Kachin, as it is inscribed in a wider pattern of oppression by the military. It also serves to reinforce their sense of victimhood under Burman domination, and, crucially, their support for the KIO/KIA, which has managed to present itself not only as a bulwark against the Burmese army, but also against drugs. Thus, the particular war on drugs waged by the KIO and other Kachin organizations is also a nationalist war.

Gam Ba told me that his centre has treated 1,700 addicts since it opened in 2010. He believed that, in most cases, the treatment dispensed by the KIO was successful, and claimed that the majority of those treated had conquered their addiction for good. Only fifty people had been readmitted, he said. 'But many people go to government-controlled areas after leaving here, and then we cannot keep track of them', he acknowledged. The main weapon employed in combating addiction in the rehabilitation centres was religion. Drug users are encouraged to embrace the Christian faith in order to be saved from their addiction. They were directed to heal through sermons, Bible studies and songs. They were also put to work in the local town and taught how to farm. However, there were virtually no palliatives to alleviate withdrawal symptoms, and corporal punishments were often used to subdue rebellious addicts.

Some of the drug users in the KIO centres were volunteers, or were sent by their families, but most had been detained by the KIO and held there against their will. One of them was Ma Bung, a forty-eight-year-old woman who had been sent to a rehabilitation centre in Mai Ja Yang, the second-biggest town in KIO-controlled territory, after she was discovered buying drugs in a village known as an important hub of drug distribution in the area. The most surprising fact about Ma Bung was that she was not a Burmese citizen. She was an ethnic Kachin, but lived in China, where some 130,000 Kachin (classified there as Jingpo) live in Yunnan Province. She held Chinese citizenship, but the KIO did not seem to care, and kept her in the rehabilitation centre for six months. 'She is poor, and the authorities in China would not care about her', a worker at the centre told me. Official borders between nation-states are often meaningless in northern Burma, and are easily overridden by ethnic allegiances.

*　　*　　*

The war in Kachin state soon reached an apparent stalemate, which bombings by the Burmese military, including that of Laiza over Christmas of 2012, did not break. The KIO's territory shrank during the years of Thein Sein, but, as Colonel Maran Zaw Tawng told me in 2012, it was proved that an outright defeat was impossible. Meanwhile, the KIO managed to regain wide popular support from the Kachin population after the years of the ceasefire, during which many Kachin criticized KIO leaders as more interested in economic gain than defending the political rights of their people.[20] With the war, and some changes in the KIO leadership, many Kachin again saw the organization as the defenders of their interests. As a consequence, Kachin nationalism has also been greatly reinforced by the war – a process to which the crimes of the Burmese military against civilians have undoubtedly contributed.

Meanwhile, Burman activists in Rangoon and elsewhere in central Burma have made some gestures of solidarity towards the Kachin. The '88 Generation' students – the leaders of the popular uprising in 1988 – organized trips to Myitkyina and issued calls for peace.[21] The Free Funeral Service, a civil society organization based in Rangoon, sent donations to the people displaced by the war.[22] But there is little awareness among most of the Burman population in the heartlands about the conflicts in the periphery. These conflicts seem almost as distant as if they were happening in another country.[23] The Burman majority enjoys a set of unofficial privileges that often go unrecognized even by the politically involved Burmans, making them more pervasive.[24] It is no wonder that many Kachin feel they have little support from the Burman population at large. Both may have been victims of the military dictatorship, but they have not been victimized in the same ways or to the same degree.

Throughout the Thein Sein administration, Aung San Suu Kyi remained aloof regarding the conflict in Kachin. As part of her strategy of reconciliation with the generals, she refused to commit herself on the issue. 'There are people who criticized me when I remained [silent] on this case. They can do so as they are not satisfied with me. But, for me, I do not want to add fire to any side of the conflict', she said in 2012 in London.[25] 'It is up to the government. This case is being handled by the government at the moment', she would say later – a strange comment from an opposition leader who seemed to wash her hands of a fundamental issue in the country she aspired to govern one day.[26]

The refusal of Suu Kyi to adopt any position on the issue elicited a variety of responses from the Kachin. When I asked a Catholic priest in Laiza in 2012 whether he trusted Suu Kyi, he replied that she was just another Burman, and as such could not be trusted. Soon, another conflict flared up on the other side of the country, further revealing the limits of her moral commitments and leadership.

3

Days of Fury in Arakan

By June 2012 the democratic transition seemed to be progressing smoothly, at least in central Burma. Aung San Suu Kyi had become a member of parliament in April; some political prisoners had been released earlier that year; and new laws liberalizing the media and trade unions were in the pipeline. Thein Sein was applauded internationally, and even Hillary Clinton had visited the country as US Secretary of State in late 2011 – a move by which the most powerful country on earth was giving its blessing to the new regime. The war in Kachin State seemed to be the only intractable problem in what might otherwise have looked like the beginning of a promising new era for the country. Then a new crisis suddenly erupted in Arakan State – a crisis that would only get worse in the coming years, and would have profound implications beyond the state.

In late May, a twenty-seven-year-old Buddhist Rakhine woman called Thida Htwe was brutally raped and killed on Ramree Island, in central Arakan. The alleged perpetrators, two Muslim men and an orphan Buddhist adopted by a Muslim family, were arrested the next day by the police, but villages and towns throughout the state were swept by media reports and pamphlets denouncing the crime, and emphasizing the religion of the perpetrators. Over the following weeks, this triggered a spiral of intercommunal violence that snowballed throughout the state and broke, perhaps irremediably, the fragile coexistence between the Muslim and Buddhist communities. A few days later, on 3 June, in Toungup, a town in the south of the state, a mob of several hundred Buddhists stopped a bus, dragged ten Muslim men from central Burma from it, and beat them to death.

Five days later, thousands of Muslim Rohingya in Maungdaw town, in the predominantly Rohingya north of the state, near to the border with Bangladesh, went on a rampage after Friday prayers, destroying a number of buildings and killing several Buddhists. The violence soon spread to the state's capital, Sittwe, where it was mostly perpetrated by Buddhist Rakhine against Rohingya Muslims in retaliation for the rape and assassination of the Buddhist girl in Ramree and the attacks in Maungdaw. On 12 June, the army stepped in and restored order in the state. By then, hundreds of houses had been destroyed, over 100,000 people, most of them Rohingya, had been displaced to make-shift camps. The government claimed that seventy-eight people had been killed – a figure that was, in all probability, a gross underestimate.[1]

The government portrayed the violence as an eruption of spontane-ous sectarian hostility between two communities incapable of living together – a convenient narrative that allowed the Tatmadaw to portray itself as the pacifier. The rape and killing of Thida Htwe had been widely publicized in the state, playing up stereotypes circulated widely among the Buddhist population that depicted Muslims as brutal sexual predators. An individual criminal case was blown out of proportion; collective blame was assigned to the Rohingya community as a whole for the alleged actions of just three men. Not all Rakhine participated in the violence, or even supported it; but the invocation of collective responsibility played into pre-existing intercommunal tensions. It made thinkable and justifiable the retaliation against ten innocent men a few days later, and subsequently against the whole Rohingya community.

Intercommunal tensions had existed in the state for decades, but that was only part of the story. The violence was not entirely spontaneous; strong indications emerged that there was some element of planning on the Rakhine side. According to a well-researched report by the International State Crime Initiative, based at Queen Mary, University of London, local Rakhine businessmen, Rakhine civil society organiza-tions and politicians of the Rakhine Nationalities Development Party (RNDP) had organized mobs from Rakhine villages and taken them on buses to Sittwe, where they attacked the quarter of Narzi, mostly inhabited by Rohingya Muslims, and burned it to the ground.[2] Moreover, at first the police did nothing to stop the violence, allowing it to escalate, and then often took sides with the Rakhine, shooting at the Rohingya and helping Rakhine mobs to torch Rohingya houses. The impunity that Rakhine attackers enjoyed also belies the notion that the authorities were impartial pacifiers; while many Rohingya in Maungdaw and Sittwe were jailed, not a single Rakhine was arrested.

The violence did not come out of the blue. In the immediate context of the transition, Rakhine nationalists had lashed out against the Rohingya after they were allowed to vote in the 2010 election. In September 2011, several Rakhine associations held a seminar in Rangoon protesting the 'Rohingyanization of Arakan'.[3] One month later, the RNDP organized a series of public conferences in several towns in Northern Arakan with the same theme. 'We have no intention to breed racial or religious hatred among the peoples living together on our land', said U Aung Mra Kyaw, an MP for the RNDP. But the reaction of some people in attendance seemed to belie his words. One participant in one of the conferences was reported as saying: 'Many people did not want to return home, even after concluding the conference ... because they were embittered with the feelings that their land and valued heritages are being insulted by those groups of Chittagonian Bengali Muslims with their made up histories of Rohingya.'[4]

I visited Sittwe for the first time a few weeks after the first wave of riots. The government had imposed strict segregation between the two communities, with the ostensible rationale of preventing further violence; but the reality was that the city had been almost completely ethnically cleansed of its Muslim population, and it has remained so ever since. The overwhelming majority of Rohingya had been taken to a complex of camps near the city, mostly built around pre-existing Rohingya villages. Only two Muslim enclaves remained within Sittwe: Bumay, on the edge of the city, and Aung Mingalar, the Muslim ghetto downtown.

Those in the camps were, in one sense, more fortunate than those in Aung Mingalar: the 'registered' interns in the camps received food from UN agencies, while those 'unregistered' did not. Meanwhile the inhabitants of the ghetto were not officially regarded as IDPs, so they did not receive anything. I could not visit Aung Mingalar on that occasion, but

I managed to speak on the phone with some residents, and they told me that they were forced to buy food from the police at as much as ten times its market price. Many of them received remittances from relatives in Rangoon or abroad, but, given that the money had to go through the police guarding the neighbourhood, the officers always got a substantial commission.

My interactions with Rohingya people were scarce and brief on that first trip. Having few contacts in Arakan, and with the camps closely guarded, I had to visit them with a military truck accompanying me and my Rakhine translator. Still, I managed to talk privately with a couple of them, who told me about how they had witnessed the police shooting relatives and neighbours in the recent violence. The camps where they had been confined were only a few weeks old, but there were already some suspicions that the displaced would not be able to return to their homes for a long time.

There were a few thousand displaced Rakhine, too, most of them sheltered in Buddhist monasteries; but their numbers were smaller than the displaced Rohingya and, unlike Muslims, they enjoyed freedom of movement. The traces of the recent violence were visible virtually everywhere. In the bustling market near the port, many shops were closed, their Muslim owners being confined in the camps or in Aung Mingalar and Bumay. In successive visits, I found most of those shops had been taken by Rakhine people. Meanwhile, Narzi quarter, the majority-Muslim area that had been attacked by Rakhine mobs and subsequently evacuated by the authorities, was a desolate landscape of debris in which no building had been left unscathed. It was a ghost town where I could see teams of monks and Buddhist laymen clearing the rubble during the day. President Thein Sein had declared a state of emergency on 10 June, and there was a strict curfew from eight in the evening to six in the morning. At night the streets were eerily empty except for a few checkpoints, and stray dogs.

It was easier to interview Rakhine people than Rohingya. It was then that I got a sense for the first time of the deeply ingrained siege mentality within the Buddhist community, with damning rumours about the other community constantly circulating. I also started to glimpse where those fears came from. When I interviewed some Buddhist monks, the abbot of Budawmaw, a monastery sheltering a dozen Rakhine families, told me that the Muslim community had been infiltrated by al-Qaeda and other international jihadist outfits. To prove his point, he showed me a VCD with stills of violence and 'Muslim extremists' undergoing training. Those images could have been taken anywhere, but he claimed they were all 'Bengalis' preparing to wage jihad in Arakan. No violence waged by the Rohingya during the recent clashes revealed any sophisticated training, and fire-arms had not been used; but the facts seemed to be irrelevant. On the VCD, there was a picture of the Thai army detaining Malay insurgents in southern Thailand. When I pointed that out, he was adamant that it was the Myanmar army.

The abbot of another monastery, U Pinnyarthami, laid out to me the theory that al-Qaeda was using international NGOs working in Arakan and the United Nations to supply local terrorists with weapons. I heard this kind of wild conspiracy theory innumerable times in the following years. Underlying them all was a widespread distrust among the Rakhine towards international NGOs and the UN, who many believed work exclusively for the Rohingya and neglected the Rakhine people. It is fair to assume that those men truly believed what they said. But they were not just channeling anti-Muslim sentiments – they were amplifying them within a community whose reverence for Buddhist monks often lends great weight to whatever words they utter.

In those early days after the riots, the triangular conflict between Burmans, Rakhine and Rohingya seemed to have flattened into a two-sided conflict pitting the first two against the latter – the two 'national races' against the weaker 'interlopers from Bangladesh'. Back then, it was not uncommon to see Rakhine people wearing tee-shirts bearing the sentence, 'We support our President Thein Sein', in both English and Burmese, in the streets of Sittwe. One month after the riots, the president said that the Rohingya were not welcome in the country, and asked the UNHCR to place them in camps or send them to another country.[5] The UN agency immediately refused the petition, but it nonetheless garnered Thein Sein some support in Arakan. 'We will take care of our own ethnic nationalities, but Rohingyas who came to Burma illegally are not [one] of our ethnic nationalities and we cannot accept them here', he said. He also made a bizarre distinction between 'Rohingya' and 'Bengali', according to which the former were illegal immigrants who had arrived in Arakan after independence in 1948, and the latter those who had arrived during the colonial period, and were thus entitled to

Burmese citizenship. But his stress on taking care of Burma's 'national races' made implicitly clear that even the 'Bengali' citizens were not a priority.

The riots hardened prejudices against the Rohingya throughout Burma. It is impossible to asses with certainty how many people shared those prejudices, but the incipient Burmese public sphere was increasingly filled with anti-Rohingya news and commentaries portraying them as a demographic threat to the nation, denying both their identity and their right to live in the country. While the Rohingya were portrayed in international media as the main victims, sometimes ignoring the Rakhine, Burmese media almost invariably focused on the violence committed by the Royingya, often blaming them for things they had not done, and ignoring the discrimination they had suffered for decades. The Rohingya, or 'Bengalis', were not regarded as a 'national race', while the Rakhine were, and that coloured many perceptions of the whole crisis. There were very few dissenting voices, at least among the Burman ethnic majority or the Rakhine, and their numbers dwindled in the coming years as the situation in Arakan grew increasingly polarized. Furthermore, anti-Muslim sentiment linked to extreme forms of nationalism extended throughout Burma.

Arguably, there was only one person with enough moral authority to tackle the issue, and at least to open a debate that might have led to a different perception of the Rohingya inside the country: Aung San Suu Kyi. Many people in Burma, albeit probably not so many in Arakan, would have listened to what she said, even if it went against the official discourse voiced by a government then still dominated by the distrusted military. For a while, it was somewhat of a mystery what the position of Suu Kyi and the NLD was on the Rohingya. She generally avoided the issue, and when she addressed it her statements were ambiguous at best. She and her party had talked about democracy and human rights for years, and it was puzzling that they were silent on such flagrant violation of the rights of around a million people within the borders of her country. Many abroad assumed that her silence was due to the strategic logic of avoiding alienation from her party's supporters by defending what seemed an utterly unpopular cause. But it soon became clear that the NLD's thinking on the Rohingya, and on who belonged to the Burmese nation, were not too dissimilar to that of the generals.

This position was most clearly articulated by the former journalist Win Tin. He was perhaps the second most important figure in the NLD, and undoubtedly its second most popular after Aung San Suu Kyi. Here was a man of unyielding principles who never wavered in his fight against the military junta – a person who I deeply respected and admired. I had already interviewed him at length in late 2010, then in hospital a year later, and we had a cordial relationship. Then, two years after our first encounter, I met him again in his humble house. The situation had changed. Win Tin was loyal to Aung San Suu Kyi, but he was critical of her approach of getting close to the generals. For him, the military was still the enemy. Our interview was going smoothly until I touched upon the crisis in Arakan State. 'The problem there is created by foreigners, the Bengalis. That is a problem we have had for a very long time. All the people in the country regard these people as foreigners – they are Bengalis who cross to this country, over land and by sea and by river', he said.

He went on to repeat the official narrative denying the Rohingya identity: 'The word "rohingya" cropped up only after, some years back, maybe thirty years, these people want to claim the land, they want to claim themselves as a race, they want to claim to be a native race, and that is not right, that is the problem.' He also repeated a myth that is rather common in Burma. In 1978, the government launched Operation Dragon King in Arakan, with the alleged intention of detecting illegal immigrants. The heavy-handed tactics of the army and the police sent more than 200,000 Rohingya Muslim refugees into Bangladesh; but, after some international pressure, the government was obliged to accept them back. Win Tin claimed that more people returned than those who had left in the first place – a false allegation. But he also added something else: 'What the authorities from Bangladesh did was to put beggars, prostitutes and criminals they wanted to get rid of with the so-called Rohingyas, Bengali refugees, and sent everybody to Burma.' Finally, the solution that Win Tin proposed to the 'Rohingya problem' was quite similar to that suggested by President Thein Sein:

The problem is these Rohingya foreigners, and we have to contain them one way or another; something like what happened in the United States during World War II with the Japanese. The US government contained them in camps, and after the war they were sent to

Japan or they could apply for citizenship. We can solve this problem that way. We cannot regard them as citizens, because they are not our citizens at all, everyone here knows that. My position is that we must not violate the human rights of these people, the Rohingya, or whatever they are. Once they are inside our land maybe we have to contain them in one place, like a camp, but we must value their human rights.

I challenged Win Tin on his views, and he grew increasingly irritated. Eventually, he abruptly interrupted our conversation and told me I had to leave, as he had visitors waiting for him. When I left, there was nobody waiting outside. We never met again, and he passed away two years later, wearing until the very end the blue shirt he used to wear while in prison as a symbolic reminder to the world that his country was not yet free. There was no doubt that he had expressed his real opinions without reservation. He was an honest man who cared deeply for his people. But that did not detract him from his racism: it was clear that the Rohingya were excluded from what he regarded as his people.

During that visit to Burma, I discovered that his opinions were far from unique within the party. They were the consensus within the NLD and the Burman pro-democracy elite. A few days later I interviewed Ko Ko Gyi, a student leader in the 1988 uprising who led a high-profile Civil Society Organization. The Rohingya 'pretend they suffer so much', he told me in another increasingly heated encounter. 'If the international community [exerts] force or pressure on this Rohingya issue, it will have to face not the military government but most of our people', he concluded. He had said on another occasion that he and the members of his organization, the 88 Generation Students, were willing to take up arms alongside the same military that had kept him behind bars for years against the 'foreign invaders'.[6]

Like Win Tin, Ko Ko Gyi claimed to speak in the name of the majority of Burmese citizens – but no polls about the Rohingya had been conducted among a population that, until recently, had had virtually no access to reliable information even about their own country. Most Burmese had never met a member of the Rohingya community, which had been confined in northern Arakan State for decades. Far from responding to a supposed popular sentiment on which nobody could have certainty, it is more likely that these members of the pro-democracy elite were in fact contributing to the shaping of such sentiments. Voices like theirs were at least as responsible for it as were statements from the widely despised former generals who ruled the country, if not more so, as they were looked up to as heroes and listened to by many Burmese.

Ko Ko Gyi was not given the chance to fight alongside the military, but on the very same day I interviewed him he was appointed to take part in an official commission of inquiry to investigate the violence in Arakan that had taken place in June – a sure sign that an important sector of the old rebellious opposition to military rule was being absorbed into mainstream politics in the new Burma. Significantly, there was no Muslim from Arakan among the members of the commission.

Other pro-democracy activists echoed anti-Rohingya sentiments over the next few years. The few people defending the Rohingya were silenced or ostracized, or changed their minds, as the crisis worsened, the situation in Arakan growing increasingly polarized and the pressure to 'take sides' increasing. The largest enigma was still the silence of Aung San Suu Kyi, and I began to believe that this was due to a political calculation, but that most analysts had failed to grasp which audience she was struggling not to alienate. Her political career had been based since the beginning in 1988 on the support of the Burman public, and that of international human rights organizations and Western governments, which had led her to win the Nobel Peace Prize in 1991, transforming her into the 'Nelson Mandela of Asia'. If she defended the Rohingya, she risked alienating her domestic base; but attacking them would probably alienate her foreign supporters – and she needed both during the transition.

Nonetheless, she was criticized for not speaking out on the Rohingya, as she had been criticized for not speaking out on the Kachin – the most common narrative being that she had become a politician, casting aside her persona of human rights icon.[7] In 2013 she remarked: 'I'm always surprised when people speak as if I've just become a politician. I've been a politician all along. I started in politics not as a human rights defender or a humanitarian worker, but as the leader of a political party. And if that's not a politician then I don't know what is.'[8] There was something deeply disingenuous about that statement, not least because she was introducing a false dichotomy between the exercise of politics and the defence of human rights. After all, she had told me two years previously that her idea of democracy was based on the Universal Declaration of Human Rights.

Noting the apparent consensus within her party and her ambiguity on the issue, I suspected that she was avoiding expressing her real feelings unequivocally because she did not want to be labelled abroad as a racist. Later developments, particularly after her rise to power, confirmed that suspicion. But, reading between the lines of her public statements in 2012, it was possible to glimpse her true thoughts. In an interview with an Indian newspaper in November 2012, she complained that 'there were those who were not pleased, because they wanted me to condemn one community or the other', when nobody had asked her to take sides between the two communities. Then she adopted an equidistant position, saying that 'both communities have suffered human rights violations, and have also violated human rights. And human rights have been grossly mishandled in the Rakhine by the government for many decades.'[9] She was reducing the issue to a problem of intercommunal violence poorly handled by the military junta. As on so many other occasions, she insisted on the necessity to uphold the 'rule of law' to solve the problem. But the most telling passage of the interview was when she was first asked about the issue, when she replied: 'Of course we are concerned. I think in many ways the situation has been mishandled. For years I have been insisting, and the National League for Democracy also, that we have to do something about the porous border with Bangladesh because it is going to lead some day or the other to grave problems.' Framing the issue as a problem of illegal immigration, she echoed the sentiments of Win Tin; but she expressed herself more obliquely.

After the riots in June 2012, intercommunal relations steadily deteriorated in Arakan, as a result of a campaign of virulent anti-Muslim propaganda voiced by local Buddhist monks' associations and the RNDP. Several organizations had distributed pamphlets among the Rakhine population warning them of the danger posed by the 'Bengali invaders', and calling them to avoid any interactions with their Rohingya neighbours. A statement released on 9 July by the monks' association of Mrauk-U, the ancient capital of the Arakanese kingdom, read:

> The Arakanese people must understand that Bengalis want to destroy
> the land of Arakan, are eating Arakan rice and plan to exterminate

Arakanese people and use their money to buy weapons to kill Arakanese people. For this reason and from today, no Arakanese should sell any goods to Bengalis, hire Bengalis as workers, provide any food to Bengalis and have any dealings with them, as they are cruel by nature.[10]

Such calls were heeded by many in the Rakhine population, often with chilling zeal. In some parts of the state, those Rakhine who were discovered dealing with the Rohingya were publicly humiliated, and their pictures posted in Facebook. A picture dated in August, supposedly taken in Myebon, showed a man with his hands tied being paraded in the town with a placard hanging around his neck with a sign reading: 'I am a traitor and a slave of Kalar' – a derogatory term often used to refer to people of South Asian origin.[11]

The central government was doing very little to improve intercommunal relations in the state. In late August, Thein Sein sent a report to the country's parliament that was leaked to Agence France-Press. It read: 'Political parties, some monks and some individuals are increasing the ethnic hatred. They even approach and lobby both the domestic and overseas [Rakhine] community ... [Rakhine] people are continuously thinking to terrorise the Bengali Muslims living across the country.'[12] But the government did not take any measures to stop or counter such hate speech. The report may have been accurate, but it was also self-serving, as it contributed to the larger narrative of a primeval intercommunal hatred between the two communities that the government was striving to control, but could not eliminate. It also suppressed the role that the central government was playing in stoking those hatreds.

During the violence in June, Zaw Htay, the director of the president's office, had posted on Facebook: 'It is heard that Rohingya terrorists of the so-called Rohingya Solidarity Organization [ARNO] are crossing the border and getting into the country with the weapons. That is Rohingyas from other countries are coming into the country. Since our Military has got the news in advance, we will eradicate them until the end! I believe we are already doing it.'[13] None of it was true. ARNO, a Rohingya armed group that had operated from Bangladesh in the nineties and had been inactive for decades, never made any incursion into Arakan, and no armed Rohingya crossed from Bangladesh. But the Facebook post served to confirm the fears of a terrorist assault expressed by the Buddhist monks I had interviewed in my first visit to Sittwe.

The narrative of an intractable intercommunal conflict and a government trying its best to solve it was convenient not only for the Thein Sein administration, but also for Western countries trying to establish relations with Burma. The United States was at the forefront of initiatives to end the isolation of Burma, as part of its 'pivot to Asia', designed to counterbalance China's growing power in the region. After her visit in December 2011, Hillary Clinton claimed some credit for nurturing 'flickers of progress into a real opening' in the country.[14]

Then, in November 2012, Barack Obama became the first US president to visit the country, in a brief trip to Rangoon during which he gave his blessings to the transition. He gave a speech at Rangoon University, a traditional hotbed of student protests since colonial times. He defended the Rohingya, saying that they 'hold themselves – hold within themselves the same dignity as you do, and I do'. But he also praised 'the government's commitment to address the issues of injustice and accountability, and humanitarian access and citizenship'.[15]

There was no reason to believe that the government had any serious intention to address such issues. On the contrary, its policies had contributed to worsening the situation in Arakan. At the very least, they had failed to prevent a second wave of violence only three weeks before Obama's visit; but the US president refused to call out the Burmese government on this score.

The strict segregation of the two communities imposed after the riots in June had the stated purpose of preventing further violence, but had the perverse effect of making the rumours of nefarious Muslim plots seem more credible to the Rakhine. In many areas of the state ignorance grew within each community about the other; with intercommunal interactions reduced to a minimum, or even completely nonexistent in some areas, it had become more difficult to see the members of the other community as human individuals. On the contrary, they were feared as part of an undifferentiated mass.

Then, in late October, violence exploded throughout the state once again. On this occasion, it spread more widely than in June, encompassing several townships in central Arakan that had been spared in the past. The violence unfolded as a series of attacks on Muslim villages and quarters in nine of the seventeen townships in the state.[16] By all accounts, the violence was mostly carried out by Rakhine mobs against Muslims. Moreover, this time there was a much higher level of coordination and organization than in June.[17]

The violence unfolded in various ways, depending on the location, but a common pattern would emerge in later investigations: a Rakhine mob would gather around a Muslim village or quarter and, after shouting insults and threats, attack it by throwing Molotov cocktails and *jinglees* (small arrows made with bicycle spikes and launched with slingshots). Many witnesses, both Muslim and Rakhine, reported that they could not recognize most of the attackers, indicating they had been taken from other areas. As in June, the police stood aside, or participated actively in the attacks against the Muslims. When the riots finished, many Muslim settlements had been razed to the ground again; an indeterminate number of people (mostly Muslims) had been killed, including around seventy in a single incident in Mrauk-U; and approximately 30,000 had been displaced from their houses, most of them Muslims.

I travelled to Arakan for the second time shortly after the October riots. On that occasion, I was able to travel to Kyaukpyu, on Ramree Island, with the Wan Lark Foundation, a local organization delivering donations to Rakhine people displaced by the violence. On the edge of the town lies the Muslim quarter, East Pikesake, which had been turned into a devastated landscape of debris and burnt trees, with the ashes of arson still covering the roads and what was left of the houses.[18] The destruction was almost completely limited to the Muslim quarter, with only a few houses beyond its margins destroyed.

Local Rakhine witnesses alleged that the Muslims had initiated the attack, so I asked them why only Muslim houses had been burnt. They replied that the Muslims had torched their own homes before fleeing in boats. That night, in the hostel where we stayed, a young member of the organization proudly showed me a video of Rakhine people of all ages training with sticks to the tune of a patriotic song. 'We have to protect ourselves', said an older member, visibly embarrassed that I had been allowed to see those images. Then he changed his tune, somewhat contradicting himself: 'But this is just for show, it's not real training.'

In the Muslim camps around Sittwe there were many recently arrived refugees, and they were telling a very different story. According to most accounts, it was they who had been attacked; and while their houses were burning, the fire brigade had stayed outside the perimeter of the Muslim quarter, only trying to stop the fires from spreading to the houses of Buddhists.

It was very difficult to ascertain exactly what had happened from the contradictory accounts. But the notion that the Muslims would torch their own houses – a trope often repeated in Burma – supposedly to get access to the camps and the international aid they would receive there, seemed absurd. It fitted too neatly into the preconceived discourse circulated by many Rakhine of the Rohingya as abject 'beggars'. People holding these views seemed to think that Muslims in the camps were well provided for, but very few Rakhine ever set foot there. Complete segregation, again, nourished stories about the other group that served to further demonize it.

While it was difficult to find out with certainty what had happened during the violence, it was clear that the authorities were dispensing very different treatment to the displaced from the different communities. Most of the displaced Rakhine in Kyaukpyu had been sheltered in a Buddhist monastery, Than Pyu, while others stayed in the houses of relatives and friends. There were 150 people sheltered in the monastery, and the government had sent two military doctors and two nurses to attend to them.

In contrast, healthcare was woefully inadequate in the vast zone of camps for Muslims near Sittwe. According to IDPs in one of the camps, the government sent just one doctor once a week, and he only provided paracetamol to treat any ailment. In Tat Kal Pyin, a village surrounded by a camp, there was a makeshift clinic staffed by seven volunteers from Rangoon who were overstretched attending hundreds of patients every day. Some international NGOs, including Médecins Sans Frontières, were visiting the camps, but they were facing hostility from the local Rakhine population, and could not go every day. At that stage, aid in the camps was not yet well organized, and Muslim people in the camps were dying of preventable diseases. Malnutrition was also rife.

The violence in October had not only affected the Rohingya. Most of the Muslim victims, particularly in Kyaukpyu and Myebon, but also in other townships, had been Kaman – a Muslim ethnic group that arrived in Burma in the late seventeenth century and that, in contrast to the Rohingya, is officially recognized as one of Burma's 135 'national races'. As citizens, the Kaman had until then been able to participate in Burma's social and political life, but they were starting to share the fate of the Rohingya. Among the Kaman affected by the violence was Khin Shwe, a forty-six-year-old mathematician who had until then been the only Muslim professor at Sittwe University. She was originally from the township of Pauktaw, where she found herself during the riots in October. When the violence broke out, she tried to escape in a commercial boat, but the army did not allow her to embark, alleging that it was not safe for her. She then decided to take one of the rickety boats that Muslims were using to flee what was virtually a war zone. The boat sank on the way to Sittwe, and thirty-eight of its fifty passengers perished, including her. One of the survivors was her younger brother, Mohammed, who I spoke to in one of the camps in Sittwe, where he told me what had happened to her.

Khin Mar Saw was another Kaman woman displaced by the violence. This small, dignified forty-two-year-old woman hailed from the devastated quarter in Kyaukpyu I had seen a few days before. She had previously worked as a clerk in the local police station, but during the violence in June, feeling unsafe, she decided to take leave, and moved with her two children to Shan State, in the north of the country, where she had some relatives. She returned in October, thinking that the situation in Arakan had calmed down. A few days later her neighbourhood was in flames. When she was fleeing, she was told by a cousin that her son had been shot while he was trying to put out the flames in the local mosque. While I was interviewing her, her husband was on a beach near Sittwe with other displaced people. They had been stranded there, surrounded by the military, for days. Bursting into tears, she asked me how she and her family could get asylum in Europe. 'We Muslims have no future in this country anymore', she said.

A few months before, when I had visited Sittwe for the first time, Rakhine ethno-nationalists had been adamant that they did not have any problem with Muslim people, only with 'Bengali' people, pointing out that there had not been any clash with Kaman people. After the violence in October, they would say that Kaman had the right to stay in Arakan, but that many of them were 'fake Kaman', and in fact 'illegal Bengali immigrants' who had somehow managed to bribe officers to obtain documents. It seemed that the circle of the 'undesirable' population had been widened from a specific ethnic group to include all members of the Muslim religion. And that circle would be widened even further in the coming months, extending beyond the mountains that mark the border between Arakan and the rest of the country.

4

'We Will Build a Fence With Our Bones if Necessary'

During late 2012 and early 2013, a seemingly innocuous symbol began to spread in cities and villages throughout Burma. Thousands of stickers appeared in shops, street stalls and taxis in cities and villages showing the multi-coloured Buddhist flag in the background, the wheel of Dhamma at the centre, the pillars of Asoka – an Indian king who spread Buddhism throughout the Indian subcontinent in the third century BC – with three lions at the top, and 969 in Burmese numerals. This number stood for the attributes of the three jewels of Buddhism: Buddha, the Dhamma (his teachings) and the Sangha (the monastic community). The stickers were used to signal that the owners of the business were Buddhists, but the underlying message, which everybody implicitly understood, was to make clear that they were not Muslims. The stickers were part of what came to be known as the '969 Movement', a somewhat loose association of Buddhist monks and lay people devoted to protecting their religion against the purported threat of Islam.

The logo was launched by some monks on 30 October 2012, on the full-moon day of Thadingyut, one of the main festivals of the Buddhist calendar, in Moulmein, the capital of Mon State, in the east of the country. A few months later, I interviewed its designer and the secretary of the organization, Ashin Sada Ma, the abbot of Mya Sadi monastery. A soft-spoken man in his late thirties, he claimed that the campaign was intended to educate the youth about the value of their Buddhist heritage: 'In the modern age, the young people don't know the jewels of Buddhism; this logo is designed to remind them.' He made an effort during our interview to present the movement in the most positive light and dissociate it from any anti-Muslim message. He denied that the recent conflict in Arakan had anything to do with the decision to launch the campaign, but it was evident that the issue worried him.

At one point he argued that the 'Bengalis' were fuelling conflict by 'migrating' to Burma. 'If they come, they can easily influence our country. They are trying to improve their lives in our country and our lands. So this symbol and campaign is intended to defend ourselves. I fear that some Bengali Muslims are terrorists and have a mission to Islamise our country', he said. 'Only small parts of Asia are Buddhist now; in the past Indonesia, Bangladesh, Afghanistan and many other places, including Turkey and Iraq, were Buddhist countries, but now they are lost', he added, showing me a map of Asia that I had seen in one of the corridors of the monastery and would see again in many places, with the majority religion in each country. 'We will build a fence with our bones if necessary', was its slogan.

Ashin Sada Ma and a few other monks were the prime movers and organizers of the 969 Movement, but its most famous and vociferous representative was Ashin Wirathu, the abbot of the sprawling Ma Soe Yein monastery in Mandalay, the country's second-biggest city. Wirathu had been arrested in 2003 for inciting anti-Muslim riots in his hometown, Kyaukse, which had left eleven dead and fourteen injured.[1] He had been sentenced to twenty-five years in jail, but was released in early 2012 as part of a series of amnesties ordered by President Thein Sein to boost his reformist credentials. Wirathu visited Maungdaw, in northern Arakan, after the riots in June.[2] Unsurprisingly, he focused solely on the violence committed by the Rohingya, placing all the blame on the 'Bengalis'. When he returned to Mandalay, he organized a three-day-long march in Mandalay supporting the president's proposal to expel the Rohingya from the country.[3] The protests went unhindered by the authorities, while that very same month the government brought charges against the organizers of a march in Rangoon calling for peace in Kachin State.[4] Wirathu and the 969 Movement were also instrumental in organizing a series of protests in various Burmese cities against the government's decision to allow the Organization of Islamic Cooperation to open an office in the country.

Those protests were successful, and Thein Sein announced in October 2012 that he would revoke the decision.[5]

The government was highly selective as to which popular demands it would meet and which it would suppress. In this way, it was contributing to the shaping of what was acceptable and what was not when it came to participatory politics in the country, and at the same time could shield itself behind a nebulous idea of 'popular will' to deflect responsibility for discrimination against the Rohingya and other Muslims. This emboldened Wirathu and the 969 Movement to carry their message throughout Burma, which was directed not only against the Rohingya, but against Muslims in general. Apart from the increasingly ubiquitous stickers designed by Ashin Sadama, monks associated with the movement toured the country giving sermons about the need to protect Buddhism from the Muslim threat, and VCDs with those sermons, often accompanied by gruesome images of brutal crimes purportedly committed by Muslims, were made widely available in markets throughout the country.

The rhetoric of Wirathu was particularly virulent. In April 2013, I went with two other colleagues to interview him in his monastery. Sitting beneath several huge portraits of himself, he spoke with a calm demeanour and a boyish, expressionless face that sometimes showed an elusive smile, or even a grin of pain when explaining the 'Muslim conspiracy' that he claimed was threatening to engulf Burma. A man of contradictions – there was a portrait of Aung San Suu Kyi behind him, but he accused her and her party of being controlled by Muslims and supported Thein Sein – he seemed consistent only in his loathing of Islam. At one point he claimed that all rapes in the country were committed by Muslims, a ludicrous accusation for which he only referenced vague reports he assured us he had in his possession.

'If Burmese Buddhists do not take action, by 2100 the whole country will resemble the Mayu region of Arakan State', he explained, referring to northern Arakan. His solution was a simple formula: 'Buddhists can talk with Muslims, but not marry them; there can be friendship between them, but not trade.' In this formulation, Wirathu condensed how he and other 969 monks portrayed the alleged Muslim threat as that of a monstrous horde bent on economic and demographic domination. What motivated Wirathu to get involved in his personal anti-Muslim crusade was something of a mystery, as he had given conflicting accounts to different interviewers. But, sincere or not, the explanation that he gave us was revealing of his ideology and that of the 969 Movement. He claimed that two decades before, a Muslim who had converted to Buddhism had given him a 'secret message' circulated among Burmese Muslims with the plans to Islamise the country: the alleged strategy was to take over the economy in order to lull as many poor Buddhist girls as possible into marrying Muslim men and converting them, and thus slowly to make Burma an Islamic country.

The origins of both 969 and Wirathu's personal crusade, which seemed to have the blessing of the military regime, can probably be traced back to the early 1990s. According to an investigation by the British journalist Andrew Marshall, the movement was inspired by Kyaw Lwin, a former monk and government official who died in 2001.[6] In 1991, the military junta created the Department for the Promotion and Propagation of the Sasana ('religion' in Pali) (DPPS), under the Ministry of Religion, and appointed Kyaw Lwin as its head. One year later, the DPPS published Kyaw Lwin's book, *How to Live as a Good Buddhist*. The book was republished in 2000 under the title *The Best Buddhist*, with a cover showing an early version of the 969 logo. Kyaw Lwin, who had close relations with the military junta, including its highest authority, Senior General Than Shwe, met Wirathu and other future 969 leaders, and stayed in touch with them over the years. It was after his death that Wirathu started the anti-Muslim preaching that would send him to jail. But incarceration did not deter him. A few months later, I would meet a former political prisoner who had shared some time in jail with him in Obo prison, in Mandalay. According to the former political prisoner, who at that time was working as a teacher for Burmese migrant workers and refugees in Mae Sot (Thailand), Wirathu had access to materials that other prisoners could not possess, such a mobile phones and books, enjoyed a degree of freedom of movement between the parts of the jail, and continued preaching in jail, often to hardened criminals.

It is unclear whether the 969 monks and Wirathu were supported by the military, but there are strong suspicions that this was the case. In any case, most of the extremist monks seemed to be true believers in their cause, rather than cynical opportunists. And the phenomenon of Buddhist monks engaging in nationalist politics, stoking anti-Muslim or xenophobic sentiments, was not new in Burma.

Not all Buddhist monks adhered to the principles of the 969 Movement. Many stayed away from politics, and there was a small minority of monks who vocally opposed 969; but they seemed to have less means to voice their message of tolerance. One of them was Ashin Pum Na Wontha, the fifty-six-year-old abbot of a monastery in Rangoon with a history of political activism dating back to 1988. He was a member of the Peace Cultivation Network, an organization established to promote understanding between different faiths. In an interview in his monastery, he told me that Ashin Wirathu was merely a puppet 'motivated by his vanity and thirst for fame.' He was convinced that Wirathu and the 969 Movement received financial support from the 'cronies', a group of businessmen who had gotten wealthy during the military dictatorship through their connection with the generals. According to him, some Muslim businessmen had huge assets, and the 'cronies' were trying to get their hands on them. Those claims were impossible to verify, but it appeared evident that wealthy people were donating to the 969's propaganda juggernaut. With the political opening and the increasing availability of mobile phones and access to the internet, the message of 969 was spreading dangerously fast and wide. Moreover, the recent violence in Arakan, and the way it had been framed by the local media, provided the movement with plausibility in the eyes of many Burmese Buddhists.

Historically, there had been five groups of Muslims in Burma: the Rohingya, the Kaman, the Panthay (Chinese Muslims who mostly settled in Shan State), Muslim immigrants from the Indian subcontinent during the colonial period, and less numerous Burman Muslims. The overwhelming majority of all of these groups are Sunni, with only a tiny proportion of Shia Muslims in central Burma. The largest group is the Rohingya, who – as a consequence of the apartheid regime imposed on them by the state since the late 1970s – are also the least integrated into Burmese socioeconomic life. Muslims elsewhere in the country are comparatively well integrated, but they have also suffered discrimination. Many of the descendants of Indian migrants have kept their distinctive culture, dress and customs, and sometimes even the languages of their ancestors; but it would be extremely difficult to find one who does not speak Burmese, as most have attended public schools and universities.

Many others are of mixed descent, whether Indo-Burman, Indo-Karen or Indo-Shan; and others still are simply Burman, or Shan, or belong to other groups. These Muslims are basically indistinguishable from the rest of the Burmese, their religion being their only distinguishing characteristic. But ethnicity is so intertwined with religion in Burma that, in informal conversations, the 'Muslims' are often counterposed to 'Burmese' or 'Burmans' – a conflation of religious and ethnic/national categories reflected in the old adage that 'to be Burmese is to be Buddhist'.

This conflation also works at the official level. The Citizen Scrutiny Card that all Burmese citizens have to carry includes both their ethnicity and their religion. Thus, Burma's state polices contribute to fixing the identities of its citizens; though all of them are supposed to have the same rights,[7] the cards make it easier to discriminate based on ethnicity or religion. Moreover, the authorities often arbitrarily ascribe ethnicity on the basis of religion. The cards were originally issued by the Ministry of Migration and Population (later renamed as Ministry of Labour, Immigration and Population by the Suu Kyi administration), whose motto is: 'A race does not face extinction by being swallowed into the earth, but from being swallowed up by another race.' Muslims, regardless of their ethnicity, are routinely classified as 'Indians', 'Pakistanis' or 'Bengalis', depending on the whim of the official who issues their card. Theirs is always defined as a foreign ancestry. In some cases, the process of classification may reach absurd extremes. In one example reported by the Burmese scholar Sai Latt, two different siblings were classified as 'India + Burmese + Islam' and 'Pakistan + Shan + Burmese + Islam' respectively, even though they shared the same parents, neither of whom had any connection with India or Pakistan.[8]

The intercommunal tensions between Muslims and Buddhists are very different in central Burma from those in Arakan. In the two cases, religion and ethnicity play a different role. Yet the conflicts have fed each other over the years. The 2012 riots in Arakan reverberated throughout Burma, contributing to rising hostility against Muslims elsewhere. Conversely, the anti-Muslim wave largely provoked by the 969 Movement contributed to a hardening of anti-Rohingya sentiment in Arakan. The living conditions of Muslims are also generally different. In Arakan, most of the Muslim population is rural, and largely concentrated in the north. There have been urban Muslims in places like Sittwe, and even a

Rohingya middle class of traders and merchants; but the overwhelming majority of Rohingya are extremely impoverished farmers. Both Rakhine and Rohingya claim the same territory as their ancestral land, based on divergent historical narratives. In central and upper Burma, most of the Muslim population live in cities like Rangoon and Mandalay. They may concentrate in certain neighbourhoods in the cities, but they are scattered throughout the country.

Most Muslims in central and upper Burma are far from wealthy, but they are overrepresented in trade, as a consequence of strong networks and having inherited a somewhat advantageous – though later increasingly precarious – position from the colonial period, while Buddhists are mostly impoverished farmers. Real economic domination in the country is exercised by the generals, Chinese companies and businessmen, and the billionaire 'cronies'; but the country's wealthiest people are out of sight of the general population. Muslim traders, usually owners of shops of small and middle size, are more visible to the general Burmese population than the super-rich businessmen, and their marginally better economic position has sometimes caused resentment among the Buddhist population. Chinese traders and small businessmen have flooded several cities in upper Burma in recent decades, most conspicuously in Mandalay, where they exercise huge control over the economy that is resented by many of its Burmese citizens.[9] But there has not recently been any sustained anti-Chinese campaign comparable to the 969 Movement against Muslims. Due to the strong links that the military government has maintained with China and Chinese corporations, it has been in its best interests to avoid anti-Chinese sentiment from exploding into violence. In short, the fact that Muslims have a certain degree of control over small trade in towns and cities may make the notion of a Muslim economic threat peddled by the 969 Movement plausible to many Buddhists in central Burma.

In the climate of intercommunal distrust fostered by the 969 Movement, violence did not take long to explode. The first place to fall was Meiktila, a commercial town with a population of around 100,000 in Irrawaddy Division, 140 kilometres south of Mandalay. Wirathu had mentioned Meiktila in one of his sermons, which was uploaded to YouTube during the violence, saying that the NLD office in town was controlled by Muslims – though it is unclear when and where he gave the sermon, and how many people in the town had heard it.[10] In the weeks before the violence, a pamphlet was distributed around the town in the name of 'Buddhists who feel helpless'. The pamphlet claimed that strange 'kalars' (a derogatory term used to refer to people of South Asian origin) had been seen around town and that 'using money Saudi allocated to mosques, they have been buying land, farm and houses both in and out of the town with incredible amount of money under the Burmese names'. These mysterious Muslims were allegedly bribing officials to gain control over the city and marry Buddhist women.[11] Such accusations may have had a ring of truth for many because the retail trade in Meiktila was mostly in the hands of Muslims.

The trigger for the violence took place in one of those Muslim-owned shops. Everything started with the breaking of a gold hair-clip.[12] On 20 March 2013, a Buddhist woman from a village near Meiktila went with her husband and sister to a downtown gold shop to sell a gold hair-clip. When they were bargaining with the owner of the shop, the hair clip got broken, and a quarrel ensued in which the owner slapped the woman. According to several witnesses, the clients were expelled from the shop and beaten up in the street by three clerks. The police detained the owner and the woman; but a crowd of Buddhists gathered around, soon becoming enraged and attacking the shop, shouting anti-Muslim slurs. Tensions mounted as the story of the incident quickly became known everywhere in the town. That same evening, four Muslims allegedly attacked a Buddhist monk travelling on the back of a bike. They hit him in the head, and when he fell they doused him with fuel and set him on fire. He died in hospital a few hours later. That evening, the Muslim-majority quarter of Mingalar Zay Yone was in flames, when Buddhist mobs attacked the Muslim population in retaliation.

Mon Hnin, a twenty-nine-year-old Muslim woman, told me a couple of weeks later that she had spent the night when everything had started with her daughter and mother-in-law, hiding in terror in the bushes on the fringes of that neighbourhood. Her house had been destroyed by a Buddhist mob, and she and her relatives had to take refuge in the first place they could find. The bushes where they had hidden are in front of a local madrasa, where the worst atrocity of that pogrom took place. According to several eyewitnesses, the next morning a mob of Buddhists attacked the madrasa and killed at least twenty students and four teachers.[13] Mon Hnin told me that she saw about thirty policemen arriving in trucks in the morning. From her hiding place, she saw how the students and teachers of the madrasa gave up the weapons they had improvised to defend themselves. A group of them was offered the chance to be evacuated from the area in police trucks, but they were attacked by the mob before reaching the vehicles. One of them was her husband, a halal butcher who was stabbed to death. The policemen in the area did nothing to stop the carnage. Shortly afterwards, Mon Hnin, her daughter and her mother-in-law were given shelter in the house of a Buddhist neighbour.

Win Htein was then the local MP for the NLD. A former army officer who had spent several years in jail for his political activities, he had been the man responsible for the security of Aung San Suu Kyi after she was released from house arrest on November 2010. 'I saw with my own eyes two people already dead and five more put to death in front of me', he told me a few weeks later in the ramshackle local NLD office, explaining what he had witnessed in the madrasa. He assured me that he had tried to protect the Muslims, but the mob had threatened him. Then he called the chief minister of Mandalay Division, General Ye Myint, imploring him to stop the riots. 'He said he'd already given orders to the police to take action, but there was no action at all', he told me.

A local video journalist from Mandalay went immediately to Meiktila. When she arrived at the scene of the massacre in the madrasa, she saw a pile of several dozen corpses a few metres away. When she went back four hours later, the pile had been set on fire. In the meantime, in the intersection of the main road, she filmed a group of Buddhists slit the throat of a Muslim man before dousing him with petrol and setting him on fire while he was still alive. The police were there, but they did nothing. She continued recording despite being told to stop, but eventually had to flee the scene on a motorbike when several men chased her. According to her, during the time she spent recording the riots in Meiktila, she saw only Buddhists carrying weapons, and the violence was fundamentally one-sided, the Muslims being always on the receiving end.

Win Htein told me that the attacks were spontaneous and perpetrated by the Buddhist residents of the city; but other witnesses said that the attackers were unknown to them, and seemed to be following a well-coordinated plan. It is difficult to know exactly who carried out the violence, but it is possible that some mobs from outside had led the riots, with local residents joining in. Some of the perpetrators seemed to be Buddhist monks; many Burmese, horrified with the violence, were adamant that those could not have been monks, but must have been thugs dressed as such.

Amid the carnage, there were also stories of heroism, as some monks gave shelter to Muslims in their monasteries. But for two days, Buddhist mobs roamed free through the city, destroying hundreds of houses and killing, according to official figures, at least forty-two people, until the military intervened and restored a semblance of order. Some members of the 88 Generation visited the town to calm the situation down. Ashin Wirathu also visited the city when order had largely been restored, and called for an end to the violence.

The landscape in Meiktila after the violence looked eerily similar to the razed quarters I had seen in Sittwe and Kyaukphyu the previous year. The Muslim quarter was another landscape of ruins and ashes as far as the eye could see. Around 12,000 people, most of them Muslims, had lost their houses and were sheltered in temporary camps. Among them was Mon Hnin, the woman who had seen a mob kill her husband, living with her family in an unofficial camp ten kilometres away from town. In the immediate aftermath of the violence, the government announced it had plans to rebuild the destroyed houses within two months, but few believed in its ability or even willingness to do so. Many Muslim refugees feared their situation might become permanent, as had happened to Muslims in Arakan.

The violence soon spread to other towns and villages in central Burma. In the coming weeks, around twenty towns and villages saw anti-Muslim pogroms of lower intensity, tracing a line that threatened to reach Rangoon, the country's biggest city. When I visited the country I interviewed some refugees who had been displaced to Rangoon from Minhla, a town 160 kilometres to the north. A group of eighty Muslims were sheltering in a derelict building owned by a Muslim. Maung Win, a teacher at the local madrasa, recounted how a mob of Buddhist extremists had attacked the mosque shortly after afternoon prayers. He and other refugees from Minhla told me that the attacks had come out of the blue, without any prior threat or warning. But they also said that relations between the two communities had steadily soured after a monk had visited the city one month before, when he had given a sermon telling Buddhists to shun Muslims and their shops.

The violence never reached Rangoon, but its Muslim residents feared that the worst could also come to them. Residents told me that people roamed the streets in cars at night, shouting threats and anti-Muslim slurs. After the attacks in Meiktila, the residents of Mingalar Taungyungnunt, the main Muslim quarter in Rangoon, were on edge. The community had taken charge of its own security. At night, men patrolled the streets, and every entrance to the neighbourhood from the main streets was blocked with makeshift barricades. Nobody seemed to trust that the authorities would protect them if what they called 'Buddhist terrorists' attacked them.

Many Muslims felt that Aung San Suu Kyi had also abandoned them. Muslims throughout Burma have long supported her in the hope that she would strive to stamp out discrimination against them. Win Htein, the NLD lawmaker who had tried to calm the situation during the riots in Meiktila, denounced the violence in subsequent weeks, and he was denounced by Buddhist extremists as a 'friend of the kalar'. Meanwhile, Suu Kyi kept silent. A few days after the riots, on 27 March, she surprised observers and Burmese citizens alike by attending a military parade in Naypyidaw for the first time, as part of a celebration of Armed Forces Day.

When I asked Win Htein about her silence, he said that the party was willing to 'accept the blame for not taking the necessary steps on behalf of the Muslims', and he added that they would 'repair the damage later, by getting involved in religious ceremonies and asking committees to get together, but it will be a hard task'. He also told me that he had told Suu Kyi not to go to Meiktila during the riots. 'I advised her not to come here, because people were blaming me when I supported the Muslims.' After admitting that this decision was born out of political calculation, he added, 'She wouldn't be able to give a reasonable answer to the conflict – that's why I told her not to come.' It seemed that he was shielding her from the political damage that defending Muslims might bring.

I visited Meiktila again one year later, and the situation had not changed substantially. Little reconstruction had been undertaken in the Muslim quarter, and around 8,000 people, including Buddhists and Muslims, remained in camps for the displaced. Muslims enjoyed a freedom of movement that was denied to their coreligionists in Arakan, but it was more difficult for them to return to their homes than it was for Buddhists.

Even many of those whose houses had not been destroyed were unable to return. The local authorities did not give them permission to go back to Buddhist-majority quarters, arguing that their presence might exacerbate tensions between the communities. The house of War War, a forty-two-year-old mother of four, still stood in downtown Meiktila. Her husband commuted every day from the camp outside Meiktila to work, but the chairman of the quarter refused to grant them permission to live in their home again. 'We have been asking him for months if we can go home, but he says that the Buddhist people there don't want us to return. He said there had been an incident involving another Muslim family. But we have visited the old quarter and our neighbours have told us that they want us to come back', she told me.

The chairman was a sixty-year-old man called U Chaw. 'Muslims cannot come back because this is a Buddhist-majority neighbourhood', he said. 'But they will be allowed back when everything has been rebuilt.' He claimed that he was following both orders from above and the requests of the Buddhist population of his quarter to prevent Muslim families returning home. 'People are afraid that returning Muslims will do something. It will take a long time to rebuild trust between the two communities', he said.

When I visited the quarter and talked with its Buddhist residents, their sentiments turned out to be more complicated. One of them was Kyaw Myaing, a middle-aged man who assured me that he did not blame their Muslim neighbours for the violence, and claimed that it was the local authorities who did not wish to see the Muslims returning. But, like many of his neighbours, he was not pressing the issue, and he thought that 'there might be trouble' if Muslims returned to the quarter. Talking with him and other neighbours, I came to the view that they did not harbour any hatred towards the Muslims with whom they had lived in close proximity for many years, but were afraid of a repetition of the riots – and the government and local authorities were not doing anything to dispel such fears. Meanwhile, some people had given up and left. Among them was Mo Hnin, the woman who I had interviewed the previous year. When I tried to find her, the leader of the camp told me that she had left the country and was living in Qatar, working in a textile factory. 'She couldn't stand the sadness of living here and had to move away. She now sends money home to her family', he explained.

Most of the displaced people have returned home over the years. The communities have gradually come to live together again, thanks to the initiatives of local civil society organizations working on interfaith dialogue.[14] As in Arakan, Buddhists and Muslims had lived side by side and interacted for generations; but, unlike in Arakan, after the violence the authorities had not kept the communities apart.

Muslims in Burma have not only been demonized by the 969 Movement, but also actively persecuted by the authorities. They have been falsely portrayed by the Burmese government as a potential terrorist threat since the US Bush administration launched its 'war on terror' after 9/11, in what was probably a desperate attempt to curry international favour at a time when the Western powers were isolating the military regime. During the Thein Sein administration, that insidious association between Islam and terrorism came back with a vengeance. In May 2015, the police arrested twenty Muslims who were going to attend a wedding in Taungyyi, in southern Shan State. They were eventually sentenced to several years in jail on terrorism charges, including a seven-year term for a fifteen-year-old boy. No evidence was produced by the prosecution at the trial.[15]

That same year, with the journalist Veronica Pedrosa, I investigated a similar case in Mandalay.[16] At least a dozen people had been accused of belonging to a hitherto unknown organization called 'Myanmar Muslim Army'. There was a powerful reason why nobody had heard of such a group: it did not exist. One of the defendants was Soe Moe Aung, a twenty-four-year-old man. He was arrested in November 2014 and held incommunicado, and without access to a lawyer, for ten days during which, according to his mother and his lawyer, he was tortured to extract a confession that was used in the subsequent trial. 'They accuse him of undergoing training in a camp, but I don't think that's possible', her mother said in an interview in Mandalay. 'He's sick – he suffers from gout – so how could he have received any training?' While investigating the case, we were able to obtain the authorization for the one of the arrests signed by the minister of home affairs, indicating that the case was, at the very least, given the green light from the highest authority. 'That's a big burden for the accused, because the court is afraid of not following orders from the minister himself', Aung Naing Soe, the lawyer of another accused, told me.

The lawyer of Soe Moe Aung and four other people accused of belonging to the 'Myanmar Muslim Army' was a Muslim woman named Nandar Myint Thein who had received threats for taking up the case. She assured me that no evidence beyond the confessions was ever submitted during the trial. 'When I asked the prosecution's witnesses [all of them members of the police] for evidence about the Myanmar Muslim Army, they answered that they couldn't speak about it before the court, that this information came from above', she said. She and Aung Naing Soe, lawyer of others accused of belonging to the same ghost organization, said that the accusation alleged that the evidence for the defendants' involvement with the 'Myanmar Muslim Army', or even proof of the group's very existence, was withheld on the basis that revealing it in court would jeopardize 'national security', making any defence virtually impossible.

We managed to talk on the phone with Zaw Htay, the director of the president's office, and he echoed this argument. 'The Home Affairs Ministry has all the evidence on these activities, but we can't make it public because this is a national security issue', he told us. To the question of how the defendants would be able have a fair trial when the evidence against them was not produced, he simply replied, 'They have the right to appeal in upper courts.' He justified the arrests by saying, 'There are many activities outside the country and they want to promote their terrorist attacks with some people inside the country, so right now we are doing a pre-emptive strike to protect ourselves against any possible attack.' The talk about a 'pre-emptive strike' had echoes of the rhetoric used by the US government in its war on terror, like Zaw Htay's assertion that 'we have to balance our security with the defence of our freedoms'. Eventually, the twelve accused were sentenced to seven years in jail for belonging to an armed group whose existence was never proved.[17]

Meanwhile, Wirathu was acquiring international fame. He appeared on the cover of *Time* magazine under the headline 'The Face of Buddhist Terror'.[18] The cover provoked the fury of Buddhists in Burma, with demonstrations against the magazine, and even managed to offend some of Wirathu's most vocal detractors, including the former monk Ashin Gambira. A leader of what was internationally known as the 'Saffron revolution' in 2007, Gambira did not defend Wirathu, but found it insulting to find the words 'terror' and 'Buddhism' in the same sentence.[19] The president defended both Buddhism and the controversial monk. After describing Wirathu as a 'son of Buddha' and a 'noble man' committed to peace in a post in his Facebook page, he said, 'The article in *Time* magazine can cause misunderstanding about the Buddhist religion, which has existed for millennia and is followed by the majority of Burmese citizens.'[20] As was already happening in relation to the conflict in Arakan State, domestic and international perceptions about the country and its intercommunal tensions were steadily diverging, leading to a belated discovery abroad that followers of Buddhism – widely seen in the West as a peaceful faith – were also capable of committing violence in the name of their religion. Within Burma itself, a growing siege mentality among Buddhists, who began to feel that foreigners did not understand the country's culture and challenges, was slowly setting in. This attitude would grow in the following years, helping to entrench a xenophobic variety of nationalism increasingly prevalent in Burma.

It was unclear to what extent the ethno-nationalist monks had been directly involved in the anti-Muslim pogroms. Surely monks like Wirathu had contributed to the creation of a climate of intercommunal tension, but they had been careful to distance themselves from the violence. Wirathu invariably placed the blame on the Muslims themselves, refusing to acknowledge that his sermons had stoked the flames of anti-Muslim hatred, and insisting that he was 'just informing the public'. But there was one case in which there was little doubt that his words had contributed to unleashing deadly riots. On 30 June 2014, Wirathu posted on his Facebook page a denunciation of an alleged rape by three Muslims of a Buddhist girl working for one of them in the coffee shop they owned in Mandalay.[21]

The next day, according to several witnesses, a group of twenty-five to thirty unknown men roamed around the Muslim quarter downtown, hurling insults at Muslims and damaging vehicles and shops, all unimpeded by the riot police who were already present in the area. Some Buddhist monks managed to bring the crowds under control, and three days later the police stopped the riots. Two men had been killed: one Buddhist and one Muslim. It turned out that the rape allegations were false. Even then, Wirathu found a chance to blame Muslims. 'The rape of Ma Soe Soe on June 28, 2014 at the hands of Sun Cafe owners Nay Win and San Maung is not just a criminal offence but an offence aimed at instigating violence in our country. The July 1 and 2 incidents in Mandalay are not a clash of religions or races but a Jihad. They are gathering in mosques in Mandalay under the guise of Ramadan but in reality they are recruiting and preparing for Jihad against us', Wirathu posted when the riots were over. He was never prosecuted by the authorities for instigating these riots, as he had been in 2003.

After the riots in Mandalay, episodes of intercommunal violence receded in central Burma; by this time the 969 symbol had almost disappeared from view. The Sangha Maha Nayaka Committee – a body of senior monks appointed by the government to regulate the monastic community – banned its political use in September 2013. But that did not put an end to the activities of nationalist monks like Ashin Sada Ma or Wirathu. In January 2014, in a massive conference of monks in Mandalay, they founded a new organization that replaced the 969 Movement. It was named A-myo Batha Thatana Saun Shauq Ye a Pwe, or Association for the Protection of Race and Religion, better known by the Burmese acronym Ma Ba Tha.[22] The Association helped to organize Buddhist 'Sunday school' classes for children throughout Burma, selling curriculum books to any interested Buddhists. The aim of the schools was to impart Buddhist values to the new generations. Their teachings were usually not explicitly anti-Muslim, but the underlying message was clear: it was necessary to protect Buddhism and, as many Ma Ba Tha monks made clear, the main threat was Islam.[23]

The crowning achievement of Ma Ba Tha was the passing of four 'Race and Religion Protection Laws' in 2015.[24] The first law bans polygamy. The second makes religious conversion dependant on obtaining approval from a Registration Board for religious conversion at the township level, and punishes forced conversions. The third law regulates the marriages of Buddhist women to non-Buddhist men, mandating local registrars to post marriage applications for fourteen days in public, in order to determine whether there are any objections to the proposed unions – and the couple may marry only if there are no objections. The fourth law imposes a limit on the number of children a woman can bear, but only in certain regions. Muslims are not mentioned explicitly in the laws, but it was clear to everybody that they were directed at them, while the Population Control Bill was to be applied in Arakan to the Rohingya community exclusively. The laws had wide popular support.

A draft of the interreligious marriage law was circulated in the summer of 2013, and monks organized demonstrations in support. A campaign to gather signatures was launched around that time, with stalls set up all around the country, and it was claimed that 2.5 million people signed. There was opposition from some quarters – especially from women's groups, who regarded the laws as inimical to women's rights.[25] Ma Ba Tha responded with a condemnation of 'those critics, who are backed by foreign groups, for raising the human rights issues and not working for the benefit of the public and not being loyal to the state', and some of the critics received death threats.[26] But many women had also participated actively in the promotion of the laws, as they now had an opportunity to take a public role.[27]

The nationalist monks not only succeeded during this period in getting their laws passed, but also managed to determine to a large degree the issues that were considered of national importance and would take centre-stage in public debates throughout Burma.

Meanwhile, other kinds of mobilizations, for workers' rights or against rampant land-grabbing, were virtually relegated to the margins. Some of them acquired brief prominence, including a series of student protests in early 2014 against a new education law that was to give the government tight control over the universities. The students organized nationwide, coordinating a big march to Rangoon. But they were blocked by the police in Letpadan, 100 kilometres north of the city, and were eventually beaten with great brutality. Many of them were arrested and put in jail for two years.[28] The new education law was eventually passed with overwhelming parliamentary support, including that of Aung San Suu Kyi, who during the protests had done little to hide her annoyance, saying: 'Whether it is in this country or in any country, the best method to resolve problems is to discuss and negotiate.'[29] In the context of those protests, of the demonstrations against the Letpadaung Copper Mine, and other mobilizations, the government of Thein Sein was sending a clear message: only movements to protect race and religion were to be allowed in the new 'discipline-flourishing democracy'. For the rest, the old apparatus of repression was still very much in place.

Ahead of the elections in November 2015, Ma Ba Tha threw its support behind the party in government, the USDP, and actively campaigned against the NLD, accusing it of being controlled by Muslims and being too soft on defending 'race and religion'. The NLD eventually won the elections, but it was not a victory over the Buddhist ethno-nationalism expounded by Ma Ba Tha. The NLD had yielded to them; not wanting to endanger its chances of winning, the party did not file a single Muslim candidate. As a result, there would not be any Muslims in the new parliament.

5

The Counted and the Excluded

The census is one of the main instruments the state has to shape the nation, as well as to control its populations. In many senses, the Burmese nation is still a work in progress. Seven decades after independence, many members of the ethnic minorities still feel little allegiance to an overall Burmese identity they see as a project of Burman supremacy. During the Thein Sein period, the state was undergoing a crucial transformation in which, in 2014, the government decided to carry out a nationwide census. The way of classifying the population, particularly its ethnic make-up, would not be merely descriptive, but would have far-reaching political consequences. The list of ethnic categories had been elaborated by the military regime long before, and would potentially contribute to shaping the political voice of its varied population. According to the 2008 Constitution, political representation is based largely on ethnicity, and dividing or conflating ethnic groups could alter the balance of power between the various communities, at both the national and the local levels. The census was bound to create winners and losers, and nobody would lose more than those who were excluded.

It was the first census conducted in Burma since 1983. This was a very long gap, as in most countries censuses are conducted every ten years. It was possible that, with its stringent registration rules, the military junta that had ruled the country since 1988 already had some figures on the Burmese population; but it had never conducted a public, nationwide survey. The fact that it did not bother to do so for all those years could indicate indifference – the generals seemed more keen on cementing their power, strengthening the army and filling their pockets – but it also betrays the incapacities of a state that is extremely authoritarian but highly disfunctional in many aspects.

In the months ahead of the 2014 census, there was a campaign throughout the country presenting it as an exercise of civic duty and part of a common project of nation-building beyond political divisions. The famous comedian and pro-democracy activist Zarganar, who had spent years in prison for his anti-junta activities but had played an increasingly official role during the transition, was appointed 'census ambassador', and toured the country for three weeks. One of the activities involved the public shouting and holding signs with the official census slogan, 'Nation-wide census – let's all participate!' for as long as possible in a competition to win an official census tee shirt or cap.[1]

The census was conducted by what was then called the Union of Myanmar Ministry of Immigration and Population, with the technical assistance of the United Nations Population Fund (UNFPA), which also distributed most of the funding provided by donor countries, including Australia and the United Kingdom.[2] In the climate of international optimism about the 'democratic transition' in the country, the UN and the donor countries supported the census, alleging that it was necessary for the development of that new Burma so many people wanted to believe was being born. To this end, the UNFPA even ignored its own rule for conducting censuses only during times of peace. The peace process between several ethnic armed groups and the government was extremely fragile, and the war was still raging in Kachin State, with sporadic flare-ups in other areas. Eventually, the census was not conducted in the areas of Kachin State controlled by the KIO,[3] or in some townships in Karen State. According to the government, 46,600 people were not enumerated in Kachin, and 69,753 were left out in Karen.

There were dozens of questions in the census, but the most sensitive was that of ethnicity, or race – concepts often difficult to distinguish in the Burmese context. The Burmese word, *lumyo* literally means 'type of people', and is used indistinctly for both. In common usage, *lumyo* implies closed groups of descent not only with a common culture and language, but also with common physical and psychological features. In a country plagued by several violent ethnic and intercommunal conflicts, most of which are unresolved and some even deteriorating, there was fear that the census question relating to ethnicity risked exacerbating those conflicts, and some organizations even suggested dropping it altogether.[4]

There were several problems with the question. The respondents could only identify themselves with one ethnic group, so the final result did not reflect the fact that many Burmese are of mixed descent. Also, the list of groups was large, but closed. It was based on a more than two-decades-old classification of 135 'indigenous races' (*taingyinthar lumyo*), with the possibility of choosing 'other *lumyo*', which, by definition, meant foreign. If ethnicity is a social construct, in this case the government classification imposed a state-directed construct of categories that reflected poorly the complex and fluid realities of ethnic allegiances in the country, and undermined the wishes of many people on how to identify themselves.

Again, this contravened the standards of the UN, whose *Principles and Recommendations for Population and Housing Censuses*, published by the United Nations Statistics Division, recommends that categories should not be fixed. Moreover, the classification of 135 groups was not accepted by the representatives of many ethnic groups. There are two tiers in the classification: eight 'major races', the Burman and the seven groups from which the seven states in the country take their names (Mon, Rakhine for Arakan, Kachin, Chin, Shan, Kayah for Karen, and Kayin for Karenni); and 135 'subgroups' living in those states and subsumed in the 'major races' in a way that was often arbitrary and seldom reflected how people identify themselves.

Some subgroups are only geographically related to the major races of which they are supposedly a part – such as, for instance, the Wa, who live in Shan state but have little relation to the Shan ethnic group. In other cases, the subgroups would be better characterized as tribes or clans of the 'major races', like the Kachin subgroups (with the possible exception of the Lisu). In the case of the Chin, the major race had been divided into fifty-three different subgroups – a division that many Chin leaders regard as false.[5] In at least one case, one group was under two different 'major races': the Mro are a subgroup of the Rakhine in Arakan, and a subgroup of the Chin (to whom are really related) with another name (Wakim) in Chin State.

Not unsurprisingly, civil society leaders, intellectuals and politicians of most ethnic groups protested against such classification, alleging that it had been created artificially to split and distort the political representation of the minorities.[6] On top of that, and given that it was the enumerators who would fill in the forms without the respondents being able to check that it had been done correctly, there was ample room for mistakes and manipulation.

A few months after the census, the government announced that it would not release the data on ethnicity until after the election. It alleged that it was too technically complex to do it quickly[7] – though it is more likely that it feared the findings might provoke further conflict that it could not manage. At the time of writing – years later and with another government in charge – the results are still unknown. Nevertheless, Min Aung Hlaing, the commander-in-chief of the armed forces, gave a speech on October 2016 commemorating the nationwide ceasefire signed with eight armed groups, in which he revealed very precise statistics about Shan State and Kachin State. It turned out that, in Kachin State, out of a total population of 1.6 million, the Kachin were less than 50 per cent. It is unclear if that was a veiled warning to the Kachin nationalists and the KIO, who had not signed the ceasefire yet; but for some served to confirm old allegations that the government had been pursuing plans to dilute the Kachin population in their own state.

The results of the census that proved to be far less sensitive than expected were those on religion, released two years later, in July 2016. There was some fear that intercommunal violence could flare again if the new figures showed a marked growth in the Muslim population since 1983. But a quick look at the last three censuses showed clearly that, if Buddhism were under threat in Burma, Islam would be an unlikely menace. According to the 2014 census, there were 2,237,495 Muslims in the country, comprising 4.3 per cent of the total population, while Buddhists comprised around 87.9 per cent. In both the 1973 and 1983 censuses, Muslims accounted for 3.9 per cent of the population, and Buddhists for 88.8 and 89.4 per cent, respectively.[8] Meanwhile, the Christian population grew from 4.6 per cent in 1973 and 4.9 per cent in 1983 to 6.3 per cent in 2014.[9] According to the 2014 census, the total population in Burma was 51,486,253 (including those not enumerated, but excluding many among the up to 4 million migrants in neighbouring countries). The total population in 1983 was 35,307,913. The total population had grown by 45.8 per cent, the Buddhist population by 43.9 per cent, the Christian population by 83.4 per cent, and the Muslim

population by 62.5 per cent. But the higher growth of the Muslim population was due to that of Arakan, as we shall see below. The Muslim
population elsewhere in Burma – a total of 1,118,764 – grew by 40.9 per
cent, from 793,950 in 1983, which was a lower rate than any other religious group, and lower than the overall growth rate of the country as a
whole. But, while these data disproved the notion of a Muslim threat
voiced by Buddhist ultra-nationalists, the prevalence of anti-Muslim
rhetoric did not change after the results were announced.

The most problematic aspect of the census was the Rohingya issue. The
Rohingya are not included in the list of 135 'national races', as only those
ethnic groups that were allegedly settled in Burma before the beginning
of the colonial period in 1824 are regarded as *taingyinthar*, and the official narrative on the Rohingya claims that they arrived later, as labourers
from Bengal during the colonial period – and some even later still, as
illegal immigrants after Burma's independence in 1948. Thus, the term
'Rohingya' itself is rejected in Burma, on the assumption that it is a
recent invention by which the 'Bengalis' have contrived an indigenous
identity in order to gain political rights to which, as 'foreigners', they are
not entitled.

Meanwhile, Rohingya activists and politicians allege that their presence in Burma, and the term Rohingya itself, pre-date the arrival of the
British by several centuries, and that they are as indigenous as any of the
other 135 'national races'. In principle, the question of whether the
Rohingya are *taingyinthar* or not should not by itself determine their
citizenship status; but the distinction between *taingyinthar* and citizenship had become increasingly blurred in public discourse. This issue
acquired more prominence than ever after the sectarian violence in
2012; by the time of the census, a seemingly academic debate on the
Rohingyas' place in the history of Arakan had become a matter of life
and death.

The Burmese government had given assurances that everybody
would have the right to self-identify, including the Rohingya.[10] It was
never clear whether the final results would include the word; given that
the enumerators would fill the forms themselves, they could write
'Bengali' when the respondents answered 'Rohingya' to the question of
ethnicity. The government had even negotiated with a Rohingya Census
Supporting Committee about employing Rohingya enumerators in

Muslim-majority areas in the state; but eventually they were dismissed, alleging pressure from the Rakhine community. The mere possibility that the census might give some legitimacy to the Rohingya was unacceptable to Rakhine nationalists, and they organized protests throughout Arakan, and even threatened to boycott the process.[11] The government announced at the last minute that it would not enumerate those who self-identified as Rohingya. The enumerators would visit Rohingya houses accompanied by security forces, would ask the ethnicity question, and then leave immediately if they heard the proscribed word. The UNFPA issued a feeble protest, suggesting the postponement of the census in Arakan or the dropping of the ethnicity question altogether, but the government went ahead. Despite the fact that the government had broken its promise of respecting the right of the respondents to self-identification, the UNFPA did not withdraw its assistance. Thus, the overwhelming majority of the Rohingya population was not enumerated. Only a tiny minority accepted the label 'Bengali'. The Rohingya were reduced to a simple number of 1,090,000 "non-enumerated" people in Arakan, as reflected in the census final figures.

As a result of the protests against the census, tensions had mounted in Arakan. In January, they were compounded by an incident in a remote village in Maungdaw Township called Du Chee Yar Than. Villagers claimed that the village had been attacked by the police, and that up to forty-four people had been massacred. The government forcefully denied such accusation and closed off the area to external observers. The truth of what went on in Du Chee Yar Than has never been established, but it seems clear that there was some sort of outbreak of violence. A couple of weeks later, Médecins Sans Frontières (MSF), one of the most important providers of healthcare in the country and virtually the only one in Northern Arakan, made a public statement saying they had treated twenty-two people from the village with knife wounds. One month later, the government expelled MSF completely from Arakan, alleging that it had privileged the 'Bengalis'. As a result, up to 750,000 people were deprived of vital access to healthcare.[12]

Protests organized by Rakhine nationalists soon targeted other international organizations, which they accused of being biased in favour of the Muslim population. To signal support for the boycott of the census, Rakhine nationalists hoisted Buddhist flags in many buildings in Sittwe.

A few days before the census, a foreign aid worker for the NGO Malteser International took down the Buddhist flag from its office in Sittwe, as the rules of the organization prohibited the use of religious symbols. The rumour circulated in town that she had disrespected the flag by putting it in the back pocket of her trousers – though a subsequent investigation determined she had not done so.[13] The protests against the census turned into violence against the offices of NGOs and UN agencies, and a girl was killed by the police during the riots. Foreign organizations evacuated their international workers from Arakan for several weeks, and, during the census, the government also stopped its mobile clinics. As a consequence, aid and services like healthcare were virtually nonexistent in Rohingya camps for more than one month.[14]

The Rohingya had been subjected to various types of violence over the years. Direct attacks like those suffered during the riots in 2012 had been relatively rare, and up to that point they had probably been less destructive than other kinds of violence that were more insidious and less likely to grab media headlines. During the period in 2014 when the NGOs and UN agencies were not delivering aid, many died of starvation or as a consequence of preventable diseases that might not have killed them if MSF and other organizations had been able to attend to them.

I travelled to Sittwe a couple of weeks after the evacuation, when all the foreign staff for international organizations were out of the state. Visiting the Rohingya camps on the city's outskirts for a few days entailed witnessing horror after horror. This included stories like that of Ruk and Kun Suma, twins who had been born five minutes apart two weeks before. Their mother was an emaciated forty-year-old woman named Noor Begum who suffered from tuberculosis and was unable to breastfeed. The girls looked like tiny skeletons gasping for air, with all their bones visible through their thin skin. The parents were so poor that they could not afford to buy milk for them, so, for the first two weeks of their lives, Ruk and Kuma had only received cheap coffee creamer from the tip of their mother's finger.

In a camp for 'unregistered IDPs' there was a small hut made with tarpaulin where a family of nine lived, sleeping on the dirt. A woman was lying down in this hut, unable to feed another child. She and her husband could not afford another mouth to feed, and she had had an abortion one week before. She had been bleeding, unable to move and with no doctor around to see her. There was little one could do in those circumstances. The only aid worker around was an American working for a small NGO who had sneaked into Sittwe and the camps, and I would refer such cases to him. We wondered how the little twins could have survived for so long, and he gave them some nutrients, but they would die a week later. Everywhere, it was common to see children and adults with diarrhoea, because the water was insufficient or dirty. Many children died as a consequence. It is unclear how many people perished during that period in the camps or in northern Arakan, but it is probable that the number ran into the hundreds.

Back in Sittwe, I visited Satyokyak, a camp for Rakhine IDPs. The camp sheltered around 3,000 people living in houses built by the government. The houses, one for each family, had electricity and were elevated to avoid flooding during the rainy season, unlike the dwellings for the Rohingya IDPs. The head of the camp committee was Tun Sein, a man who seemed willing to talk with me only because I was accompanied by a member of a respected local organization. He claimed that the World Food Programme had previously provided a sack of rice for every family each month before the evacuation, but 'the situation is the same since the NGOs left the state – we don't have any problem, because the NGOs didn't help us before anyway', he said. He voiced the same complains about the INGOs being pro-Rohingya, to the detriment of the Rakhine, and would not listen to my arguments that the needs of the two communities were different. Rakhine politicians and the state and central governments were lending credence to such accusations, as when they justified the expulsion of MSF on the basis that it was biased towards the Rohingya. 'We don't want aid from NGOs. They give very little to the Rakhine community and much to the Kalars. We don't want any help from them', he said. He acknowledged that there were 'no cases of malnutrition in the camp or any important health issues here'.

The difference in how the two communities lived – and died – had only grown since the establishment of the camps a couple of years before. But I wondered to what degree Rakhine people were aware of what was happening on the other side of the divide. That very same evening, I met a Rakhine friend I had known since my first visit. He was a decent man, but he shared many of the prejudices against the Rohingya so widespread in his community. During our conversation, I told him about the horrors I had witnessed in the Rohingya camps. He just stared to me in silence. Many Rakhine would dismiss such reports as exaggerations, and the common narrative voiced by the local media, monks and other intellectual elites was very different.

Rakhine nationalists often referred to the Rohingya as 'guests' in a land that properly belonged to the Rakhine. As guests, the Rohingya were expected not to abuse the hospitality of their hosts. But they had committed the unpardonable sin of making claims over the land. As a result, the guests were now at the mercy of their hosts, and when NGOs and UN agencies returned to the state, the government created a new committee, the Emergency Coordination Centre, comprising state and central government officials, representatives from the United Nations, NGOs and civil society leaders of the ethnic Rakhine community, to which the aid groups would need to submit their proposals at least one week before their planned activities.[15] Among the representatives of the local Rakhine, there were people with strong prejudices against the Rohingya – and no Rohingya were involved in those deliberations.

By that point, it mattered little what the Rohingya did to be accepted as citizens. In July 2014, the government launched a pilot programme of citizenship verification for the Muslim population in Myebon, a township in central Arakan State. Around 3,000 Muslims lived in the township, all of them in a camp near the main town. Muslims were required to show the citizenship cards of their parents or grandparents, a family registration list, or other documents; in other words, they were assumed to be illegal immigrants unless they could prove otherwise. Producing such documents could be extremely difficult in a country where, according to the census, 27 per cent of the population above ten years of age lacked any identity document.[16] Also, the applicants had to accept the designation 'Bengali' and renounce the term Rohingya. The right of self-identification is probably less important for people on the ground than activists and politicians – Rohingya or foreigners – often assume, provided that, by renouncing it, Muslims living in Arakan could regain their citizenship, freedom of movement, and access to education or healthcare. Virtually all the Muslims in Myebon applied for citizenship, but very few attained it. Only ninety-seven were granted full citizenship, while 969 received naturalized citizenship. In practical terms, little changed for them.

I visited Myebon almost three years later, in early 2017. This small town of around 12,000 people on the bank of a river is only reachable by boat from Sittwe. Many of its inhabitants make their living by fishing. Taung Pa, the Muslim camp, is not far from town, and is heavily protected by the army and police, as much to prevent anybody from attacking it as to stop its inmates from leaving. 'I heard the word Rohingya from my parents when I was a child, but it's not accepted by the immigration department. They laughed at me and told me to go when I pronounced it once in their office. Bengali means we are from Bangladesh, and I am from Burma, but I'm willing to accept it if I can get citizenship and rights', Gulban told me. She was a fifty-three-year-old woman whose wrinkles and exhausted demeanour testified to an entire life of suffering that made her look older than her real age. The designation 'Bengali' was not only applied to the Rohingya, but also to some Kaman, even though this Muslim ethnic group is recognized as one of the 'national races'. Maung Zaw, a forty-five-year-old father of three, showed me the pink card the authorities had given to him. He was categorized as Bengali, but he also showed me his family book stating that both of his parents were Kaman. Both Gulban and Maung Zaw were given citizenship, but they were still confined in the camp, not permitted to leave for hospital, or to send their children to the school downtown, though the government and MSF sent in doctors, and there was a school in the camp.

Mahla, another Rohingya woman who had been granted citizenship, was worried about her children. 'They can only receive primary and middle education here. I'm very worried about their future. They can't get educated properly, and they will languish if they can't get out of here', she told me. Gulban said that she did not wish to go anywhere outside Myebon. 'I'm poor, and I wouldn't have anywhere to go, but I don't want to be confined in this camp', she said. 'I don't know what human rights are. I just know I would like to have food at my table, freedom of movement, education for my children, access to healthcare, and for my family to live without fear.' Gulban's words provided a definition of human rights that surpasses those of dozens of scholars.

'We gave them citizenship according to the 1982 Citizenship Law, even though they are not naturally citizens', said Tin Shwe, the general administrator of Myebon township, who had been in charge of the pilot programme, when I spoke to him in his office before visiting the camp. 'They don't belong to any of our indigenous races', he replied when I asked what distinguished them from 'natural citizens'. 'They can move whenever they want, they can go to Sittwe, or from there to Yangon, but to go to Yangon they need to inform the immigration authorities', he explained. However, the people I interviewed in the camp told me that travel permits were extremely difficult to get, and that they had to pay exorbitant bribes to the police that very few of them could afford. Tin Shwe was an ethnic Burman from central Burma, and he placed the blame squarely on the local Rakhine population for the restrictions of movement imposed on Muslims. 'When the programme was implemented it was met with strong protests from the indigenous community. I tried to explain the law to them, but it's difficult for the government, because we found ourselves between both communities. Local people don't allow Muslims to go to the hospital, so we send doctors to the camp', he said.

Since the moment when the programme was launched, the Arakan Women's Network had organized protests against it. The main organizer of those protests was Khin Thein, the local chair of the Arakan Women's Network. 'The Kalar don't belong here. With the previous military government, they used to come from Bangladesh and bribe the local officials to get legal documents because they had a lot of money. That's why we cannot accept most of them, and we protested', she explained at the jewellery shop she owned in downtown Myebon. It was a ridiculous claim, given how poor the Muslim community in the township was.

Like many Rakhine nationalists, Khin Thein was as resentful of Burman domination as she was of the purported invasion by 'Bengalis'. 'Our biggest enemy is the Myanmar government. I support the Arakan army and I want the Fatherland of Rakhine to be independent', she told me. But beyond the divergences between Rakhine nationalists like her and government officials like Tin Shwe, all of them seemed to agree that the Rohingya were not 'natural citizens'. And, once again, the government was shielding itself behind a popular sentiment it had encouraged in order to avoid having to protect a vulnerable minority. It mattered little if some of the members of that minority were officially recognized as citizens. Both Khin Thein and Tin Shwe offered the same recipe to ease intercommunal tensions: time.

'It is impossible to live together now, but it may be possible within five or ten years', said Bananda Phyabawga, the sixty-year-old abbot of Pyanabakeman, a local Buddhist monastery. Beyond that, nobody seemed able to suggest any concrete strategy to restore the fragile coexistence that had existed before 2012. The passage of time had different meanings for the Rakhine and the Rohingya communities. For the former, it could mean put the violence of 2012, and even the Rohingya themselves, behind them; for the latter, it could only mean the confirmation that their confinement and ejection from Burmese society, and the impossibility of finding work to fend for themselves, would be made permanent.

Such grim prospects induced many Rohingya men and women to flee Arakan for other countries. From 2012 to 2015, most of them tried to reach Malaysia, a predominantly Muslim country that is more economically developed than Burma. Many people leaving Arakan were young men trying to find work in construction and other sectors, but there were also many young women joining their husbands already in Malaysia, or moving there to meet their future husbands – often in marriages arranged by their families. All of them placed themselves in the hands of ruthless transnational networks of human smugglers, who transported them with migrants from Bangladesh along clandestine routes to the coasts of Thailand and Malaysia in overcrowded boats. Some of them paid a fee at the outset, but many others would have to work for years to pay the debt they had incurred.

It was a booming business for human smugglers, as there was no shortage of desperate Rohingya trying to flee the miseries of apartheid in their home country. According to the United Nations High Commissioner for Refugees (UNHCR), around 125,000 Rohingya fled to Malaysia between 2012 and 2015, while an indeterminate number of people would have crossed during that period into Bangladesh.[17] If we accept the figure of 1,090,000 non-enumerated people in Arakan given in the 2014 census, almost 10 per cent of the Rohingya population in Arakan left during those three years. Due to the harsh conditions in the boats, thousands died, their bodies unceremoniously thrown into the sea.

Many others – mostly those who had not paid in advance – ended up in clandestine camps in southern Thailand and northern Malaysia.[18] The human traffickers would become their captors in those camps, whose human cargo were sometimes sold by Thai police and immigration officials who had intercepted them at sea.[19] The Rohingya who ended up in those camps were often beaten and tortured by their captors, who called their relatives in Arakan or Malaysia demanding ransoms of up to

US$2,000 to free them. Many of those who could not pay were killed. The existence of these camps was known from late 2013, but the Thai authorities did little to close them. One year later, the *Guardian* revealed that thousands of slaves throughout Asia were a key part of the Thai prawn industry, supplying supermarket chains in Europe and the United States.[20] Some Rohingya were sold as slaves through the same networks that had set up the camps in southern Thailand, but most were Cambodians or Burmese or other ethnicities.[21]

The European Union and the United States threatened sanctions potentially harmful to Thailand's economy and international reputation.[22] The Thai government was compelled to act, and cracked down on the networks trafficking Rohingya people. In May 2015, the Thai police discovered and dismantled a camp that contained twenty-six buried bodies in the southern province of Songkhla.[23] Two days later they began to make arrests, including that of a Rohingya man called Anwar, suspected of running the camps.[24] As a consequence of the crackdown, many smugglers abandoned the boats they were then sailing, and the Thai, Malaysian and Indonesian authorities pushed all boats trying to approach their coasts back onto the high seas. In a two-week period, 10,000 Rohingya refugees and Bangladeshi migrants were abandoned to their fate in the sea, with no food or water, and unable to disembark on any coast.

It was the fishermen of Aceh, a semi-autonomous region in the north of Indonesia, who decided to take action, organizing an operation to rescue the boats approaching their coast. 'We didn't even know who these people were, but we had to save them', said Teungku Tahe, an influential Acehnese community leader who coordinated the rescue operations, when I spoke to him a few weeks later in Langsa, a city in southern Aceh Province sheltering most of the rescued refugees. In rescuing the Rohingya, the Acehnese fishermen were following ancient customary law in contravention of direct orders from the Indonesian navy and authorities, who had threatened legal action, and even sent boats to block them. 'We received SMSs telling us not to save the boats if we saw them, but our obligation is to take to the shore anybody who is in the sea. Even if it is a corpse or an animal what we find, we have the obligation to save it', he explained.

The fishermen rescued three boats carrying around 3,000 people, including Bangladeshi migrants and Rohingya refugees, many of them women and children. Among them was Mohammed Idris, a Rohingya man who had been confined in three different boats for six months, enslaved and beaten by his captors, while the human traffickers demanded a ransom for his freedom that his family could not pay. He hailed from Maungdaw and, as in many other cases, it was economic strangulation that had compelled him to embark upon the dangerous journey to Malaysia. 'Before 2012 we were poor, but we could eat. Then there was a curfew in our village and I couldn't get out to work. I was too afraid of Rakhine people and the army, and two people were killed when they went out of our village to fish', he told me in a refugee camp in Aceh. His family had to sell some land to pay for his ransom, but it was not enough to pay what the traffickers demanded, and he was kept for months on a huge prison ship in international waters. 'I didn't know it was going to be like this. If I had known, I would have stayed in Burma', he said. Eventually, when the authorities cracked down on the human smugglers, he was transferred to one of the boats that was rescued by the Acehnese fishermen. 'We feel happy here, because these people are treating us like brothers, but we are still worried about our families in Burma', he said.

These Rohingya had been received with open arms perhaps for the first time in their lives. The Bangladeshi migrants were slowly repatriated, but it was less clear what would happen to the Rohingya. The Acehnese appeared ready to receive them permanently. They had suffered a cruel war with the central Indonesian authorities that had lasted decades, and had been victims of the devastating tsunami that hit the coasts of Southeast Asia in 2014. Among them, there was a widespread sentiment of solidarity with the Rohingya. 'We Acehnese have suffered a lot – that's why we understand well the plight of the Rohingya. My husband disappeared during the conflict and we have never seen him again', said Yanah, the owner of a humble restaurant on a road near one of the camps. 'I feel that they are part of our family, part of the Acehnese society, because they have suffered as much as us. It's better if they stay permanently here.'

'We are ready to take the Rohingya permanently, as our own brothers. We have enough land and resources for them. We can make them work and provide for them', Teungku Tahe told me. But Aceh is a poor province where employment opportunities are limited, and many of the refugees had relatives waiting for them in Malaysia. When I asked

Mohammad Idris if he wanted to go to Malaysia, he replied, 'I like to be here, but I need to go to a place where I can make a living.' Eventually, most of the Rohingya were taken by human smugglers to Malaysia, while others were relocated to third countries by the UNHCR – a process that takes years.

In response to international pressure, and perhaps partly spurred by the example set by the Acehnese fishermen, the authorities in Thailand, Malaysia and Indonesia eventually allowed the Rohingya stranded in boats to disembark in their countries, on the condition that they be relocated to third countries by UN agencies after one year. With refugees flowing en masse to Europe and other places, and the UN bureaucracy incapable of tackling the global crises giving rise to mass migration in all their magnitude, this was almost impossible, and many Rohingya refugees still languish in immigration detention centres in Southeast Asia.

The networks that had previously transported the Rohingya to Malaysia had now been disrupted for good by the Thai and Malaysian authorities, while at home the Rohingya were further disenfranchised. The government had been planning to hold a referendum to amend the Constitution, and President Thein Sein had promised that those holding national verification cards – the 'white cards' held by non-citizens like most Rohingya – would be able to vote, as they had done in the 2010 election. But, yielding again to popular pressure, the government backtracked and announced that holders of white cards would not vote.[25] The referendum was eventually cancelled, and the government even revoked the white cards in order to initiate a citizenship verification process akin to that tested in Myebon.[26] The verification process was never fully implemented, having met opposition from many in the Rohingya community, distrustful of the government and the obligation to accept a label, 'Bengali', that they saw as a trap to render permanent their status as alleged foreigners in their own land.

Excluded from the census and from participating in the quasi-democratic system that was emerging in Burma, and with little or no freedom to conduct any meaningful economic activity as a result of the segregation imposed upon them, the Rohingya had been ousted altogether from Burmese social life. They were treated as unwelcome 'guests', and the survival of many of them depended on the good will of 'hosts' who regarded them with deep suspicion, and on the largesse of international organizations.

At this point the Rohingya could be tolerated grudgingly in Burmese territory; but it had become clear that they had little or no protection from being killed with impunity if their hosts decided they had become unruly. The situation of the Rohingya population and the relations between them and the Rakhine were not alike throughout the state, but depended on local conditions. The camps near Sittwe had been 'normalized' up to a point, some inmates now trading with Rakhine merchants. At the same time, corruption was rampant among some of the camp leaders, who were making illicit profit through the distribution of aid.[27]

But, while not all Rohingya individuals were victimized in the same way by the system of apartheid imposed on them, the community as a whole had been socially erased in the country. By the time of the election in late 2015, the overwhelming majority of the Rohingya in Arakan had not only been condemned to a life of absolute poverty and stagnation, but their political voice had been completely gagged. The only escape route left to them – the possibility of throwing in their lot with human traffickers and risking everything on the dangerous journey to Malaysia – had been closed off. Reduced to utter impotence, there was only one thing left to do: wait and see if things changed with a new government led by Aung San Suu Kyi.

6

The Burmese Cage

The overriding political category in contemporary Burma is ethnicity. This is such an obvious and widely held assumption on the part of both Burma watchers and Burmese themselves that it often goes unexamined in analyses of the country. One of the consequences of the pervasiveness of ethnicity is the almost total absence of class politics in the country, at least in public debates. This is particularly puzzling in a country with such staggering inequalities, stemming from a highly exploitative economic model based on the extraction of natural resources, which privileges a plundering elite of generals and their cronies, who accumulate enormous wealth at the expense of the overwhelming majority of the population.[1]

Such exploitation is particularly acute for the hundreds of thousands of farmers who, over the last two decades, have been evicted from their lands to make way for huge development projects. While many of those farmers have taken advantage of the political opening to protest strongly against land-grabbing throughout the country,[2] their demands have never coalesced into a nationwide movement. For instance, the protests against the Letpadaung Copper Mine did not extended much beyond Salingyi township. Responsibility for this lies partly with Aung San Suu Kyi, who contributed to the deactivation of their potential power in the name of a supposedly superior 'national interest'. Ethnic and nationalist politics are not inherently inimical to other kinds of politics demanding social justice or the redistribution of wealth; but, in Burma as elsewhere, nationalism has often served to delegitimize political movements of that kind. And nationalism in Burma, as in many other places, is strongly predicated on an ideal of unity that serves to discipline the population and silence sectoral demands, which are condemned as 'selfish'.[3]

The pervasiveness of ethnic conflict in Burma is accompanied by the dominance of an idea that all ethnic groups seem to expound: the notion of 'national races' (*taingyintha*). This comes with the corollary that only members of the groups identified as such legitimately belong in the country. Underlying this belief is an understanding of race and ethnicity that separates ethnic communities into discrete and almost watertight groups, attached to a particular territory and endowed with cultural and even psychological traits that are virtually unalterable. What we may call the *taingyintha* ideology has failed to provide a sense of common nation-hood to the various ethnic groups living in Burma, but it does serve as an idiom common to all, determining who can make political claims. Not figuring on the approved list of 'national races', the Rohingya are thus excluded from the country's political life.

The *taingyintha* ideology is, of course, interpreted and acted upon in different ways by different groups, and even by different people within each group. For many Burman ethno-nationalists – and the mainstream of Burmese nationalism is mostly formed by Burmans – it often serves implicitly to justify a civilizational hierarchy that puts their group at its apex, with other groups below, even if some might truly believe in equal-ity between groups. Thus, the Burman majority represents the apex of Burmese civilization, while peoples like the Kachin, the Karen, and so on, are seen as 'younger brothers', 'hill tribes' in need of civilizing by their eldest brothers, the Burmans.

Meanwhile, Kachin ethno-nationalists, for instance, see themselves chiefly as the *taingyintha* of Kachinland (or 'Wunpawng Mungdan' – the Kachin country), and only secondarily as *taingyintha* of Burma as a whole. Rakhine nationalism, with all its distinctive aspects, is thus akin to Kachin nationalism to the extent that it claims that Arakan state does not belong to Burma, and the Burmans do not belong in Arakan. But the Rohingya are excluded, and their exclusion has served at times to unite Rakhine and Burman ethno-nationalists against the 'common enemy' in a way not too different from how anti-black sentiment and policies served to unite the English and Afrikaner nations in the early process of the formation of the (white) South African nation, or Americans in the southern and northern states after the Civil War and in post-reconstruction America.[4]

But where the whites in South Africa and the United States succeeded in creating nations largely based on the exclusion of another race, any success in uniting Rakhine and Burmans has been fleeting and unstable. The intercommunal crisis of 2012 pushed some Rakhine nationalists to side with the Burmese military and government – both generally seen as forces of colonial oppression – but only to the extent that they were thought to take their side against the Rohingya. Ultimately, this did not prevent the emergence of a new Rakhine armed group, fighting in Arakan against Burmese security forces. In 2015, the Arakan Army, which had been training and fighting in KIA-controlled territory for a few years, descended on Arakan and began a low-level insurgency straddling the border between Arakan and Chin states, attacking military positions and police outposts.[5] Popular support for the Arakan Army grew in subsequent years, further complicating an already extremely tense situation in the state. In short, the violence in 2012 and the vilification of the Rohingya have not made Rakhine ethno-nationalism any less inclined to define itself against Burman domination.

For the most part, Rohingya demands are limited to citizenship and recognition as a 'national race', despite claims by Rakhine and Burmese nationalists that their ultimate goal is a Muslim state in Arakan. Many Rakhine and Burmans share an ingrained fear of the Rohingya, and by extension of the Muslim 'other', but such fears are felt in different ways. While the Burmans fear Muslims as a threat to Burma as a whole, for many Rakhine the Rohingya pose a threat to them primarily as Rakhine. Rakhine nationalists may establish strategic alliances with the Burman-dominated government in their fight against the Rohingya; but many also think that, ultimately, both are their enemies. Here lies the tragic irony of the conflict in Arakan: the Rohingya are rejected by the Burmese nation they wish to belong to, while Rakhine nationalists reject the Burmese nation they feel they are forced to belong to.

In analysing ethnic conflicts in Burma, we must be very careful to avoid reifying ethnicity and casting such conflicts as inevitable clashes derived from irreconcilable cultural differences between groups, even if the actors themselves see it that way. Boundaries between ethnic groups are as important in defining them as the specific cultural characteristics of each particular group, if not more so.[6] Moreover, the cultural attributes that serve to differentiate one group from another are somewhat arbitrary, largely depending on contingent circumstances that may change over time. For instance, what distinguishes the Rohingya from the Rakhine and the Burmans is mostly religion and language; but those elements can hardly distinguish the Rakhine from the Burmans, as both are Theravada Buddhist and their languages are very similar. In the latter case, small cultural and dialectal differences that would not distinguish a Burman person from upper Burma from another in the south are seen as strong distinguishing markers that underpin claims to the land and a distinct history. As we shall see in subsequent chapters, those boundaries between groups have shifted and hardened over time; but for those in the thick of these inter-ethnic conflicts, such boundaries are often seen as an eternal and ineluctable consequence of cultural differences that are held to be immutable.

The underlying assumption of this conception of ethnicity is that it is an inescapable 'natural fact' beyond any possible individual choice. One is supposedly born into one's ethnic group and has little say on the matter. In that sense, ethnicity is lived as a 'primordial attachment' to the '*assumed* "givens" of social existence', as described by the anthropologist Clifford Geertz:

> immediate contiguity and kin connection mainly, but beyond them the givenness that stems from being born into a particular religious community, speaking a particular language, or even a dialect of a language, and following particular social practices. These congruities of blood, speech, custom, and so on, are seen to have an ineffable, and at times overpowering, coerciveness in and of themselves.[7]

In reality, while it is true that ethnic identity is most often acquired at birth, it can also be chosen – though, as the sociologist Orlando Patterson puts it, 'it is a choice predicated on the strongly held, intensely conceived belief that the individual has absolutely no choice but to belong to that specific group'.[8] The freedom to make such a choice depends largely on social conditions: the stronger the ethnic polarization and the more fixed inter-ethnic boundaries are, the more difficult it is to choose. But, as a general rule, ethnicity 'differs from voluntary affiliation, not because the two are dichotomous, but because they occupy different positions on a continuum', in the words of the political scientist Donald L. Horowitz.[9] How far the ethnic identity of an individual is from voluntary affiliation on that continuum will depend largely on how sharp the boundaries are between different groups, which may itself vary in different places and times. Such boundaries become sharper when and where there is a conflict between two or more of them. Ethno-cultural differences may or may not lead to conflict but, as David Keen has pointed out and we shall see in the following chapters, 'conflict generates ethnicity'.[10]

Even in a country as extremely polarized along ethnic lines as Burma, there are geographical and temporal variations in the nature and intensity of different inter-ethnic conflicts that affect the way in which different groups see themselves. It is always risky to make generalizations, but it seems fair to say that, in the case of Kachin State, the enemy for many if not most Kachin nationalists is not the Burmans as a people but the Burmese government. The fact that the All Burma Students Democratic Front (ABSDF, a group of Burman activists created in the aftermath of the 1988 uprising against the dictatorship of General Ne Win) has a base in KIO-controlled territory confirms this.

Probably the highest levels of polarization were to be found in Arakan in the years after the intercommunal violence in 2012. In this case, the perceived enemy of most Rakhine ethno-nationalists was not any institution or armed group representing the Rohingya, but the community as a whole. It is also in Arakan that some have taken the identification between race and ethnicity with religion to its most absurd extremes. In 2014, at a conference of Rakhine nationalist organizations held in the state, a speaker proposed to roaring applause that the blood of Muslims 'should be tested' to make sure they were identified and kept apart from Buddhists – as if religion were a physical or genetic attribute.[11]

Yet, despite the hard boundaries between different groups, despite the codification and imposition by the state of such identities through ID cards, censuses and official registers, it is still possible for some people to choose the group they want to belong to – even in Arakan, where such choice is potentially lethal.

This is the case of a man I met by chance in 2014, whom I shall refer to as Mohammed Saed. In fact, he had two names, reflecting two different identities. A sturdy man in his late thirties, Mohammed Saed was living as a Rohingya in one of the camps for Muslims near the state capital, Sittwe; but he had been born as a Rakhine, and his ID card stated that he was a Rakhine Buddhist. He made a living going to the market in downtown Sittwe to buy food and other products to sell in the Muslim villages and the surrounding camps. On regular trips, he switched to his Rakhine identity every time he crossed the checkpoints separating the two communities. Saed had been born in a Buddhist family, and spent his childhood living in the Muslim-majority quarter of Narzi. 'My parents always got along very well with Muslims, there was never a problem between [the] communities when I was a kid', he told me. He lost his parents when he was fifteen years old, and he was adopted by a Rohingya woman living in his neighbourhood. 'Nobody else did anything for me', he said. Living with this woman would bring Saed closer to the Rohingya community, until he decided to convert to Islam in 2009 in order to marry Fahima, a Rohingya woman from his neigh-bourhood. They had two children, a boy and a girl, and when their neighbourhood was swept by the violence, and its Muslim population evacuated by the security forces to the camps in 2012, Saed felt he had no choice but to join them.

It was a dangerous choice, and his life was arguably at risk every time he crossed the checkpoint to downtown Sittwe. He could be lynched if extremist Rakhine found out about his life as a Rohingya. He and his wife regarded their children as Rohingya, but they had decided to register them as Rakhine Buddhists so that they could obtain documents and access to education not afforded to others. Saed's Rohingya neighbours treated him as one of them, and he claimed proudly to be a Rohingya. He had not chosen to be born as a Rakhine, but he had freely chosen to be Rohingya. Nevertheless, this decision presented itself to him with the same inevitability as the iden-tity he had received when he was born, as it was the only way to stay with his family. The Rakhine identity reflected in his citizenship veri-fication card was purely instrumental.

The case of Mohammed Saed may show that, even in the context of extreme ethnic polarization prevalent in Arakan, some had a measure of freedom to choose the group they wanted to belong to; but it also under-scores that nobody is free to choose *not to belong to any group*. Ethnicity is ultimately inescapable in contemporary Burma, and all the more so in Arakan.

The almost total segregation of the Rohingya community from the Rakhine majority imposed by the government in places like Sittwe and Myebon had the effect of further polarizing and estranging the two communities. Having little or no contact with each other contributed to the dehumanizing of the Rohingya in the eyes of the Rakhine – and vice versa. Each community felt it was the victim of the other, and of the Burman government – though that sense of victimhood, not without reason, was stronger among the Rohingya. As the oppression against the Rohingya worsened, victimhood became one of the main marks of Rohingya identity, and contributed to cementing the very same Rohingya identity that the government was so determined to obliterate.

This sense of absolute victimhood, coupled with segregation from the Rakhine community, also explains the prevalence of rumours about the Rakhine among the Rohingya community that were no less lurid and unfounded than those circulating among the Rakhine about the Rohingya – some of them are potentially lethal. One rumour that journalists would hear often in the camps was the allegation that Rohingya patients going to the Sittwe General Hospital were systematically killed by Rakhine doctors and nurses. The most common story was that a doctor or nurse had injected to a Rohingya patient with a green liquid that had killed them. During several visits to the camps, I would repeatedly hear such stories, and at some point I even interviewed a woman who claimed that her husband had been killed with the dreaded lethal injection – although she had not witnessed it directly.

It was a terrible story that I decided not to publish, partly because it seemed far-fetched, but mostly because I had no way of corroborating it. It was highly unlikely that any doctor or nurse would confess to having done something like that, or would become a whistle-blower after witnessing one or several of such killings. At the same time, there were the cases of people I knew who had been in the hospital and had returned unharmed to the camps or to the Muslim ghetto of Aung Mingalar. Then, in late 2015, a colleague and I met a woman in the camps who had been to the hospital with several patients who did not have any relative to go with them. She had made a sort of job out of providing such services, and charged her customers for doing so. She had accompanied a total of seventeen people to the hospital, and all of them had returned safely to the camps.

The rumour of the killings in the hospital seemed to have little basis in fact. It is true that both Rohingya and Rakhine people die in a hospital whose facilities are woefully deficient, as would be expected in the second-poorest state in one of the poorest countries in Asia, whose government has always allocated an extremely paltry budget to public healthcare. Also, access to healthcare is much more complicated for Rohingya than for Rakhine patients, increasing the likelihood that they will arrive at hospital in a more advanced stage of their illness.[12] It is plausible that a Rakhine doctor having two patients, a Rakhine and a Rohingya, might give preferential treatment to the former. All of these conditions increase the possibility that a Rohingya suffering from a serious condition might die in the hospital; but that is a far cry from being deliberately killed by the doctors. It is only natural that distressed relatives of the deceased might think that they had been victims of assassinations – all the more so in the climate of extreme distrust between the two communities. But, for those who had not gone through that, the rumour only made sense within the context of an overarching narrative of absolute Rohingya victimhood and extreme Rakhine sadism. The rumour was so widespread that some seriously ill patients refused to be taken to the hospital for fear of being killed. Possibly some have died as a consequence.

The Rohingya camps and communities were abuzz with rumours of this kind, which portrayed the Rakhine as an undifferentiated mass of enemies of Muslims. As a consequence of segregation, individual or other identities were erased. Doctors were not doctors anymore, but killers, and an increasingly insurmountable gap was created between the communities – a gap that would have taken years to narrow, even if there had been political will to do so. But such political will was completely absent.

Ever since the first wave of sectarian violence in 2012 in Arakan, the subsequent anti-Muslim riots elsewhere in Burma, and the emergence of extreme nationalist Buddhist movements across the whole country, there have been two opposing views on the root causes of these conflicts. On the one hand, many see these phenomena as a direct consequence of the democratic transition, which purportedly gave free rein to old intercommunal hatreds that had been repressed by the military during the decades of dictatorship.[13] On the other hand, some argue that the military had orchestrated the violence behind the scenes from the very beginning, and had been skilfully brainwashing the Rakhine and Burmese population for decades, directing popular anger against the Rohingya and other Muslims.[14]

The first explanation falls into the trap of *groupism*, which social scientist Rogers Brubaker warns is 'the tendency to treat ethnic groups, nations and races as substantial entities to which interests and agency can be attributed'.[15] It also forgets, or ignores, that most ancient hatreds in ethnic conflicts throughout the world are in fact more modern than liberals attached to the idea of progress would care to admit.[16] The second reading simply concedes too much power to the military to manipulate the minds of the Burmese public. One of the most striking features of the military dictatorship in Burma was its almost total absence of popular legitimacy – all the more so after the popular uprising of 1988, the downfall of General Ne Win, and the establishment of the military junta. Very few people believed the propaganda of a regime relying almost exclusively on coercion, but they seemed willing to believe anti-Muslim propaganda, and that happened because it fell on fertile ground, that is, on a society where anti-Muslim prejudices were already pervasive to a large degree. Of course, the military cannot, and should not, be exonerated from responsibility for its criminal policies; but we should also understand the social and historical context in which they have been developed.

In challenging these excessively reductive interpretations, I am not denying that racism against Rohingya and other Muslims is deeply embedded in Burmese society, or that the military has played an important role in stoking the flames of sectarian violence. But we must bear in mind that individual Burmese may react in widely different ways to such racism, taking account of the small number who oppose it. Many activists and Buddhist monks have spoken out against anti-Muslim rhetoric, but their voices have often been drowned out by those of the ultranationalist movements. Perhaps the most extraordinary example I have found is that of Sai Han Htike, a Buddhist from Shan State who, at considerable risk to himself, set up an NGO to help Rohingya children in Sittwe.[17]

But perhaps the most common reaction among Burmese people towards racism is to ignore it most of the time, except for off-hand casual remarks. The Burmese state has acted for decades as an enforcer of ethnic classifications through censuses, registration cards and laws. But it would be misguided to assume that the government is merely force-feeding extreme ethno-nationalism to a reluctant population, as is demonstrated by the apparently broad popular support for the 2015 passage of the 'Race and Religion Protection Laws'.

At least one of these laws was used in ways unintended by its sponsors. One of the laws banned polygamy, and it was aimed at Muslims – but it has often been used by Buddhist women against Buddhist husbands who have abandoned them to live with other women, or had extramarital affairs. In Burmese society, women are often socially stigmatized if their husbands leave them – blamed for their inability to retain them. Many abandoned women found in the new monogamy law a way to remedy their situation. In the four months after the law was enacted, on 31 August 2015, a total of twenty-nine complaints were filed in Rangoon alone, according to figures from the local police. Virtually all of them were directed against Buddhist men, and only three cases were brought against women.[18] As the Burmese saying goes, it was a case of 'a trap set for rabbits that caught cats instead'. This also shows that, as prevalent as ethnic cleavages are in Burma, the daily lives of millions of people are occupied with other worries that can only be addressed in creative ways when the state and the law provide so little protection.

But, careful as we should be to refrain from sweeping generalizations, it is undeniable that the dominant discourse about Muslims in Burma is one of hostility. The military has portrayed the Rohingya and other Muslims as a threat against national sovereignty, and has treated them as such. The motives of the generals may well be cynically instrumental (indicating a divide-and-rule strategy, an attempt at diversion, and so on) or ideological (suggesting they truly believe in the threat of a 'Bengali-Muslim invasion', as many others do in the country); they might perfectly well derive from both sources. Ultimately, each explanation – deeply embedded 'social racism', and racism encouraged from the top – is unsatisfactory taken in isolation. At best, each only tells part of the story. To understand the phenomenon of the rise of Buddhist nationalism, we have to look at these two forces as feeding and reinforcing one another in the context of a political culture where ethnicity plays a central role, and the notion of *taingyintha* ('national races') is almost always accepted without question.

In the second volume of his monumental tetralogy *The Sources of Social Power*, the sociologist Michael Mann described the modern nation-state as a 'cage' whose 'inmates cared more about conditions within their cages than about the cages themselves'. The shape of such cages depended on political, institutional, economic and ideological 'crystallizations' that were the contingent products of complex, and to some extent random, historical processes.[19] The cage that is contemporary Burma is a fractured space in which politics revolve mostly around ethno-nationalist allegiances. Ideologically, such a cage is made of solid ethnic bars; and, as Mann pointed out in another work, 'ethnic hostility rises where ethnicity trumps class as the main form of social stratification, in the process capturing and channelling classlike sentiments towards ethnonationalism'.[20]

In January 2002, the head of Burma's ruling military junta, Senior General Than Shwe, proclaimed in a public speech: 'Thanks to the unity and farsightedness of our forefathers, our country has existed as a united and firm Union and not as separate small nations for over 2,000 years.'[21] This extraordinary assertion did not merely reflect the opinion of the most powerful man in Burma at the time; it constituted the official view of history held by the state.

When studying the history of any nation, we should take with a healthy pinch of salt whatever nationalist historians and ideologues have to say. As Eric Hobsbawm remarked, 'no serious historian of nations and nationalism can be a committed political nationalist', since 'nationalism requires too much belief in what is patently not so'.[22] As I hope to demonstrate in the next chapters, statements like that of General Than Shwe and others contained in Burmese history textbooks are patently false. They are part of an ongoing project of nation-building and reinvention of the past in which the Burman polities in central Burma play the leading role, and other ethnic groups are relegated to subordinate roles. They imagine an eternal Burma in which all ethnic groups are part of a common nation that has survived heroically for centuries, against all odds. They therefore tell us much about contemporary Burma, but very little about its past. Of course, the invention of history is a feature of most nationalist projects, and we should not expect the Burmese to be an exception. In Burma, as elsewhere, the myths are important in legitimating territorial claims and national integration; hence in the formation of adequate markets for their products. And, on a more general level, the myths help to define the national 'public' which forms the audience for intellectuals and intelligentsia; they foster a sense of ethnic community and citizenship among the 'middle classes'. And, finally, such is the malleability of an historical ethnic myth, we may find it being adapted by populist intellectuals to the alleged needs of peasants and workers.[23]

We may add that such myths are also weapons used against other groups to dominate them, as in the case of the Kachin and other minorities; to get rid of foreign domination, as was the case in relation to the British during the anticolonial struggle; or to exclude them altogether from a contested territory, as is the case for the Rohingya.

Ernest Gellner defined nationalism as the political principle 'which holds that the political and the national unit should be congruent'.[24] All nations and nationalisms are relatively recent, but the nationalist ideologies of most of them are predicated on having deep historical roots – on having been *always there*. As Gellner pointed out, nationalism 'preaches and defends continuity, but owes everything to a decisive and unutterably profound break in human history'.[25] This break befell Burma, like many other countries that emerged from the ashes of European imperialism, during the traumatic colonial encounter with the British Empire. There were states in what we know now as Burma before the British conquest, but no congruence between them and nations, and none had the same borders as they do now. Moreover, the nations of the time – if such a concept makes any sense at all before the British period – were extremely fluid and porous communities that barely resemble their supposed contemporary heirs.

In contemporary Burma, the categories of 'nation' and 'ethnic group' have been reified to the point of being synonymous with 'races' – not just political communities, but biological entities. And the concept of race itself, at least as it is now understood in Burma, is also largely a product of colonialism. As the historian Patrick Wolfe has written, 'race itself is a distinctive configuration of ideological elements that we do not find configured in this way before the late eighteenth century, but that we do find so configured, and mutually reinforcing, from that time on. Moreover, this configuration is a specifically European (or Eurocolonial) invention.'[26] Rather than ahistorical entities, races in Burma and elsewhere are the products of histories of domination and the struggles against it. They are, borrowing Wolfe's words once again, 'traces of history'. It is to that history that we shall now turn, in order to gain a sense of how Burma and its 'national races' came to be the overriding social realities they are today.

PART II
History and Its Traces

7

The Worlds of Precolonial 'Burma'

Burman civilization was historically located along the Irrawaddy river, which crosses Burma from north to south through the heartland of the country. The Irrawaddy basin is surrounded by a ring of mountain ranges, including the Arakan Yoma in the south-west and the Kachin hills in the north. These mountains are more sparsely populated than the basin, and escaped the control of successive Burman kingdoms for most of their history. The basin is divided into two areas with different climates: the Irrawaddy Delta, or Lower Burma, where the Irrawaddy discharges into the Andaman Sea, is a wet area prone to heavy rains and flooding. The plains of Upper Burma are a dry zone where the climate is more forgiving. The centres of power oscillated between these two areas throughout the history of precolonial Burma, with the northern region taking precedence for most of the time.[1] But throughout that period, 'Burma' as we know it today never existed, neither as a state unified under a single political power within the present borders nor as a single 'nation'.

The earliest civilizations in these areas were those of the Pyu in Upper Burma and the Mon in Lower Burma. The Pyu spoke a Tibeto-Burman language, while the Mon spoke an Austroasiatic language related to Khmer. Both practised a syncretic religion that mixed Brahmanism and Mahayana Buddhism. The Pyu civilization fell at the end of the first millennium of the present era, and there is little left of it. Another civilization would emerge, that of the Burmans – another Tibeto-Burman speaking people who may have emigrated from an area in the west of China between the Gobi Desert and Tibet around the ninth century. It is likely that the Pyu were culturally absorbed by the emergent Burmans, who founded Pagan, the capital of the first Burmese kingdom, in the year 849.[2]

The man who founded the Empire of Pagan, and has gone down in Burmese nationalist historiography as the first great Burmese king, was Anawrahta, who ruled from 1044 to 1077. Anawratha greatly expanded his domains from what until then was just a small area in central Burma, conquering the Mon capital of Thaton in the south and borrowing much of its culture by taking to Pagan Mon scholars and artisans. Anawrahta also reinforced the patronage of the *sangha* – the Buddhist monastic community – and began to set the tone of relations between the monarchy and the Buddhist clergy.[3] At its height, the power of the Pagan kingdom stretched from Bhamo, in what is today southern Kachin State, to the coast of Tenasserim, in the south.[4] But the authority of Pagan was not uniform. Its power in the Chin, Kachin or Shan hills was negligible, and the extremities of the Irrawaddy basin were considered alien territories that were called 'conquered lands' up to the decline of the Pagan dynasty in the fourteenth century.[5] Arakan remained outside of Pagan's control, protected as it was by the almost impassable Arakan mountain range.[6] Moreover, most of the kingdom was not even ruled directly by the king, but by nobles appointed by him – generally members of the royal family who were granted control of their regions in exchange for the payment of taxes to the central government.

In precolonial Burma – not only during the Pagan period, but also in subsequent dynasties – the most prevalent form of political organization, common in Southeast Asia, consisted in what the scholar Stanley J. Tambiah described as the 'galactic polity':

> Not only in Java but also elsewhere in Thailand, Burma, and so on, it was commonly the case that the names of kingdoms were those of capital cities (e.g., Sukhodaya, Ayutthaya, Pagan, Pegu, Madjapahat, Singhasari). This concept of territory as a variable sphere of influence that diminishes as royal power radiates from a center is integral to the characterization of the traditional polity as a mandala composed of concentric circles, usually three in number.[7]

It is therefore anachronistic to talk about borders, as we understand them now, before the arrival of the colonial powers, with their ideas of uniform nation-states. Power was concentrated around the royal capitals, and diminished gradually as one moved away from them, while outlying states just paid tribute to the central courts – often to different courts at different times, and at times even simultaneously – while preserving a high degree of autonomy.[8] As the British anthropologist Edmund R. Leach put it, precolonial Burma was a 'wide imprecisely defined frontier region lying between India and China' where

> the indigenous political systems which existed prior to the phase of European political expansion were not separated from one another by frontiers in the modern sense and they were not sovereign Nation-States . . . The political entities in question had interpenetrating political systems, they were not separate countries inhabited by distinct populations.[9]

Theravada Buddhism was the dominant religion in the central plains of Burman from at least the times of Pagan. At first sight, it might appear that Theravada Buddhism, a religion primarily concerned with personal salvation, has little to do with politics, but it was effectively the state religion in Burma for centuries. Theravada Buddhism was possibly introduced in the Irrawaddy basin and Pagan by the Mon, but that is very much in dispute. What is less controversial is that Pagan received a strong religious influence from Ceylon (modern Sri Lanka), and the Pagan kings sent several missions there in order to purify the *sangha*.[10]

The basic doctrine of Buddhism is encapsulated in the 'Four Noble Truths'. The first is that life is suffering (*dukkha*, in Pali). The second is that desire is the cause of suffering. We suffer because we desire things, but our desire can never be fulfilled because everything is impermanent (*anicca*) – impermanence being, with suffering and non-self (or the absence of essence in living beings, *anatta*), one of the three conditions of existence – and desire causes us to be reborn again and again. The Third Noble Truth is that it is possible to cease suffering by eradicating desire. Finally, the Fourth Noble Truth consists in the 'formula' for eradicating desire: the 'Noble Eightfold Path', a progression from morality to wisdom through meditation. It is then possible to interrupt the cycle of rebirths and attain *nibbana* – the Enlightenment and 'salvation' of those who have realized the Four Noble Truths.[11]

According to Buddhism, everything is subject to the laws of *kamma*, an inexorable law of cause-and-effect with moral consequences. According to *kamma*, our actions in one life determine how we will be born in the next life. If we act according to the *dhamma* – the teachings of the Buddha, a word that could also be translated as 'morality' – we will gain merit, and our rebirth will happen in conditions more conducive to attain *nibbana*. If we act against the *dhamma*, our store of merit will decrease, and we will be reborn in worse conditions, even as animals, moving away from the possibility of attaining *nibbana*. But it is fair to say that the ultimate goal of *nibbana* is far from the minds of most Buddhists. It is mostly reserved to monks, who can only own a few possessions, and otherwise depend on donations from lay Buddhists.

A Buddhist is defined merely as someone who has taken refuge in the three jewels of Buddhism – Buddha, the *dhamma* and the *sangha* – whose respective attributes furnish the numeral 969, which Burmese Buddhists would use to differentiate themselves from Muslims in 2012 and 2013. Most Buddhists are more interested in improving their *kamma* through meritorious actions, and thus being reborn in a better condition, or improving their conditions in the present life. That is the difference between 'Nibbanic Buddhism', which only a few practise, and 'Kammatic Buddhism', the religion actually practised by most Buddhists.[12]

Theravada Buddhism in central Burma was at the beginning a royal cult, but developed over time as a popular religion.[13] At a popular level, monasteries came to be an important part of the landscape in the villages and towns of precolonial Burma, and monks played an important role in village life, enjoying unparalleled moral authority as 'fields of merit' to be supported by lay people in order to improve their *kamma*. The monasteries were also historically centres of education, where children could learn to read and write in Pali, the language of the religion. Theravada Buddhism also coexisted, as it does today, with the indigenous cult of *nats*, spirits with power to do either good or evil to people.[14] At first, King Anawrahta tried to eliminate the worship of *nats*, but this proved impossible. Instead, he incorporated it into Buddhism through the creation of a pantheon of thirty-seven *nats* subservient to the Buddha in the main pagoda of Pagan, reasoning: 'Let the people come to worship their old gods, and then they will discover the truth of the new faith of Buddhism.'[15] Other kings would issue their royal lists of *nats*, up until King Bodawpaya (r. 1781–1819).[16] The cult of *nats* survives to this day, and *nat* festivals are crowded and raucous affairs where supernatural beings are propitiated to attain luck in gambling or improve prospects in professional life. The irony is that this most indigenous cult in Burma is followed by people of all faiths, including those, like Muslims, who are regarded by many Buddhists as foreign.[17] Even the *nats* themselves belong to different religions and ethnic backgrounds.

For lay Theravada Buddhists, nothing is more meritorious than donating to the *sangha*, thus helping monks to attain *nibbana* and preserve the *sasana* – the Buddhist religion. In precolonial Burma, the main protectors and patrons of Buddhism and the *sangha* were the kings, and there was a symbiotic, if often fraught, relationship between political and religious power. The paradigm of this relationship for rulers in the Theravada kingdoms of mainland Southeast Asia and Sri Lanka was King Asoka, the first Buddhist emperor who managed to unify large swathes of the Indian subcontinent in the third century BC.[18] After a bloody war of conquest that lasted for eight years, King Asoka decided to renounce violence in favour of the *dhamma*, and turned from being a *cakkavati* – a world conqueror – to become a *dhammaraja* – a benevolent universal ruler who would follow the prescriptions of the Buddha. He published a series of edicts written on rocks and pillars scattered throughout his kingdom, in which he laid down rules for a moral life based on Buddhist values like *metta* (loving kindness) and *karuna* (compassion).

One of Asoka's main worries was the purification and unification of the *sangha*, inaugurating a role that kings in the Burmese kingdoms also took for themselves. Asoka also attempted to propagate the *dhamma* among purportedly less civilized peoples who lived on the margins of his empire – the so-called 'hill tribes' or 'forest people'. In the words of Tambiah, 'the Asokan pronouncements on the spreading of *dharma* to these peoples partly serve as a historic precedent and charter for the policies of domestication, political incorporation, and even conversion to Buddhism, followed by the governments of Burma, Thailand, and others, toward their allegedly primitive and bothersome hill tribes'.[19] Nevertheless, Asoka also issued edicts pleading for religious tolerance towards other faiths, such as Hinduism of Jainism, and the coexistence of different sects – a plea that seemingly entered into contradiction with his missionary project and attempts to unify the *sangha*.

The *dhammaraja* model of moral king was, of course, an ideal rather than a reality for most of Burma's history. But this ideal served as the legitimizing foundation of the whole system of power. According to Buddhist cosmology, the morality of the king would be reflected in the well-being of the whole kingdom, and some kings even claimed to be *boddhisattvas* – individuals on the path to Enlightenment. As was true for Asoka, who had attained his empire through conquest, there was a tension between the violence necessary to establish the kingdom and the pacifist teachings of the Buddha, which was often resolved by regarding such violence as a necessary evil in the quest to spread the *dhamma*. Meanwhile, the position of every member of society was attributed to their *kamma*, and the king, at the apex of the social pyramid, was deemed to have accumulated the best *kamma* of all. But this was a double-edged sword, as there were no well-established rules of succession, and every king was at risk of being attacked by usurpers. If they managed to do so successfully, the doctrine of *kamma* would automatically serve to justify their victory, as it would prove a posteriori their superior merit.[20]

As *dhammarajas*, the kings of the Burmese precolonial period were expected to be the ultimate protectors and patrons of religion, including the monastic orders. The complex of magnificent temples and pagodas from the Pagan period, built between the tenth and the thirteenth centuries, bear witness to that. But the patronage of religion was another double-edged sword. If it boosted the legitimacy of the king, it could also put the kingdom itself seriously at risk.[21] The population and the king, as the chief donor, earned merit mainly through the donation of lands and slaves to the monastic orders, and this had two consequences – one detrimental to the *sangha* and the other to the state itself. On the one hand, it provoked moral decay among monks, whose vow of poverty was increasingly compromised as they received donations. On the other hand, it also meant a depletion of the resources available to the state, as the lands given to the clergy were tax-exempt, and therefore lost to the state as a source of revenue. And the donation of slaves to the religion also saw a depletion of the manpower available to the court.

The only instrument that the king had to alleviate this problem was the purification of the *sangha*, which was chronically divided not so much by doctrinal controversies as on points of practice. Kings tended to favour the sects that adhered more strictly to the *vinaya* – the monastic code – and those less prone to acquiring land and intervening in politics.[22] But the problem was ultimately irresolvable, as the kings were obligated to continue donating to the *sangha*. As a consequence, Pagan was mortally weakened.[23]

One of the titles of the Burman kings was Sri Nittya Dhammadhara – the 'Fortunate Possessor of the Principle of Permanence',[24] a bold title in the context of Buddhism, one of whose central tenets is the principle of impermanence (*anicca*). Implicit in the title was the idea that the king was the only guarantor of stability and continuity; but such 'permanence' was not a characteristic of the state as such. Precolonial Burma was by no means an era of uniform political order and stability, as modern nationalist historiography would have it. In fact, not even central Burma was always ruled by a single political authority, and during the centuries between the fall of the Pagan dynasty and the beginning of the colonial period, in the nineteenth century, central authority was only gradually asserted, at every point confronting many difficulties and including long periods of anarchy in which petty states competed for power. As Victor Lieberman has remarked, 'the post-Pagan era of civil wars (conventionally dated 1287–1555) is usually regarded as a mere interlude; but in chronological terms, surely, it is equally valid to view Pagan as a temporary break in the normal polycentric pattern.'[25]

This pattern was interrupted when the Toungoo dynasty managed to assert its power in the mid sixteenth century, initiating an expansion that would mean the end of Mon independence, reducing Manipur (in western India) and the Shan states in the north-west to tributary status, and even conquering Ayutthaya, the powerful capital of the kingdom of Siam (present-day Thailand), for the first time.[26] Nonetheless, over-stretched and unable to maintain its internal cohesiveness, the first Toungoo Empire collapsed in 1599, when the imperial capital was raided by the king of Arakan and a disgruntled Toungoo vassal.[27] But this fragmentation was short-lived compared with the period of civil wars after the fall of the Pagan Empire, and the restored Toungoo dynasty would soon recover part of its past splendour and its capital in Ava, near Mandalay.

The new empire was smaller but more cohesive, and less vulnerable to the overstretching of its forces. The Burman sphere of influence then remained more or less stable until the late eighteenth century.[28] But eventually, in the mid seventeenth century, the restored Toungoo dynasty would fall, after several decades of slow but steady decline, to be replaced in 1752 by the Konbaung Dynasty. King Alaungpaya (r. 1752–1760) managed to reintegrate central Burma, and started a process of expansion, continued by his heirs, that would lead to the total destruction of Ayutthaya in 1767, and to the conquest of Manipur, in India, and Arakan in 1784. Thus, when the British started their conquest of Burma in 1824, the Konbaung dominions formed the largest empire ever held by Burmese rulers.

The task of tracing the institutional changes and evolution of the various Burmese polities during that long period is beyond the scope of this book. The institutions that underpinned the social order in Burma were not static, and the changes they underwent were just as influenced by external forces as by internal dynamics. But the conceptual framework I have described for Pagan was very much unaltered: the concepts of galactic polity, *dhammaraja*, and the relations between the kings and the *sangha* remained basically unaltered throughout most of the precolonial period.

The late kingdoms of precolonial Burma were relatively 'multicultural'. Alongside Burmans, Shans and Mons, there were Chinese, Indians, Armenians, Portuguese and other foreigners, sometimes playing important roles in the court as advisors or mercenaries. Court ministers devised their own systems of what we would today call 'ethnic classification'. Court records in the early seventeenth century include a list of 'one hundred and one *lu-myo* in the world', meaning groups sharing a common descent and culture.[29] They were subsumed under five overarching categories: Myanma (or Burman), Tayok, Shan, Mon and Kala.

The criteria were not very consistent. The Rakhine were included inside the Myanma category; the Kachin under the Shan; Tayok meant roughly people from beyond the eastern highlands, referring mostly to the Chinese; Kala did not have the derogatory connotation it has today, and referred to foreigners to the west, from India and beyond, including Europeans. Popular perceptions of such classifications are a mystery, and it is doubtful that there was a widespread sense of belonging to a 'Burmese' identity. In any case, society was structured on the basis of class divisions rather than ethnic distinctions. The *dhammasat* texts, legal and ethical treatises dictating appropriate social practices, categorized people into classes and, for instance, showed a preference for class endogamy in marriages, but went silent on marriages between different religions or races, which were accepted.[30]

In the Konbaung era, the economy was based on taxing cultivators and external commerce – both maritime and, more importantly, overland with Yunnan, in China.[31] It is estimated that, by the early nineteenth century, 4.5 million people lived in the Burmese Empire, and 70 per cent of them were based in the Irrawaddy basin. Many of them were war captives from outlying areas, including Manipur, Lower Burma and the Shan Hills, but they also included immigrants from other surrounding areas.[32] The social system was based on the distinction between the *ahmudan* – hereditary crown servants who owed labour services to the court, including military service – and the *athi*, who provided taxes instead of labour. There were also slaves, called *kyun*. Some of them were hereditary slaves, who could never escape their condition, but most of them were redeemable slaves bonded to a master who would be released once their debts were paid.

Rural Burma was organized around clusters, or 'circles', of villages called *myo*, each ruled by a *myothugyi*, a hereditary chief who acted as intermediary between the population and the court through members of the aristocracy called *myo-za*, who collected the incomes from different areas. The *myothugyi* enjoyed a certain degree of autonomy, which increased the further his *myo* was from the centre at Ava.[33]

Burman culture became gradually predominant in central Burma during the precolonial period, and wars between different polities were almost permanent; but it would be a mistake to regard these groups as closed and mutually exclusive 'nations' during that time. That is a view put forward by historians who read backwards sharper divisions that only emerged and solidified later on, with the arrival of the British and their concepts of race, ethnicity and nation.[34] The loose control exerted from the centre in the more distant areas made it impossible to create the modicum of cultural homogeneity necessary to form a 'nation', and the relative isolation of the different *myos* meant that the rural population had little sense of belonging to a larger polity.

Allegiance to the king was what really mattered, and so the ethnicity of the subjects was of little importance: *ahmudans* of different ethnicities coexisted in and around the court. Power was based on control over people, rather than territory, as Burma was not densely populated, and the kings needed a large labour force for their large-scale projects and armies. As a consequence, they were not choosy about the 'ethnicity' or 'race' of the people they ruled. In the wars between Mons and Burman it was not uncommon to find Mons fighting alongside the Burman kings, and vice versa, and it was even more common for Mons to 'become Burman', individually or collectively, when a territory had been taken by the enemy. Moreover, the universalistic Buddhist character of kingship also rendered the ethnic identity of the king himself secondary. As universal and moral ruler, it was more important for him to support the religion and the *sangha*. Thus, in the fourteenth and fifteenth centuries there were Shan kings in Burman-majority Ava who were accepted as legitimate.

Burmese kings often showed a remarkable tolerance towards other religions, including Islam and Christianity, even if at times they could be extraordinarily stern, to the point of cruelty, in enforcing religious orthodoxy among their Buddhist subjects. Muslim traders started to arrive in coastal cities in the ninth century. The Muslim population grew steadily during the next centuries through immigration of new traders and mixed marriages with Buddhist women. Muslims also settled in the Irrawaddy basin and, from the sixteenth century, many of them served as soldiers and bodyguards for the king, while others took administrative posts. The language employed by the Burmese kings in their dealings with foreign powers, at least until the First Anglo-Burmese war (1824–26), was Persian, and the translators were usually Muslims who had mastered the language.

Some Muslims were deported from Manipur in the eighteenth century and relocated in villages in Central Burma, where their descendants are still living today. At the end of the century there were Muslim quarters and mosques in every major town in Burma.[35] Some kings forbade Muslims from sacrificing cattle, as it offended Buddhist sensitivities; but some were particularly supportive of their religion. King Mindon (r. 1853–78) helped Muslims to build mosques, and even funded the construction of a hostel in Mecca for Burmese pilgrims doing the *hajj*.[36]

*   *   *

Political integration, however fragile for most of the time in the plains of central Burma, never happened in the uplands surrounding them, which were characterised by mostly rugged terrain where communications were extremely difficult. The peoples living in those mountains were more isolated, and developed cultures different from those of the peoples in the Irrawaddy basin. They were mostly animists rather than Buddhists, practising slash-and-burn cultivation instead of the wet-rice cultivation employed in the plains, and many were nomadic or semi-nomadic. Most never founded states, and they often lacked the written culture of their neighbours in the lowlands, albeit not complex cosmologies and forms of social organization that tended to be more democratic and egalitarian than the monarchies in the plains.

Most of those peoples lacked a written language until the arrival of British missionaries in the nineteenth and twentieth centuries, so their history only figures, if at all, in royal chronicles produced by the Burman, the Shan or the Chinese, who tended to exaggerate their control over them and their 'barbarity' compared to their own civilizations. This has led to the incorrect impression of their being primitive peoples without history, who did not evolve over time. But recent scholarship has challenged this view, trying to situate those peoples in the general history of the region. The territory they inhabited has been named 'Zomia' by some scholars: an area of around 2.5 million square meters on the fringes of mainland Southeast Asia, China, India and Bangladesh, which includes vast territories in outer Burma and is home to hundreds of ethnolinguistic groups.[37]

According to the most enthusiastic advocate of 'Zomia studies', the American anthropologist James C. Scott, many of its inhabitants arrived there after fleeing the exactions of the states in the valleys, including those in Central Burma. But the hill peoples of Zomia 'actually sought, sometimes quite eagerly, relationships with valley states that are compatible with a large degree of political autonomy'.[38] Thus, the Kachin were never completely dominated by the pre-modern Burmese or Chinese states, but maintained commercial relations with them, mostly through the slave trade they controlled in their region.

Fragments of Zomia are now integral parts of nation-states like Burma, China, Thailand, Laos and India. Burma's peoples are members of ethnic groups like the Kachin, the Chin and the Karen, that have been fighting ethno-nationalist struggles against the central government since independence. Their ethno-nationalist ideologies, like those of the Burmans or any other group for that matter, are predicated on myths of common descent, and the notion that they have existed since time immemorial as the discrete ethnic groups belonging to that place. But their origins are infinitely complex, due partly to the fact that ethnic allegiances were much more fluid in precolonial times than most ethno-nationalists, the Burmese state, and many historians care to admit. For instance, the term 'Kachin' was used by the Burmans in central Burma, up to the nineteenth century, as a vague category 'applied to the barbarians of the northeast frontiers', including various tribes that spoke different languages.[39]

The social systems of these communities grew in complexity throughout history partly through interaction with the political systems in the valleys. The British anthropologist Edmund R. Leach, in his classic *Political Systems of Highland Burma* (1954), studied the interactions between the Kachin and the Shan peoples in northern Burma. According to him, the main difference between the two peoples was that 'the Shans occupy the river valleys where they cultivate rice in irrigated fields; they are a relatively sophisticated people with a culture somewhat resembling that of the Burmese', whereas the Kachin 'occupy the hills where they cultivate rice mainly by the slash and burn techniques of shifting cultivation'.[40] The differences also included language, religion (the Kachin were animists, and now are overwhelmingly Christians; the Shan have been Buddhists since at least the sixteenth century), and their forms of political organization (more democratic in the case of the Kachin; more similar to the centralized kingdoms of Burma in the case of the Shan, who had small states in the valleys). But both groups were 'very much mixed together', and boundaries between them were enormously porous, to the point where it was possible for people to change their ethnicity over one or two generations.[41]

The anthropologist F. K. Lehman, who did extensive fieldwork on the Chin of eastern Burma, suggested half a century ago that, when people identified themselves as members of an ethnic group, they were merely 'taking positions in culturally defined systems of intergroup relations', and that 'ethnic categories are formally like roles and are, in that sense, only very indirectly descriptive of the empirical characteristics of substantive groups of people'. Therefore, local or regional groups were 'inherently likely to have recourse to more than one ethnic role system and more than one 'identity''.[42] In precolonial times, ethnicity was performative, and to a certain extent voluntary, rather than ascriptive; consequently, it was more fluid that is admitted now by ethno-nationalist ideologues. As a consequence of the fluidity of these roles and the constant mixing of 'different' peoples through migrations and intermarriages, Lehman concluded that

> we cannot reconstruct any demonstrable discrete ancestral group for some 'ethnic category'– no matter whether we define such a possible ancestral group as a discrete dialect group, or as a group with relatively sharp discontinuities from its neighbors. In this case there should also be evidence that the category has never achieved the degree of cultural and/or linguistic discreteness from its neighbors that it may claim for itself or have claimed for it by observers treating it as having a global culture consequent upon a distinctive history.[43]

These considerations are as valid for the states in central Burma as they are for Zomia. A similar argument led Leach to argue that 'Shan culture, as we know it, is not to be regarded as a complex imported into the area ready made from somewhere outside, as most of the authorities seem to have supposed. It is an indigenous growth resulting from the economic interaction of small-scale military colonies with an indigenous hill population over a long period', and that 'large sections of the peoples we now know as Shans are descendants of hill tribesmen who have in the recent past assimilated into the more sophisticated ways of Buddhist culture'.[44]

But, contra to Leach, the 'Kachin' culture was not less sophisticated than the Shan, and also evolved over time. The anthropologist Mandy Sadan has shown that what she calls the 'Jinghpaw social world' (the ethnolinguistic group that would form the nucleus of Kachin ethnonationalism in the twentieth century) was, by the end of the eighteenth century, 'an established, clearly distinguishable, socially and culturally sophisticated system of considerable complexity' based on hereditary chieftainship, which 'functioned as a "mature" system in relation to the many different Asian cultural and political systems of governance and authority with which it interacted'.[45]

If Leach described precolonial Burma as a 'wide imprecisely defined frontier region lying between India and China',[46] we could describe

Arakan as a 'frontier region' lying between Burma and Bengal. Arakan is separated from the rest of Burma by a range of mountains, something that served to keep it relatively protected from the depredations of the kingdoms in the Irrawaddy basin. But there are not the same natural barriers between Arakan and Bengal. Consequently, the areas of influence of both kingdoms often overlapped at their edges, and were constantly fluctuating. For most of its history, Arakan maintained closer relations with the kingdom of Bengal, in the west, than with the Burmese kingdoms in the east, and developed a culture distinct from that of the Irrawaddy valley, despite sharing some common features like religion and language.

Little is known about the history of Arakan in the first millennium of the common era, but it is likely that the earliest inhabitants of Arakan were the Mro, the Khami and other 'hill tribes' linguistically related to the present Chin ethnolinguistic group.[47] From around the fourth to sixth centuries, Arakan was ruled by the Candra dynasty, from north-east India, in what was known as the Kingdom of Vesali.[48] These rulers left inscriptions in Sanskrit very similar to others found in Bengal. The political organization and the religion in Vesali were shaped by a mixture of Hinduism and Mahayana Buddhism.[49] After the fall of the Candra dynasty, power was held by local chiefs; and then, in the eighth century, Vesali fell under the influence of the Pala Empire, whose centre was in Eastern Bengal,[50] until its fall in the twelfth century. Over that period, Arakan was mostly under the political and cultural influence of East Bengal, rather than of the Irrawaddy valley; but it would slowly gravitate towards the Burmese orbit over the course of the next centuries.

Rakhine ethno-nationalists often portray themselves as the inhabitants of Arakan since time immemorial. But, according to the historian Pamela Gutman, 'the Rakhaing [Rakhine] were the last significant group to come to Arakan'[51] – that is, if we except the Rohingya, who probably emerged *as a distinct ethnic group* later; but the ancestry of both groups is extremely complex, and cannot be reduced by identifying the speakers of languages in the past with those of their successor languages today. The Rakhine language is very close to Burmese. Rakhine ethno-nationalists sometimes claim that they are an older branch of the 'Burmese race', while others are adamant that the Rakhine are an Indo-Aryan 'race', on the basis that the language of Vesali was Indo-Aryan.

This reasoning is always aimed at proving that its proponents are the 'original' inhabitants of Arakan. Against these arguments, Rohingya intellectuals and historians, as well as their defenders, often point out that it is the Rohingya who speak an Indo-Aryan language, and claim that this proves they were in Arakan before the Rakhine.[52] Both positions stem from contemporary debates on ethnicity and the 'national races ideology' so pervasive in contemporary Burma. But, as we have seen, a position that regards present ethnic groups as primordial, discrete entities is untenable. And linguistic and cultural characteristics are not necessarily indicative of descent.

The date of arrival of the 'Rakhine' in Arakan is somewhat hazy, but no serious historian doubts that the first Burman-speakers arrived from central Burma, perhaps during the Pagan period.[53] The most likely hypothesis is that those 'Burmans' mixed with the peoples already there, and, through a long process of acculturation and intermingling, absorbed them into a Rakhine culture that became dominant – a culture that had originated in the Irrawaddy basin, but otherwise developed separately. Thus, given this mixing of populations, some of the ancestors of the present-day Rakhine would be the Burman-speakers who started to arrive around the ninth century, and some others would already have been there before then.

A new kingdom, with its capital in Mrauk-U, flourished in Arakan between the fifteenth and the eighteenth centuries, and was during some periods particularly powerful. Throughout this period, Arakan borrowed political and cultural elements from both central Burma and Bengal. Thus, between the fifteenth and seventeenth centuries, the Arakanese kings, heavily influenced by the sultanates of Bengal, took Muslim titles, despite being Buddhist themselves, and issued coins with the *kalima* – the Muslim profession of faith.[54] Such Muslim titles have led some authors to assume erroneously that those kings were themselves Muslims.[55] One of the first kings of the Mrauk-U dynasty, Narameikhla (r. 1404–34), was defeated by the Burmese in 1404, and took refuge in Bengal; but he was able to retake the throne with the help of Bengali commanders.[56] For a long period, the Mrauk-U dynasty even extended its domination – in the diffuse sense we have seen for central Burma – to significant parts of Bengal, while at other times the Bengali kings extended theirs to large areas that had been ruled by the Arakan kingdom, in a geopolitical tug-of-war that was never decisively and permanently won by any side. Thus, the Arakanese king Basawpyu (who bore the Muslim/Bengali name Kalima Shah) occupied Chittagong (now part of Bangladesh) in 1459, and Arakan controlled it up to 1666.[57] At that time, Bengal and Arakan were shifting political entities within the same cultural and social world.

The topography of Arakan made it extremely difficult to maintain internal unity. The region is a thin strip of land between the mountains and the sea, a rugged landscape of malaria-infested jungles fragmented by innumerable rivers. This difficult terrain complicated internal communications enormously, presenting an obstacle to the Arakanese kings' exercise of full control over various regions. That compelled them to be tolerant of the religious beliefs of different communities under their rule. As the scholar Michael Charney put it, 'In Arakan the royal center was not simply indifferent to promoting one particular religious identity over another, but rather was one of the chief barriers restricting the emergence of a Theravada Buddhist orthodoxy in the Arakan littoral.'[58] In this way, the Arakanese kings showed a high degree of religious tolerance that stands in stark contrast to the positions of most contemporary Rakhine nationalists who claim them as their predecessors. They did not try to establish a 'Buddhist kingdom', but worked through local patron–client networks and acted as the protectors of whatever religion was practised at a local level, be it Buddhism, Islam or even Catholicism in some Portuguese communities on the coast. For centuries, this practice prevented the creation of communal identities based on religious beliefs.

The origins of the Rohingya Muslims are as hazy as those of the Rakhine Buddhists. The Rohingya ethnicity, like the Rakhine, is strongly predicated on religion, but that does not mean the ancestors of any of them adhered to the same religions they profess today. The first Muslims arrived in the coastal towns of Arakan, as elsewhere in Burma, around the ninth century, and some attained important positions in the Arakanese court; but their numbers were small. We have to look forward several centuries to find a demographically significant presence of Muslims in Arakan.

In the sixteenth and seventeenth centuries, the Arakanese kings, and Portuguese mercenaries settled in their dominions, conducted raids in Bengal to snatch slaves, whom they resold to foreign merchants, allotted to royal service groups in the court, or settled in the Kaladan valley, in what is now northern Arakan State. This was a highly lucrative trade for the Portuguese, who were allowed to sell the slaves to the Dutch, after their arrival in the Bay of Bengal, on the condition that they handed at least one in four of them to the Arakanese court. For the Arakanese kings, the trade was a way to obtain manpower and populate a sparsely populated area. The well-educated among those slaves were taken to Mrauk-U to serve in the court as functionaries. The exact number of those slaves is unknown, but the Portuguese kept detailed records of their spoils. According to Charney, they took around 147,000 captives between 1617 and 1666. Many died on the way, while others fled back to Bengal or were sold to the Dutch. But 'a conservative estimate for the number of Bengalis who survived their resettlement to Danra-waddy [Northern Arakan, including Sittwe and Mrauk-U] by the end of the seventeenth century was perhaps sixty thousand, probably much higher'.[59]

Before the Burmese conquest of Arakan in 1784, there was already a substantial rural Muslim population in the region. By then, Northern Arakan was said to be predominantly Muslim, with Muslims comprising up to three-quarters of the population in that area.[60] There is no reason to believe they did not mix with pre-existing populations there. Thus, those slaves were some of the ancestors of present-day Rohingya; some would arrive later, during the colonial period; and some had already been there for centuries.

Other Muslims were descendants of the followers of Shah Shuja, the prospective king of Bengal, a Moghul who had been defeated by his brother Aurangzib in the struggle for the throne, and had taken refuge in the court of Mrauk-U at the invitation of Arakanese King Sandathudamma (r. 1652–84). Shuja tried to overthrow the Arakanese king, but his plot was foiled, and he was executed. His followers were spared, however, and retained as archers of the king. They would exert considerable political influence in subsequent years, at times even murdering and installing puppet kings. New arrivals from northern India joined them, and in 1692 they burnt the palace and ravaged the countryside at will. Their rebellion was suppressed by the next king, Sandawizaya (r. 1710–31), who deported them to Ramree Island.[61] They were the Kaman – some of the ancestors of the Muslim group of the same name, which, as we have seen, is included in the official list of 'indigenous races' by today's Burmese government.

By 1784, internal divisions were weakening the Mrauk-U kingdom enormously, and the ambitious Burmese King Bodawpaya (r. 1782–1819) took advantage of this situation, launching an invasion under the pretext of establishing order and purifying the *sasana*. After a short campaign, Arakan fell fully under Burmese control.[62] The Burmese invasion was extremely violent, and changed the Arakanese world forever. After the conquest, the Burmese took back to the court in Amarapura the Arakanese royal family and up to 20,000 people.[63] It was a traumatic blow to the Arakanese, who saw their political and religious world turned upside-down. The Burmese not only brought to Amarapura the ancient Mahamunni statue – a gigantic representation of the Buddha that was a symbol of Arakanese Buddhism – but also 'tried to centralize Buddhist Arakanese religion under their authority in various ways, most of all by burmanizing Arakanese Buddhism through Burman monks, texts, and a *sangha* organization that reached from Arakanese villages to the Burman court', in Charney's words.[64]

The Burmese largely succeeded in that endeavour: up until today, the monastic practices of Arakan are mostly indistinguishable from those of central Burma. A ferocious insurgency against Burman rule led up to one quarter of the population, both Buddhists and Muslims, to flee Arakan across the border to Bengal, which was then part of the British Empire.[65] The Burmese conquest and subsequent wars with insurgents severely reduced the population of Arakan, but there is no reason to believe that the waves of refugees and forcible transfer to the court in Ava substantially altered the demographic ratio of Buddhists to Muslims.

It was around that time that the first known written record of the term 'Rohingya' appeared, in reference to the Muslim inhabitants of Arakan. In an article about the languages spoken in the 'Burma Empire', published in 1799, the Scottish physician Francis Buchanan wrote: 'I shall now add three dialects, spoken in the Burma Empire, but evidently derived from the language of the Hindu nation. The first is that spoken by the Mohammedans, who have long settled in Arakan, and who call themselves Rooinga [*sic*], or natives of Arakan.'[66] Apparently, Buchanan's informants were Muslims forcibly transferred to the Burmese court at Ava. He did not use the word in any of his other writings, and it does not appear in any work by other writers of the era, except those quoting Buchanan. Those who deny Rohingya ethnicity are keen to point out the uniqueness of that document; but its existence is undeniable, and the rare appearance of the term should be understood in light of the fact that scholarship on Arakan was almost nonexistent at the time. The term 'Rohingya' derives in all likelihood from 'Rohang', the Bengali word for Arakan, and thus was just another way to say 'Arakanese'. Charney suggests tentatively that 'Rohingya may be a term that had been used by both Hindu and Muslim Bengalis living in Rakhaing [Arakan] since the sixteenth century, either as resident traders in the capital or as war captives resettled in the Kaladan River Valley.' But he is careful to point out that, in the past, 'Rohingya and Rakhaing [Rakhine] were not mutually exclusive ethnonyms. Rakhaing's topography may have led to Rohingya and Rakhaing emerging as separate versions of the same term in different geographical contexts that came, in the eighteenth century, to be associated closely with the predominant religious makeup of the local area concerned.'[67] Ethnic identities, in Arakan, as well as in Burma, would only crystallize later.

The conquest of Arakan meant that the Burmese kingdom bordered a Western power for the first time in history. The Naf river marked the limit between Arakan and the British-administered province of Chittagong, in Bengal. But borders did not have the same meaning for those on either side. Eastern Bengal was not only geographically coterminous with Arakan, but, for the Burmese, it seems to have been part of a sphere of influence they had some right to reclaim from the British. Already in 1797, before diplomatic relations between the British and the Burmese were irredeemably poisoned, the Burmese court entertained the idea of claiming East Bengal from the British, on the grounds that the Arakanese kingdom had ruled the region for long periods in the past. A junior minister suggested informally to the British envoy in Rangoon that the British and the Burmese should share the revenues of the region.[68] Moreover, in June 1818, the governor of Arakan sent a letter to the British governor of India demanding the British surrender Southern Bengal to Burma, and even threatening to take it by force, on the very same grounds.[69]

During the first years after the Burmese invasion of Arakan, diplomatic relations between Burma and British India were mostly friendly, despite some misunderstandings – unavoidable in the encounter between two such different cultures that had hitherto had little contact with each other, and the occasional arrogance of some British envoys.[70]

Almost from the beginning, however, Arakanese insurgents used the Chittagong province controlled by the British as their base to launch attacks in Arakan, and Burmese soldiers often crossed the border to chase them.[71] At the beginning, the frictions between British India and Burma that those incidents provoked were resolved diplomatically. But relations soured when, in 1811, a new Arakanese leader, Chin Byan, launched an attack from Bengal, in which his forces managed to capture Mrauk-U, and asked the British governor in Calcutta for support in holding the kingdom under British suzerainty. The Burmese accused the British of supporting Chin Byan, and retook Arakan; but the Arakanese leaders managed to escape, and found safe haven again in Bengal. From then on, relations between Burma and British India would steadily deteriorate, also as a consequence of tensions in the Indian province of Assam, which the legendary Burmese general Mahabandoola conquered in 1819. The enmity between the British and the Burmese definitively exploded in the First Anglo-Burmese war (1824–26), after which Arakan, Assam and Tenasserim (in southern Burma) passed to British hands, and the kingdom of the Konbaung dynasty began to unravel.

8

Burma Under the British

The British declared war on the Burmese kingdom on 5 March 1824. In May, they took Rangoon without encountering much resistance, but it took longer to conquer Arakan and other areas because it was monsoon season. On 24 February 1826 all sides signed the Treaty of Yandabo, and the war came to an end. The Burmese had to cede the provinces of Arakan and Tenesserim, in Southern Burma, as well as Assam and Manipur, in Northeast India. They were forced to pay crippling reparations of war amounting to £1 million, and to receive a British resident as permanent ambassador. The British retired to Rangoon after they received the first instalment of the reparations, and then left the Burma Delta completely after the second.[1] During the campaign, at least 15,000 of the British expeditionary forces perished, most from fever and dysentery. But the war was far more destructive for the Burmese, for whom the defeat meant the beginning of the end of what had hitherto been an expanding regional empire.

At first, the Arakanese did not oppose the British invasion, and many even took an active part in it. The magistrate of Chittagong raised a levy of Arakanese refugees, the 'Mug Battalion', who entered their old kingdom alongside British and Indian troops in 1824.[2] The leaders of those refugees had expected that the British would restore their old kingdom, but were soon disappointed to learn that they had merely exchanged their old conquerors for new ones. Discontent swiftly grew among Arakanese elites, and they organized a rebellion in 1836 to expel the colonial power, but it was crushed without difficulty.[3] Most refugees returned from Cox's Bazar in the aftermath of the war.

In April 1826, Charles Paton, the sub-commissioner of Arakan, wrote a confidential report after surveying the country and ordering a census, in which he stated that the total population of Arakan did not exceed 100,000 people, and estimated that 60 per cent were 'Mughs' (a somewhat derogatory term for Rakhine), 30 per cent were 'Mussalman' (Muslims) and 10 per cent 'Burmese'.[4] These were rough and highly tentative figures, but they indicate that there was a substantial Muslim population in Arakan before the arrival of the British – something that Rakhine and Burmese nationalists deny. The report also contains a list of villages in Arakan with the names of their chiefs, including many Muslims among them.

Following the conquest, the British East India Company set out to exploit its new possessions in southern Burma. The kingdom of Arakan had been a large exporter of rice in the seventeenth century, but years of instability, as well as a nationwide ban from the Burmese crown, had put a stop to exports. The British re-established the exports and, with the return of tens of thousands of war refugees from Chittagong province, agriculture thrived again. From 1830 to 1852, the rice acreage in the new province expanded four-and-a-half times.[5] Over time, Akyab (Sittwe, now the capital of Arakan State) became an important commercial hub. But the economic recovery of Arakan did little to improve the lives of its inhabitants. The British imposed an onerous taxation system that contributed to impoverishing the population,[6] and did nothing to develop the province. They never built a railway from Akyab to central Burma, and they built virtually no roads.[7]

Defeat in the first Anglo-Burmese War had been a traumatic and humiliating blow to the Burmese kingdom. And the loss of Lower Burma in the second Anglo-Burmese War was further confirmation that their status as a regional power was evaporating in the fact of a technologically superior army. Moreover, the motivation behind the British declaration of war only served to underscore the lack of respect accorded to the Konbaung dynasty. In late 1851, the Burmese authorities had imposed a fine of 1,000 rupees on two British ships for allegedly violating the port rules in Rangoon. The British decided that this was an affront to their prestige and, after a diplomatic tug-of-war in which the British made overblown demands on the Burmese, the British declared war and took the province of Pegu, in Lower Burma. The conquest allowed the British to connect Arakan and Tenasserim, and rendered the Burmese kingdom a landlocked country. As a result, the Burmese economy was severely disrupted: the government lost its control on the rice surpluses from Lower Burma, and now it had to buy them at international prices. The Burmese government made more stringent the exactions on the farmers in Upper Burma, in order to maintain the royal family and the aristocracy, and many of those farmers emigrated to the south – a tendency that had started before the war, but was accentuated after 1852.[8]

One year later, King Mindon took the throne in Ava through a palace coup. Like the kings Mongkut and Chulalongkorn in neighbouring Siam, Mindon was a modernizer who introduced technological, administrative, military and economic changes in an attempt to adapt his kingdom to a new reality in which it was part of the international economic system to an unprecedented degree. His reforms were less successful than those of his Siamese counterparts: the aristocrats were not willing to renounce to their privileges, and he never managed to create a modern bureaucratic state.[9] Mindon adopted a more conciliatory stance towards the British, in the vain hope of recovering Lower Burma. He also tried to balance his relations with other European powers, particularly with France – the main rival of the British in Southeast Asia. This aroused the suspicions of the British, who regarded Burma as part of their Indian sphere of influence. Every attempt made by the Burmese to be treated as a sovereign state on an equal footing with Great Britain, and to deal directly with the government in London, was humiliatingly snubbed in favour of the viceroy of India. King Mindon was forced to make several concessions to the British, including legal extraterritoriality (which entailed that British citizens could not be judged by Burmese courts for offences committed in Burmese territory) and trade agreements, which meant in effect that the Burmese government lost control of its economy.[10]

Mindon, at a moment when his political authority was severely curtailed, decided to bolster his legitimacy by reinforcing the old links between state and religion. He tried to increase his control over the *sangha*, reducing the power of the highest echelons of the Buddhist clergy and subordinating it to his authority. As a part of his religious policies, in 1871 he organized the Fifth Great Buddhist Council, in which learned monks from all over Burma, as well as some from Siam and Sri Lanka, convened for three years to produce an authoritative 'official' Pali version of the *Tripitaka*, the sacred scripture of Theravada Buddhism. The final version was inscribed in 729 marble slabs that still lie at the foot of Mandalay Hill.[11] The Fifth Council ultimately failed to unify the monastic community, but it contributed to reinforcing the identification between state and *sangha* – between politics and religion – and served as an inspiration for a very similar Council organized by Prime Minister U Nu after independence.

Eventually, in 1885, the British conquered Upper Burma – seven years after the death of Mindon and the bloody ascent to the throne of his son, King Thibaw. Their excuse was the imposition by the Burmese government of a high fee on a British company for logging; but it is more likely that the real reason was growing concern that the Burmese kingdom was becoming dangerously close to France.[12] In October, the British declared war, and on 11 November 10,000 troops crossed the border in a campaign that took them to Mandalay at the end of the month. Having fought a couple of battles on the way, the British invaders found little resistance when they reached the royal capital. King Thibaw surrendered on 29 November, and was taken to Ratanagiri, on the west coast of India, where he died thirty years later as a state pensioner of the British Crown. On 1 January 1886, the viceroy of India, Lord Dufferin, announced that Upper Burma had become part of the British Empire. In February, Burma formally became a province of British India – a decision whose consequences still reverberate today.[13]

The British had thought they would be received by the population as liberators from a cruel and capricious king. But, after their quick conquest of Mandalay, they had to face an insurgency in the countryside led by hereditary local chiefs, bandits and former members of the royal court. In many villages in central Burma, virtually every household contained at least one male fighting against the British. The rebellion expanded to Lower Burma, and even Buddhist monks engaged in the fighting. The resistance was carried out mostly in an uncoordinated manner by local leaders, but various aristocrats of the ancient regime acted in concert with each other.[14] By February 1887, during the height of the 'pacification' campaign, 45,000 British and Indian troops were deployed in the country.[15] The response of the British was as brutal as in many other colonies: entire villages were torched, and suspected rebels were tortured and summarily executed. In order to quell the resistance, the authorities carried out the forced relocation of thousands of Burmese, in order to leave the guerrillas bereft of popular support.[16]

By the end of the 1880s most of central Burma had been 'pacified'. The British did not face any serious insurrection in those areas for another fifty years, so they could concentrate on the administration of their new possessions. They dismantled the existing political and social structures in central Burma and replaced them with others that had little to do with the culture of its inhabitants. In 1887, the chief commissioner of Burma, Sir Charles Crosthwaite, passed the Village Act, which broke up the old *myos* – the clusters of villages that had until then been the smaller administrative units – and dismissed their hereditary chiefs, the *myothugyis*. The new system imposed heavy duties of taxation and policing on local headmen, but gave them few rights and no autonomy. Their position was thus untenable, as they found themselves squeezed between the demands of the colonial state and a population over which they had little moral authority.[17] At that time, the colonial administration in India was dominated by utilitarians, who followed the philosophy of Jeremy Bentham as if it were gospel. They believed that it was possible to write laws according to scientific and universal principles applicable everywhere, regardless of the local social systems and cultures they encountered. They had devised the Indian Penal Code and introduced it in Burma, abolishing virtually all precolonial law and erasing in a single stroke most of the legal traditions that had been accumulated for centuries in Burma.[18]

The British government lacked legitimacy in the eyes of most Burmese, not only because it was the result of a foreign invasion, but also because it failed to fulfil what had for centuries been one of the most important functions of rulers in central Burma: patronage in support of Buddhism and the monastic community. The British had adopted a policy of religious neutrality in their Indian colony since the late eighteenth century, and that approach was largely extended to Burma.[19] There was some recognition of the position of the *thathanabaing*, a Buddhist primate chosen by the king who had some moral authority over large parts of the *sangha* – though he had never managed to achieve full control of the diverse sects during the Konbaung period; but his decrees were rendered even more toothless by the British administration. At first, during the insurgency that followed the fall of the Konbaung dynasty in 1885, he tried to persuade rebellious monks and laymen to accept British rule in exchange of recognition of his ecclesiastical jurisdiction. But the British did not provide him with the means to make it effective, and monks fell under the jurisdiction of the police and secular courts for the first time in Burma's history.[20]

The British also tried to use Buddhist monasteries, which had provided religious education in the villages for centuries, to build a modern education system on the cheap. But that plan never worked. This failure was due to a complete misinterpretation of the nature of monastic schools. For the British, education was a tool of modernization that taught children to be productive workers in the colonial system. But monks understood the education they provided in an almost opposite way: their goal was to instil Buddhist ethics in the children and preserve religion in a world that was changing fast and threatened their religion's survival.[21] The government then decided to promote lay and missionary schools providing education in English, and many parents enrolled their children in those schools, where they could acquire skills to advance socially in the modern world. But anxiety about the fragility of Buddhism grew during the colonial period, providing the first rallying points among Burmese Buddhists against colonial domination (see Chapter 9).

The key motivation of the British colonial project in Burma was economic profit and development. The new rulers mostly concentrated their efforts in Lower Burma, where they introduced a system of 'industrial agriculture' to replace the agriculture of subsistence prevalent before their arrival. Lower Burma had been traditionally less populated than Upper Burma, but that changed with the development of the region by the colonial power. The export of rice from the region grew from 162,000 tons in 1855 to 2 million tons in 1905. This growth was accompanied by a huge increase in population, which quadrupled between the Second Anglo-Burmese War in 1852 to reach 4 million at the turn of the century.[22] Part of this demographic growth was due to internal migration from Upper Burma, which contributed to the Burmanization of a zone that had been predominantly Mon until recently.

Immigration from India also played a role in demographic change. As early as 1852, colonial officials had suggested that Lower Burma could be used as a 'safety valve' for impoverished and densely populated regions in India, such as Bengal,[23] and India that would provide an apparently inexhaustible pool of cheap labour to develop Burma along British lines. In the 1880s, the British started to subsidize migrant labourers from the depressed Indian province of Madras.[24] By 1918, 300,000 immigrants were arriving each year at the port of Rangoon.[25] According to the census conducted in 1881, there were 243,123 Indians in Burma. In 1931, the numbers had swelled to 1,017,825, or 6.9 per cent of the total population, most of them living in Lower Burma.[26] The overwhelming majority worked in the rice mills and on the docks, earning miserable salaries and living in overcrowded and unsanitary barracks, where the annual death rates were as high as thirty-seven per thousand residents.[27]

As Burma was administered as a province of India, immigration was not regulated, unlike in other British colonies such as Malaya and East Africa, and the labourers were often exploited by ruthless agents. The Indian migrants would be increasingly resented by the local population as competitors in the labour market, particularly during times of economic crisis.[28] The authorities also found it more profitable to employ Indians in the administration, commerce and industry than to train Burmese, who were less experienced in the British colonial system. Most foreigners were concentrated in port cities like Rangoon and Moulmein; by 1931, almost 50 per cent of the urban population was Indian.[29] Indians also dominated the medical profession, and held a monopoly of employment on public works, railways and river steamers.[30] The financial and commercial sectors were dominated by European firms that preferred to hire Indian and Chinese employees.[31]

Particularly resented among the Burmese rural population in times of crisis were the *chettiars* – moneylenders from Tamil Nadu, who made loans to farmers and small businesses at much lower rates than their Burmese counterparts and had more contacts with international banks.[32] The *chettiars* established offices throughout Lower Burma, and played a crucial role in the development of the economy; but when the Great Depression hit Burma in the 1930s, lowering the price of rice, they had to seize lands as collateral for debts that the farmers were unable to pay. Thus, having occupied 6 per cent of the land in rice-growing districts in 1930, they occupied 25 per cent by 1938.[33]

The Burmese had been thrown into an economic system imposed by their conquerors, for which they were badly prepared. In central and Lower

Burma, the labour market and the economy were roughly divided along racial lines, and most Burmese had difficulty finding their place in a system beyond their control. The British had created what the colonial administrator and scholar J. S. Furnivall famously described as a 'plural society', in which 'the various peoples met in the economic sphere, the market place; but they lived apart and continually tended to fall apart'.[34] Europeans were at the apex of the system, directing it from above; but most Burmese were more likely to have more direct contact with Indian policemen, *chettiar* moneylenders, Indian and Chinese traders, or coolies working in the docks, who often lived in far worse conditions than them. The Indians, as much as the British, were increasingly resented as foreign invaders. These tensions would flare up in bloody episodes of sectarian violence in the 1930s, generating an anti-Indian sentiment that political and intellectual elites, as well as popular culture, have kept alive until today.

Immigration from Bengal to Arakan during the colonial period is the object of much controversy. There is little doubt that the Muslim population in Arakan grew during the period, and that this demographic growth was mostly due to immigration from the district of Chittagong in Bengal. Chittagong was more densely populated than Arakan,[35] and many Chittagonians sought the opportunity to work as farmers in Arakan. While some were seasonal labourers who returned to their places of origin after the harvest, many settled for good, mostly in the Akyab district (the present townships of Maungdaw, Buthidaung, Rathedaung, Mrauk-U and Sittwe).

Rohingya historians and activists tend to downplay the extent of such migration in an attempt to deny claims by Rakhine and Burmese nationalists that the Rohingya are not a 'national race'. But a look at colonial censuses reveals that the volume of migration in colonial times was significant: in 1881 there were 113,557 'Indians' in Arakan , and by 1931 there were 217,801; and while 62.6 per cent of those 'Indians' in 1881 had been born in India, that figure had fallen to 23.2 per cent by 1931.[36] These figures for 'Indians' include a small percentage of Hindus, and some others from elsewhere in India; but the overwhelming majority hailed from Muslim-majority Chittagong. These immigrants joined a sizable Muslim population in Arakan, well established since at least the fifteenth century. According to the 1931 census, there was a total of 51,612 'Arakan-Mohammedans' in Arakan.[37]

The censuses of the time made clear-cut distinctions between Chittagonians and 'Arakanese Muslims'. Some commentators at the time even attributed different personal traits to each group, describing the latter as 'as indolent and extravagant as the Arakanese themselves', while the former 'have not been sapped of their vitality'.[38] This distinction, alongside the fact that the term 'Rohingya' itself does not appear in any colonial record or census, is often used to deny claims of indigeneity advanced by the Rohingya.[39] These arguments are highly problematic for a variety of reasons. Most importantly, they take at face value colonial ethnic classifications. But, while colonial records might be a valuable source of information when it comes to demographic estimates, their systems of ethnic classification were highly spurious. The main problem is that there was a conscious effort to pin down 'racial' identities that were enormously fluid, assuming, and often imposing, sharp boundaries between different groups.[40]

As we have seen, in precolonial times Arakan and southern Bengal formed a diffuse frontier area where two kingdoms, and two cultures, overlapped and nourished each other. Given the migration flows in both directions for centuries, it is perfectly plausible that many 'Chittagonians' were descendants of 'Arakanese Muslims', and vice versa. The claim that there had been hard boundaries between polities and human groups in that borderless area is an anachronism. Moreover, during the British period there was no border between Arakan and Bengal, as both were part of the same empire. But, paradoxically, it was during this period, when they were part of the same political system, that sharp distinctions were introduced between those human communities that had been mixed for centuries. Ultimately, censuses were not just descriptive – they contributed to reinforcing, solidifying and sometimes even creating ethnic identities, not only in Arakan, but also in central Burma and the highlands of 'Zomia'.

The British 'pacification' of the mountainous areas surrounding central Burma after the third Anglo-Burmese war was no less violent than that in the territories hitherto under the Konbaung kingdom. In what is now Kachin State, Jinghpaw tribes opposed the colonial power for nearly thirty years,[41] and some areas were not brought under British control until the 1920s.[42] Once these areas had been 'pacified', the administration imposed in them was completely different from the rest of Burma.

Instead of direct rule, in the 'hill tracts' the British introduced a system of indirect rule through co-opted traditional chiefs, like the Shan *sawb-was* or the Kachin *duwas*, who were accountable to the highest administrative officer of Burma, the chief commissioner, and were responsible for the administration of civil, criminal and revenue matters.[43]

For the first time in history, the territory known as Burma was under a single political authority, but it was now divided into two different areas – Ministerial Burma, or 'Burma Proper', including the Irrawaddy basin and Arakan; and the Frontier Areas, also known as the Scheduled or 'Excluded Areas', in the peripheries. The Karenni (or Kayah) areas were treated as a separate feudatory state not included within the borders of Burma. There were further distinctions, and the Shan, seen by the British as more civilized than other groups, enjoyed representation from 1897 through a new lieutenant governor's council. In 1922, the colonial government created a Burma Frontier Service, separated from the government of Burma, and also two federations of Shan states and a Federal Council of Shan Chiefs. Thirteen years later, it established two territorial categories in Ministerial Burma: 'excluded areas' and 'partially excluded areas', under the jurisdiction of the new parliament, created when Burma was separated from India in 1937. The result was a variation on what the scholar Mahmood Mamdani, referring to colonial Africa, called a 'bifurcated State', in which direct and indirect rule coexisted as 'complementary ways of native control'. While the former was 'about the exclusion of natives from civil freedoms guaranteed to citizens in civil society', the latter was 'about incorporating natives into a state-enforced customary order'.[44] This complex patchwork of administrative units contributed to entrenching differences between groups that had until then mingled more freely.

When the British arrived in the frontier areas of Burma, they found a bewildering variety of ethno-linguistic groups whose identities were enormously fluid. In order to administer such a complex human landscape efficiently, colonial administrators carried out censuses that imposed rigid grids of ethnic classification, in which they conflated the languages spoken and religions professed by the people with the categories of 'tribe' or 'race',[45] oblivious to the fact that language and religion were not necessarily indicative either of ethnic or racial identity, or of permanent political allegiance.[46] These taxonomies were not merely descriptive, but were actively enforced. Thus, according to Leach,

One of the few continuing elements in British administrative policy towards the Kachins was the policy of treating Shan and Kachin as separate racial elements. Even to the last – in 1946! – British officials were engaged in surveying precise boundaries between Kachin and Shan territory. The political dependence of Shan and Kachin or vice versa was excluded by edict; economic relations between the two groups, though not prohibited, were made extremely difficult. Everything possible was done to deter the more sophisticated Kachins from settling in Shan territory in the plains. This policy originated from a desire 'to establish peace and security within the settled districts', and it achieved its end, but at a high cost.[47]

These administrative systems and classifications have often been described as 'divide and rule' strategies. But there is no reason to believe that the colonial administrators were cynical about the way in which they classified the peoples they ruled. They held a set of views on race strongly influenced by the social Darwinist prejudices of the time, and attributed innate characteristics to different groups: the Karen and Kachin were stereotyped as simple and honest people, but also good warriors, and were included within the 'martial races'; whereas the Burman were seen as devious and undisciplined, not fit for combat. On the basis of these spurious classifications, when they started to recruit indigenous soldiers in earnest during World War I, they favoured non-Burman groups, and formed mono-ethnic units. Thus, in 1931, the Kachin, Karen and Chin ethnic groups, who represented around 13 per cent of the total population, made up 83 per cent of the indigenous sections of the army in Burma, while only 12 per cent were Burman, Shan or Mon, though these groups comprised around 75 per cent of the population.[48]

This process of ethnic polarization was not unique to Burma, but unfolded in many colonized countries that, after independence, found themselves ensnared in seemingly intractable ethnic conflicts. As the political scientist Donald Horowitz remarked, 'the colonialists set in motion a comparative process by which aptitudes and disabilities were to be evaluated', and, 'like the new polity and economy in which the disparities were embedded, the evaluations took hold'.[49] The Colonial experience created the basis of the modern Burmese state through two forces pulling in opposite directions: one was centripetal, as the British put territories that had never been unified under a single political authority for the first time; the other was centrifugal, as their colonial policies and practices deepened interethnic divisions, solidifying identities that had historically been more diffuse. But it would be a mistake to infer that the peoples inhabiting colonial Burma were mere passive recipients of the classifications imposed by the British. To paraphrase E. P. Thompson, the various ethnic groups in Burma made themselves as much as they were made, and they made themselves as nations in a modern world of nation-states.

9

The Emergence of Nationalisms

Nationalist politics emerged in Burma in the context of the colonial encounter. The British greatly contributed to the solidification of ethnic identities, but in doing so they also helped to give birth to political forces that turned against them. In the first decades of the twentieth century, the 'nation' itself became a political actor, or at least claims began to be made in its name. This was unprecedented in Burma, and came at a moment when the nation-state model was spreading throughout the world and nationalism was one of the main idioms of politics – a development of which educated and politically minded Burmese of all ethnicities were well aware. The emergence of various nationalist movements in Burma was largely shaped by the conditions imposed by the British, but also by its precolonial history. Several nationalist movements, virtually one for each group, emerged in the cauldron of the anticolonial struggles.

In his classic study, *Imagined Communities*, Benedict Anderson explored the role that education systems played in the emergence of young nationalist intelligentsias in several countries colonized by European powers. Using Indonesia as an example, he explained how students hailing from a great variety of backgrounds shared a common experience going through the standardized education system set up by the Dutch. All of them followed a similar path, from local primary schools in villages scattered throughout the colony, where they studied the same curriculum, to tertiary education institutions in the cities of

Batavia and Bandung. Their 'common experience, and the amiably competitive comradeship of the classroom, gave the maps of the colony which they studied . . . a territorially specific imagined reality which was every day confirmed by the accents and physiognomies of their class-mates'. The Dutch East Indies was a vast archipelago with innumerable ethnolinguistic groups that had never been politically unified before the colonial period; but, out of that shared experience, boys and girls hailing from numerous distant islands acquired a common sense of nationhood from which emerged, as Anderson put it, 'the spectacular butterfly called "Indonesian"'.[1]

That was not going to be the case in Burma – also a land of great ethno-linguistic diversity that was politically unified for the first time during the colonial period. As in Indonesia, students also played a prominent role in Burmese nationalism, but there was a crucial differ-ence between the two colonies: the 'bifurcated state' imposed by the British, with its separate systems of administration, made virtually impossible the emergence of a Burmese nationalist movement with which all the ethnic groups could identify. The experience of the peoples in the 'scheduled areas' under British indirect rule was completely differ-ent from that of the Burman, Mon and Rakhine living in 'Burma proper' under British direct rule, and this set them on divergent paths. In central Burma, a Burman-centric nationalism emerged with 'pan-Burmese' aspirations, while several nationalist movements appeared in the 'excluded areas' representing various ethnic groups, including the Kachin, the Shan, the Chin and the Karen.

By the turn of the twentieth century, there was a widespread perception among Buddhist Burmese that their religion was suffering a dangerous decay – that the young generation thrown into the modern world was losing its Buddhist morals.[2] It was left to the lay community to fill the void, as the protector of Buddhism had left when the last king was deposed. Thus, hundreds of Buddhist organizations sprang up during the last decade of the nineteenth century in central Burma and Arakan – what the British called 'Burma proper'. These associations were devoted to collecting donations for the *sangha*, upholding Buddhist ethics and morals, providing Buddhist education to children attending lay or missionary schools, and organizing Pali examinations. Many of them were locally based, while others had branches throughout the country.

These associations gave common laypeople a prominent role that they had rarely had in the past, and fostered a new sense of community and engagement in public affairs. This was facilitated by the arrival of what Anderson called 'print capitalism' and the burgeoning of a local press.[3]

The Buddhist associations did not yet form a nationalist movement as such, as their concerns were primarily religious and their members were acting as Buddhists rather than Burman, Rakhine, or Mon. But they provided a fertile breeding ground from where popular nationalism could grow. They generated an 'imagined community' that might potentially see itself as a nation dominated by heathen foreigners, and could be mobilized to recover its independence. The first nationalist movements in 'Burma proper' emerged from that soil around the second decade of the twentieth century, and the Buddhist religion was their key unifying characteristic.

Buddhism also had the potential to be used to assert particular ethno-nationalist identities, as in the case of the Rakhine. The recent history of Arakan had been one of humiliation, first under the Burmans and then under the British, after its having been a regional power for centuries. In a Burman-centric religious historiography, the kingdom was simply ignored. Moreover, the Arakanese monastic community had been almost completely erased and replaced by the Burmese after the invasion in 1784.

Probably in reaction against that humiliation, around the time of the Fifth Council convened by King Mindon, in 1872, there emerged an anonymous text called *Explanation on the Venerable Sasana of Arakan*, which made two extraordinary claims: that the Buddha himself had visited Arakan and had chosen it as the land where his followers would preserve his teachings; and that Arakan was the stronghold of Theravada Buddhism, from where even Sri Lanka took inspiration and guidance, reversing the roles that the two kingdoms had played throughout history.[4] The *Explanation* did not mention central Burma, but it contained an implicit rebuke to the Burman-centric Buddhist chronicles. Its portrayal of the Rakhine as a 'chosen people' identified by the Buddha himself already contains the main themes of Rakhine nationalism that would emerge later: the strong identification of the Rakhine with Buddhism, and its rivalry with the Burmese central state. But at the beginning of the twentieth century Rakhine nationalism had not yet coalesced into an independent political force.

The first modern nationalist organization in 'Burma proper' was the Young Men's Buddhist Association (YMBA), founded in 1906 in Rangoon by a group of middle-class young men with the purpose of promoting '*Amyo, Bartha, Thathana* and *Pyinnyar*' (race or nation, language, Buddhism and education).[5] During its first ten years of existence, the YMBA limited itself to religious, cultural and educational issues, but in 1916 it assumed the leadership in a campaign against the British. The issue was both religious and a matter of national pride. In Burma, as in many other Buddhist countries, anybody entering a pagoda has to remove their shoes as a sign of respect; but the colonial authorities exempted Europeans from doing so, causing resentment among the local population. A lawyer from Prome demanded that the government legally enforce the removal of footwear in the pagodas, and the fifty YMBA branches in the country soon took up the issue.

At first the government rejected the demand, and for three years there was a confrontation between the authorities and the YMBA that only served to inflame nationalist sentiments further. Eventually, in 1919, after a group of Europeans entering a pagoda with their shoes was attacked by angry monks, the colonial government yielded, issuing a resolution granting the abbot of each pagoda the right to lay down his own rules – albeit exempting soldiers, policemen and magistrates sent by the authorities.[6] It was a partial victory, but a victory nonetheless, and the first against the British authorities by an incipient Burmese nationalist movement that had proved capable of mobilizing large sectors of the population.

Throughout the 1920s, Buddhist monks were at the vanguard of Burmese anticolonial movements. They enjoyed enormous moral authority among the Buddhist population, proving to be a formidable mobilizing force. In principle, the involvement of monks in worldly issues goes against the *vinaya* (monastic laws); but as the British had eliminated any meaningful religious authority, there was nobody who could discipline the 'political monks'. Moreover, for many of them the struggle for independence had religious overtones that justified such an apparent breach of the rules. They reasoned that the British had reduced Buddhists to the condition of 'slaves' in their own land, and slaves could not attain *nibbana*; it was therefore necessary to get rid of the British to restore Buddhism, and give the Burmese the chance to attain salvation.[7]

The most prominent nationalist monk was U Ottama, who is widely regarded as the first martyr of Burmese nationalism – though in fact he was not Burman, but Rakhine.[8] Born in Akyab (now Sittwe) in 1879, he was a cosmopolitan man who had studied in Calcutta, where he was involved in anti-British demonstrations and linked up with the Indian National Congress. He also had lived in Japan, and travelled to several countries in Europe and Asia. In 1919 he returned to Burma and began his fight for independence. He contributed articles to several papers, toured the country giving speeches against colonial rule, and organized several campaigns against the British. In his approach he was inspired by Gandhi, advocating tactics like non-payment of taxes and boycotts.

Ottama was instrumental in the creation of the General Council of the Sangha Samettgyi (GCSS), an organization of anticolonial monks that went on to establish a network with a presence in villages all over 'Burma proper'. The GCSS often worked in collaboration with the General Council of Burmese Associations (GCBA), a lay organization that emerged from the YMBA. U Ottama understood that the anticolonial movement in Burma was connected to other movements for national liberation. He advocated the unity of Muslims, Hindus and Buddhists in their struggle against the British, declared that the Burmese and Indians were friends, and publicly supported an anti-British Muslim rebellion that took place in India in the early 1920s.[9] He was accused of sedition by the colonial authorities and jailed on several occasions during the 1920s. He eventually died in prison in 1939, and was subsequently mourned as a martyr.

In the early 1930s, the British faced the first violent insurrection in 'Burma proper' since the aftermath of the Third Anglo-Burmese war. On December 1930, organized bands attacked the headmen and police forces of several villages in the Tharrawaddy District of Lower Burma. The attacks soon spread to other rural districts, in what came to be known as the Saya San Rebellion, after its instigator, a former monk, traditional healer and member of the GCBA who claimed to be a king who would re-establish the old order in Burma by expelling the British.[10] Many of the insurgents wore traditional tattoos and amulets, in the belief that they would make them invulnerable. This led the British to think that it was merely a millennial revolt, with little or no relation to modern, urban nationalist movements. This provided them with cover to deny the very real and legitimate socioeconomic grievances of Burmese agriculturalists, for whom the process of modernization imposed by their colonial masters had been enormously distressing.[11] Most farmers were deep in debt, and many were losing their lands to Indian moneylenders – especially after the Great Depression hit Burma in the early 1930s. As a consequence, the insurgents often directed their fury as much towards Indians as towards the British administration and its Burmese collaborators. The revolt extended to most rural areas in Lower Burma and some districts in central Burma, and was not completely quelled until 1932. By then, almost 2,000 people had perished in the disturbances.

The revolt was supported by some urban nationalists, including the members of the Dobama Asiayone (We Burmans/Our Burma Association), an organization created in 1930 by a group of Burman intellectuals in Rangoon.[12] Initially a small group that was often scorned by the older guard of the GCBA, the Dobama Asiayone grew in influence over the decade, as it managed to mobilize workers and peasants through strikes and demonstrations. Its members addressed each other with the title *thakin* (Lord, or Master), indicating that the Burmese were the true rulers of their own country. Their slogan was: 'Burma is our country, Burmese literature is our literature, Burmese language is our language. Love our country, praise Burmese literature, cherish the Burmese language.' But their sources of inspiration were not only indigenous. They were avid readers who took ideas from figures as diverse as Sun Yat-sen, Jean-Jacques Rousseau, the English Fabians, and the Irish Fenians. Marxism also played an increasingly prominent role, especially in the second half of the decade, when a new generation of more progressive students joined the association. Among them was Aung San, the father of Aung San Suu Kyi, who would lead the nationalist movement and found the Burmese army in the 1940s, and his friend U Nu, the first prime minister of independent Burma.

The *thakins* self-consciously chose the word 'Bama' instead of 'Myanma', in an attempt to include all the 'indigenous races' in the country, not only the Burmans – even though both words had basically the same connotation. The basic distinction they made was not between different ethnic groups, but between those Burmese who collaborated with the British and those who preserved Burmese culture and opposed the invaders; but the movement was nevertheless dominated by

Burmans.[13] With the *thakins*, the leadership and ideological underpinnings of Burmese nationalism veered towards secularism, though Buddhism never quite lost its central place as a marker of Burmese identity.

Many Mons and Rakhine were eager to participate in mainstream Burmese nationalism, and some even played leading roles. U Ottama was the most prominent example, but not the only one. There were some organizations devoted to advancing the interests of the Mon and Rakhine peoples, including the Association for Awakening and the Patriotic Association, created after World War I to promote Rakhine culture and demand that the colonial authorities work for the development of 'neglected Arakan'.[14] But those organizations still maintained close links with the GCBA or the Dobama Asiayone, and they were more concerned about preserving their culture, traditions and languages in the context of an increasingly strong and vocal Burmese nationalism than with advancing any separatist agenda. A full-fledged Rakhine nationalist movement with autonomist ambitions would emerge later on.

The *thakins* and other nationalists encouraged the consumption of Burmese products, such as cheroots (Burmese cigars) instead of cigarettes, as part of a revival of a culture they perceived as being in peril. They advocated wearing Burmese instead of Western clothes – but there was more pressure on women to do so than on men, as women were seen as the bearers of tradition. At the end of the 1930s, there were violent incidents in which women wearing Western clothes were assaulted by young Buddhist monks, who tore their blouses.[15] Women were at the centre of debates among nationalists, and Westernized women and those who married foreigners – particularly Indians – were often the object of scorn in a way that had no precedent in precolonial Burma, as mixed marriages between Burmese women and foreigners were now seen as threatening the Burmese race.[16]

Such anxieties about the behaviour and status of Burmese women were also linked to a crisis in masculinity, as the scholar Chie Ikeya has brilliantly shown.[17] Under the colonial order, men had been displaced from some occupations by newcomers, as well as by modernized women who could study and advance their careers as professionals. Burman men were generally regarded by the British as lacking the 'virile' qualities of the 'martial races', and were largely excluded from the army. That was taken as an affront to the 'manliness' of many Burmans, and there was a proliferation of novels and literature depicting Burman men as courageous soldiers, or rescuing from oblivion the deeds and past glories of Burman military leaders.

In the 1930s, there was a proliferation of *tats* (paramilitary armies), created to instil a martial ethos among the youth and organize the nationalist movement. The Dobama Asiayone founded its own *tat* in 1935, the Burma Letyone Tat (Burma Strength Army); but most political organizations had one, including student unions.[18] The 'soldiers' of the tats were not allowed to carry firearms, but usually underwent training and war exercises with bamboo poles. They were the predecessors of the militias that would create havoc throughout the country during and after World War II, and during the first years of independence.

One of the significant debates in Burmese politics during the 1920s and 1930s was about its relationship with India.[19] In 1923, the British established in the colony a system of diarchic government in which the Burmese had some representation. In the early 1930s, they started to make preparations to separate Burma from India to rule it as a separated colony. There was a heated controversy about this question in nationalist circles, with many opposing separation because they suspected it was a ruse of the colonial power to delay Burma's independence.

In 1935, the Rule of Burma Act passed, sealing its colonial divorce from India, which came into effect in 1937. Some members of nationalist old guard, mostly former leaders of the GCBA, saw an opportunity to lead the country gradually to independence, after it had passed at some unspecified point through a stage of dominion status, and decided to run in the legislative elections held in 1936. The *thakins* despised this gradual approach, demanding full independence as soon as possible and labelling the old nationalists as lackeys of the British. They also formed their own party, with the intention of rejecting all ministerial posts once in parliament, and thereby eroding the system from within. But the former GCBA members won, and in 1937 the veteran Ba Maw was elected to the largely ceremonial post of prime minister.

Nobody doubted that Burma did not belong to India, and very few nationalists thought that the roughly 1 million Indians living in the country belonged to Burma. The resentment against the Indians who had arrived in the wake of the British invasion had been steadily growing, and was most acute in the 1930s, when the impact of the Great Depression impoverished thousands of Burmese farmers and workers. Many farmers lost their lands to Chettiar moneylenders, of whom a large number migrated to Rangoon, where they found few employment opportunities, as coolies from India had taken most of the jobs in the docks. Tensions between them exploded in late May 1930, when the Indian coolies working in the docks organized a strike demanding higher wages, and Burmese labourers were hired to replace them for a few days. The Indian coolies attacked the Burmese workers in the docks, the Burmese retaliated, and violence soon spread to other parts of the city, with mobs attacking Indian shops and living quarters. When the police were able to impose order a few days later, at least one hundred people had been killed.[20]

In July 1938, a new wave of communal riots engulfed Rangoon, then extended to other cities in Lower and central Burma. This time, the anger of many Burmese was aimed at Indian Muslims. The riots were even more violent and destructive than those of 1930 – 113 mosques were burned and, according to official estimates, 240 people were killed, more than half of them Muslims.[21] The immediate trigger for the riots was a book deemed insulting to Buddhism that had been published by a Muslim writer. The book had first been published in 1931, but had attracted little attention at that time, or even when it was republished five years later. But tensions between Muslim Indians and Buddhists had grown at the end of the decade, and the book provided an excuse to further inflame anti-Muslim sentiment when, in June 1938, a Buddhist journalist denounced it, publishing its most offensive sections. As a result, some monks organized an anti-Muslim rally at the Shwedagon Pagoda.

In truth, the root cause of such tensions was the issue of mixed marriages between Indian Muslim men and Burmese Buddhist women. Often the women involved did not receive as much inheritance as they expected, or any at all. In some cases, the men they married were only temporarily in Burma, and when their husbands left for India they discovered that, according to Muslim law, they were not married at all. The issue was taken up and amplified by some nationalists in anti-Muslim propaganda campaigns.

As a consequence of these tensions, an important segment of Burmese nationalism acquired a strong anti-Indian and anti-Muslim component.

Despite the fact that there had already been sizeable Muslim communities in precolonial times, the origins of the idea that Islam was a foreign religion can be traced to this period, when Burmese nationalism became strongly associated with Buddhism. In 1930, the *thakins* reacted immediately to the riots; in the first pamphlet distributed by the Dobama Asiayone, they praised the common Burmese folk, including young monks, who defended their Burmese compatriots against the Indians and attacked the snobbish 'smart Burmese' who had criticized them.[22] In press articles, pamphlets and cartoons, Indians were depicted alongside Chinese as greedy parasites displacing Burmese from their lands and reducing them to a subordinate position in the economic order.[23] The fact that Indians had representation in parliament, however toothless it was in practice, also caused resentment among many Burmese nationalists. The irony was that the government regarded the Indian community with suspicion, thinking they were the instigators of Burmese nationalism.[24] Nevertheless, it would be a mistake to portray Burmese nationalism as homogenously anti-Indian. As we have seen, U Ottama advocated the unity of Muslims, Hindus and Buddhists in the struggle against the British, and maintained close links with the Indian National Congress that the younger generation of *thakins* of Aung San and U Nu would maintain in the late 1930s and beyond.

In September 1938, the leftist intellectual Thein Pe published a short book on the recent anti-Muslim riots titled *The Indo-Burman Conflict*, which was explicitly endorsed by Aung San and U Nu.[25] The book appears at first sight to be a diatribe against Indians, including statements like: 'As for the Indians, they come to Burma solely to make money and to exploit as much as they could'. It also contains denunciations of unrestricted migration and the lack of protection for Buddhist girls married to Indian men. But Thein Pe paid as much attention to class as to ethnicity, arguing that 'the Indians who are obstructing and working against Burmese interests belong to the capitalist and middle class', and defending the 'ordinary poor Indians' who 'don't treat the Burmese as their enemies and sometimes they work together with the Burmese for better or for worse'. The book concludes by stating that Burmese nationalists can work with the Indian National Congress as long as it is dominated by leftists like Nehru, and not by others like Gandhi. Thein Pe was one of the founders of the Communist Party of Burma (CPB), alongside Aung San and others, on 15 August, 1939.[26]

The Communist Party of India provided help at the beginning to the CPB, and two of the six founding members of the latter were of Bengali extraction.[27]

Roughly speaking, *thakins* more influenced by Marxism and socialism, like Aung San, Thein Pe and U Nu, tended to be more internationalist and less xenophobic towards Indians, while the 'right-wing' *thakins*, more reluctant to accept socialist ideas, tended to be more anti-Indian and xenophobic. Eventually, in 1938, the two factions of the Dobama Asiayone split apart. A young postal clerk called Shu Maung, by then a very minor figure in nationalist politics, joined the right-wing faction.[28] Shu Maung later came to be known as General Ne Win, the commander-in-chief of the armed forces who put an end to democracy in Burma and ruled it as a military dictator from 1962 to 1988.

The development of these competing strands of Burmese nationalism in 'Burma proper' was largely separated from the emergence of other nationalisms among the ethnic groups in the outlying areas of what was called Burma. The first was probably the Karen nationalist movement, in eastern Burma, whose origins can be traced to the opposition to Burman insurrections against British rule in the 1880s.[29] The Karen had resented the attempts of the Burmans to dominate them in precolonial times, and many enrolled in the British army to fight against Burman insurgents before and after the Third Anglo-Burmese War. Most Karen were animists or Buddhists, but some had already been converted to Christianity by British missionaries, and had received a modern education in missionary schools. These educated Christians formed a political and intellectual Karen elite, and in 1881 founded the Karen National Association, an organization aimed at unifying Karens of all religions and linguistic groups. Arguably, Karen nationalism was born in opposition to the Burmans, rather than the British. It grew stronger after World War I, and in the 1930s successfully campaigned for communal representation.[30]

The British regarded the Kachin peoples in the border region between China and Burma as one of the marital races – as they usually did inhabitants of the peripheries of the kingdoms they conquered. As soon as they pacified the region, they tried to lure them, through recruitment into the army, away from resistance and into allegiance to the colonial order. Most of the recruits belonged to the Jingphaw group.

According to the anthropologist Mandy Sadan, experience in the British army – especially in World War I, when many were sent to Mesopotamia – provided these soldiers with new knowledge of the workings of the empire and the modern world.[31] They also acquired a self-confidence and prestige that sometimes clashed with the authority of the local leaders when they returned home. The Jingphaw had no written language, but a Swedish-American Baptist pastor and linguist had developed a Jingphaw orthography, and helped to found the first Jingphaw-language newspaper, *Jingphaw Shi Laika*, in 1914. At the end of World War I, the newspaper began to publish texts by soldiers returned from the war, in which they expressed their ideas on how Kachin society should develop.[32]

On December 1924, more than one hundred Kachin chiefs and elders travelled to Rangoon and petitioned the governor of Burma for Kachin autonomy. They complained that the colonial government had not developed their region, and had put it in a disadvantageous position in relation to 'Burma proper'. They stressed the need for access to modern education, in English or Burmese, to enable them to work and assert their position in the Burmese state.[33] These leaders were aware of the requirements not only of the colonial system, but also of the modern world, and wanted to enter into it on an equal footing with other groups.

A new, modern ethno-nationalist conscience was emerging and, while it was often led by the Jingphaw, it aspired to include the various groups subsumed under the label 'Kachin'. The term Kachin, however, was not itself used locally by those groups. It was a term first used by the Burmese in precolonial times, which the British appropriated, and which encompassed several ethno-linguistic groups inhabiting the mountains of northern Burma.

In 1927, a secular Kachin organization was created called Pawng Yawng Hpung. It was established to work for the development of all the groups living in Kachin State. The organization fostered a Kachin identity under the native term Wunpawng, and tried to instil a sense of community between the various groups (the Jingphaw, the Lisu, the Rawang, and so on).[34] The predominant language was Jingphaw, which had been put into writing and was spoken by the most powerful group. The Kachin – or more appropriately the Wunpawng – were entering the contentious world of nationalist politics.

The period between the world wars saw similar nationalist awakenings among other peoples in Burma (the Chin and the Shan, for instance) and elsewhere. The exception were the Rohingya, who were largely politically inactive as a separate group at that point. Mainstream Burmese nationalists paid little attention to these developments, and when they did so it was often to accuse the Karen or the Kachin of being stooges of the British. The main concern of Burmese nationalists was to attain independence as soon as possible; they gave little thought to what would be the status of groups from the 'excluded areas' in a future independent Burma, or what system might better accommodate their demands for autonomy. The underlying assumption was that they should belong to Burma – something that was not necessarily part of the plans of the nationalist movements concerned. The nationalisms of the peripheries and Burmese nationalism were entering upon a collision course that would lead to violent confrontation, and ultimately war. The crucial turning point would be provided by World War II.

10

World War II and the
Road to Independence

Burma was a crucial Asian theatre of battle during World War II. By 1942 it had become the farthest point of Japanese expansion, and was the last line of defence of the British and the Allies, who were holding their own in India. The war devastated the country. When the Japanese invaded from Thailand in early 1942, the British employed a scorched-earth policy on their retreat, destroying harvests and infrastructure to deprive the invaders of supplies. In 1945, when the British retook Burma after having bombed it intensively for three years, the Japanese carried out similar scorched-earth policies in their turn. Beyond the destruction and staggering loss of life, the war also had a profound effect on relations between the various ethnic groups in Burma, leaving many wounds that remain open today. The conflict deepened older inter-ethnic rifts and generated new ones, as different groups took sides and, in some cases, the war pitted Karen or Kachin against Burman or Muslims against Buddhists in Arakan.

In 1939, a group of young nationalists were already planning to launch an armed struggle against the British. At the age of twenty-five, Aung San had already taken a position of leadership in the nationalist movement.[1] He had tried unsuccessfully to establish contact with the Communist Party of China (CPC) to prepare for the insurrection. Meanwhile, the Burmese prime minister, Ba Maw, was asking the Japanese for support against the British. In late 1940, Aung San and his comrade Bo Yan Aung embarked on a Norwegian freighter in Rangoon headed to Amoy, in China. It is not entirely clear whether their real purpose was to establish contact with the CPC, the Japanese or whoever might be willing to help them. They were intercepted by an agent of the Kempeitai (the Japanese secret police) and ended up in Japan, where they agreed to fight alongside the Japanese to attain independence as part of the Japanese Greater East Asia Co-prosperity Sphere. Aung San returned clandestinely to Burma with a Japanese agent to recruit fighters among the younger *thakins*.[2] Between March and July 1941, thirty of those young *thakins* from various factions, including a young Ne Win, travelled to Japan, where they received military training on the island of Hainan. Led by Aung San, they would go down in history as the 'Thirty Comrades'.

By the end of 1941, the Thirty Comrades had completed their training and travelled to Thailand – at the time an ally of the Japanese. In Bangkok, on 28 December, the Thirty Comrades held a traditional ceremony in which they drank their blood mixed with liquor in a shared bowl, assumed new names, and pledged eternal loyalty to each other and to the cause of national liberation. They also founded the Burma Independence Army (BIA), from which the Tatmadaw – the modern Burmese army – would later be born. For the next month, they recruited up to 3,500 volunteer fighters along the border. At the beginning of the next year, the BIA entered Burma accompanying the conquering Japanese troops. After its devastating defeat in Singapore, the British government fell quickly. Its hasty retreat to India proved that it was not invincible; it would never command the same respect, or fear, among the Burmese that had enabled it to rule the colony.

Japanese rule deepened the racial divisions that had festered during the British period.[3] All the Thirty Comrades who founded the Burmese army were Burman, as were most of the soldiers they recruited. From the beginning of the war, the Japanese portrayed their expansionist policies as a holy war 'to liberate the 130 million tropical people from the colonial policy of the white peoples', and repeated the slogan 'Asia for the Asians'. The Japanese made half-hearted attempts to win the minorities to their side, but they also stressed their ties with the Burmans by calling them 'fellow Buddhists', arousing suspicions among Christian, Muslim and animist minorities.

Nevertheless, the occupying forces treated all ethnic groups with equal harshness, born of their feeling of racial superiority – though the minorities had the perception that the Burmans were favoured by them, as the puppet 'independent' government was headed by a Burman, Prime Minister Ba Maw. It did not help that Ba Maw adopted as the official slogan for his government: 'One blood, one voice, one leader'. Despite the attempts of Ba Maw to reach out to the Karens, including his appointment of a Karen to the Privy Council, the slogan seemed to many to refer only to Burmans.

The Japanese formally proclaimed the independence of Burma on 1 August 1943. This independence seemed increasingly hollow as the Japanese tightened their domination and acted as occupiers, with the BIA under their command. Many young nationalists, including Aung San, soon realized that the Japanese would never grant their aspirations for independence, and began to organize clandestinely to fight them. In August 1944, the leaders of several organizations, including the Communist Party of Burma (CPB) and the Burmese National Army (BNA – renamed from the BIA), met in Pegu to form the Anti-Fascist Organization (AFO – later renamed as the Anti-Fascist People's Freedom League, AFPFL).[4]

Aung San was named its leader, and began to make contact with the British to join them in the fight against the Japanese. At first, the British distrusted the seemingly treacherous young dissident. Later on, when the British were making advances in northern Burma, Aung San met several times with General William Slim, the commander of the British forces that would retake Burma. Slim accused him of asking for British help only because he saw that the British were bound to win, to which Aung San retorted that it would have been pointless to approach them if they were losing.[5]

Such frankness gained the trust of the commanders on the ground, and the British came to the conclusion that it would be better to have Aung San on their side if they wanted to avoid a massive insurrection when they retook the country. Eventually, in March 1945, after working underground for months to undermine the Japanese, Aung San and his army joined forces with British and US forces to drive the Japanese out.

From the beginning of the war, while Burman nationalists were collaborating with the Japanese, most of the ethnic minorities in the mountainous areas threw their lot in with British and US Special Forces. In the words of the scholar Martin Smith, World War II was 'the major formative political experience' for all ethnic groups in the country,[6] and the fact that the various groups took different sides often made irreconcilable their subsequent readings of such an important period. In the official Burman historiography, taking sides with the Japanese at the beginning was a shrewd tactical move. This version of events tends to exaggerate the importance of the BNA in the campaign to expel the Japanese, and is often received with derision by members of those groups that predominantly fought the Japanese from the beginning. 'It's a funny thing to say that the BIA liberated Burma from Japanese occupation. The Allied Forces and the Kachin, the northern Kachin rangers, expelled all the Japanese in conjunction with some hill peoples', the Baptist reverend Ja Gun, an influential Kachin historian and linguist, told me in 2012 in Laiza, headquarters of the KIO.

The Kachin, the Karen and the Chin take as a badge of honour having fought alongside the Allies from the beginning of the war. From the point of view of some Burman nationalists, it just shows their naive allegiance to the colonial power and lack of political sophistication. But the motivations of the men who joined the British army were more complex, as Mandy Sadan has persuasively argued. The Kachin and other groups had suffered at the hands of the Japanese, and many fought to defend their land, not the British Empire. Their cause was not necessarily that of their 'colonial masters', to whom they pledged allegiance; rather their reasons for fighting with the Allies were as pragmatic as those of the Thirty Comrades in joining the Japanese.[7] In the case of the Karen, British and especially US officers made vague promises that they would be given a separate state after independence as a reward for their loyalty during the war – a promise not backed by their superiors in London or Kandy (Ceylon, modern Sri Lanka), where the Allied Southeast Asia Command was headquartered.

The Burmans and these ethnic minorities not only took different sides during the war, but sometimes fought each other directly.[8] The most virulent case was that of the Karen, who were geographically closer to the Burmans than the more isolated Kachin, and in some areas of western Burma lived side by side with them. Many Karen had already helped the British in the pacification campaigns of 1886, or the anti-insurgency campaigns during the Saya San Rebellion in the early 1930s. When the BIA entered the country from Thailand, many of its soldiers took revenge, committing several atrocities against Karen villagers. According to official figures, BIA soldiers killed more than 1,800 people and destroyed 400 villages in a single district. In a notorious incident, BIA troops murdered 152 people, including a pre-war cabinet minister, Saw Pe Tha.[9] After the war, Aung San tried to reconcile with the Karens and other ethnic groups, but the seeds of future conflicts had already been planted.

Meanwhile, in Arakan state, the war opened up conflict between Muslims and Buddhists. Until then, relations between the two communities had been largely peaceful. There had been some tensions between them during the colonial period, but never any serious episode of sectarian violence. The Rakhine were the one non-Burman group that cooperated more enthusiastically with the BIA/BNA at the onset of the war.[10] At the same time, the Muslim community worked with the British army, who distributed arms among them to foil, or at least delay, any Japanese attempt to advance into Bengal. Some officers on the ground made vague promises to the people they armed that they would grant them a Muslim National Area after the war, but such promises were not official British policy.

With both sides armed and willing to vent old grievances, the wider conflict soon generated a brutal civil war between the Muslim and Buddhist communities. Until today, both sides accuse the other of committing genocide during those years. When the British were retreating and the BIA advanced over Arakan, Rakhine Buddhist gangs attacked Muslim villages in southern Arakan, killing thousands of Muslims there, and paying little attention to moderate Rakhine elders who tried to stop them.

Meanwhile, the Muslims, armed by the British, were already attacking the Buddhists in northern Arakan, and the violence was compounded by the retaliation provoked by the stories of Muslim refugees fleeing from the south.[11] The situation got worse after the failed attempt by the Allies to retake Arakan in 1943, when British Indian army Baluch troops brutalized the local Buddhist population as a punishment for the anti-Muslim violence the previous year.[12] We do not have exact figures of how many were killed during those years, but the final result was a double ethnic cleansing that effectively divided Arakan in two areas: one predominantly Muslim, in the north (the Mayu region); and another predominantly Buddhist, in the south.

*   *   *

One of the forgotten tragedies of the war was the disastrous exodus of the Indian community from Burma upon the arrival of the Japanese.[13] When the Japanese began to bomb Rangoon in December 1941, many Indians decided to leave, but they were persuaded by the authorities to go back to the city. That proved fatal for many, as the British, in their hasty evacuation of Burma only a few weeks later, failed to organize the evacuation of hundreds of thousands of poor Indians who were still in the country. The masses of downtrodden coolies and labourers who could not afford to buy passage by steamer from Rangoon or Sittwe to the ports in India were particularly vulnerable.

Around 450,000 Indians took gruesome journeys by foot to the east through Arakan or the north, and many died on their way as a consequence of Japanese air attacks, disease, malnutrition or sheer exhaustion. According to Hugh Tinker, himself a witness of the exodus, up to 50,000 died during the journey; more recent research points to a figure of up to 80,000 dead.[14] While, according to Tinker, some of the evacuees were treated with kindness by the local Burmese population they encountered on the way, others suffered looting and violence. Chettiar moneylenders were often attacked by their creditors, and many Burmese decided to settle scores with the despised Indian community. According to an Indian doctor, Burmese went on a murderous rampage against the Indians, only to be stopped by the arrival of the Japanese.[15] In a separate episode Aung San himself executed the headman of a village near Moulmein – a Muslim man of Indian origins called Abdul Rashid – after BIA soldiers had starved and held him captive in a cart with a pig for eight days, according to the unfortunate headman's widow.[16] Most of these Indians never returned. While some remained, the exodus marked the end of the prominent place that Indians had occupied in Burma during the period of British rule.

At the end of the war, after retaking Burma in 1945, the British planned to re-establish their power, with the intention of granting dominion status after a few years. But it soon became clear that the nationalist forces that had fought against them at the beginning of the war and were now well trained, armed and organized, would not accept that. There were calls from some in the British government to arrest Aung San and other leaders for murder and high treason, but Lord Mountbatten, Allied supreme commander in Southeast Asia, was afraid that doing so could trigger a massive revolt, in the knowledge that the British could no longer rely on the Indian army to buttress their power in the region.

Thus, Mountbatten pushed to rehabilitate Aung San, accepting him as the main representative of Burmese nationalists. Meanwhile, to put pressure on the British, Aung San and the AFPFL organized mass rallies and strikes that posed a serious challenge to the British, and created the People's Voluntary Organisation (PVO), a paramilitary corps that reached a membership of more than 100,000 by independence.[17] British domination in Burma was coming to an end; the only thing left for it to do was negotiate the terms of the transfer of power.

Aung San was leading a deeply divided movement in a country devastated by the war. In March 1946, the CPB split into two factions, one of which, the 'Red Flags', led by Thakin Soe, broke up with the AFPFL and launched an armed struggle, accusing the latter of being a lackey of the imperialists. In September 1946, the AFPFL accepted the positions offered by the British in the governor's Executive Council, and Aung San assumed prime-ministerial power. The remaining faction of the CPB, the 'White Flags' led by Than Tun, Aung San's brother-in-law, was sidelined within the AFPFL, and Aung San definitively took the reins of the mainstream nationalist movement, leading negotiations with the British in late 1946.[18]

The thorniest question was that of the status of non-Burman peoples in the future Burma. After the war, the British indicated that no decision would be made on the frontier areas without the full consent of their inhabitants; but they were more concerned about the fate of India and Pakistan, and paid relatively little attention to developments in Burma. They trusted Aung San's assurances that he would obtain such consent from the minorities, and allowed him and the AFPFL to oversee them.

When they invited the young leader and a group of delegates in early 1947 to London for the crucial talks on the transfer of power, they did not extend the invitation to any delegate from the ethnic minorities, prompting Karen, Kachin and Shan leaders to cable warnings that they would regard any agreement as non-binding.[19] The negotiations culminated in the Attlee–Aung San agreement, signed in London on 27 January 1947. This included a road map leading to Burma's independence, after elections for a constituent assembly and the drafting of a constitution, within one year.

*   *   *

Aung San not only played a crucial role in the years leading up to independence; he also became a national symbol whose legacy many would try to appropriate after independence. He was more a man of action than a political thinker, but he expounded some of his ideas in writings and speeches.[20] They may at times give the impression that he contradicted himself, or at least that he adapted his ideas to changing circumstances. But he was a man of his time who was not advocating a return to pre-colonial political institutions; rather, he wanted to build a modern and independent nation-state based on socialist principles. He believed in democracy, but not in its classical liberal sense. The Soviet Union was for him the highest form of democracy. He thought socialism should be the final goal for Burma, but that it was unattainable for the moment.[21]

In 'Problems for Burma's Freedom', his inaugural address at the AFPFL convention in January 1946,[22] Aung San exposed a conception of nationalism in which 'race, religion, and language are by themselves not primary factors which go into the making of a nation, but [it is] the historic necessity of having to lead a common life that is the pivotal principle of nationality and nationalism'. In that spirit, he offered an open hand to the Indians and Chinese living in the country: 'we have no bitterness, no ill-will toward them . . . If they choose to join us, we will welcome them as our brethren.' But, in an ominous foreshadowing of the way in which they would always be under suspicion, he warned: '[T] hey must be careful not to be made pawns in the game of our internal politics . . . They must choose and choose once and for [whether] all they will be our friends or foes. They cannot be both.'

In that same speech, Aung San also expounded on the role that religion should play in Burma: 'If we mix religion with politics, this is against the spirit of religion itself, for religion takes care of our hereafter and usually has not to do with mundane affairs, which are the sphere of politics.' After that, he seemed to backtrack a little, describing Buddhism as 'more than a religion itself', and 'possibly the greatest philosophy in the world', exhorting the *sangha* to 'purify it and broadcast it to all the world so that all mankind might be able to listen to its timeless message of love and brotherhood till eternity'. No mention was made of any other faith.

Aung San endorsed Stalin's famous definition of a nation as 'a historically evolved stable community of language, territory, economic life, and psychological make-up manifested in a community of culture'.[23]

After establishing a distinction between 'national community' and 'political community', he added that 'strictly speaking there can be only one' nationality in Burma. But, relying on Stalin's narrow definition of nationality, he claimed that, 'by stretching a point', only the Shan could be regarded as a national community, apart from the Burmans. He thereby denying a national identity to the Karen, the Kachin and the Chin, on the basis that none of those groups had their own common, single language. Aung San concluded that, 'in a community of nations there must be the right of self-determination'. But he warned that 'this right must not be overindulged regardless of time and circumstances'.

The ideal of 'unity' was a constant in Aung San's speeches. Significantly, he closed an address to the AFPFL in 1947 with the words, pronounced in the Buddhist religious language, Pali: 'Unity is the foundation. Let this fact be engraved in your memory, ye who hearken to me, and go ye to your appointed tasks with diligence.' These calls for unity were necessary, given the odds faced by the nationalists in their struggle for independence against the colonial power; but they also served to justify anti-democratic tendencies within the AFPFL that demonized any form of dissent as an expression of self-interest.

This stress on unity traced its roots in the first nationalist movements, and even further back, to precolonial ideologies of kingship based on Buddhist notions of social harmony and selflessness.[24] This idea of unity would become an absolute moral value deeply embedded in Burmese political culture. It has also served to justify authoritarianism both on the part of the military regime during the dictatorship and within the democratic opposition.

Aung San is often credited as the man who was able to bring the various ethnic groups together. He gained the trust of some non-Burman leaders, reportedly assuring them that 'if Burma receives one kyat, you will also get one kyat' – a saying still remembered by many non-Burman nationalists to recall the original promise made by the young leader, and how subsequent governments failed to fulfil it.

Aung San's main achievement in this respect was the Panglong Agreement, signed on 12 February 1947 in southern Shan State by representatives of some of the ethnic groups and the AFPFL. This Agreement was the basis on which the Union of Burma was founded. The date is still celebrated as 'Union Day' every year, and the 'Panglong

Spirit' is often invoked in Burmese politics as a symbol of the coming together of the various peoples making up the country. But the Panglong Agreement was inconclusive, and ultimately failed to address the issue of building a nation to which all of its ethnic groups could feel they belonged. The main concession from the attending representatives of the peoples from the frontier areas was to accept 'immediate co-operation with the Interim Burmese Government' in the belief 'that freedom will be more speedily achieved' in such a way, while they received assurances that 'full autonomy in internal administration for the Frontier Areas is accepted in principle'. Not surprisingly, Burmese national leaders tend to underscore the first point, while ethnic leaders tend to emphasize the second.

The Panglong Agreement was insufficient for several reasons.[25] Only four groups signed it: the Burman, led by Aung San (who just signed his name, with no official position attached to it),[26] the Shan, the Kachin and the Chin. Groups like the Nagas and the Wa were excluded because they were regarded as too primitive to be 'able to assist in the drawing up of the constitution'. And it is debatable to what extent those who attended were truly representative of their respective groups, or could make their voices heard clearly. There were organizations among the Shan and the Kachin that were demanding both independence and democratic reforms to modernize their societies – organizations like the Shan State Freedom League and the Kachin Freedom League, who had been active collaborators of the AFPFL.

Those younger Shan and Kachin groups were also willing to join Burma while maintaining their autonomy; but Aung San and other organizers favoured less democratic leaders, with whom he could expect to reach an agreement more quickly. Thus, he chose to negotiate with the very same Shan and Kachin elites through whom the British had indirectly ruled the frontier areas during the colonial period. Meanwhile, the Chin arrived in Panglong when the Shan and the Kachin had already decided to join independent Burma, so they were under pressure to accept the conditions they had already negotiated with the Burmans. Moreover, according to the Chin historian Lian Sakhong, an error in translation led the Burman representatives to believe that they were not demanding their own state. When the Constitution was drafted, the Chin ended up getting a 'Special Division' without the right of secession granted only to the Shan and the Karenni (or Kayah).[27]

The question of the Karens was the most sensitive at the time. The Karens were the group that had suffered the most at the hands of the BIA during the war. While a few were allies of the AFPFL, many deeply distrusted the Burmans. Karen nationalists sent some representatives as mere observers to Panglong, refusing to sign any agreement, as they would later refuse to take part in the constituent assembly. Eventually, a few months after independence, they launched an insurgency. The Karenni, whose region had not been under British authority during the colonial period, did not participate either; they were incorporated in the Union of Burma a few months after independence, and many would join the Karen insurgency.

The Rakhine and Mon were not invited. Aung San did not seem to regard the Mon as a separate nation, while his position on the Rakhine was ambiguous. By the time of the Panglong Conference, there was already a strong current of Rakhine nationalism demanding a separate state. Led by the former monk U Seinda, Rakhine nationalists organized a revolt that often merged with the insurgent 'Red Flag' communists. Meanwhile, in Rangoon, Aung San claimed to accept 'in principle' Rakhine demands for statehood; but during the drafting of the constitution he asked the Rakhine MPs to drop those demands, arguing that they would 'create the impression of disunity' and might 'delay the declaration of independence'.[28]

Meanwhile, some Muslim activists were starting to demand an Islamic frontier state in Northern Arakan, but nobody paid much attention to them.[29] In May 1946, a group of Arakanese Muslims sent a letter to Mohammad Ali Jinnah, the leader of the Indian Muslim League, asking him to annex the Mayu Region to the future state of Pakistan. Jinnah did not support the idea, and even sent a letter to Aung San assuring him that he was not making any territorial claim to Arakan.[30] The supporters of annexation were mostly immigrants from Chittagong who had arrived in Arakan during the colonial period, while Muslims with older roots in the area tended to oppose the idea.[31] Those demanding annexation by Pakistan did not represent all the Muslim inhabitants of Arakan; but the petition has often been used by Rakhine and Burmese nationalists alike to sow suspicion regarding the allegiance of the Rohingya community as a whole to the Burmese nation-state, and, by implication, further their claim that the Rohingya do not belong in Burma.

*   *   *

The Constituent Assembly convened for the first time on 9 June 1947. One month later, on 19 July, Aung San was assassinated with seven other members of his cabinet, including a Karen, a Shan and Abdul Razak, a brilliant Muslim of mixed Burman and Indian ancestry who was at that time the minister of education. A political rival, U Saw, was accused of orchestrating the killing, and was subsequently executed. For many in Burma, the day Aung San was killed marks the date when things went wrong for the country, and it is still commemorated as 'Martyrs Day'. Many of those who mourn Aung San believe that, as he had proved to be the only man who had managed to gain the trust of (some of) the ethnic minorities, he might have prevented the civil wars that engulfed the country for decades, and democracy might have survived. It is impossible to know how Burma would have fared if Aung San had survived. The history of the country probably would have been different, but the problems besieging Burma at its birth were too complex to be resolved by any single person, and the Constitution he was so instrumental in bringing about was not free of serious shortcomings.[32]

The AFPFL was the predominant force in the Constituent Assembly. Out of a total of 182 delegates from 'Burma proper', 171 were members of the AFPFL, and many of the forty-five delegates from the frontier areas were either affiliated with or supported the party founded by Aung San. As a result, the Constitution was bound to be fundamentally an AFPFL document.[33] The final result was vague about relations between the central government and the states where some of the minorities lived. The Union was divided into areas roughly corresponding to the territories that the British had governed directly as 'Burma proper', as well as some of the states that coincided with the 'excluded areas' that the British had ruled indirectly. The states enjoyed some measure of autonomy, but ultimate power rested with the central government of the Union.

As a result, Union laws took precedence over state laws; the heads of each state were appointed by the prime minister of the Union in consultation with the council of each state; and land ownership was ultimately in the hands of the Union, not of each state. Moreover, not all the states had the same status. Only four were recognized: Shan, Kachin, Karenni and Karen. Of these, only the Karennni (or Kayah) and the Shan eventually received the right of secession, though the procedure was not specified. Meanwhile, the Chin were granted only the status of a 'Special

Division', to be governed by a 'minister for Chin affairs' appointed by the president. Neither the Mon nor the increasingly restive Rakhine and Rohingya in Arakan were granted separate states. Some of these arrangements would be altered in subsequent years, albeit not always to the satisfaction of the groups concerned. The semi-federal system enshrined different arrangements depending on the area. Rather than the fruit of a process of negotiation between all of the groups sitting down together to reach a mutually acceptable modus vivendi, it was the result of rushed negotiations between the AFPFL and the various groups, in which each minority had attained what its bargaining position allowed it to secure.

In other respects, the Constitution was politically progressive. For instance, it ensured the independence of the judiciary. It recognized 'the special position of Buddhism as the faith professed by the great majority of the citizens of the Union', but also recognized 'Islam, Christianity, Hinduism and Animism as some of the religions existing in the Union', guaranteed freedom of belief, and forbade the 'abuse of religion for political purposes'.

Compared with the current 1982 Citizenship Law, the Constitution was more open in its definition of citizenship. Unlike the law now in effect, it invoked only one level of citizenship, which was determined essentially according to three criteria: membership of one of the 'indigenous races of Burma', having been born in 'any of the territories ... included within His Britannic Majesty's dominions'; and having lived in Burma for at least eight of the ten years preceding independence, or the ten years preceding World War II, and wanting to reside permanently in the country – a provision clearly devised for the Indian community.

The concept of 'indigenous races' was already present from the beginning, and it was defined in the same terms as those of the 1982 Citizenship Law. 'Indigenous races' were, according to the 1948 Union Citizenship Act, 'such racial groups as had settled in any of the territories included within the Union as their permanent home from a period anterior to 1823 AD'. But, in the same way that some vague recognition of Buddhism did not detract from the freedom to practise other religions, the recognition of 'indigenous races' did not establish any hierarchy in relation to other citizens.

With a fragile government, and many divisions still unresolved, Burma declared its independence on 4 January 1948. Prime Minister U Nu declared: 'We lost our independence without losing our self-respect;

we clung to our culture and our traditions and these we now hold to cherish and to develop in accordance with the genius of our people. We part without rancour and in friendship from the great British nation who held us in fee. This Day of Independence dawns on a people not only free, but united.'[34] The *thakins*, who had made an independent Burma from the ashes of the British Empire, now had to make Burmese citizens out of people who mostly saw themselves as Burman, Rakhine, Kachin or Karen. That would prove a much more difficult task.

11

An Embattled Democracy

In 1948, the birth pangs of an independent Burma produced a weak state tasked with governing a collection of ethnic groups with little or no cohesion. Many of those peoples now found themselves under a single independent nation-state for the first time in history, and many among them distrusted the central government as a tool of Burman domination. The first fourteen years of independence were an experiment in parliamentary rule that ended up in failure because the civilian government was unable to consolidate institutionally. In hindsight, the obstacles seem daunting: riddled with factionalism and embattled on virtually every front, the AFPFL-led government had to build a country virtually from scratch in an extremely unstable environment. During those years, only the military would prove able to entrench itself gradually, until it decided to take power definitively in 1962.

The government of Prime Minister U Nu was besieged on three fronts. The first was the insurgencies led by the Communist Party of Burma (CPB) and the People's Voluntary Organization (PVO) – the paramilitary organization founded by Aung San, which ran out of control after the death of its leader. The second came from an array of ethnic guerrillas fighting for independence. The third came from abroad: rump Kuomintang (KMT) troops that, after being defeated by the People's Liberation Army in China in 1949, crossed into northern Burma.

There was no shortage of weapons readily available to all of these groups. After World War II, thousands of weapons had been left scattered throughout the country by the British and the Japanese, and the American CIA provided material and logistical support for a few years to the KMT.

The 'Red Flag' faction of the CPB had already launched its insurgency before independence, with bases in the Arakan mountains. Only two months later, 25,000 partisans under the mainstream CPB, the 'White Flag' Communists, launched a new insurgency in central Burma. They were led by Thakin Than Tun, one of the Thirty Comrades. The main disagreement with the government seemed to be about issues of national sovereignty. Than Tun had harshly criticized the U Nu–Attlee agreement signed on October 1947 in London, by which the terms of Burma's independence were agreed. He condemned it as a 'fake' agreement designed to impose 'national humiliation and permanent enslavement' on the Burmese, and threatened to attack the 'Anglo-American imperialists and their running dogs, the collaborating AFPFL leadership'.[1]

The agreement had granted full independence to Burma, which also refused to join the Commonwealth, but U Nu had made a few concessions that the Communists deemed unacceptable, including a commitment to give entry to Commonwealth naval vessels and air force planes.[2] By mid 1948 fighting had reached the outskirts of Rangoon, and the government was on the verge of collapse. The predominantly Burman government was saved from disaster by loyal troops mostly made up of Chin, Kachin and Karen regiments under a Karen commander-in-chief, General Smith Dun. Over the second half of 1948, they managed to recapture important areas of central Burma, giving breathing space to the army to reorganize itself for a different war.[3]

Dissatisfaction in the Karen National Union (KNU), the main Karen nationalist organization, had been brewing since the approval of the Constitution in September 1947. The Constitution granted a Karen state in areas with a Karen-majority population, but the KNU also wanted some other areas in Lower Burma.[4] Tensions between the government and the KNU escalated during the first months of the Communist insurgency. The fact that Karen and Kachin troops were fighting the Communists in central Burma generated resentment among the local Burman population, while militias from all sides often operated under no authority. The violence was often communal in character, pitting Burmans against Karens, sometimes within the same village.[5]

The Anti-Fascist People's Freedom League (AFPFL) created an irregular paramilitary force, the Sitwundan, and put it under the command of the War Office, bypassing the command structure of the regular army. The government wanted to reinforce its military strength, distrustful of a Karen-dominated regular army whose allegiance to the Burmese state it did not completely trust.[6] In December, while the Karen Rifles of the Tatmadaw were fighting a hard battle against the Communists in central Burma, a group of paramilitaries perpetrated a massacre of Karen villagers in Lower Burma. It was a turning point that prompted the Karen Rifles to defect and join the Karen National Defence Organization (KNDO), the armed wing of the KNU, which was about to launch its insurgency. At the end of January 1949, the KNDO took Insein, on the outskirts of Rangoon.

The unresolved war between the Burmese government and the Karen insurgents had re-ignited. On 30 January the government outlawed the KNDO, and two days later U Nu placed all the Karen officers of the Burmese army 'on leave' and replaced Smith Dun with the General Ne Win as chief of staff, giving him the title of supreme commander. Karen soldiers joined the uprising or were interned in 'Armed Forces Rest Camps'.[7] From then on, the military was dominated by Burman officers.

There were also smaller rebellions of ethnic guerrillas fighting for the Mon, the Pa-Os and or the Karennis. In Arakan, Communists, Rakhine guerrillas and Muslim *mujahideens* were also fighting. But the biggest threat was posed by the KNDO. The Tatmadaw's First Kachin Rifles also joined the Karen rebellion when Ne Win ordered them to attack the Karen, though most Kachin soldiers initially remained loyal to the government. Nevertheless, many of them began to feel conflicted about fighting against their World War II allies for a government and army that were increasingly dominated by Burmans. As a consequence, Kachin enrolment in the army diminished throughout the 1950s, and de-enlistment reached a peak in the late 1950s and early 1960s.[8]

By the beginning of 1949, the Tatmadaw had lost 42 per cent of its manpower in defections to various guerrillas.[9] At a certain point there were more armed men fighting against the government than defending it; it became known as the 'Rangoon government', since its control hardly extended beyond the limits of the capital. But it did not fall within the first two years of independence thanks to the lack of coordination between the groups attacking it, but also to the crucial aid it received from abroad through the port of Rangoon, mainly from India and Britain.[10] Eventually, in 1950, the government managed to regain control of large areas of central Burma, pushing the insurgents far from the main urban centres. But if help from abroad was crucial to avoiding the complete collapse of the state, a major threat soon came also from outside.

In 1949, after the Communist victory in China, around 2,000 troops of the KMT crossed from the Chinese province of Yunnan to Shan State, in northern Burma. At the beginning, they were little more than a nuisance for a government fighting more important battles; but as their numbers swelled, reaching 12,000 by 1952, they grew to be more of a threat.[11] The KMT forces had the support of the CIA, which flew supplies of weapons and ammunitions through Thailand in an attempt to open a new front against Communist China.[12] The Burmese grew increasingly nervous about the presence of the KMT in its territory, fearing that Communist China might invade northern Burma to crush it. It declared martial law in parts of northern Shan State in 1950, and the Tatmadaw launched several unsuccessful offensives against the KMT. Burma brought the issue to the UN, and in April 1953 it was agreed that the KMT troops should be evacuated. But many of the supposed KMT members, who ended up in Taiwan, turned out to be locals from the Shan or Lahu ethnic groups.

The KMT were not expelled from Burma until the early 1960s. The invasion had three major consequences. It contributed to the triggering of ethnic insurgencies – both directly, through the alliances of the KMT with Mon and other rebels, and indirectly, as the military presence of the Tatmadaw in Shan State and its heavy-handed treatment of the local population generated resentment against the central government among ethnic groups that had until then had little contact with it.[13] Secondly, the KMT monopolized the opium trade in Shan State as a means of raising funds, thereby boosting it spectacularly. From 1949 to 1961, the production of opium in Shan State grew by almost 500 per cent. Opium became a huge industry that would survive and thrive long after the KMT had left, making Shan State the biggest producer in the world before Afghanistan took the lead in the early 1990s.[14]

Lastly, this external threat persuaded both civilian and military leaders of the necessity to overhaul the military and transform it from 'its post-resistance, decentralized guerrilla character into one capable of defending the sovereignty of the Union', in the words of the scholar Mary Callahan.[15] Such an overhaul would include giving army officials more control over operational and military issues; the establishment of educational and training institutions like the Defence Services Academy, modelled on West Point; and the creation of the Defence Services Institute, a company owned by the Tatmadaw exempted from paying taxes, whose ostensible purpose was to provide materiel to the soldiers, but which became a profitable corporation that, by 1960, included banks, shipping lines and the largest import–export operation in the country.[16]

The years between 1948 and 1962 are sometimes idealized as a period when democracy flourished in Burma. There was a multi-party system, and relatively free elections were held in 1951, 1956 and 1960; the judiciary was relatively independent; and there was a vibrant press, often highly critical with the government. But the government did as much as it could to stifle dissent. It invoked emergency provisions to arrest not only Communist and Karen rebels, but also political opponents. Elections were often marred by violence, as the local paramilitary groups created by the AFPFL 'campaigned' for their party using violent methods. Political assassination was not unheard of, at least at the local level.[17]

As a result, the AFPFL failed to build a viable civilian state. In the countryside, the party relied on local patronage networks, and strongmen who often joined the party out of mere convenience.[18] This strategy strengthened the local leaders, rather than the party itself. Where those networks were absent, the party had little presence, and politics became a violent contest for power between local factions. That was the situation in central Burma, while the control of the state was almost nonexistent in the rugged mountains of the borderlands.

Meanwhile, the Tatmadaw was gradually consolidating itself as an institution. Throughout the 1950s, the military grew steadily stronger as the civilian government became weaker. Army officers often travelled abroad in the mid 1950s on shopping trips to acquire weapons and equipment. In the first three years after independence, the only supplier was the United Kingdom. But in 1952 the army began to visit other countries: India, Pakistan, Yugoslavia, Israel, and China.[19] These trips were also study missions on which they searched for models for their own army. Their two main models were Yugoslavia and Israel, as they both provided a blueprint for building an army capable of both waging guerrilla war and defending the country against foreign aggression.

In 1956, the Directorate of Psychological Warfare (also known as the Psy-War Directorate) began to assume a political role that went beyond the duties usually expected of an army. As part of its counterinsurgency campaign against Communists and ethnic guerrillas, the Tatmadaw designed programmes of propaganda to win the hearts and minds of the population.[20] To this end, it used traditional performances, radio programmes and the press. Sensing that the civilian government was failing in its mission to create Burmese citizens, the generals took that responsibility into their own hands.

In 1958, Prime Minister U Nu offered an amnesty to insurgent groups, in a call for 'arms for democracy'. Similar initiatives had been ignored before, but this one was relatively successful. In cities and towns through-out the country, 5,500 armed insurgents were officially pardoned and greeted by local government officials.[21] The amnesty entailed the disso-lution of armed groups like the Arakan People's Liberation Party. Also, many PVO members relinquished their weapons, and the CPB was reduced. The exception was the KNU, which saw its power grow. For all its shortcomings, the amnesty seemed at the time like an encouraging step in the direction of solving various armed conflicts. But a new conflict soon emerged.

That very same year, internal divisions in the AFPFL reached break-ing point during a vote to elect a new secretary-general. In April, the party irremediably split into two factions: the 'Clean' AFPFL, led by Prime Minister U Nu, and the 'Stable' AFPFL.[22] It was not a split over ideology, but a consequence of personal feuds for power; the AFPFL was basically a socialist party, though U Nu had turned gradually to the right. The split exacerbated instability in both the cities and the country-side, where both factions jockeyed for control of the party's militias.

The split also affected the army, most officers siding with the 'Stable' faction, as a reaction to the criticism that U Nu had been directing against the army's increasingly powerful role in politics. He had intro-duced measures to increase civilian control over the Tatmadaw, and many field commanders believed that he wanted to include some

Communist leaders in the government. Some officers began to make preparations for a coup. In order to prevent it, fearing it would lead to bloody clashes, colonels Maung Maung and Aung Gyi decided to stage their own 'soft coup'. On 26 September 1958, they forced the prime minister to accept a transfer of power to a new caretaker government headed by the general Ne Win. In principle, Ne Win would have six months to impose law and order; but in the event his government lasted for a year and a half before returning to a parliamentary system.[23]

The caretaker government fulfilled its mission of restoring a modicum of order. When it relinquished power and organized a new election in 1960, Burmese citizens were able to cast their votes in 95 per cent of the electoral districts – more than in previous elections.[24] But perhaps the main consequence of that brief military government was that it convinced the generals that it was their mission to build the nation-state. The army's distrust of parliamentary democracy, and of the Burmese population at large, deepened after what it regarded a successful government of its own. Such distrust had been exposed in a document published three weeks after the coup by the Psy-War Directorate, in which it suggested that the Burmese were not ready for democracy, as they were 'left in the grip of their instincts alone, which generally are not of too high standards'.[25] This mentality has permeated the culture of the Tatmadaw until the present.

Buddhism played a crucial political role during the turbulent democratic period. The Constitution prohibited the use of religion for political purposes, and Aung San had wished to keep religion separate from politics; but U Nu was a different kind of politician. He presented himself as a pious Buddhist, and the government as the protector of religion, in the old Dhammaraja tradition of universal moral rulers. He even convened a Sixth Great Buddhist Council in 1954, eighty-eight years after the last king of Burma had convened the Fifth. The government allocated considerable resources to the event, which lasted for two years and was publicized as a moment of national pride.[26] U Nu's politicization of Buddhism may have been a product of opportunism, of a genuine belief in the religion, or a combination of the two. Nothing suggests his piousness was insincere, but the results were ultimately damaging for any inclusive project of nation-building in a country with several religious minorities. Probably without intending it (there were prominent Muslims in his cabinet), U Nu contributed to reinforcing the idea that only Buddhists were real Burmans, or even Burmese.

Religion was used in propaganda campaigns against Communism, often organized by the Tatmadaw.[27] In May 1958, the month of Buddha's birthday, the Psy-War Directorate published and widely distributed a pamphlet called *Dhammarantaya* ('Buddhism in danger'), which portrayed communists as destroyers of the religion. For the illiterate population, the Directorate placed billboards in prominent places depicting evil Communists slaughtering Buddhist monks and torching temples. The Tatmadaw also used Islam and Christianity in its anti-Communist crusade, publishing pamphlets for Muslim and Christian audiences; and it organized hundreds of meetings at which Buddhist monks warned of the evils of such anti-religious doctrines. Muslim and Christian leaders often spoke alongside the monks.

One of U Nu's main promises during the election campaign of 1960 was to make Buddhism the state religion. After winning the election, his party presented the bill in parliament in August 1961. It won by an over-whelming majority, and the Constitution was amended to guarantee that the Union government would 'promote and maintain Buddhism for its welfare and advancement'.[28] The amendment caused a great deal of anxiety among adherents of other religions. U Nu decided to present another bill in parliament – the Fourth Constitutional Amendment – aimed at protecting other religions as well.[29] Radical Buddhist monks opposed it fiercely, arguing that it entailed the recognition of all other faiths on an equal footing with Buddhism.

A group of young radical monks reacted with fury to the amendment's approval, and occupied a mosque under construction in a Rangoon suburb for a couple of weeks. At first, the authorities refused to deploy any force against them; but the crisis escalated, and the monks ended up destroying the mosque and burning another one. There was a riot when a Buddhist mob attacked Muslims, killing two of them. Two Buddhists were shot dead by the police when they eventually stepped in. The monks accused the authorities of brutality, and U Nu did his best to make amends, holding ceremonies and making donations. Extremist monks had proved a a fearsome force during the anti-Muslim riots in 1938, and they showed their strength again – this time against a government afraid to confront them.

*   *   *

Engulfed by political instability and nationwide armed conflicts, the embattled central government was initially largely neglectful of what was happening in Arakan. The brutal sectarian violence that had pitted Buddhists against Muslims in World War II had left a legacy of deep distrust between the two communities. In the first months after independence, the government replaced Muslim civil servants and policemen with Rakhine, who often vented their resentment against the Muslims, carrying out arbitrary arrests and humiliating their leaders. Immigration authorities imposed restrictions of movement on Muslims from Northern Arakan to Sittwe. Meanwhile, some 13,000 Rohingya refugees from the war living in India and Pakistan were not allowed to return.[30]

In April 1948, a *mujahid* revolt exploded in northern Arakan in reaction against such discrimination. Led by the popular singer Jafar Hussein, the *mujahideen* pledged to fight for an Islamic state in the Mayu region.[31] The rebellion spread quickly because the government was overstretched by having to fight other guerrillas in central Burma; but its appeal among the Muslim community was far from universal. Muslim leaders condemned their activities as un-Islamic, and tried to persuade them to desist. They addressed the government, explaining that the *mujahideen* were few in number, and that their uprising was due to injustices committed against the community. Moreover, these leaders accused the rebels of threatening Muslims as much as Buddhists, and on several occasions even requested weapons to fight against them. But their demands were rejected.[32]

The authorities claimed that the *mujahideen* were encouraging illegal immigrants from overpopulated East Pakistan to Arakan; but the Muslim leaders who opposed the rebellion denied such accusations, arguing that the government was making up the story in order to prevent Rohingya refugees from returning.[33] The charge of illegal migration from East Pakistan (later Bangladesh) continues to this day. The border has always been porous, and during some periods hardly controlled at all. Nonetheless, there is little evidence that massive waves of migrants from East Pakistan crossed during the parliamentary period into Burma. And such immigration was possibly offset by emigration in the other direction: in 1951, the Pakistani government sent a note of protest to the Burmese government complaining that 250,000 Muslims had crossed into their country fleeing the violence in Arakan.[34] The figure is likely a gross exaggeration, but there is no reason to believe that thousands did not cross the border.

Charges of illegal immigration were sometimes denied by a judiciary that was still capable of preserving its independence. Thus, in 1960 the Supreme Court overturned a decision by the immigration authorities in Maungdaw to arrest several dozen alleged 'illegal immigrants' it wanted to expel. The authorities had claimed that the detainees did not speak Burmese – an allegation that continues to be made in the present to assert that the Rohingya are foreigners. The Supreme Court ruling argued that in Burma 'there were races who could not speak the Burmese language and whose customs were different from the Burmese but who nevertheless were citizens of the Union under the provisions of the Constitution'.[35]

There were three different revolts in the region in the first years of independence: in the south, the Rakhine rebels of the Arakan National Liberation Party (ANLP), whose leaders were all former monks, and the Arakan People's Liberation Party (APLP), led by the monk U Seinda;[36] the 'Red Flag' Communists hiding in the Arakan Mountains; and the *mujahid* insurgency in the north. These insurgencies were somewhat interlinked.

Rakhine politicians in Rangoon pushed for an autonomous Arakan state throughout the democratic period. Meanwhile, Rohingya politicians were afraid of the retribution their community could meet if they fell under the control of their Rakhine neighbours for the violence during World War II, and demanded their own separate state in the north.[37] Muslim MPs from the Mayu Region did not oppose the creation of an Arakanese state, as long as Maungdaw, Buthidaung and parts of Rathedaung were excluded and formed a separate administrative unit.

In 1961, after winning his third elections, U Nu was ready to yield to the demands of the Rakhine, and also the Mon, for their own state. Before that, in May that year, he established the Mayu Frontier Administration (MFA) to allay the fears of the Muslim community. The MFA was placed under the control of army officers, and was ruled directly from Rangoon. The solution seemingly satisfied Muslim representatives. Meanwhile, the Rakhine insurgencies had mostly subsided by the late 1950s and early 1960s, as some groups accepted the amnesties offered by U Nu in his 'arms for democracy' programme in 1958 and the government showed its willingness to yield to the demands for statehood in Arakan made by Rakhine politicians.

Around the same time, the *mujahid* insurrection was in its last throes. In July 1961, the last *mujahideen* surrendered their weapons to the government in a ceremony in Maungdaw presided over by Brigadier General Aung Gyi, vice chief of staff of the army. Aung Gyi made a speech that was both conciliatory and threatening.[38] He recognized that Muslims in Northern Arakan had suffered persecution in the past, but he stated that such persecution was over, and 'emphatically and categorically recognized Rohingyas as an ethnic minority of the Union of Burma, making efforts for the progress and development of the Rohingya ethnic minority'. He explained that the Rohingya minority straddled the borders between Burma and Bangladesh, in the same way that other minorities, like the Kachin, straddled the borders between Burma and China, and issued a warning: 'Although you might have family ties, in-laws, and even children in West Pakistan, your family ties must not interfere or lessen your allegiance to the Union of Burma. For as you are all members of the Union of Burma your allegiance and loyalty must, with no equivocation, lie with our Union.'

This recognition of the Rohingya as an ethnic minority of Burma directly contradicts current official narratives that deny their very identity. Rakhine and Burman nationalists often accuse the Rohingya of making up an identity with a separatist agenda in mind, arguing that the term only appeared in the 1950s, or even later.[39] The argument, supported by a few scholars sympathetic with Rakhine nationalism, is that the term 'Rohingya' does not correspond to any real ethnic group, but to a 'political movement'.[40] If there is such thing as *a* 'Rohingya movement', it is the most unlikely of movements, as it has historically pulled in several directions, often mutually contradictory: from separatism to integration in the Burmese nation-state. As we have already seen, the term itself already existed in precolonial times, referring to the Muslim population in Arakan.

But it may well be the case that Arakanese Muslims only started to use it as widely an ethnonym in the 1950s, and the reasons are probably political. Yet ethnicity is inherently political, and not only in the case of the Rohingya. The dichotomy between ethnicity and politics is predicated on the assumption that ethnic groups are primordial entities, rather than social constructs that evolve over time. In any case, it is disingenuous to apply such a dichotomy only to the Rohingya, and not to other ethnicities, which have usually been accepted without question.

Other groups in Burma had begun to assert a distinctive ethnic identity to make political claims only a few decades before, as was true of the Kachin or the Rakhine themselves. It that sense, borrowing from Marxian terminology, they evolved from being groups 'in themselves' to become groups 'for themselves' – that is, groups consciously acting as such to defend their interests. The difference for the Rohingya is simply that such consciousness arrived slightly later than for most of the other groups in Burma. Their leaders and intellectuals had not previously felt the need to assert their ethnicity politically; but by independence it was clear that politics in Burma revolved predominantly around ethnicity.

The speech of General Aung Gyi was not the only sign that the government was willing to accept the Rohingya as a Burmese ethnic group, notwithstanding the accusations that there had been some illegal immigration from East Pakistan: there were legally registered associations in Rangoon University representing Rohingya students; the name appeared in some official documents; and, three times a week, the national radio broadcast brief programmes in Rohingya and Urdu (the language of education for many Muslims in Northern Arakan), as it did in the languages of other groups living within the borders of the country.[41] It was only later, during the military regime of General Ne Win, when the term 'Rohingya' became anathema to the Burmese state. At this time, Rohingya were labelled non-indigenous 'Bengalis', and the community began to be treated as an existential threat coming from abroad, which had to be contained at any cost.

Rohingya old enough to have lived through that period still remember it as a time when they felt they belonged in Burma. This was true of Kyaw Hla Aung, an elderly Rohingya lawyer I met on several occasions after successive waves of sectarian violence swept Arakan in 2012. The house of Kyaw Hla Aung in downtown Sittwe was destroyed during the riots in June 2012, and he and his family had to relocate to the area on the outskirts of town, where tens of thousands of Rohingya are still confined. Before fleeing his house, Kyaw Hla Aung was able to rescue a batch of documents that showed how established his family was in Arakan during the late colonial period and the first decades after independence. Now, whenever he receives a journalist in the rickety house he shares with his daughters, he will produce a folder full of those documents: pictures of relatives belonging to the Rohingya Students Association in Rangoon University, identity cards for him and relatives, property titles, his certificate from the Lawyer's Association, and count-less other worn papers and photocopies he treasures as if his life depended on keeping them.

All of these documents, ignored by the present government, are for him and other Rohingya, vital proof of a time when many of them were accepted as citizens and participated in the country's social life – a time that is fading from memory, and seems less likely to return with every passing day.

The Kachin had for the most part maintained their loyalty to the central government since independence, some of them fighting against the Karen and Communist insurgencies. Like the Shan, they were signato-ries to the Panglong agreement, and at first hoped they might find their place in the new country, along with political representation. Like the Shan, they saw their hopes crushed throughout the 1950s. Eventually, each launched their own insurgency in the late 1950s and early 1960s.[42]

The Kachin youth had grown increasingly restless after independ-ence.[43] Kachin State was severely neglected by the central government, and urban centres like Myitkyina were economically dominated by Burmans. The experience for countless Kachin people in those places was one of restricted opportunities and discrimination. Decisions that deeply affected them were made without listening to their voices, includ-ing a border realignment with China in 1956, by which some Kachin villages were transferred to China and thousands of villagers were relo-cated. They also felt they were unrepresented by the political leadership in their state. The first head of the state, Sama Duwa Sinwa Nawng, was widely seen as too authoritarian in a culture that had traditionally prac-tised a democratic form of politics based on consensus. There was also some discontent with U Nu's decision to make Buddhism the state reli-gion, despite the fact that the majority of Kachin were not yet Christian.

In 1960, a group of Kachin students at Rangoon University that were later known as the Seven Stars formed a Kachin Literature and Culture Committee. The group provided a platform for the young Kachin gener-ation to discuss politics. They belonged to a well-educated elite living far from home, and soon they reached the conclusion that they could not trust the existing political institutions to ensure that the voice of their people was heard. It was necessary to launch an armed struggle. Soon dozens, if not hundreds of school students in Kachin joined them, and they founded the KIO on 5 February 1961, declaring an armed struggle against the Burmese government to create an independent Kachin state.

For fifteen years, Kachin nationalists had fought in three different wars for three different sides. First, they had fought against the Japanese in World War II; then they had joined the allies of their former enemies, the Burmans, against Communists and other ethnic insurgents; and finally they had decided to wage their own war against the central state. Few people embody those shifts as well as Lazum Htang, a Kachin veteran I met in 2014. He was a frail ninety-two-year-old man who had joined three armies in his youth. At first, he enrolled in the British army shortly after World War II. After independence, he joined the Tatmadaw, and was wounded fighting the Karen insurgency. Finally, he joined the Kachin Independence Army (KIA) after 1961. 'I did what I thought I had to do for my people at every turn', he explained.

For thousands of Kachin like him, these wars had been struggles for the survival of their own people against shifting enemies. Half-deaf and barely able to walk, Lazum Htang was living with his wife in a hut in the Nhkawng Pa Camp for displaced people, in KIO-controlled territory. 'We're just staying here to die. We don't want to die in the camp. We want to die at home', he told a colleague who interviewed him a few days later.[44] Both my colleague and I were unable to track him down later on. He had seen the very beginning of the war that had displaced him and his family, but he would likely never see its end, still far from view.

In early 1962, the new government of U Nu was making preparations to create two new states: Mon and Arakan. He was also making overtures to the political leaders of other minorities. In mid February he convened a conference with Shan and Karenni representatives in Rangoon, in which they made some demands for greater autonomy. It was during those meetings, on 2 March, that the Tatmadaw staged the definitive coup that gave power to General Ne Win, inaugurating five decades of military dictatorship – one of the longest in the world. The 1962 coup was very different from that in 1958, as it entailed the mobilization of troops throughout the country, instead of pressing the prime minister to cede power to the generals.

It is often assumed that the meeting between U Nu and the minority leaders, and the concession of statehood to Mon and Arakan, were the motives behind a coup staged in order to preserve national unity. The generals themselves encouraged this idea. 'Federalism is impossible, it will destroy the Union', General Ne Win told the minister of the Chin Special Division the night of the coup. General Aung Gyi explained: 'We had economic, religious and political crises with the issue of federalism as the most important for the coup.'[45]

But U Nu and the AFPFL had showed little willingness during all their years in power to make any but token concessions to the minorities. The Burmese state had been strongly centralized, and there is little reason to believe it was ready to modify its deeply ingrained mentality of national unity and centralization. It is more likely that the coup was the result of a decade-long double process in which the generals had grown increasingly distrustful of parliamentary politics, and had managed to build a strong and cohesive army.[46] The generals had come to believe that they were the only ones who could carry out the task of building the Burmese nation-state, and decided to take on the mission only when they felt they had finally built an institution strong enough to do so.

The coup was relatively peaceful at first compared with other military takeovers in the region, such as the bloodbath that accompanied the coup by Suharto in Indonesia only three years later. Only one person was killed, the son of Sao Shwe Thaike, an ethnic Shan who had been the first president during the first U Nu administration. The former president was himself jailed, with dozens of other politicians, and it is believed that he died in prison a few months later.[47] The coup elicited little resistance at first among a population tired of instability and conflict, but the brutality of an ever more paranoid military regime that saw enemies everywhere would become increasingly manifest over time. Such brutality would fall mostly, but by no means exclusively, upon the ethnic minorities.

12

The Burmese Way to Socialism

The Tatmadaw soon dispelled any illusion that it would establish another provisional government. Two days after the coup, on 2 March 1962, General Ne Win assumed all powers as chairman of the eight-member Revolutionary Council. Placing all the blame for Burma's woes on parliamentary democracy, the regime abolished it and began to seize control over all aspects of public life in the country, declaring illegal any political opposition, banning all political parties, and taking the reins of every institution. Ne Win also expelled foreign organizations in a campaign of cultural 'purification' – part of his policy to close off the country from the rest of the world. Through his radical isolationist policies, the dictator wanted to avoid being sucked into the Cold War that was ravaging other countries in Southeast Asia. He largely succeeded in that, but at the steep price of stunting Burma's development and turning it into a hermit nation that seemed to be frozen for five decades.

Ne Win's regime soon made clear that it would ruthlessly suppress any kind of opposition. In July, four months after the coup, students protested at the University of Rangoon. The government accused the students of being under the orders of the CPB, and sent in the army. The soldiers shot at the protestors, and then used dynamite to blow up the building of the Students' Union – a legendary hotbed of activism where students, including a young Aung San, had organized their resistance against the British in the 1930s. According to official figures, fifteen students were killed and seventy-seven wounded; but witnesses and students reported that hundreds of dead bodies lay scattered on the university compound after the crackdown.[1] After that, many students went underground and joined the CPB or one of the ethnic guerrillas. The regime closed the university for a few months – something it would do again and again in subsequent years whenever the students became restless.

One of the first decisions of the Revolutionary Council was to centralize the state further, reversing U Nu's decision to grant statehood to Mon and Arakan. Two years later, it also dissolved the special border districts, including the Mayu Frontier Administration in northern Arakan.[2] Ne Win ostensibly sought to confine the domain of ethnicity purely to cultural expression, ignoring the political demands of the ethnic minorities in the peripheries of the country. But the strong push towards centralization, the fact that the Tatmadaw was in full control of the state, that most members of the Revolutionary Council, the central government and the military were Burmans, and that the cultural revival encouraged by the regime was carried out mostly in Burman terms, all signalled that, in reality, the regime was embarking on a project of Burman supremacy. This only served to encourage stronger resistance from the ethnic armed groups. It also implied the rejection of whole groups, who were branded as foreigners.

In an effort to legitimize its rule, the regime created an official ideology that it referred to as the 'Burmese way to Socialism' – a mixture of Buddhist and Marxist concepts explained in two texts: 'The Burmese Way to Socialism', the policy statement of the Revolutionary Council issued in April 1962, and *The System of Correlation of Man and His Environment*, which expounded a more elaborate philosophy, published in January 1963.[3] The doctrine was vague enough to allow various interpretations and changes of policy according to circumstance, but the principle of one-party rule was non-negotiable.

Ne Win's 'Burmese Way to Socialism' was a smokescreen that served three interlocking purposes. The first was to justify his attempt to exert almost total control over Burmese society. The pamphlet blamed 'the absence of a mature public opinion', among other factors, for losing sight of 'socialist aims' during the parliamentary period. According to the British ambassador to Burma, Ne Win was an 'undoubted patriot', but he could not disguise 'his contempt for what he regards as the laziness and pusillanimity of the average Burman'.[4] It was perhaps such contempt that explains Ne Win's authoritarianism, as he probably thought that such a population needed to be ruled by an iron fist in order to be properly disciplined. The regime also engaged in an artificial revival of Burmese culture to 'cleanse' it of foreign influences. For instance, it banned horseracing, as well as both music and dance contests, as decadent 'Western imports'.[5] Nevertheless, Ne Win himself seems to have enjoyed a Westernized style of life, particularly in his trips abroad, and was famously a regular at horse races whenever he ventured outside Burma.

A socialist doctrine also allowed the regime to navigate the minefield of the Cold War. The regime was not communist, so the Capitalist Bloc could rest assured it was not joining the other side. Ne Win visited Lyndon B. Johnson in 1966, in order to reassure the Americans about his stance. He abstained from criticizing American involvement in Southeast Asia, and after his visit he reportedly said: 'Maybe the Americans are finally going to appreciate a guy who can keep his mouth shut'.[6] They seemed to appreciate his discretion, and maintained cordial relations with him. But by adopting 'socialism', Ne Win could also forestall the hostility of the Communist Bloc.[7] For that, Tin Pe, the advisor to Ne Win on ideological matters, had been ordered to produce a leftist ideology within days, so he had to rush to the university library and collect all the books on Marxism he could find. 'What did I know about ideology?' he would confess years later.[8]

Lastly, socialism was an instrument to realize the Dobama Asiayone's claim of Burma for the Burmese. Ne Win told a British observer in 1966 that he wanted to 'give the Burmese people back their country'.[9] When the regime embarked on its nationalization programmes in the mid 1960s, the results were not so much to redistribute wealth among the poor as to deprive so-called foreigners of their share in the economy. The nationalization affected mostly Indian, and to a lesser extent Chinese, traders and shopkeepers in central Burma, who lost their businesses and properties virtually overnight.[10] As a result, as many as 300,000 Indians who had lived in Burma for decades were pushed to the subcontinent. After the nationalization, the population of Indian origin was reduced to a quarter of a million.[11]

Ne Win eschewed a personality cult for himself, but encouraged the cult of Aung San and claimed to be the bearer of his legacy, as a member

of the fabled Thirty Comrades led by the martyred hero. The justifica-
tion for one-party rule from Aung San was found in 'The Blueprint for
Burma', a pamphlet he had purportedly written while undergoing training in Japan in 1941.[12] The 'Blueprint' espouses a neatly fascist ideology,
according to which 'there shall be only one nation, one party, one leader',
and 'no parliamentary opposition, no nonsense of individualism.
Everyone must submit to the State which is supreme over the individual.' Socialism is not mentioned anywhere. The 'Blueprint' is out of step
with other writings by Aung San, both before and after the war, and, if
authentic, probably reflected more a wish to please his Japanese hosts
than his real ideas. Moreover, in its final form it was likely written by the
Japanese officers, and not by Aung San himself.[13]

Ne Win returned to the secular politics that Aung San had advocated,
reversing the decision to declare Buddhism the state religion almost
immediately. Religion was to be a purely private matter once again.[14]
Only three weeks after the coup, the government dissolved the Buddha
Sasana Council and cut off state funding for the *sangha*. In a statement
issued in 1964, the Revolutionary Council announced that it 'would not
solicit the support of the monks in running the affairs of the state or in
political activities and would also expect that monks stay aloof'.[15] The
Buddhist clergy were seen as a potential threat and, over the first year of
the dictatorship, several attempts were made to control the monkhood,
but all of them were unsuccessful.

The regime had to tread carefully, however, as its shaky legitimacy
could be open to challenges from the Buddhist clergy, which managed
to maintain its autonomy for the first two decades of the dictatorship.
High officials had to give public assurances that they did not wish to
attack Buddhism; but Ne Win himself was not particularly pious, at least
until his old age. In private, he dismissed Buddha as that 'Kalar boy' – a
racially charged epithet to refer to people from the Indian subcontinent
indicating both his disdain for religion and his racial prejudices.[16]

Nonetheless, Ne Win became interested in Buddhism in the mid
1970s, when he reportedly studied the scriptures, was ordained as a
monk for a few months, and built several pagodas.[17] In 1980 he attempted
to unify the Buddhist monastic community through what was called the
'Congregation of the Sangha of All Orders for Purification, Perpetuation
and Propagation of the Sasana'. The State Sangha Maha Nayaka
Committee was then created, and through it the state exerted control

over the monastic community in the following decades. From then on, the government played an increasing role in promoting Buddhism, sending missionary monks to the states and giving more coverage to Buddhist religious issues in the state newspapers.[18] But the regime was still fundamentally secular, and Ne Win himself rarely participated in public religious activities.

The Revolutionary Council ruled by decree for the first twelve years. The Burma Socialist Programme Party (BSPP) was built over these years in what was essentially a military regime, but a transition to a civilian government began in the mid 1970s. In 1972, a drafting committee finished the first draft of a new constitution, and Ne Win and most government officials retired from the military. In January 1974, the Constitution went into effect after a national referendum. On paper, the transition to civilian one-party rule had been effected, with a largely toothless People's Parliament, and a Central Executive Committee, headed by Ne Win himself, as the highest organ of the BSPP and the state itself.[19] The aim of Ne Win was to build a strong party that would allow him to spread his political base and give more legitimacy to his regime, but he ultimately failed. The leadership of the party was composed of retired officers, and all political decisions were in the hands of Ne Win himself. Unable to resolve tensions between military officers squabbling for power, the BSPP operated as a mechanism for providing them with comfortable positions after retirement, so as to tame them in the present.[20]

In 1963 the Revolutionary Council organized peace talks with the various armed groups fighting throughout the country.[21] But any political demand from the ethnic organizations was dismissed out of hand, and the talks broke down quickly. The regime withdrew any political recognition from the armed groups, treating them as bandits, saboteurs and extremists, and tried to crush them with unprecedented brutality. The Tatmadaw created the infamous 'Four Cuts' strategy, which consisted of counterinsurgency campaigns designed to starve armed groups of their four main means of survival: food, funding, intelligence and recruits.[22] Inspired by the strategies deployed by the British against Communist insurgents in Malaya, the Four Cuts entailed the forced relocation of farmers to 'strategic villages' were they could be controlled. Whole areas were cordoned off to carry out concentrated military operations in which the army would confiscate villagers' food, torch their houses and shoot anybody in sight. It was civilians who bore the brunt of these military sweeps, as insurgents could usually retreat to the jungle or to safe havens in Thailand, Bangladesh, China or India. Up to the present, hundreds of thousands of civilians have been killed, and many more have been displaced, in operations employing variants of the Four Cuts strategy.

The heavy-handed tactics of the Tatmadaw and the uncompromising attitude of the Revolutionary Council ultimately conspired to drive more people towards the armed groups, hardening ethno-nationalist movements among the minorities, and even generating new insurgencies. These included a new Rohingya armed group, the Rohingya Independence Front (later renamed as the Rohingya Patriotic Front, RPF), which was created in 1963. The new movement benefited from receiving supplies of weapons during the Bangladeshi War of Independence in the early 1970s, and at some point was the second-largest insurgent force in Arakan after the CPB.[23] The RPF collaborated initially with the Arakan National Liberation Party (ANLP). But the main force among the Rakhine, particularly in the countryside, was the CPB's 'Red Flag' faction, whose promises of 'land for the tiller' had some appeal among an extremely impoverished peasantry.[24]

The powerful 'White Flag' faction of the CPB made its base in Northern Burma after being expelled from the central territories. There it enjoyed support from the Chinese government almost immediately after the coup in 1962.[25] Relations between China and Burma under Ne Win were complex and quite contradictory, reflecting a certain inconsistency in Chinese foreign policy. On the one hand, Ne Win managed to preserve a good relationship with the Chinese state, according to the principle of 'Pauk Phaw' ('fraternity'). On the other hand, China conducted a policy of supporting Communist parties overseas to export its Revolution, and this is what it did with the CPB, though such support was relatively feeble during the first years of Ne Win's regime.

Chinese support to the CPB was considerably boosted after 1967, partly as a consequence of the wave of brutal anti-Chinese riots that swept Rangoon that year.[26] One year before, China had launched the Cultural Revolution, which crossed the border into the Chinese community in Burma. Some Chinese students wore badges of Chairman Mao and recited the sayings of the 'Great Helmsman'. The Burmese authorities banned such activities, but the students remained defiant. In June, there were some scuffles between Chinese students and their teachers that soon escalated into full-blown anti-Chinese attacks by Burmese mobs in Rangoon. Hundreds of Chinese lost their lives, and tens of thousands fled the country. Those who remained hid their Chinese ancestry for fear of retaliation.

The riots happened at a time of deep economic crisis in Burma, and growing discontent with the regime. The government adopted a strong stance against both China and the Chinese community, and the security forces allowed rioters to attack their Chinese neighbours without intervening. The regime had not created popular resentment against the Chinese community, who had been vilified since colonial times as foreign exploiters, but it was effective in amplifying it so as to deflect attention from its own mismanagement and boost its patriotic credentials. It was a strategy that would repeatedly prove useful to Ne Win and his successors in the future.

The riots provoked a deep crisis in relations between Burma and China. With the Cultural Revolution, the most radical Maoists had taken control of foreign policy in China, and they greatly expanded their support of the CPB. In January 1968, the CPB launched an offensive in north-eastern Shan State, with the help of Chinese weapons and thousands of Chinese volunteers, most of them members of the same ethnic minorities on the other side of the border. The Burmese military was overrun in many areas.[27] In subsequent years, the CPB would gain more territory with each battle, making alliances with tribal warlords. By 1974, it controlled a territory of 20,000 square kilometres along the Chinese border. In some respects, the CPB's composition was not dissimilar to that of the Ne Win regime itself: the political leaders were mostly Burmans, while the soldiers belonged to local ethnic minorities.[28]

The CPB adopted an uncompromising Maoist line, first conquering the countryside, which held little appeal to urban intellectuals. Many students had joined after the anti-coup protests at Rangoon University in 1962, but a large number were executed in brutal purges of 'revisionists' and 'right-wing opportunists' throughout the 1960s.[29] In 1974, the major cities of central Burma were rocked by massive anti-government protests organized by workers against inflation and food shortages.

The army reacted with characteristic brutality, shooting at the protestors and killing dozens of them. New protests flared in Rangoon around the funeral of U Thant, the former secretary general of the United Nations. The government declared martial law, quelling the protests using lethal force once again.[30] The government pinned the blame on the CPB, but the party had little to do with either wave of protest, and most of the Burman students who fled joined the Parliamentary Democracy Party that U Nu had formed along the border with Thailand after his release from prison in 1969, not the CPB.

Chinese support for the CPB began to decline in 1976, when the reformist Deng Xiaoping, who was not so interested in exporting the Maoist Revolution, began to amass power in Beijing. China gradually scaled down its support for the CPB, recalling its volunteers and sending back to Burma the party's broadcasting station, which had previously operated from Chinese soil.[31]

After the coup, the Kachin Independence Organization (KIO, political wing of the Kachin Independence Army) began to emerge as the main representative of the Kachin. The KIO had to reshape Kachin society in a double project of nation-building and war mobilization. One of its first measures was to abolish the powers of traditional chiefs, the *duwas*. There were suspicions that some of them were blocking villagers from joining the insurgency, and their authority was now reduced to that of local intermediaries between the KIO and the local communities.[32] Some of the reluctant *duwas* were executed. The KIO substituted traditional structures of authority by dividing the territories it controlled into military and administrative units, creating a structure akin to a state.

Around that time, most of the Kachin population was already converted to Christianity, reflecting the completion of a process initiated by foreign missionaries at the turn of the century. This phenomenon further entrenched a distinctive Kachin identity in opposition to that of Buddhist Burmans.[33] The identification between Kachin nationalism and Christianity provided a unifying identity to the various ethnolinguistic groups and tribes that made up the Kachin nation.[34] But some groups were reluctant to accept a Kachin nationalism that was dominated by the Jinghpaw. The Rawang saw themselves more as Rawang than as Kachin, partly as a consequence of their adherence to small evangelical movements instead of the Kachin Baptist Convention. The

KIA sometimes deployed violence to bring those communities under its control.[35] An overarching Kachin national identity was sometimes enforced in a way that was not too dissimilar to how the Burmans had attempted to enforce a Burmese identity.

The KIA initially had to fight on two separate fronts – against both the Tatmadaw and the CPB.[36] In 1972, the chairman of the KIO, Zau Seng, even joined the World Anti-Communist League. This anti-communist stance was partly a consequence of religiosity, and arguably contributed to reinforcing it; but a change in the leadership entailed a new relationship with the CPB. In 1975, Zau Seng and two senior KIO leaders were killed by young KIA soldiers. The soldiers were furious at the corruption and luxurious lifestyle of their leaders, who spent most of their time in Thailand, away from the hardships of armed struggle in Burma.[37]

A new generation of leaders took the leadership. The new chairman was Brang Seng, former headmaster of a Baptist high school in Myitkyina. He is still regarded as the most prominent leader of the KIO, and as the man who managed to unify all of the organization's various groups, advancing the Kachin struggle both at home and internationally. In 1976, Brang Seng travelled to China and met the CPB Politburo. They signed a military agreement by which both pledged to join in their struggle against the Ne Win regime. The KIA benefited greatly by receiving new Chinese weapons, and it was able to overrun many outposts of the Burmese army, consolidating its control over a larger territory in the following years.[38]

Underpinning the enforcement of unity among the different ethnic groups was the notion of *taingyintha* ('national races'), which came to occupy a central position in official rhetoric and practice during the Ne Win era. U Nu had already used the 'national races' card in calls for unity during his premiership, but it was not until Ne Win that such discourse became hegemonic.[39] In 1964, the government founded an Academy for the Development of the National Races, and official scholarship began to posit a vision of Burma's history in which all the national races stemmed from a common heritage, and had been unified before colonial times. That unity had supposedly been broken by the British, and the historical mission of the state was to restore it. Such myths were the cornerstone of a state-directed project of nation-building that attempted to 'restore' a unity that had never existed, and were used to delegitimize the political movements among the minorities.

The other side of the 'national races' ideology was the exclusion of those groups that, according to government criteria, did not qualify as such. The 1982 Citizenship Law was designed to exclude such groups. The law created three tiers of citizenship – full citizenship, associate citizenship and naturalized citizenship – giving full political rights only to the first. On paper, full citizenship would only be granted to members of the national races – those ethnic groups that were already settled in the territory of Burma in 1983 – but also to those people who were already citizens according to the 1948 Citizenship Law, even if they were not members of the recognized national races. But the law did not specify what groups were regarded as *taingyintha*, giving only a non-exhaustive list of the eight 'major races', and endowing the Council of State with the prerogative to decide on what groups were 'national races'. A full official list of 135 'national races' would not be composed until 1990.

The process of drafting the Citizenship Law began in 1976, and involved mass meetings throughout the country in which suggestions were accepted from the public.[40] The government claimed that 1.9 million people participated in those meetings, but it is unclear to what extent those critical to the law were present in such a repressive political context – or whether, if they were present, they were listened to at all. But the regime, through this process, managed to provide the new law with a veneer of popular legitimacy. Nevertheless, it caused a great deal of anxiety among those who might lose their citizenship. By 1980, it was already clear that full citizenship would be granted almost only to the members of the national races; foreign diplomats in Burma calculated that 3 million people were thereby at risk of becoming stateless.[41]

In August 1982, Ne Win presented the new law in a meeting of the BSPP Central Committee.[42] He claimed that it had been enacted to solve 'the problems [related to] the *foreigners* who had settled down' in colonial times, as well as those who had arrived after independence, and how to distinguish between them.[43] Non-*taingyintha* citizens had to be accepted, as the government was 'not in a position to drive away all those people who had come at different times for different reasons from different lands'. But 'leniency on humanitarian ground cannot be such as to endanger ourselves . . . If we were to allow them to get into positions where they can decide the destiny of the State and if they were to betray

us we would be in trouble.' Thus they would be associate citizens, without the right to occupy public positions. Ne Win even veered into
outright racism when he said, in reference to Indians and Chinese, 'We
are aware of their penchant for making money by all means, and knowing this, how could we trust them in our organizations that decide the
destiny of our country?'

The scholar Robert Taylor, who wrote a sympathetic biography of the
dictator, claims that, 'What Ne Win was addressing was a problem left
over from colonialism, the plural society that J. S. Furnivall described in
1948'.[44] It is entirely possible that this was the problem Ne Win *thought*
he was addressing, but such a problem simply had not existed for years
when the law was discussed and enacted. The Indian community had
been drastically reduced by the exoduses provoked by World War II and
the nationalizations of the mid 1960s, and tens of thousands of Chinese
had fled the country after the 1967 riots. Both communities had lost
their economic power, and arguably those who had decided to stay in
the country were proving their loyalty to it by that very decision. In fact,
the law resurrected a 'problem' that was long dead, and contributed to
entrenching intercommunal divisions and further dividing Burmese
society along ethnic lines. The process of public consultation probably
served less as a means of hearing the voice of the Burmese population
than of encouraging and amplifying already widespread prejudices
against alleged 'foreigners'.

Despite all the publicity surrounding the drafting of the 1982 Citizenship
Law, its enforcement was extraordinarily slow. The law was enacted on 15
October 1982, but the procedures to carry it out were not spelled out until
one year later. Its implementation only began in March 1985, when the new
ID cards for citizens – the Citizen Scrutiny Cards – began to be issued. For
the first time, these cards included the religion and ethnicity of their bearers.[45] Even then, the process of enforcing the new citizenship rules was
carried out slowly and unsystematically.[46] The state, besieged by internal
enemies and economic problems, inefficient and underfunded, was too
overstretched and it only implemented the much touted Citizenship Law
slowly and unsystematically over the next six years.

According to the 'national races' ideology, the Rohingya were the
foreign intruders par excellence – though the 1982 Citizenship Law
would not be enforced in Arakan until the early 1990s. Nevertheless,

the casting of the Rohingya as foreigners began long before that, and it was not predicated merely on denying that they were a national race, but on the claim that many, if not most of them, were illegal immigrants from East Pakistan/Bangladesh who had arrived in Burma after independence. Such accusations were not new, but the Ne Win regime ratcheted them up after the 1971 Liberation War in which Bangladesh attained its independence from Pakistan. Four years later, in early 1975, 15,000 Muslims from Arakan fled to Bangladesh with stories of persecution by the local Buddhist population.[47] But much worse was to come.

In subsequent years, the Burmese government complained to Bangladesh that the influx of illegal immigrants was growing, alleging that some of them were bandits who had attacked police stations and villages in remote areas. Then, in February 1978, the regime decided to launch Operation Naga Min ('Dragon King') in Arakan, after doing so in other border areas around the country.[48] Naga Min was supposed to be an operation to detect illegal immigrants and properly register legal residents. In Arakan it unfolded with a brutality that failed to match its alleged purpose. More than 200,000 Rohingya fled to Bangladesh in a few months, many recounting stories of rape, murder and arson in their villages. The government denied the allegations, instead blaming 'armed bands of Bengalis' for the chaos.[49]

The number of alleged illegal immigrants apprehended by the government during Operation Naga Min was not particularly high, totalling 2,296 throughout Burma, including Arakan, Chin State, Sagaing Division and Mandalay Division. An immigration official who took part in the operation said years later that only 349 undocumented migrants were found in Sittwe, and 228 in Maungdaw and Buthidaung districts, in Northern Arakan. But the government claimed that those who had fled to Bangladesh were 'illegal Bengalis' who had escaped for fear of facing legal action, and went as far as to accuse some of them of torching their own villages – a canard that would be repeated again and again in subsequent years.[50]

The exodus caused by Naga Min marked the first time that the Rohingya received attention outside Burma, provoking an international uproar. In 1979, under intense pressure, Burma finally announced that it had reached an agreement with Bangladesh on the repatriation of the refugees, who were interned in camps in Cox's Bazar that were managed by the Bangladeshi government with the assistance of the UNHCR. Death rates in the camps were unusually high, and, by March 1979, 12,000 refugees had perished. According to Alan C. Lindquist, head of the UNHCR sub-office in Cox's Bazar at that time, there were no logistical or funding factors that could account for such high death rates. The reasons were political.[51]

The Bangladesh government wanted to rid itself of the refugees as soon as possible. To put pressure on them, it reduced food rations to a minimum, leading to thousands of deaths by starvation. 'Well, gentlemen, it is all very well to have fat, well-fed refugees. But I must be a politician, and we are not going to make the refugees so comfortable that they won't go back to Burma', a Bangladeshi official said during a meeting. According to Lindquist, 'none of the UN agency heads raised any objection to using food as a political weapon.'[52]

Most of the refugees eventually returned to Burma, even though they received little guarantee of their safety. Some decided to migrate to countries such as Pakistan and Saudi Arabia, while a few stayed in Cox's Bazar. Among those who returned to their country, many were unable to go back to their original villages, finding that their lands had been taken by Buddhist Rakhine villagers. Some returned once again to Bangladesh.[53]

The Rohingya already had few friends in Burma. 'Even President Ne Win's most bitter domestic enemies vigorously deny the allegations of religious persecution, racial discrimination and systematic apartheid', as one journalist wrote for the prestigious *Far Eastern Economic Review* from Rangoon.[54]

How valid are the claims of the arrival of massive waves of 'illegal immigrants' from East Pakistan/Bangladesh after independence? The border between Bangladesh and Burma was extremely porous, and had been poorly guarded on both sides for long stretches of time. Smuggling of all kinds of goods, including narcotics, had been a common phenomenon there, often relying on the connivance of corrupt officials.[55] Moreover, the grip of the Burmese state in the border areas has been very tenuous, and northern Arakan is no exception. The Burmese government, and institutions linked to the government, have repeated claims of illegal immigration over and over again, and they are believed by many Burmese.[56]

But nobody has shown any strong evidence of such massive waves of 'illegal Bengali migrants'. It is important to recall here that, in the strict sense, 'illegal immigration' only refers to migration that may have occurred after Burma attained independence in 1948. According to colonial laws, before 1948, migration from any part of India to Burma was perfectly legal; and no law enacted after independence by the Burmese government, not even the 1982 Citizenship Law, made immigration during the colonial period retroactively illegal.

Official censuses carried out by the British in 1931 – the last whose complete results are preserved – and by the Burmese government itself in 1983 do not show the inordinately higher demographic growth of the Muslim population compared with other groups in Arakan, or Burma as a whole, that could be reasonably expected if massive waves of 'illegal immigrants' had crossed from Bangladesh during the period. In 1931, there were 255,361 Muslims in Arakan: 25.9 per cent of a total population of 987,117. By 1983, there were 582,984 Muslims: 28.5 per cent of a total population of 2,045,559.

Elsewhere, I have argued that comparing the demographic growth of Arakan Muslims with that of other communities in Arakan, and taking into account several other factors – such as perfectly legal migration between 1931 and the beginning of World War II, and likely higher birth rates among Muslims – shows that no more than 5 per cent of all the Muslims living in Arakan in 1983 could have been migrants who arrived after independence.[57] That amounts at most to 1.4 per cent of the total population in Arakan that year – hardly a massive wave of 'Bengali invaders'. Moreover, whatever illegal immigration there may have been until that point, it was severely reduced as a result of tighter control of the border imposed from then onwards.[58] Subsequently, it was offset by emigration in the other direction – that of Rohingya fleeing increasingly vicious persecution.

In November 2015, Aung San Suu Kyi, asked about the accusations of a genocide against the Rohingya during a press conference, said: 'I think it's very important that we should not exaggerate the problems in this country.'[59] But that is what most governments in Burma, including hers, have been doing regarding massive waves of 'Bengali illegal immigrants', which only exist in their imagination as exaggerations of what in reality was a very small influx. This is not a phenomenon unique to Burma.[60] But by convincing themselves and the Burmese public that there was an invasion of 'illegal Bengalis', successive Burmese governments acquired a self-imposed 'Rohingya problem' that would lead to apartheid, statelessness, and ultimately murderous ethnic cleansing.[61]

But accusations of 'illegal immigration' operate as a smokescreen, albeit perhaps self-imposed. They represent the exclusionary ethnonationalism that lies at the root of the self-inflicted 'Rohingya problem', which makes its adherents perceive the Rohingya as foreigners regardless of when their ancestors arrived in Arakan. Given that the Rohingya community as a whole is seen as a 'foreign race', all of its members are seen as foreigners by default.

The state built by the Ne Win regime was ultimately unable to tackle the problems it had to face, whether self-imposed or inherited. This inability was due to a combination of bad political decisions, sheer incompetence and lack of resources. The Ne Win regime, like the military dictatorship that replaced it, has sometimes been described as 'totalitarian'; but totalitarianism was more an aspiration than a reality. Ne Win had a deep impact on Burma, but he failed to shape the country in the ways he intended. Even his project of a one-party state that would replace a military dictatorship ended up in failure. His regime only managed to control the regions of central Burma, where its apparatus of surveillance and repression managed to prevent the emergence of any serious opposition to its rule for more than two decades – except for bouts of protest that were brutally quashed almost immediately. Its control in the border areas was shaky, at best. The Ne Win regime managed to build a state apparatus capable of self-preservation, but little else. It was incapable of extending its tentacles uniformly throughout the country, and its failure to fulfil the promise of becoming a developed country meant that Ne Win failed to attain legitimacy among the Burman majority.

By the mid 1980s, the economic model of the Burmese Way to Socialism lay in tatters. Scarcity of all types of goods prevailed, and most Burmese had to turn to the black market, which accounted for an extremely large share of the economy and served to fund the armed groups through their control of the smuggling routes in the border areas. In 1987 the government had to apply to the United Nations for the status of 'least developed country' in order to receive badly needed foreign debt relief. That same year, the regime lifted restrictions on trade

– but it also announced the demonetization of the highest-denomination banknotes in an attempt to cut off funding for insurgents, rendering between 60 and 80 per cent of Burmese money entirely worthless. As a result, millions lost the paltry savings they possessed, and scores of students found themselves unable pay their university fees.[62] The popular discontent that had been brewing for years in central Burma eventually exploded in a mass uprising the following year, which shook the pillars of the system built by Ne Win and would lead to the end of the Burmese Way to Socialism.

13

A Long 'Caretaker Government'

In 1988, popular discontent with the Ne Win regime finally exploded in Burma, and what had begun with small protests by university students in Rangoon soon snowballed into a mass uprising.[1] The regime failed to stop the protests, and at some point Ne Win seemed to yield, resigning from his position as chairman of the Burma Socialist Programme Party (BSPP) and the Council of State in late June.[2] He was now officially out of the picture, but left with a chilling warning: 'I want the entire nation, the people, to know that if in the future there are mob disturbances, if the army shoots, it hits – there is no firing into the air to scare.'

Protestors were emboldened, but seemed to lack a clear direction. Apart from a few student leaders, known as the '88 Generation', the movement was largely acephalous, and without a clear ideology beyond the loathing of the regime and calls for 'democracy' – a concept probably understood in many different ways.[3] But the uprising soon got its leader.

On 26 August, Aung San Suu Kyi made her entrance into Burmese politics. That day, she gave a speech in the grounds of Shwedagon Pagoda, a historical site for political activism since the times of the anti-colonial struggle. Up to that moment, she had never been involved in her country's politics, as she had lived outside Burma for most of her life. She was married to Michael Aris, a British professor of Tibetan studies at Oxford University, and was living in Oxford at the time. She found herself in Rangoon during the uprisings by chance, having travelled there to take care of her ailing mother.[4] As the daughter of Aung San, she had been persuaded by some activists to support the protests, and up to half a million people attended her 26 August speech, anointing her the leader of the pro-democratic opposition.

By then, however, the uprising was sliding into chaos.[5] The security forces had withdrawn from the streets, and political prisoners had been released – along with hundreds of hardened criminals. Meanwhile, the Directorate of Defence Services Intelligence (DDSI) was infiltrating the protest movement, often acting as agents provocateurs. Suspected DDSI agents were beheaded almost every day in Rangoon by angry mobs, and arson and looting of government buildings and factories was a common occurrence.

Eventually, on 18 September, the chief of staff of the armed forces, General Saw Maung, announced on the radio that the military had taken power and established the State Law and Order Restoration Council (SLORC) – a military junta that would impose order and rule the country until conditions were stable enough to hold an election. Over the next two weeks, the army swept the major cities with methodical brutality, killing hundreds of protestors and arresting many more.

Hundreds of students and demonstrators fled to the borders, most of them taking refuge in Manerplaw, the headquarters of the Karen National Union (KNU) near the border with Thailand. In Rangoon, Aung San Suu Kyi founded the National League for Democracy (NLD) in late September with Aung Gyi, a former ally of Ne Win, and Tin Oo, a former commander-in-chief of the army. The lines had been drawn for a struggle between the military dictatorship and the pro-democracy camp, led by the NLD, that would last for more than two decades.

One year after the uprising, General Khin Nyunt, the powerful head of Military Intelligence since 1983, held a long press conference in which he portrayed the 'disturbances' of 1988 as an attempt by the Communist Party of Burma (CPB) 'to seize State power'.[6] The Communist conspiracy was largely an invention. Some hitherto dormant Communist cells in Rangoon and Mandalay had been involved in mobilizing some students, but their role had been minimal.[7] The number of students who fled to CPB-controlled areas after the military coup in 1988 was small – about fifty or sixty, compared to the thousands who fled to the Thai border, or areas controlled by the Kachin Independence Organization (KIO) along the border with China.[8]

By this time the CPB was living on borrowed time, with little political influence in central Burma, and struggling to survive in its strongholds in northern Shan State. Support from China had been terminated in 1985. The party had to soften its political line and rely on the opium trade, and it ended up doing business with the remnants of the anti-Communist Kuomintang (KMT) and the infamous drug kingpin Kun Sha, harbouring heroin refineries in its area, and taking 'protection taxes'.[9] But narcotics were not enough to maintain its civilian administration, and it began to unravel. Eventually, in March and April 1989, a series of insurrections against the leadership broke out, most importantly on the part of soldiers of the Kokang and Wa ethnic minorities, and the Burman party leaders had to flee to China.[10]

Out of the party's ashes emerged the most powerful ethnic armed group in the country, the United Wa State Army (UWSA), which would go on to make considerable profits from the narcotics business. The downfall of the CPB was the definitive defeat of Communism in Burma, and showed how politics in the country had increasingly gravitated towards competing ethno-nationalisms since independence.

The SLORC immediately suspended the 1974 Constitution, and presented itself as a mere transitional government somewhat similar to Ne Win's 'caretaker government' of the late 1950s, tasked with restoring order until it would relinquish power to an elected government. Two years later, it organized an election. The BSPP was transformed into the National Unity Party (NUP), and the NLD was allowed to run – but its leaders, including Aung San Suu Kyi and Tin Oo, were placed under house arrest. By the time of the election, in May 1990, there was much confusion over how a transfer of power would be carried out, and even over what the election was about. SLORC members made contradictory public statements indicating that its purpose was to elect either a new government or a constituent assembly.[11]

The NLD won by a landslide, taking 60 per cent of the vote and, due to the first-past-the-post system, 80 per cent of the representatives. The military junta refused to cede power, claiming that the purpose of the election had been to elect a assembly to draft a new constitution. Not much changed for three years, except that hundreds of activists and

NLD members were jailed and General Saw Maung resigned, to be replaced by General Than Shwe. In 1993 the junta organized the National Convention to draft a new Constitution, but its composition did not reflect the results of the election, as most of its members were appointed by the military. In 1996 the NLD boycotted the drafting process, and the Convention was suspended for eight years. In 1997, the SLORC changed its name to the more friendly-sounding State Peace and Development Council (SPDC), but its rule was left untouched. That 'provisional' military junta ended up ruling the country for more than two decades, in a permanent state of exception.

The new regime repudiated the 'Burmese way to Socialism'. From 1995 onwards, it embarked on a process of economic deregulation and privatization along neoliberal lines, which was to be carried out 'to promote emergence and prosperity of national economic enterprises in the hands of the national entrepreneurs', while avoiding any 'monopolization by a private group in distribution of national wealth'.[12] But the latter is exactly what happened. Most of the country's wealth was transferred from the state to a group of businessmen who took advantage of their close relations with the generals. They were the infamous 'cronies', and military-owned conglomerates, such as the Union of Myanmar Economic Holdings Company Ltd (UMEH).[13]

After almost three decades of isolation, the regime also tried to attract foreign investors. Some big companies from Western countries invested in the country, particularly in the extraction of its abundant natural resources. The most controversial was the French Total, which signed a contract with the US company Chevron in 1992 to exploit the Yadana gas field in the Andaman Sea.[14] But massive foreign investment failed to materialize, as a consequence of an uncertain legal environment and – perhaps more crucially – the sanctions imposed by the United States and the European Union during the 1990s and the early 2000s as punishment for the dismal human rights record of the regime.

Like many of the policies of Western countries on Burma, the sanctions regime was largely based on recommendations by Aung San Suu Kyi, who at some point in the mid 1990s reportedly said to a confidant that the Burmese had to 'tighten our belts and think about politics'.[15] In 2003, the US government introduced the Burmese Freedom and Democracy Act, after Suu Kyi and her followers were attacked in central Burma by regime-hired thugs, resulting in dozens of deaths. The George W. Bush administration reacted by banning all imports from Burma. That had the effect of crippling the country's nascent garment industry, 54 per cent of whose exports had gone to the United States. As a result, it was estimated that between 50,000 and 60,000 Burmese lost their jobs.[16]

There was much debate in the international community over the effects of sanctions.[17] Their most dominant effect was to push the Burmese regime to embrace China and other neighbouring countries like Thailand as main trading partners. By 2004, China had become Burma's main source of foreign direct investment, accounting for 46 per cent of the total. Chinese investment was especially strong in regions like Kachin and Shan states, which were rich in natural resources like timber or precious stones.[18]

Sanctions hampered the economic growth of the country, but they did not debilitate the military. The Tatmadaw's manpower grew from around 190,000 soldiers in 1988 to almost 400,000 by the turn of the century.[19] It also upgraded its equipment despite the arms embargoes imposed by the United States and European countries, buying weapons and military technology from countries including China, Russia, Singapore, Pakistan, Thailand and Israel.[20] The expansion of the armed forces required formidable investment, at the expense of other sectors, such as education and health. The army was not only expanded, but by now also controlled most of the economy, either through companies like the UMEH or through the 'cronies'.

In 1993, the junta created its own mass organization, the Union Solidarity and Development Association (USDA), which acquired millions of members over a few months. Membership was mandatory for civil servants, and some people were included in the ranks even without their knowledge. Members were exempted from forced labour, and many people in the rural areas joined. The USDA provided social services such as courses in English or computing; but it was mostly an instrument of mobilization that was often deployed against the political opposition. Young members received military training, and were exhorted to 'crush destructive elements inside and outside the country'; and they were sometimes deployed to attack political opponents of the regime.[21] The USDA would later be transformed into the Union Solidarity and Development Party (USDP), which governed the country between 2011 and 2015.

*   *   *

As the military regime grew stronger, the moral authority of the NLD increased both domestically and internationally. The popular appeal of the party depended on Suu Kyi's charisma rather than any political platform or ideology. The leadership was made up of a central committee of former military men and elders known as the 'uncles'. Among them, nobody could rival Suu Kyi in either leadership or popularity. She was the daughter of the national hero, who projected an appealing image of gentleness, grace and firmness that contrasted starkly with the naked brutality on which the military relied. As years went by, the exemplary character of her personal sacrifices for the country, including fifteen years under house arrest, further enhanced her appeal. But the NLD never managed to build a mass movement capable of challenging the Tatmadaw.

The ideology of Aung San Suu Kyi and the NLD has always been rather vague. She has always claimed to be continuing the legacy of her father, but she has filtered out his strong socialist leanings. She has favoured a free market tempered by demands on businessmen to behave ethically. She had little direct experience of how the majority of Burmese citizens lived – most of them impoverished farmers. Her way of making contact with ordinary Burmese was by touring the country giving speeches, in which they listened to her much more than she listened to them. In 1995 and 1996, after her first stint under house arrest, Suu Kyi gave a series of 'talks over the gate' of her compound in Rangoon every weekend. During these talks, the public congregated in front of her house, and she would answer questions that people had left in writing in her mailbox over the previous week. The format was more interactive than her usual speeches, but it was the people who asked the questions and she who provided the answers – even if sometimes she admitted that she was unable to do so. 'I like the fact that they are not afraid to talk to me. And they are not afraid to disagree with me. But when I reason with them, then, they accept it', she commented about those encounters at the time.[22]

Suu Kyi has always advocated liberal democracy as the preferable form of government; but what she might do within such a system, and what her policies would be once she had gained power, have always remained a mystery. That very same mysteriousness was arguably part of her appeal over the years. The vacuity of her political discourse made it an empty space upon which anybody can project whatever they wish, according to their own assumptions about what terms like 'freedom' and 'democracy' might mean. But she had already shown the motifs that came to be recurrent in her political career in the speech she delivered at the feet of the Shwedagon Pagoda in 1988.[23] She defined the pro-democracy struggle in nationalist terms: 'This national crisis could in fact be called the second struggle for national independence.' In order to achieve the goal of a parliamentary democracy, she stressed the need for unity – an old theme in Burmese politics. Of the Tatmadaw, she said: 'I feel strong attachment for the armed forces. Not only were they built up by my father, as a child I was cared for by his soldiers.' She made an appeal to the armed forces 'to become a force in which the people can place their trust and reliance', and to the people to 'try to forget what has already taken place, and I would like to appeal to them not to lose their affection for the army'.

Ultimately, her vision was moral rather than political. One key concept for her was 'revolution of the spirit', which she explained for the first time in 1990.[24] Such spiritual awakening was to be based on Buddhist values, to the point that she once asserted in the mid 1990s that the Buddhist monastic tradition of mutual forgiveness was a 'fore-runner of the most democratic of institutions, the parliament'.[25] In one of her 'over the gate' talks, answering the question of what changes had to be made in the country, she replied:

> I think that we have to change the way people think. It is only by changing the way that people think that we can progress towards peace. I think that change is coming. I think that many people are beginning to realise now that material development is not everything. The last century has been one of material development, great material development, but I think that people are now starting to realise that material development did not bring with it more happiness as it were.[26]

It was an odd answer in the context of a country as impoverished as Burma. Her commitment to spiritual regeneration, with deep roots in Buddhist political thought,[27] hardly amounted to a politically viable programme. Her focus on morality avoided questions that were inher-ently political, such as how to tackle economic inequalities or establish a fairer social order – issues that Suu Kyi has seldom addressed. She has often protested that she has been a politician all along, and not an icon or human rights defender;[28] but it could be argued that in fact she has never been *political enough,* insofar as she has offered only moral and spiritual solutions to political problems.

Ne Win had presented himself as the heir of Aung San, but the generals who took power after him could not do so. Most belonged to a younger generation than the men who participated in the anticolonial struggle, and it was not possible to inherit the legacy of a man whose daughter was their sworn enemy.[29] Thus Aung San was almost completely erased from official propaganda, even disappearing from the banknotes issued by the government after 1988. His name was mostly conjured in attacks against Aung San Suu Kyi published in state media, in which she was branded a traitor to his legacy for marrying a foreigner.

Instead, the generals chose to portray themselves as the heirs of the ancient kings of central Burma who, according to the SLORC/SPDC historical narrative, had managed to unify all of the ethnic groups under their rule and preserved the Burmese nation for centuries. This was the bread-and-butter of the history curriculum for secondary students throughout the country. Thus, it was not uncommon to find in history textbooks fanciful assertions like, 'Pagan was based on the systematic unification of the accomplishments of ancient civilizations. In Pagan era, all the indigenous groups/national races, Pyus, Mons, Palaungs, Karens, Taugthus, Thets, Chins, Arakanese, Burmans, Shans etc., united with solidarity to build a Myanmar nation. They lived in harmony. That is why Pagan became famous and was respected by its neighbours.'[30]

As part of that project of recovering that precolonial past, the names of the country and other geographical markers were changed in 1989. Through the Adaptation of Expressions Law, the official policy was to change both 'Burma' and 'Burmese' for 'Myanmar', as well as changing the names of some states and cities.[31] In 2005, the SPDC moved the capital of the country from Rangoon to Naypyidaw, a city built from scratch in the plains of central Burma. The cost was estimated to be between $4 billion and $5 billion – in a country where annual government expenditure on healthcare was of less than $0.50 per person.[32]

The name of the new capital, which translates as 'Abode of Kings', offers a cue to the underlying ideology behind the move. By relocating the capital to the plains of central Burma, the junta was returning the centre of Burman power to where it had resided before the colonial period.[33] Naypyidaw can be seen as the symbol of the power of the military in a project of Burman supremacy inspired by the old kings, albeit adapted to a modern context. It is not by accident that the ground on which the armed forces parade take place every year is presided over by the gigantic statues of three warrior kings, seen as unifiers of the Burmese kingdom.

Assuming the role of keeper of a contrived unity that had supposedly endured since time immemorial against the convulsions of history, the Tatmadaw seemed to be claiming the title of Sri Nittya Dhammadhara – the 'Fortunate Possessor of the Principle of Permanence' – which was held by those precolonial kings whose legacy it claimed to preserve.[34] This was expressed in the 'three national causes' of the junta, later included in the 2008 Constitution as its 'basic principles': 'non-disintegration of the Union', 'non-disintegration of National Solidarity' and 'perpetuation of Sovereignty'.

The regime often defended itself from accusations of human rights violations by alleging that its uniquely Burmese laws, designed to perpetuate its sovereignty, could not be understood by foreigners. There was a double irony in this, since the junta was not above breaking its own laws when it deemed it necessary – and often used old British colonial laws to persecute its opponents.[35]

The generals made efforts to portray themselves as pious protectors of Buddhism, a tendency timidly initiated by Ne Win in the early 1980s. In 1992, the junta created the Ministry of Religious Affairs, and extended official recognition to monastic schools for the first time in the country's history since the dethronement the last king, in 1885.[36] It also introduced the teaching of Buddhism in schools and lavished money on the construction of pagodas and on Buddhist abbots, in order to tighten its control of the Buddhist monastic community.[37] Meanwhile, Military Intelligence infiltrated the monasteries to keep an eye on potential subversive activities. After Ne Win's secularism, Buddhism now became Burma's de facto state religion, albeit not officially by law.

The generals not only attempted to improve their karma by giving donations to the monastic community; they were equally concerned about improving the karma of the citizenry. Most Burmese Buddhists were so impoverished that it was difficult for them to make as many religious donations as they wanted, so the regime gave them the opportunity of demonstrating their merit by donating their time to develop the country, mostly by working on infrastructure projects. At least, that was the way the regime explained the widespread practice of forced labour that has affected many Burmese, and has been consistently denounced by human rights organizations, the UN and Burmese activists.[38]

They also attempted to use religion as an instrument of cultural homogenization among some ethnic minorities. The promotion of Buddhism included missionary projects in regions inhabited by ethnic groups defined largely by their religious identity, such as the Christian Kachin or Chin.[39] These efforts were led by the Department for the Promotion and Propagation of the Sanana (DPPS), created in 1991. According to the DPPS website, there were 457 'Buddhist Missionary Centres' in 'border and hilly regions' of the country, and 144,054 people had been converted to Buddhism by 2005.[40] Missionary efforts were often coercive, and ultimately contributed to the inflammation of ethnonationalist sentiments among the ethnic groups in the border areas.

The militant Buddhism that has exploded in recent years has historically fought a variety of enemies allegedly threatening Buddhism: the British, Indian migrants, Communism and Islam. With the British long gone and Communism defeated, the only group left to be construed as a threat were Muslims. There were anti-Muslim pogroms both in Arakan and other parts of Burma during the military dictatorship. In 2001, there was a wave of anti-Muslim violence in Sittwe and several towns in central Burma. The destruction by the Taliban of the ancient Buddha statues at Bamiyan, in Afghanistan, had provoked the fury of Buddhists, and was a contributing factor in anti-Muslim pogroms in several towns.[41]

In some areas, Buddhist monks distributed an anti-Muslim pamphlet titled *The Fear of Losing One's Race*, and were seen leading angry mobs attacking mosques and Muslim quarters. Once again, the authorities did little to stop the violence. The country was going through an economic crisis at the time, and the government may have orchestrated the pogroms to distract the attention of the public, though its role has never been fully ascertained. On the other hand, the authorities imposed curfews relatively quickly in most of the towns in central Burma affected by the violence.

At the very least, the regime bears some responsibility for hardening such prejudices among a population suffering enormous economic pressures and extreme repression. The junta was instrumental in fostering a climate of distrust against religious minorities by insisting on identifying Buddhism with Burmese nationhood, and by demonizing Muslims and people of Indian origin. The Tatmadaw did not create Islamophobia in Burma, but it actively encouraged it, whether it had a direct role in particular anti-Muslim pogroms or not.

Islamophobia in Burma largely traces its origins to the colonial encounter with the British, and in that sense it is a very local phenomenon. But at the turn of this century it found itself aligned with the 'war on terror' launched by the United States after 9/11. The regime tried to take sides in the putative 'clash of civilizations' with which Burma in fact had nothing to do. It was then that the Burmese government began to portray Burmese Muslims as a potential terrorist threat, in a desperate attempt to curry international favour at a time when Western powers were isolating it.[42] The Burmese military even shared intelligence with the US embassy in 2002 about alleged links between the Arakan Rohingya National Organisation (ARNO – a Rohingya armed group with bases in Bangladesh) and al-Qaeda.

Such links have never been proved, but, in the midst of the counter-terrorist paranoia, the US embassy staff commented in a cable sent to Washington: 'The Burmese report has enough specificity to make it generally plausible.' Nevertheless, US officials in Rangoon were able to discern the intentions behind the report of the Burmese intelligence, remarking: 'Presumably, they hope to bolster relations with the United States by getting credit for cooperation on the CT [counterterrorism] front.'[43]

The SLORC/SPDC signed a series of ceasefires with several armed groups over the years, and tried to co-opt local elites through business concessions, particularly in the border between Shan and Kachin states. The application of this strategy varied from one place to another, depending on the strength of the different armed groups, how pliable they were, and how interested the government was in exploiting local natural resources.[44] During the 1990s, as the regime signed those ceasefires, in some cases it managed to play one off against another.

Such was the case in Karen State, where the government signed a ceasefire in 1994 with the Democratic Karen Buddhist Army, a splinter group of the predominantly Christian KNU, which continued its war against the Tatmadaw. But the first ceasefires were those signed with the UWSA and the Kokang Democratic Army (later renamed the Myanmar National Democratic Alliance Army), the groups emerging from the implosion of the CPB. The government allowed them to control their own self-administered areas in northern Shan State, with little or no interference, and they built their own mini-states.[45]

The ceasefire strategy was designed and executed by the shrewd General Khin Nyunt, head of the all-powerful Military Intelligence, and was a consequence of four main factors. First of all, the downfall of the Communist Party in 1989 substantially altered the balance of forces. The economic opening, with the adoption of a capitalist model, opened the door to private investors willing to exploit the rich natural resources in the border areas, in a process of primitive accumulation that scholar Kevin Woods has termed 'ceasefire capitalism'.[46] This was supported by increasingly close relations with China, since many of the investors were Chinese. Lastly, the build-up of the Tatmadaw meant that it was able to sign ceasefires from a position of strength. As a result, authority in the border areas was divided between the central government, various armed groups, militias working with the government, and various warlords, all of them jockeying for territory and resources.

The usual procedure was to grant a concession to extract the natural resources of a particular patch of land to businessmen, often from China. Then the army would step in to secure the area, thus reclaiming more territory for the state. Large areas were deforested during this period. Chinese companies often brought their own workers from China, or the government took workers from central Burma, resulting in the displacement of tens of thousands of local villagers. It was neither war nor peace, and local communities were caught between competing groups without having much of a political voice.

To make things worse, in 1997 the military gave the order that the regional commands would have to fend for themselves locally, instead of relying on a central supply system, and local populations ended up being exploited to feed the army.[47] The resentment towards a central state that was widely seen by the ethnic minorities as extraneous, exploitative and brutal only increased with this form of capitalist development. But in the meantime the Tatmadaw managed to extend its tentacles throughout the borderlands, and, if it never fully controlled many of those regions, at least it gained the upper hand in many areas that had previously been completely outside its control.

The change of regime and the downfall of the CPB pushed the leaders of the KIO/KIA to rethink their strategy. The fall of the CPB weakened the group's position, and the rapprochement between the Burmese and the Chinese government increased its isolation, especially when two other Kachin armed groups signed ceasefires with the Tatmadaw.[48] The change of regime and its public commitment to drafting a new constitution were seen by the KIO leadership as offering a chance to reach a peaceful solution. Brang Seng, the chairman of the KIO, made overtures to hold talks with the military junta.

Thus, when the National Convention to draft a new constitution was held in 1993, the KIO participated in it. Brang Seng finally signed a ceasefire with the government in 1994, but he fell ill and passed away the next year.[49] It was a huge blow to the KIO, which had lost one of its most capable leaders. As in other areas, the Tatmadaw used the ceasefire to strengthen its presence in Kachin State, and some KIO leaders took advantage of new economic opportunities. Despite all the attempts made by the regime to quell it, Kachin nationalist sentiments only grew stronger during the ceasefire period, even though many people felt disappointed with the KIO, whose leadership was seen as disconnected from common people's concerns. It would recover its popular support in 2011, when the resumption of the war put an end to the precarious ceasefire.

The junta fully embraced the 'national races' ideology. In 1990, the SLORC started to rely officially on a list of 135 'national races'.[50] Unsurprisingly, the Rohingya were excluded, and it was around this time that the regime stripped them of Burmese citizenship en masse, using the 1982 Citizenship Law as a cover. It was not the application of the law that rendered them stateless, but the way it was applied, which arguably broke the law itself.[51] Most Rohingya held National Registration Cards (NRCs), but very few held citizenship certificates according to the 1948 Citizenship Act. That was far from unusual; the overwhelming majority of Burmese held an NRC – a document that was only issued to non-foreigners, and was accepted for identification purposes by state officials. When the 1982 Citizenship Law was enforced, citizens had to surrender their NRCs in order to receive their new citizenship documents. Like everybody else, the Rohingya surrendered their old NRCs under the promise of receiving citizenship certificates soon, but, unlike for most other Burmese, they never received their certificates. Instead, they were given 'temporary identification cards', which were not regarded as proof of citizenship and they held until 2014.

Successive governments, including Thein Sein's and Aung San Suu Kyi's, have invoked the 1982 Citizenship Law to ascertain who among the Rohingya may qualify for citizenship. But, while the correct application of that law should not have served to render the overwhelming majority of the Rohingya stateless, they face an enormous obstacle to regaining citizenship, given that they are not regarded as a 'national race' and would have to prove they were citizens according to the previous law, something extremely difficult given that most of them have lost their documents after giving them to the authorities. Thus, regaining citizenship depends on the whim of the authorities. When a pilot programme of citizenship verification was conducted in Myebon in 2014, only a token number were granted it.[52] Summing up, the Rohingya were rendered stateless by virtue of violating the 1982 Citizenship Law; but their statelessness has been perpetuated either by inaction of the government or by the authorities' claim of following scrupulously the letter of that very same law. In short, rather than the instrument to render the Rohingya stateless, the Citizenship Law has arguably been the instrument to keep them in such legal limbo for decades.

The Rohingya were stripped of any form of citizenship as if they were 'illegal immigrants'; that is, as if they had arrived in Burma after independence. In truth, only a vanishingly small percentage of them may have migrated to Arakan after independence. But what is really at stake is a project of national 'purification' in which only members of those groups officially recognized as 'national races' have a place in Burmese society, regardless of the status they should be entitled to according to Burmese laws. The Ministry of Foreign Affairs made this clear in 1992 in a press statement:

In fact, although there are 135 national races residing in Myanmar today, the so-called Rohingya people are not among them. Historically, there has never been a Rohingya race in Myanmar. The very name

Rohingya was a creation of a group of insurgents in the Rakhine State. *Since the First Anglo-Burmese War in 1824,* people of the Muslim faith from the adjacent country have entered Myanmar *illegally,* particularly Rakhine State. Being illegal immigrants, they do not hold any immigration papers like the other nationals of the country. With the passage of time, the number of people who entered Myanmar illegally has greatly inflated.[53]

This statement ignored the fact that many of the ancestors of the present-day Rohingya were already settled in Arakan before colonial times. But that only bears a relative importance from a strictly legal point of view, as the law recognizes, on paper, the citizenship of the descendants of migrants during the colonial period. The most astonishing claim was its branding as 'illegal immigrants' those who had arrived during colonial times, without making any distinction between them and those who arrived after independence – a distinction clearly established in Burmese law. Nevertheless, the Burmese authorities have not always blurred this distinction.

In 2012, President Thein Sein stated: 'According to our laws, those descended from [migrants] who came to Burma before 1948, the "Third Generation", can be considered Burmese citizens.'[54] But that recognition came too late. The problem is that the numbers of those who arrived after independence have been grossly exaggerated, and the government deals with the Rohingya by consistently placing the burden of proof upon them to demonstrate that they are not illegal immigrants.

The Ministry of Foreign Affairs released the press statement quoted above as a response to international condemnation of another exodus of hundreds of thousands of Rohingya the previous year. This time, the exodus was provoked by the heavy-handed way in which the NRCs had been collected, but also by the way in which the government militarized the region in counter-insurgency campaigns against an armed group that had emerged in 1982, the Rohingya Solidarity Organization (RSO). As a result, at least 260,000 refugees fled to Bangladesh.[55]

As had been the case fourteen years earlier, the Bangladeshi government wanted to push them back into Burma as soon as possible, and used aid as a tool to do so, confiscating their ration cards and even physically threatening them. The UNHCR assured the refugees that it would provide help to them once they returned to Burma, but that was a promise it proved unable to fulfil, as access to northern Arakan was severely restricted. As it had done in 1978, the UNHCR again betrayed one of its core tenets: the principle of non-refoulement, against sending refugees back to a country in which they are bound to suffer persecution. Most of the refugees had returned by 1995. Two years later, only 22,000 of them remained in Bangladesh; but many more would flee Burma in the coming years.[56]

The government established a special security force in 1992, known as the Na Sa Ka, that operated exclusively in northern Arakan, and was responsible for most of the human rights violations against the Rohingya.[57] The government progressively tightened the noose around them, with increasingly oppressive policies. These included an almost complete deprivation of freedom of movement, educational opportunities and healthcare services. According to a report of the UN Special Rapporteur on the human rights situation in Myanmar, in 2010 there were only three doctors per 430,000 persons in Maungdaw, and two per 280,000 persons in Buthidaung.[58] Access to education had been so limited that the illiteracy rate among the Rohingya was estimated at 80 per cent in 2012.[59]

The plight of the Rohingya thereafter was documented by several human rights organizations, but few within the international community paid much attention. The big story in the global media was that of Aung San Suu Kyi and her struggle for democracy, with some occasional coverage of the armed conflicts in the border regions. For their part, Aung San Suu Kyi, the NLD and the wider pro-democracy camp kept silent about the Rohingya. 'The Lady' never publicly denounced their statelessness or the oppression they were suffering, and she did not address the issue until 2012; nor has she ever challenged the basic tenets of the 'national races ideology'.

These apartheid policies imposed on the Rohingya were implemented in a somewhat erratic manner. While every Rohingya individual was affected in one way or another, the impact of the policies varied greatly depending on several factors, from geographical location to the whims of local officials and the socioeconomic positions of Rohingya individuals themselves. Access to education was much more open in Sittwe than in rural areas in Northern Arakan: while Rohingya students attended

Sittwe University up to 2012, in the rural areas of Maungdaw or Buthidaung, many children never attended primary school. Restrictions on movement had less severe effects on Rohingya who were wealthy enough to pay bribes than on impoverished villagers, who had often never travelled far beyond their villages. In Maungdaw town, close to the border with Bangladesh, Rohingya businessmen made a living, and some became relatively rich, through cross-border trade. In urban centres there was a Rohingya middle class of sorts, made up of shop-keepers and traders.

This is not to deny the destructive impact that discriminatory policies had on the Rohingya community; nevertheless, such policies were not implemented in a systematic and uniform way. The ideology of exclusion underlying such policies was potentially genocidal, but the policies themselves were not necessarily so. The regime was badly overstretched and besieged on many fronts, and it lacked the capacity and commitment to carry such an ideology to its ultimate conclusion. Its measures added up to an overall policy of containment and neglect, rather than a carefully orchestrated project of ethnic cleansing or 'slow-burning genocide', as some have argued.[60] The fortunes of the 'Na Ta La villages' programme are symptomatic of this fact.

Named for the Burmese acronym of the Ministry of Progress for Border Areas, National Races and Development, the Na Ta La villages were part of a project to settle 'national races' in northern Arakan, in order to alter the demographic balance in the region.[61] The settlers were poor Rakhine from other parts of the state, or impoverished Burmans from central Burma. Some were petty criminals who received the offer to settle in one of the villages for a few years instead of completing their jail terms. Buddhist Rakhine from Bangladesh were also welcomed.[62] The government provided land, houses and some money to the newcomers, and even paid their expenses to move to the villages; thousands of Rohingya farmers were evicted from their lands to build them. But this project of social engineering never really took off, failing in its aim to change the demographic balance in the region substantially. According to government media, in 2017 there were thirty-nine Na Ta La villages in the townships of Maungdaw, Buthidaung and Rathedaung, out of a total of around 880 villages.[63] The Na Ta La project failed in its stated goal of social engineering, mostly because there were few takers, and because the government abandoned those who did sign up. But it contributed to the souring of interethnic relations in those areas where the villages were built.

One of the main rationales for this repression was the claim of illegal immigration from Bangladesh. Such migration was negligible between independence and 1983. In the period between the 1983 and 2014 censuses, it was even more unlikely, given that the regime greatly increased its oppression against the Rohingya. And whatever immigration there may have been, it was surpassed by the well-documented high volume of emigration in the other direction – that of Rohingya fleeing to Bangladesh, Malaysia, Saudi Arabia and other countries. Moreover, all relevant indicators show that, as underdeveloped as Bangladesh is, Burma has fared even worse, and this gap is even wider in relation to Arakan, the second-poorest state in the country. It would thus make very little sense for a Bangladeshi to seek a better life in a region more impoverished, where they would suffer severe oppression.[64]

Meanwhile, the 2014 census revealed that population growth in Burma as a whole since 1983 had been much lower than expected, due to lower birth rates and emigration to neighbouring countries.[65] The growth rate of the Muslim population in Arakan was higher than that in the country as a whole, but also higher than its own growth rate during the period between 1931 and 1983, despite the fact that no significant immigration from Bangladesh took place after the late seventies. The annual growth rate between 1931 and 1983 had been 2.47 per cent, whereas between 1983 and 2014 it stood at 2.96 per cent – higher than Myanmar as a whole (1.48 per cent), Arakan (1.80 per cent) or the Rakhine Buddhist population in the same state (1.34 per cent). The Muslim population in Arakan grew to roughly 1,120,000 – 35 per cent of a total of 3,118,807, as compared with the 28.5 per cent share it represented in 1983.[66] The Rohingya are arguably the most oppressed ethnic group in Burma, but their numbers increased more than those of others. Why?

The explanation for this puzzle is to be found in the very same oppression the Rohingya suffered over this period. First of all, they have been confined in Northern Arakan. In contrast, the Rakhine enjoy freedom of movement, and many have moved to Rangoon and other places in the country searching for better economic opportunities.[67] Still, the growth rate of the Rohingya population is higher than the national rate. The main cause is to be found in higher birth rates than the rest of the population, not in immigration from Bangladesh. Repeated studies all over the world have shown that poverty, combined with lack of education, is strongly correlated to high birth rates.[68] Northern Arakan State is one of the poorest regions of Burma, and the Rohingya community has less access to education than any other either within the state or in most other areas of Burma.

The tragic irony is that the very same policies implemented by the Burmese state over four decades to contain the Rohingya population have contributed to an increase in its demographic growth. Conversely, such growth has fuelled conspiracy theories about 'demographic jihad' among Burmese and Rakhine nationalists alike. State officials have given credence to such stories over the years. For instance, in 2013 the authorities gave orders to Muslims in northern Arakan not to have more than two children.

'The population growth of Rohingya Muslims is ten times higher than that of the Rakhine Buddhists. Overpopulation is one of the causes of tensions', Win Myaing, Arakan State's spokesman, said at the time.[69] It was an exaggeration, as their growth rate was in fact about twice as high. But it was an exaggeration that contributed to a widespread perception of the Rohingya as a demographic threat. It could be argued that it was not so much demographic growth among the Rohingya that was causing intercommunal tensions in Arakan, but constant repetition by local media, state officials, politicians of all stripes and Buddhist monks that such growth posed an existential danger. Once again, the self-infliction of the 'Rohingya problem' by the regime only caused to exacerbate it – even by the regime's own criteria.

At the turn of the twenty-first century, the SPDC seemed to be firmly entrenched in power despite its deep unpopularity and partial international isolation. In 2003, General Khin Nyunt announced plans for a 'Roadmap to a discipline-flourishing democracy', to be carried out in seven steps. The first of them was to re-establish the National Convention, which had been suspended in 1996, and the last would be to hand power to an elected government under the Constitution drafted by the Convention, which would be submitted to a national referendum. The NLD refused to participate; while some parties among the ethnic minorities took part, their voice was barely heard, and the Tatmadaw drafted the Constitution on its own. Khin Nyunt was purged one year after he had made the announcement. His powerful department of Military Intelligence was dissolved, and up to 600 of its officers were jailed. The purge was the result of a power struggle between Kyin Nyunt and Than Shwe, the junta's supremo. Nevertheless, the junta continued to pursue the former's roadmap.[70]

Three years later, a new wave of protests shook the country.[71] In August 2007, the government removed subsidies on fuel and natural gas, and the prices of some basic commodities increased by 500 per cent almost overnight. The 88 Generation students organized protests in Rangoon, but they were soon arrested and jailed. A new organization emerged, the All Burma Monks Alliance, which coordinated new protests. In mid September, monks marched in the main cities of Burma, and were joined by tens of thousands of laypeople. A few days later, police and army battalions were deployed in Rangoon and other cities to crack down on the demonstrators. At least thirty-one people were killed, while hundreds were arrested.[72] Wide international coverage of what became known as the 'Saffron Revolution' put Burma on the front pages of newspapers throughout the world for the first time in decades. The brutality against the monks showed that the junta was willing to pay any cost to cling on to power, even if that implied attacking the most respected group among Burmese Buddhists.

One year later, the regime again showed its ruthlessness, when a deadly cyclone devastated large areas of Lower Burma, killing up to 130,000 people. The government neglected the victims and refused entry to international aid agencies for weeks, while it went ahead with the referendum over the Constitution, which was deferred only in the areas most severely affected by the cyclone. But the generals backtracked when the international uproar became increasingly intense, eventually allowing some international aid into the country.

Given these examples of repression, the fact that the Tatmadaw appeared to cede some power voluntarily after 2011 may seem surprising. With hindsight, it seems that the junta decided to relinquish part of its power and implement its 'road map to a discipline-flourishing democracy' simply because that is what the generals had planned all along. If it took more than two decades, that was because they wanted to control the process and guarantee a prominent role for themselves in the country's politics, ensuring a privileged place for their idea of national unity and the protection of their interests.

The transition had to be carried out on the Tatmadaw's own terms, and it dedicated the long 'caretaker government' between 1988 and 2011 to preventing the emergence of any powerful opposition capable of displacing it, as well as to strengthening itself politically, militarily and economically. In fact, the generals did not renounce their power, but instead designed a system with a veneer of democratic legitimacy, implementing it only when they were sufficiently confident that they would not lose control. This was the framework within which Aung San Suu Kyi's party was allowed to run for election in 2015.

PART III
A Diarchic Government

14

The Election

When it finally arrived, 8 November 2015 was a day of promise in Burma. For the first time in decades, citizens all over the country were to be given the chance to elect their parliament and, indirectly, their government. The election seemed to be the culmination of four years of deep social and political change, and an apparent confirmation that the country's transition to democracy was not a mirage.

The stakes were particularly high, and the election seemed to have the character of a founding event for a still fragile new political system. But, like any other election, it had different meanings for different people. For the military it was the end of a process, the culmination of their roadmap to what they had termed a 'discipline-flourishing democracy', laid out as far as 2003. For the prospective winner, the National League for Democracy (NLD), it was the beginning of a process of change towards a democratic system. It did not seem to matter that nobody had spelled out clearly what that democratic system might look like or how the party would make it happen. Millions of Burmans seemed to trust that its leader would be able to change the country.

For the ethnic minorities, the election seemed to increase the possibility of a political settlement and the attainment of some autonomy for their states. For the Rohingya, the sentiments were more conflicted: while many harboured hopes that their lot might change with a new government, they were not allowed to vote for the first time in Burma's history as an independent country. For non-Rohingya Muslims else-where in Burma, the election was a bittersweet moment. Most of them supported the NLD and Aung San Suu Kyi, but the party had not filed a single Muslim candidate, yielding to pressures from ultranationalist Buddhist monks and lay leaders who were implausibly accusing it of being controlled by Muslims. Western diplomats and businessmen read the election as definitive confirmation that it was licit to engage with a country whose dictators had turned it into a 'pariah state' in the past. They could soon invest there with a clear conscience and enter into that very rare thing: a virgin market.

The political opening of the transition had made more visible than ever deep inter-ethnic divisions and communal conflicts that seemed intractable, and Suu Kyi and her party had mostly appeared as passive spectators. It was unclear how Suu Kyi might tackle these conflicts once in power, as she had given only extremely vague indications of what her policies would be once in power; but many made a leap of faith, assum-ing that she had kept silent in order not to alienate the generals, and would come up with a strategy once in power.

In the days ahead of the election, Rangoon was full of portraits of Aung San Suu Kyi, and the red flag with a yellow peacock, which repre-sented the party, could be seen everywhere. The party was so certain of its victory that it had not bothered to issue a well-articulated party manifesto. The economic policy platform, for instance, was a paltry document of three pages, including the Burmese original and its English translation, and was based on 'five pillars': fiscal prudence, lean and effi-cient government, revitalizing agriculture, monetary and fiscal stability, and creating a functioning infrastructure. Hardly anybody could argue against those goals, but there was little detail on how to reach them.[1] It was difficult to ascertain whether the party was keeping its cards close to its chest or simply did not have a plan. In any case, few doubted she would win, and it mattered little that, according to the Constitution, she was barred from being the president.

A few days before election day, she gave a press conference in the garden of her villa in Rangoon, where she assured everyone that she would be 'above the president' if her party won the election. When she was asked if such an arrangement was unconstitutional, she replied: 'No. The constitution says nothing about somebody being above the presi-dent.'[2] In fact, Article 58 of the Constitution says that 'the President of the Republic of the Union of Myanmar takes precedence over all other persons throughout the Republic of the Union of Myanmar'.[3]

I was in the country covering the election as a freelance journalist. I found it difficult at times not to become carried away by the enthusiasm of many Burmese, even as a foreign observer infected by some scepticism about the whole process, having covered the darkest and most violent aspects of the democratic transition for the previous few years.

Before attending Suu Kyi's press conference in her villa I had travelled to Salingyi, a rural township in southern Sagaing Division, in Upper Burma. I was curious about what people had to say there, for two reasons. I thought it would be interesting to try and gauge the mood in a rural area, as 70 per cent of Burma's roughly 51.5 million people lived in the countryside, mostly in impoverished villages where the supply of electricity and clean water was unreliable and often nonexistent. Salingyi seemed to be as representative of the Burman rural population as any other place. But in one sense it was not representative at all. I had been there a couple of years before, shortly after its inhabitants had heckled Aung San Suu Kyi after she had supported the Letpadaung copper mine – a massive project built on the backs of evicted farmers, which had caused environmental destruction that had ruined the lives of many of the people in the area.[4]

Things had not improved much for the farmers in Salingyi when I visited the township one week before the election. They had continued to oppose the project, and one year before a woman had been shot dead by the police during a protest.[5] But the political mood had changed, at least regarding Aung San Suu Kyi and the NLD. I had travelled there expecting to find one story, but had found a completely different one. I thought I would hear the same complaints about her, but it soon became clear that she and her party had regained their old support among the villagers.

'I will vote for the NLD. I was angry at Aung San Suu Kyi when she came, but then I read the report [prepared by the Commission chaired by Suu Kyi three years before] and now I support her. We have to get rid of the dictatorship. She can do better for the country', said Than Swe, a farmer who had been evicted from his land. Virtually everybody I talked with expressed similar opinions. Ma Thwe Thwe Win, a young local activist who had been organizing the villagers against the project for years, also expressed her support for the NLD: 'I don't blame Aung San Suu Kyi. The recommendations of her report are good, but the problem is that the government is not following them', she told me. Many villagers echoed her words, stating that the problem was not Suu Kyi, whose recommendations they claimed to support. When I asked what recommendations they supported, most of them did not give me an answer.

The general mood seemed to be that it was better to support Suu Kyi against the military and its proxy party, the Union Solidarity and Development Party (USDP). After all, it was the generals who had been oppressing them for decades, and the NLD appeared to be the only alternative available. But the enthusiasm of the people for Suu Kyi herself was also evident. When an NLD convoy was campaigning in a road near Ton village, where two years before I had been unable to find anybody with a kind word for Suu Kyi, it seemed that the whole village had gone to the road to cheer it. Even the local USDP candidate, a sturdy forty-four-year-old local trader called Aung Naing, had to acknowledge that 'people here changed their minds about Aung San Suu Kyi'. His own campaigning seemed to arouse very little enthusiasm. If even people in Salingyi supported Suu Ki so strongly, there was little doubt that she would get most of the votes elsewhere the country, at least among the Burman population.

In Arakan the stakes, and the players, in the election were different. Aung San Suu Kyi did not enjoy there the wide support that she could take for granted in central Burma. The main political force was the Arakan National Party (ANP), an ethno-nationalist party representing the Buddhist Rakhine. The Rohingya population were not represented by any party. I covered the election in Sittwe, the capital of the state, and by then an almost completely ethnically cleansed city. Most Muslims had been confined since 2012 in a vast area of camps for internally displaced people not far from the town; in a neighbourhood called Bumay on the edge of the city, not far from the camps; and in Aung Mingalar, a ghetto of around 4,000 Muslims in downtown Sittwe surrounded by the police and the army since the waves of sectarian violence of 2012.

At the time of the election, the conditions of the Rohingya had marginally improved since the camps had been established three years before; but aid, food and healthcare services were still insufficient. Some people were still dying of treatable diseases. By then, it had long been evident that the camps were permanent. Without the possibility to leave, and little to do except receive handouts, a fatalistic resignation and despair had set in among their population. The community was weakening not only physically, but also morally. Ozan, the head of one of the camps, told me: 'I worry about the children; their character has changed. Now they are used to begging because they see that everybody lives from handouts by aid organizations, so they don't feel the need to work. The schools are not good because they are staffed with people from the camps without proper preparation, and it's difficult to keep children going.'

For many Muslims in Arakan State, election day held a vague promise of improvement if the NLD formed a government, but it was also a day on which the expulsion of the Rohingya from national life as undesirable pariahs would be confirmed, as they had been barred from voting. A few days after the election Kyaw Hla Aung, a retired seventy-six-year-old Rohingya lawyer, told me: 'My heart was broken in many pieces because we couldn't vote. Now we are afraid of not having any representatives or any voice in parliament. It means we are definitely excluded in Burma.' The hut where he has lived with his daughters was in That Kal Pyin, one of the villages around which the confinement camps had been built, since his house in downtown Sittwe had been destroyed in 2012. He was a well-respected elder in his community, and it was not difficult to see why. Gentle and cultured, deeply committed to his people, he had spent several years in jail for his political activism, and had experienced in his own flesh how his people went through a process of gradual social degradation. He had gone from working in the courts as a lawyer belonging to a family of good standing in both the Muslim and Buddhist communities to living as a refugee near the city where he had spent most of his life, where he was unlikely ever to return again. Given his profession, he was a firm believer in rule of law, but he had seen how the law had been applied selectively, misapplied, and often directly violated so as to strip his people of their rights.

Aung San Suu Kyi had been repeating the mantra of 'rule of law' as an apparent solution for everything since the beginning of the transition, but Kyaw Hla Aung was sceptical that a new government resulting from the elections would strive to change the oppressive policies carried out by the military against his people. 'She has never come here, but she is denying the existence of the Rohingya. She is denying the genocide against Rohingya. She didn't come and study what's going on in this area', he told me.

Nevertheless, Kyaw Hla Aung seemed to be torn on the question of what to expect from the NLD, and he understood why some Rohingya supported her: 'We have no choice. There are two parties: USDP and NLD. USDP is torturing Rohingyas, so we have to take the other side. She won the Nobel Prize and the international community is supporting and giving advice to her, so our Rohingya people expect that we can get something from her.' One of the Rohingya who expected their lot might change with the new government was Ozan, the head of the camp. 'I feel very sad because we couldn't vote, but I think that a victory for the NLD will bring change for us. Aung San Suu Kyi's father was a friend of the Muslims, and I think she will follow in his footsteps. I think she will change the 1982 Citizenship Law', he told me.

A few days before meeting Ozan, during the same press conference in which Aung San Suu Kyi had said that she would be 'above the president', I had asked her whether she or her party had any plan to amend the Citizenship Law. 'This is something that I don't decide on my own. When it comes to laws, it is something that will be decided by the legislature in full', she had replied. The answer struck me as disingenuous. Given how centralized and hierarchical her party is, it was to be expected that she could exert a huge influence on her MPs. The overly humble tone of her answer also contrasted greatly with the self-confidence she displayed during the rest of a press conference in which she was presenting herself as the inevitable future leader of the country. My interpretation of her answer was that she had no intention of touching the citizenship law, but I did not have the stomach to say so to Ozan, and kept my thoughts to myself. At the time of writing, the NLD has not attempted to change the law.

In contrast to the Rohingya, the Kaman Muslims, recognized as one of the 'national races', were allowed to vote. Many of those living in Sittwe had lost their houses and businesses in 2012, and were now living in the camps or the Aung Mingalar ghetto. Twenty-six Kaman from Aung Mingalar, and around seventy from the camps, had the rare chance to venture outside the areas they had been confined to and go to their polling stations. Ma Ma Lay was a fifty-year-old Kaman woman who lived with seven relatives in a cramped house in Aung Mingalar. 'I voted with Rakhine people in a polling station nearby. It was the first time I saw some Rakhine acquaintances since the violence in 2012. They asked me about my family and I was happy to see them. I don't feel hatred in my heart', she said. 'I voted for the National League for Democracy and the Kaman Development Party. What we need is peace, to work and live our lives with tranquillity. I think Aung San Suu Kyi will help Muslims in Burma, but our fate is in the hands of God', she added.

The Rohingya could not vote, but they were used as political tools by some candidates. Kaung San Hla was the NLD candidate for the constituency of Buthidaung, a township in northern Arakan State, where the Rohingya are in a majority. His potential voters were Rakhine and members of other ethnic minorities recognized by the government, including the Mro or the Daignet. Kaung San Hla was a small, bespectacled fifty-year-old man with the air of a professor, who made a living working as a tourist guide.[6] A few days after the election, he told me about his campaign, which he had carried out mostly by travelling on foot to remote villages. He had tried to arrive at the villages after candidates from other parties, the military-backed USDP and the Rakhine nationalist ANP, had campaigned in them, thinking he would have the advantage of countering their attacks against his party.

He found that the candidates for both parties were using the perceived threat of a 'Muslim-Bengali invasion' to smear him and the NLD, telling people that Aung San Suu Kyi's party would allow the Rohingya to take their land. 'Then I told them that this is a democratic country, and people have sovereignty. So we would respect their desires. Then I asked them loudly: "Do you want this land to be Muslim?" And they would shout "No!" I repeated the same question two or three times, and then I would tell them: "So if that's your desire, we're going to respect it"', he explained. Nonetheless, he did not win his seat in parliament.

The NLD itself was not above using ethno-religious divisions in order to attract votes in Arakan. Aung San Suu Kyi did not campaign in Sittwe; she tried very hard to distance herself from the whole issue. But she went to Thandwe, a town in the south of the state where Rakhine nationalism was weaker. A few days before the election, another historical leader of the party, the ninety-year-old Tin Oo, at that time emeritus chairman of the party, campaigned in Sittwe in her place. Tin Oo was one of the founders of the NLD, and he had been the chairman of the party during many of the years when Suu Kyi was under house arrest.

He was a retired general who had been commander-in-chief of the armed forces until he was forced to resign in 1976, when he was jailed, accused of being involved in an abortive coup d'état against General Ne Win. Before being appointed commander-in-chief, Tin Oo had been the commander of the Western Command in Sittwe, and tried to use that experience to his party's advantage in the campaign, telling people in Sittwe: 'I led the Tatmadaw troops that drove out the East Pakistanis that invaded Rakhine State. I defended the islands at the mouth of the Naf River so they would remain the land of the Rakhine people. Now, I promise the Rakhine people that I'll defend your interests and the territorial integrity of Rakhine State.'[7]

The political manipulation of the 'Rohingya problem' extended beyond Arakan. In Chin State, bordering Arakan to the north, one of the candidates was the well-known Chin and women's rights activist Cheery Zahau. Running against an NLD candidate in her hometown, Falam, her opponent attempted to tarnish her reputation, falsely accusing her of having had a pregnancy and an abortion – anathema in the deeply conservative Christian Chin society. That did not quite work, so the NLD candidate threw the further accusation at her that that, as a human rights activist, she had defended the Rohingya, and that if she won she would introduce them to Chin State, where there is not a single Rohingya.

In response, Cheery went to a diplomatic function in Rangoon, where she met one of the leaders of the NLD – a party she had supported for years – and complained about her opponent's tactics. The NLD elder chuckled, telling her, 'This is politics – it's a dirty game.' The NLD candidate eventually won the seat in Falam.[8]

On election day itself, voters went to the polling stations in Sittwe in such huge numbers that, in some areas, it seemed not all of them would be able to vote. It was difficult to find NLD voters that day in the city, and the ANP won the majority of votes throughout Arakan State. Among voters and ANP candidates I interviewed, the tensions between Buddhists and Muslims seemed not to be the main issue at the time. Maung Thin Khane, the ANP Lower House candidate for Sittwe, told me at the party headquarters: 'This election is our chance to build a democratic federal state and share everything equally with the [Burmans].' For him, an NLD government could give the Rakhine more space to fulfil their aspirations for autonomy. 'I trust the NLD a little.

There are no ethnic minorities represented in the top of the party, it is a Burman party; but we think that they believe in the rights of the Burmese minorities. The father of Daw Suu, Aung San, believed in federalism', he told me.

That day I accompanied Tun Myint Thein to vote. A burly man in his forties, he was the co-director of Wan Lark Foundation, a local Rakhine organization working with rural communities in Arakan and loosely associated with the ANP. He told me that day: 'The problem with the Muslims happened because of the government. The Muslims are the rope that the government has put around the neck of our people. Only the ANP can defend our people. We support the NLD and we support an alliance between the ANP and the NLD, but we can't believe Aung San Suu Kyi on the Muslim issue, because she's under pressure from the western world. We don't believe the USDP can solve this problem either, because they created the problem in the first place.'

But for him, the main issue at stake was ultimately the development of the state and the benefits that its people might reap from its natural resources: 'Arakanese people don't benefit from the gas offshore. It belongs to the government; they sell the gas to the Chinese and get all the profits. We hope that the ANP will try to change that.' At that point, the Rohingya did not seem to worry him much, and he would half-jokingly express annoyance whenever I brought up the issue. 'We have peace now in Arakan State', he told me, as if to settle the issue. The price of that peace had been paid mostly by the Rohingya with their freedom, expelled as they now were from political and social life. That sort of peace was perhaps sustainable for Tun Myint Thein and other Rakhine people, but it clearly was not for the Rohingya. And it would not last for more than a year.

The Rohingya were not the only ones unable to vote in the election. In other border areas of Burma, up to half a million people in 600 village tracts were unable to cast their ballots.[9] But they were not disenfranchised in the same way as the Rohingya. Some of those areas were controlled by the ethnic armed groups that had long-established autonomous mini-states largely outside central government control, like those of the United Wa State Army, along the border with China in northern Shan State, and the National Democratic Alliance Army, also in northern Shan State.

The government argued that the election authorities had no access to those areas to compile voter lists, and suspended the elections there. In other cases, the government cited security reasons, as there had been skirmishes with armed groups such as the Shan State Army-North and the Kachin Independence Army (KIA). By the time of the election, tens of thousands of internally displaced persons were still languishing in camps, mostly in Kachin and Shan states.

Since 2011, the quasi-civilian government of Thein Sein had made attempts to reach ceasefires with most of the ethnic armed groups that were still active. The central government had shown little willingness to engage in a meaningful political dialogue to discuss their autonomist aspirations, but some groups had signed ceasefire agreements. Others, most crucially the KIA, had refused to do so. In the weeks before the election, the government tried to push the recalcitrant ones to accept a National Ceasefire Agreement that only eight of the eighteen armed groups recognized at that time as interlocutors by the government had agreed to sign. As a result, fighting flared in several areas in the border-lands during the months ahead of the election.

Nevertheless, most members of the ethnic minorities in Burma's periphery were able to vote. In many cases, there were a bewildering number of options. Every ethnic group had at least one ethno-nationalist party running in the election, and most had more than two. That partially accounts for the high number of parties running in the elections: a total of ninety-two, of which only a handful won representation in parliament.[10] In Kachin State there were six different local parties, in addition to the national ones. The differences between parties representing a single ethnic group were often minimal or nonexistent from an ideological or programmatic point of view, often reflecting networks of influence and personalities more than anything else. Of those Kachin parties, only five candidates from two parties won a seat. One of them was Ja Seng Hkawn, the daughter of one of the historic leaders of the Kachin Independence Organization (KIO – the political arm of the KIA), Brang Seng.[11]

A well-known member of the Kachin elite, Ja Seng Hkawn, told me a couple of years later, in her riverside villa next to the Irrawaddy in Mytkyina, the capital of Kachin State, that the proliferation of Kachin parties was the reason for the NLD victory in her state, and admitted that the differences between those parties were limited to their names and the identity of their leaders. A convinced nationalist who firmly believed in Kachin self-determination, she assured me that she had tried to convince candidates from other parties to join just one, in order to avoid splitting the vote, but they had not listened to her. Even in her own house, her husband had run for another party, and lost.

Everybody expected a resounding victory for the NLD in the Burman-majority hinterlands of Burma; but the party was also victorious in most of the states that were home to the ethnic minorities. The NLD eventually won 77 per cent of the contested seats[12] – a total of 887 in both houses of parliament – taking the majority of the seats in all regions of the country except two. The military-backed USDP won only 10 per cent of the contested seats, a total of 117.[13] The only exceptions were Arakan State, where the Arakan National Party received 64.7 per cent of contested seats, and the NLD only 23.5 per cent – mostly in the south, where Rakhine nationalism was weaker than in the north; and Shan State, where the Shan Nationalities League for Democracy won 21.8 per cent of the seats, the military-backed USDP 29.1 per cent, and the NLD only 19.1 per cent, amid accusations that the military had swung the votes in its favour in areas where it exerted strong control.

One reason for the NLD victory among the ethnic minorities was the confusing proliferation of ethno-nationalist parties. The victory of the ANP in Arakan seems to confirm this, as it was the only important Rakhine party in its state. Another reason may be that the NLD candidates in the states were usually members of the ethnic minorities that made up their constituencies. The first-past-the-post electoral system, which tends to benefit the biggest parties, was also a factor. Ultimately, however, it is likely that the strongest reason was that the main priority of everybody in Burma was to get rid of the military as quickly as possible, and the NLD seemed to be the most viable alternative.[14] Many members of ethnic minorities with autonomist aspirations probably thought that the NLD would be more responsive to their demands than a party controlled by the military.

But the NLD would not be able to govern alone – not while the military still maintained its control over most of the state's institutions. Whatever form of government the NLD might be able to form, it would be part of a diarchic regime in which the Tatmadaw was almost completely beyond the control of the civilian executive.

15

'The Lady' in Power

On 6 April 2016, Aung San Suu Kyi fulfilled the destiny that for years she and many others had assigned to her, almost three decades after she had begun her political career. That day, five months after the victory of her party in the parliamentary election, she became the leader of Burma. She had promised before the election that she would be 'above the president' if the NLD won, and she was true to her word. One month before, the parliament had elected as president the sixty-year-old Htin Kyaw, a close confidant of Suu Kyi, son of a respected poet, and virtually unknown outside the inner circle of 'the Lady'. Htin Kyaw had little previous experience in political activism, but possessed two key virtues: loyalty to Suu Kyi and a lack of political ambition. He knew his place, and would never rock the boat or betray her.

There was much speculation on how Suu Kyi might circumvent the constitutional clause preventing her from taking the presidency. The Tatmadaw was inflexible in its refusal to change it, and the necessary constitutional amendment was impossible without the assent of the generals. Faced with this insurmountable block, Suu Kyi began by taking for herself no less than four ministries. Eventually, the new position of 'state counsellor' was created especially for her, and she kept control over only two ministries, the President's Office and Foreign Affairs.

The position of state counsellor, roughly equivalent to the role of prime minister, entailed somewhat undefined powers that allowed Suu Kyi to oversee every aspect of the executive except those ministries controlled by the military. The president was a mere figurehead, with a purely ceremonial role. As state counsellor, Suu Kyi had to report to the parliament instead of the president, and thus she served as a bridge between the executive and the legislature; and by retaining control over the Ministry of Foreign Affairs, she guaranteed that she would have a seat on the eleven-member National Defence and Security Council.

It was an ingenious arrangement that the generals could have blocked, alleging that it was unconstitutional. They could plausibly have argued that the idea of anybody ruling 'above the president' was in breach of Article 58 of the Constitution, which states that 'the president of the Republic of the Union of Myanmar takes precedence over all other persons throughout the Republic of the Union of Myanmar'. The Union Solidarity and Development Party (USDP) – the military proxy party now in opposition – voted in parliament against the bill introducing the new position, and the bloc of MPs appointed directly by the Tatmadaw boycotted the vote. 'There is a word for this: bullying by the democratic majority. Now the situation is like that. So military MPs did not vote', complained Brigadier Maung Maung, a senior military delegate, after the vote, apparently unaware of the grotesque irony of being a soldier complaining about 'bullying' after decades of military dictatorship.[1] But the NLD had enough MPs to pass the bill.

The generals let Suu Kyi have what she wanted. They may have calculated that it was too late in the transition process to block her bid for power, which would probably have provoked a tremendous popular and international backlash. Be that as it may, the truth of the matter was that she could position herself above the president, but not above the commander-in-chief of the armed forces, Senior General Min Aung Hlaing, and the Tatmadaw itself, as they were free from any significant civilian oversight.

Suu Kyi had made strenuous efforts during the transition period to prove that she would not pose a threat to the military. Such had been her strategy of 'national reconciliation' since 2011, and it had paid off. Even her most relentless foe for decades, Senior General Than Shwe, the former head of the military junta until 2011 who had disappeared from public view since his retirement in 2011, appeared to endorse Suu Kyi. One month after the election, in December 2015, they met in his house in Naypyidaw and, according to Than Shwe's grandson, the old dictator had said: 'It is the truth that she will become the future leader of the country. I will support her with all of my efforts.'[2]

History seemed to have come full circle. 'I would not wish to see any splits and struggles between the army which my father built up and the people who love my father so much', Suu Kyi had said at the feet of the Shwedagon Pagoda, during the public speech in 1988 that had elevated her to leadership of the pro-democracy movement. Now, in her role as the representative of the Burmese people, she appeared to have mended the splits with the generals. The price she had to pay was that of ruling in a diarchic government in which the Tatmadaw would have the upper hand in any conflict with the civilian branch. The military not only possessed a monopoly on the instruments of violence; at that point, it also controlled a large part of the bureaucracy through the General Administration Department, under the Ministry of Home Affairs. Also, by letting Suu Kyi occupy a position of power, the generals gained international recognition for the semi-democratic regime they had devised. Thus, in late 2016, President Obama removed most of the remaining sanctions still in effect against the country.[3]

The new cabinet was a mixture of Suu Kyi's loyalists, relatively apolitical technocrats and stalwarts of the old regime. Apart from the three ministers appointed directly by the military, the ministers for labour, immigration and population, and religious and cultural affairs, were USDP members.[4] Zaw Htay, the former spokesman of President Thein Sein, famous for his anti-Rohingya rhetoric, retained his position as the voice of the government. The two vice presidents, one chosen by the military and the other by the NLD itself, were former officers of the Tatmadaw. The first, the retired general Myint Swe, had been nominated by the MPs appointed by the military in parliament and was a man close to Senior General Than Shwe, who, as head of Special Operations in Rangoon, had overseen the brutal repression of the popular uprising internationally known as the 'Saffron Revolution' in 2007.[5] The second vice president was Henry Van Thio, an ethnic Chin and Christian who had been a major in the army, and who had been appointed by the civilian government of the NLD in a clear attempt to present an ethnically inclusive face for the new government.

The new cabinet served as confirmation that, if the transition meant anything, it was a merger of two elites – the higher echelons of the military and the historic pro-democracy leaders – in the guise of 'national reconciliation'. The economic elites – the 'cronies' – kept their place in the new order, and Aung San Suu Kyi herself welcomed them with open arms. In October 2016, she chaired a meeting in Naypyidaw with the top taxpayers in the country. After pointing out that they had made their fortunes through their connections with the leadership of a repressive regime, she asked them to change their ways: 'We can't mend the past. But I would like to request that they act fairly at present . . . Can't those who have previously worked for their own self-interest work for others in the future? Don't they have the necessary attributes to work for others? I believe it is possible.'[6]

In the face of systemic malaises like cronyism, corruption and inequality, Suu Kyi eschewed any attempt at a systemic overhaul. Once again, she offered strictly moral recipes to address problems that were fundamentally political. Throughout her administration, she has made clear that her government would not steer away from the 'Burmese way to neoliberalism' on which the generals had tried unsuccessfully to embark in the nineties.

Many in Burma and abroad had hoped that the appointment of Suu Kyi as ruler of her country might usher in a new, more democratic and freer era. But not much has changed since then, and it has become increasingly clear that real reforms had already taken place during the Thein Sein period. The fact that the Tatmadaw allowed the NLD to assume power – something unthinkable only five years before – has simply proved to confirm both the apparent irreversibility and the limits of such reforms. The system put in place by the generals entailed severe constraints upon what the civilian branch of government could do; but Suu Kyi has failed to use the power at her disposal to improve the living conditions of the Burmese people or expand their freedoms. This failure has been a consequence of her leadership style, but also of the issues she has decided to focus on.

It is often argued that Burmese politics are strongly personalistic, with powerful characters dominating the scene over different periods, from Aung San before independence to his daughter in contemporary Burma, via U Nu and Ne Win in between. It is undeniable that political disputes have often been little more than power struggles between different personalities or cliques, and that institutions in the country are woefully weak, ineffective and lacking in legitimacy. But there is a crucial exception: the Tatmadaw.

The modern Burmese military may have been founded by Aung San, but it was built by Ne Win. While it relied strongly on personal loyalty to him during the first years of his dictatorship, it outlived him as an institution, developing its own ethos and discipline. Ultimately, it makes little difference who is its commander-in-chief; the Tatmadaw has proved to be strong enough to survive and maintain its power for decades. What it lacks in popular legitimacy, it makes up for through a high degree of internal cohesion. This is proved by the fact that, during five decades of military dictatorship in various forms, no serious challenge to its power has emerged from within its own ranks.

Once in power, and even before, Aung San Suu Kyi has failed to nurture both civilian institutions and a political culture that might serve as a counterweight to the power of the military; it could in fact be argued that she had actively blocked them. She lies at the centre of a personality cult that she has never done anything to discourage, and that has marked her leadership style, first in the opposition and then in government. In late 2016, she asserted in an interview: 'Our success, where I am as a leader, is decided by how dispensable I can make myself. And I hope that I'll be able to make myself totally dispensable, that they will not need me to go on, neither my party, nor my country.'[7] The implication that she was then indispensable was clear. There are few indications that she has made preparations to groom a new leadership for her party that could outlive her, except for the appointment of a new president after Htin Kyaw decided to step down in March 2018.

The new man below Suu Kyi is Win Myint – speaker in the lower house of parliament since 2012, and a more experienced politician than his predecessor. His appointment was interpreted as a sign that Suu Kyi was willing to delegate some authority, but so far there has been little evidence that he has more autonomy than Htin Kyaw had.[8] Often described as a 'micromanager', Suu Kyi exercises a highly centralized form of power in which, by all accounts, she makes virtually all important decisions and her ministers lack any meaningful autonomy. She has established strict party discipline to which NLD members are expected to adhere. There is little transparency about how she makes decisions. Since the election she has only given a few interviews to international media – and none to local outlets. Suu Kyi reviews the draft of every bill submitted to parliament, and pressure is placed on MPs to be more loyal to the party than to their own constituencies.[9]

Imperious and authoritarian, Suu Kyi is reportedly surrounded by a small retinue of trusted advisers who are reluctant to challenge her decisions or bring bad news to her, either out of fear or to curry favour with her.[10] Access to that inner circle is more a reward for personal loyalty than for competence. Thus, the finance and planning minister, Kyaw Win, had claimed to hold advanced degrees from 'Brooklyn Park University'. In reality, this nonexistent institution was merely a website run by a Pakistani company selling fake diplomas. The minister of commerce, Than Myint, held graduate degrees from an unaccredited American correspondence school that had closed in 2006. There was a minor scandal when their fake credentials were discovered, but the state counsellor refused to replace them.[11]

In many ways, the political culture of the NLD and its government resembles that of the Tatmadaw. Beholden to a strict discipline and rigid hierarchy, neither leaves much room for dissent or personal autonomy in their lower ranks. As I have already suggested, the politics of Suu Kyi are based on morality rather than any coherent ideology or workable programme, and her rule reflects that. She possesses the electoral mandate granted by her fellow Burmese, and is seen by many, particularly among Burmans, as the only person capable of steering Burma away from military rule. Her leadership style indicates that she agrees with this assessment of her gifts, but it remains a mystery what she intends to do with her power to change her country. Paraphrasing Jean Cocteau's famous description of Victor Hugo, one could say that Aung San Suu Kyi, like any other person 'of destiny', is a madwoman who thinks that she is Aung San Suu Kyi, insofar as she appears fully to believe in and inhabit and the role of indispensable saviour of her country that has been bestowed upon her. Equally, if the General Ne Win and the generals that replaced him saw the Burmese population as an undisciplined collective in need of stern rule, Suu Kyi's authoritarianism can be seen as reflecting a somewhat softer version of the same distrust, in which she has replaced the general's brute force with moralistic admonitions. Ultimately, her politics could well be described by the term 'discipline-flourishing democracy' expounded by the military.

The authoritarianism of the NLD government also extends to its way of dealing with the vibrant civil society that emerged in Burma during the SLORC/SPDC period. The origins of that milieu can be found in the organizations that mushroomed during the 1988 popular uprising, in which Suu Kyi emerged as the leader of the pro-democracy opposition. But, despite that historical debt, the state counsellor has often played down the role of civil society organizations, and even attempted to stifle them.[12] She has also, since at least the protests against the Letpadaung Copper Mine, shown a deep distrust of participatory politics.

Moreover, her government has kept in place draconian restrictions on protests from the era of military rule,[13] and civil and human rights have not improved under her government; in some respects, in fact, they have worsened. Freedom of expression has declined from the years of the Thein Sein administration, with the use of anti-defamation laws to silence critics of the government, the military or Suu Kyi herself. Thein Sein was obliged to prove his democratic credentials to the international community and the Burmese citizenry, while having no need to assuage the generals. But the situation is reversed with respect to Suu Kyi. She probably feels she has no need to prove her democratic credentials, and most of her political strategy is based on gaining the trust of the generals. As a result, her government has proved to be more authoritarian than that of the former general-turned-statesman.

Any government formed in Burma after the 2015 election would have faced daunting challenges. Some of them lie well within the purview of the executive's civilian branch, led by Suu Kyi: a corrupt and subservient judiciary; the underfunded education system; wholly inadequate infrastructure; virtually nonexistent public healthcare. With its majority in parliament, the NLD could have repealed oppressive laws from the years of dictatorship, or introduced new ones to guarantee more freedoms to the whole of the Burmese population.

When the political opening began in 2012, it was expected that the economy would grow and living standards be lifted; but despite economic growth and some influx of foreign investors, only a handful of well-connected businessmen benefited. Red tape, corruption and legal uncertainty resulted in fewer foreign companies investing in Burma than had been expected. The country faces a dilemma shared by many other underdeveloped nations: how to attract foreign investment while benefiting the population at large.

Yet the NLD has done little to tackle any of these issues. As we have seen, oppressive laws are still in place; land-grabbing is still endemic throughout the country; neither the judiciary nor the education system has experienced any serious overhaul; and little progress has been made in facilitating the foreign investment that might lift millions of rural and urban Burmese from poverty. This is partly a result of neglect, the style of leadership of Suu Kyi herself, and a lack of expertise in the government – but it is also a consequence of the issues that she has decided to focus on.

From the beginning, the state counsellor made the main priority of her administration solving a problem over which she has virtually no control: the perpetual wars between the Tatmadaw and the various armed ethnic organizations that have devastated Burma's borderlands since independence. In itself, this was a worthy cause for Suu Kyi to have chosen, partly for personal reasons, in that it continues and honours the legacy her father established when he signed the Panglong Agreement in 1947. But such efforts were condemned to failure from the start because, lacking any control over the military, Suu Kyi has been able, at best, to operate only as a mediator. Another obstacle in attaining peace is the Constitution, which leaves little room for federalism, the main demand of political representatives of the ethnic minorities – and an idea that Suu Kyi herself has indicated her support for in principle, though she has not spelled out how exactly it would work.

In August 2016, the government convened the 'Twenty-First Century Panglong Conference' in Naypyidaw.[14] 'Only if we are all united, [will our country] be at peace', Suu Kyi said in her opening remarks, stressing once again an ideal that has historically been detrimental to negotiations, since unity has mostly been dictated in Burman terms that the ethnic minorities have found it difficult to accept.[15] Around 750 delegates from the government, political parties, the military, civil society organizations and armed groups attended; but the conference ended up in failure. Some groups, including the Arakan Army (AA) and the Ta'ang National Liberation Army (TNLA), were not recognized by the Tatmadaw. The UWSA of the Wa, the most powerful ethnic armed organization in military terms, pulled out early as a consequence of a misunderstanding with the government organizers: they had erroneously been granted only observer status, instead of full participation in the process.[16]

This misstep with the UWSA was indicative of the lack of experience in conducting the peace process among those appointed by the new government. Suu Kyi had dismantled the Myanmar Peace Centre (MPC) formed by Thein Sein, and created another body with new personnel, the National Reconciliation and Peace Centre. The leaders and negotiators of some armed groups distrusted the MPC as a mere instrument of the Tatmadaw, but the MPC's members had built a relationship with them that had to be completely rebuilt by the new personnel led by Suu Kyi. To make matters worse, apart from this change of personnel, her approach to the peace process differed little from that of her predecessors.

After the first conference, Suu Kyi met with the commander-in-chief, Min Aung Hlaing, and the NLD decided to stand behind the National Ceasefire Agreements designed during the Thein Sein administration and endorsed by the Tatmadaw. That meant business as usual in dealing with the armed groups: a ceasefire and disarmament of the ethnic armed groups that almost amounted to surrender as a precondition for political dialogue confined within the narrow margins of the 2008 Constitution. In her strategy of 'national reconciliation', Suu Kyi prioritized good relations with the generals rather than with the ethnic armed groups. 'It seems to us, those in the ethnic political circles, that Suu Kyi is listening to the Tatmadaw most of the time instead of listening to the ethnic stakeholders', the well-known Chin activist Cheery Zahau said at the time.[17]

New rounds of talks were held in Naypyidaw in the next two years, with results as inconclusive as those of the first round. By mid 2018, eleven armed groups had signed the ceasefire agreement, while ten were still up in arms against the government.[18] But the number of signatories was misleading. Of all of them, only the Karen National Union (KNU) and the Restoration Council of Shan State (RCSS) possessed any substantial manpower and political clout. The rest – with the possible exceptions of the New Mon State Party, the Democratic Kayin Benevolent Army and the Democratic Karen Buddhist Army – lacked power and influence. In absolute terms, the non-signatory armed organizations accounted for 63,100 soldiers (93,100, including reserve forces), while the signatories only represented 21,560 fighters.[19]

Meanwhile war continued, and even worsened in the northern borderlands of Kachin and Shan states. In November 2016, shortly after the first Conference, the Tatmadaw launched heavy attacks against some of the non-signatory groups, displacing thousands and killing dozens of civilians.[20] Four armed groups formed the Northern Alliance: the KIO, the AA, the TNLA and the Myanmar National Democratic Alliance Army. The Northern Alliance fought back fiercely and made some territorial gains that were later reversed by the army. In July 2018, during the third session of the Twenty-First Century Panglong Conference, there were even skirmishes between the Tatmadaw and the KNU, one of the signatories to the ceasefire.[21]

Aung San Suu Kyi had no power to put a stop to this spiral of violence, and the worsening conflict showed clearly that any agreement with the civilian government was a dead letter without agreement from the Tatmadaw. The 2008 Constitution was another obstacle, as the army opposed any amendment to it, and Suu Kyi has toned down her demands for constitutional change since taking power. To secure the most powerful position in government for Suu Kyi, the NLD had found an ingenious way to circumvent the Constitution without needing to change it; but it had made no corresponding attempt to deliver some degree of autonomy to the ethnic minorities.

For instance, the Constitution prescribed that the chief minister in every state and region has to be appointed by the president, instead of being elected by the corresponding regional parliament. In those states where an ethno-nationalist party had won more votes than the NLD – Arakan and Shan states – the NLD government could have appointed a chief minister in agreement with them, but it decided to follow the Constitution scrupulously, in both cases appointing a member of its own party without consulting the ethno-nationalist parties. At the same time, it retained most of the USDP's high officials inherited from the Thein Sein administration. Agreeing a chief minister with the local parties would have sent a signal that the new government was serious about federalism; but the opportunity was lost, and disillusionment with Suu Kyi quickly settled in among ethno-nationalists from the states in the borderlands.

Meanwhile, Suu Kyi has attempted to rehabilitate her father as a symbol of national unity. After the years in which the military junta had erased him from official discourse, she has striven to bring him back to prominence. That has sometimes created resentment in the ethnic-minority regions. In early 2017, the new government decided to name a bridge in Mon State after Aung San, against the wishes of both local organizations and a minister in the state.[22] The symbolic gesture provoked a wave of protests that were echoed the following year in other areas, when the government decided to erect statues of Aung San in Karenni State and in a remote region inhabited by the Naga ethnic group, in Sagaing.[23]

The government argued that Aung San was the man who had managed to unify disparate ethnic groups – but this was a pre-eminently Burman-centric view that not all members of the ethnic minorities shared. And it was not surprising that, at a moment when war continued in the country and the old grievances of the ethnic minorities remained unaddressed, many ethno-nationalists from those groups felt that the central state was attempting to impose a symbolic ideal of national unity within which their voices had been ignored for decades. Reclaiming the mantle of the father of Burma might have worked for Suu Kyi and the NLD among the Burman majority, but his legacy is much more problematic for the ethnic minorities. This was a miscalculation from which the state counsellor has shown no sign of having learned.

The formation of an NLD government appeared at first to be a blow to the militant Buddhist movement Ma Ba Tha, some of whose most prominent leaders had explicitly supported the USDP in the 2015 election. These leaders had backed a losing horse that was deeply unpopular, and their credibility seemed to have been seriously diminished. But this electoral defeat for Ma Ba Tha was not its death sentence – only a warning that it had to alter its strategy and perhaps its image. For the first months of the new administration, the movement toned down its lurid propaganda.

In July 2016, the State Sangha Maha Nayaka Committee (also known by the Burmese acronym Ma Ha Na) issued a statement declaring that Ma Ba Tha was not an official organization, effectively disowning it.[24] Ma Ha Na has been seen historically as a tool of the government, and does not command absolute authority over the monastic community in Burma; but the statement revealed the new administration's position towards the rival movement. The statement fell short of dissolving Ma Ba Tha, but one year later Ma Ha Na issued a stronger statement, warning that Ma Ba Tha was in violation of monastic laws by its intervention in politics, and banned the use of the name. In a conference celebrating the fourth anniversary of the movement, the leadership announced that it was dropping the name, and renamed it the Buddha Dhamma Parahita Foundation. The organization had not been abolished, but merely been forced to change its name; some regional branches, which had always operated semi-independently, even refused to drop the name at all. The movement continued to oversee its social activities as before.[25]

The NLD government took action against Ma Ba Tha, but it did not make any moves against the underlying ultranationalist ideology animating it – perhaps for fear of alienating its Buddhist base, or because many NLD supporters and members actually shared that ideology. Despite enjoying a majority in parliament, the NLD did not make any effort to repel the discriminatory Race and Religion Protection Laws, for which Ma Ba Tha had successfully campaigned in 2015. Moreover, while there have been no major episodes of sectarian violence in central Burma during the Suu Kyi administration, discrimination against Muslims has continued unabated.

According to the Burma Human Rights Network, a human rights watchdog based in London with an extensive network of researchers in Burma, there were at least twenty-one villages throughout the country that had declared themselves 'no-go areas' for Muslims. Meanwhile, the authorities placed more obstacles than ever in the way of Muslims acquiring ID cards, passports and other official documents, and prohibited Muslims from rebuilding damaged mosques, let alone erecting new ones.[26]

Fears among Muslims were further compounded by the assassination of one of their most respected coreligionists. Ko Ni was a prestigious lawyer who worked as a legal advisor for Suu Kyi. On 29 January 2017, while arriving at Rangoon International Airport from a trip to Indonesia, he was shot in the head while he was holding his grandson at the exit.[27] During his escape, the assassin also killed a taxi driver who tried to stop him. For all the violence in Burmese politics, assassinations are relatively rare, and the killing shocked the country. The killer's motives were not immediately clear, and there was at first some speculation than ultranationalist groups might be behind his actions. Despite Ko Ni's membership in the NLD, he had criticized the leadership's decision not to field any Muslim candidates in the 2015 election, so as to placate Buddhist hardliners. He had also challenged the ruling in 2014 by which the Rohingya were barred from voting.[28] On the other hand, the lawyer was very critical of the 2008 Constitution. He was working on drafting a new one, and it was widely reported at the time that he had been instrumental in creating the position of state counsellor for Suu Kyi – something that may have infuriated some hardliners from the old regime.

The police arrested the assassin, a hired hit-man who claimed he had been coerced into killing the lawyer, and three other co-conspirators;

but the masterminds were never apprehended. It is widely believed that Ko Ni was not assassinated for religious reasons or his work defending Burmese Muslims, but rather for attempting to change the Constitution. But many Muslims in Burma cannot shake off the feeling that his religion made him an easy target, and that the police and judiciary would have been more effective in resolving the case if he had he been a Buddhist. His assassination showed that no Muslim was safe.

Thousands attended Ko Ni's funeral, but there was one glaring absence: Aung San Suu Kyi herself, who kept silent about the assassination and did not send her condolences to the family until one month later.[29]

Meanwhile, on his Facebook page, the extremist monk Wirathu did comment on the killing – to express his appreciation for the assassins and thank them for their deed. 'At this time, I feel relief for the future of Buddhism in my country. If not, the destruction of Buddhism, like in Thailand, would have gained a foothold here in five years', he wrote, warning that 'anyone who wants to kick out military representatives should be mindful. Anyone who wants to scrap the Constitution should be mindful.'[30] As a punishment, the State Sangha Maha Nayaka Committee banned the firebrand monk from giving sermons for one year. Meanwhile, Swe Win, an investigative journalist, was accused of defamation by a Ma Ba Tha supporter for criticizing Wirathu's words, in a case that would drag on for more than a year.[31]

Muslims were no less discriminated against under the new government than they had been before. At the very least, the NLD administration is guilty for that by its failure to act. Suu Kyi has been timid at best in tackling the prevalence among large sections of Burmese society of the sort of militant Burman ethno-nationalism that holds that non-Buddhists are not real Burmese; and she has made little use of her considerable moral authority to advance more open and progressive notions of citizenship and belonging that might transcend the 'national races ideology'. Activists working for interreligious dialogue and coexistence have enjoyed little protection from the government, while measures against hate speech spread by anti-Muslim campaigners have been erratic at best, reinforcing a sense of impunity among them. On the other hand, organizations like Ma Ba Tha and its subsequent reincarnations have provided many Buddhist citizens with an outlet for political expression in an atmosphere in which the NLD administration seems to regard the legitimate scope of mass political participation as extending no further than voting it into power. The vacuum generated by the NLD's depoliticization of Burmese society is easily filled by well-funded and well-organized ultranationalist organizations. And a series of tragic developments in Arakan under Suu Kyi's watch have further solidified Buddhist extremism, hatred against Muslims, and a siege mentality within which movements like Ma Ba Tha thrive.

16

'An Unfinished Job'

The NLD dispelled any doubts about its position on the 'Rohingya issue' even before the transfer of power. When asked about it shortly after the election, Win Htein, one of the senior leaders of the party, replied: 'We have other priorities. Peace, the peaceful transition of power, economic development and constitutional reform.' He repeated the old myth about illegal immigration: 'We'll deal with the matter based on law and order and human rights, but we have to deal with the Bangladesh government because almost all of them came from there.'[1] Neither the assumptions on which policies towards the Rohingya had been predicated for decades nor those policies themselves were to be substantially altered with the new government.

Two weeks after Suu Kyi's appointment as state counsellor, a tragedy in Arakan tested her position. A boat carrying around sixty Rohingya to Sittwe from an internment camp in Pauktaw Township, capsized. Twenty-one of its passengers, including nine children, were drowned. The passengers had received a special permit to visit the market in the capital, and they were killed when a heavy wave rocked the fragile boat.[2] The incident was provoked by the elements, but also by the confinement and segregation to which they had been subjected. Without restrictions on their freedom of movement, they would have been able to take the safer boats that usually circulate through the maze of rivers in Arakan.

The government did not comment publicly on the tragedy, as if Rohingya lives did not matter. But when the embassy of the United

States in Rangoon issued a statement offering condolences to the families of the victims, in which it used the term 'Rohingya', Aung San Suu Kyi asked the American ambassador to refrain from using the word.[3] The controversy over the name resurfaced once again, and hundreds of nationalists, led by Buddhist monks, protested in front of the American embassy.[4] The loss of lives went largely ignored elsewhere in Burma.

'Emotive terms make it very difficult for us to find a peaceful and sensible resolution to our problems', Suu Kyi said one month later, in an attempt to explain her petition to the ambassador to avoid the word Rohingya, as the US secretary of state, John Kerry, visited the country.[5] She found herself in an awkward position on the issue of terminology, with her domestic and foreign supporters pulling in opposite directions. She had never uttered the term 'Rohingya' in public – but she had not used the word 'Bengali' either. Her administration attempted to find a balance between the two in June 2016, ahead of a visit by the UN special rapporteur for Myanmar. The Ministry of Information circulated an order among state officials to avoid using either term, and suggesting instead the cumbersome 'people who believe in Islam in Rakhine State'.[6] On paper, the phrase was a balanced middle position that would not entirely satisfy either the Rohingya or the Rakhine, but it was not too offensive to either group. It was less neutral than it seemed, however. Prohibiting public officials from using the term 'Rohingya' was pointless, as they were not using it anyway; and the order not to use 'Bengali' was routinely violated without consequence.

'Development' as the cure for the ills afflicting Arakan was a widespread idea at the time, both within and beyond the government. It was effectively the policy of the UN office in the country, which was sorely divided between those focusing on development and those who wished to stress the human rights violations the Rohingya were suffering. The former had the upper hand, as that was the priority of the UN resident coordinator at the time, Renata Lok-Dessallien, who advocated cooperation with the government and was inclined to underplay rights abuses.[7]

This approach tended to view Arakan as the site of an intercommunal conflict between the Buddhist and Muslim communities, while eliding the role of government policies in perpetuating segregation and inflaming tensions. Ultimately, it served as an alibi for both the civilian government and the military, allowing them to evade any responsibility for the situation.

And the recipe of economic development was insufficient on its own – though Arakan, the second-poorest state in the country, was clearly in need of it. But fostering economic development without addressing the marginalization of the Rohingya was bound to benefit the Rakhine disproportionately, thus accentuating inequalities between the two communities and reinforcing intercommunal divisions.

When Suu Kyi took power in early 2016, Arakan was relatively peaceful. No major violent incidents had occurred for two years. But the illusory peace came at the expense of the Rohingya. During the visit from John Kerry, Suu Kyi remarked: 'All that we are asking is that people should be aware of the difficulties we are facing and to give us enough space to solve all our problems.' A few days later the government announced the creation of a Central Committee for the Implementation of Peace and Development in Rakhine State, chaired by the state counsellor herself.[8] Then, in late August, it established another Advisory Commission on Rakhine State, this time chaired by the former secretary-general of the United Nations, Kofi Annan. Tasked with 'finding lasting solutions to the complex and delicate issues in the Rakhine State', the latest in a long list of commissions had nine members, six Burmese and three foreigners, and was tasked with submitting its findings and recommendations after twelve months.[9]

Aung San Suu Kyi explained that her commission would be 'overseeing the tasks of ensuring stability and rule of law, scrutinising immigration and verifying citizenship, and implementing socio-economic development'.[10] In her explanation, she was ignoring the power dynamics in the region, as well as systematic discrimination against the Rohingya, focusing instead on her often-repeated mantra of 'rule of law', at a moment when the majority she commanded in parliament was doing nothing to change legislation, such as the 1982 Citizenship Law, that had been used to perpetuate the statelessness of the Rohingya. Also, she was once again taking at face value the collective illusion of 'illegal immigration' – a prism through which the issue had been grotesquely distorted for decades.

Even assuming, for the sake of argument, that Suu Kyi was sincere about confronting the conflict, she had made her calculations without paying much attention to the Rohingya themselves. The government and the Rakhine could afford to take their time to solve the issue of intercommunal tensions; but the Rohingya were offered little hope that anything would improve for them. For them, nothing had changed with the new government, which failed to introduce even a token policy – such as expanding the community's freedom of movement or access to services – that might serve as a sign that some sort of improvement was on the horizon. The military government had often established commissions that had served only to buy time and avoid confronting pressing issues, and the commissions created by the Suu Kyi administration seemed to many a mere ploy whereby it could drag its feet in tackling the situation. Deprived of any political voice, disenfranchised, and with little hope in the future, the Rohingya – especially their youth – were growing increasingly restless under a surface of apparent 'peace'.

A new Rohingya insurgency emerged into view in the early hours of 9 October 2016, when around 250 men assaulted the headquarters of the Border Guard Police (BGP) near Maungdaw town, and two security forces' positions in the townships of Maungdaw and Rathedaung. The attackers were mostly armed with spears, knives and homemade weapons, and their force was based on their sheer numbers and coordination. Nine members of the security forces were killed by the attackers, and dozens of Rohingya insurgents were shot by the security forces.[11]

The attacks had been organized by a new group called Harakah Al-Yakin ('Faith Movement'), later also named the Arakan Rohingya Salvation Army (ARSA). The Tatmadaw responded with its usual brutality. It promptly declared the three northernmost townships of Arakan 'military operations areas', and launched a 'clearance operation', along with the BGP, to hunt down the insurgents. The army claimed that 102 Rohingya militants and thirty-two members of the security forces were killed, but human rights researchers put the toll of dead Rohingya much higher, and determined that it included non-militants. During the operations, the military and the BGP committed a wide array of atrocities, including burning whole villages to the ground, arbitrary detentions, execution of civilians, and the gang-rape of Rohingya women. Within just a few weeks, 80,000 Rohingya had fled to Bangladesh.

I visited Arakan a few days after the insurgent attacks. Northern Arakan, with military operations still ongoing, was completely sealed off to foreigners, and I could not travel beyond Sittwe. The city was at peace, far from the fighting; but rumours about what was going on a few kilometres to the north ran wild. For many Rakhine, already distrustful of the Rohingya, the attacks were a confirmation of some of their worst fears, which framed the Rohingya as a murderous terrorist menace. The presence of Rakhine Buddhists who had fled or been evacuated by the conflict in Maungdaw contributed to the stoking of such fears.

To enquire about the authorities' position, I visited Tin Maung Shwe, the executive secretary in Arakan. As such, he was the person responsible for overseeing the General Administration Department in the state. An unfailingly polite man, Tin Maung Shwe had received me about one year earlier, before the change of government, when he had held the same position. His office was air-conditioned, clean and almost luxurious, offering a stark contrast with the rundown compound that served as the seat of Arakan State's government in downtown Sittwe. At first, he was as friendly as he had been on our previous encounter, but our conversation became increasingly tense as we talked.

Tin Maung Shwe claimed that the militants belonged to 'a terrorist organization called Aqa Mul Mujahedeen', and that they had 'a network which provides budget and support'. He added: 'They have connection with RSO [a long-extinct Rohingya armed group] and ISIS in Saudi Arabia.' According to him, the involvement of those groups had been established by monitoring remittances sent to Arakan from the Middle East – a common practice in the region – as well as through confessions made by arrested militants. At that time, sixteen alleged militants had been arrested. 'We didn't do any torture to them. They told their whole story easily. They said everything we needed to know – they explained everything thoroughly', he asserted just when I was about to raise the issue of the torture routinely practised by the security forces in the country.

When I asked him about the human rights violations allegedly committed by the security forces during counterinsurgency operations, Tin Maung Shwe denied them flatly, claiming: 'We have signed the Geneva Convention, and we carry out operations according to the law. In some villages, the villagers warmly welcome and accept our troops, so there's no problem. In some villages, the people run away. In some places some people attack, using knives and some weapons, the members of the security forces. At that time, the soldiers shoot and then they die.'

When I asked him whether it was necessary to use lethal force against someone attacking soldiers with a mere knife, he replied: 'Your concept is right, but this is an operation area. It means no consideration, no thinking. There's one instruction: if somebody responds, you shoot.' As I continued this line of questioning, he reached the limit of his patience. Eventually, he put an end to our conversation, saying: 'We have to protect our national interests, and those Muslims are not part of them. We don't care about what outsiders think. We must protect our land and our people. Humanitarian concerns are only our second priority.'

Tin Maung Shwe did not offer any evidence in support of his allegations of links between the new Rohingya insurgency and RSO or ISIS; he was merely echoing the official line adopted by the government at the time of depicting Harakah Al-Yakin/ARSA as part of international jihadism.[12] Claims of connections with transnational jihadist networks were also encouraged by Indian media and intelligence sources, which pointed fingers at Pakistani intelligence and extremist groups as associates of the Rohingya insurgents.[13] The ultranationalist Hindu government of Narendra Modi in India had an interest in isolating Pakistan and attracting Burma to its side; but it also wanted to get rid of up to 40,000 Rohingya refugees within its own borders, so such claims, invariably coming from anonymous sources, should be taken with a grain of salt. But they were widely reported by the Burmese media, and gave greater credence to the jihadist narrative many were ready to believe inside the country.

Branding Al-Yakin/ARSA as a Jihadist group served to delegitimize its political grievances and demonize the Rohingya community as a whole; but links between the insurgents and international terrorist networks were at best extremely thin, if not nonexistent. According to a comprehensive report published by the International Crisis Group in the aftermath of the attacks, 'Information from members and analysis of its methods indicate that its approach and objective are not transnational jihadist terrorism.' In public statements issued through YouTube and Twitter, the leaders of the insurgency consistently denied the allegations, asserting that it was fighting for the rights of the Rohingya community.

Al-Yakin/ARSA was reportedly led by a committee of twenty Rohingya exiles living in Saudi Arabia, plus other twenty exiles on the ground in Northern Arakan who had been providing training and organizing villagers throughout the region since the aftermath of the sectarian violence of 2012. Its leader was a man called Ata Ullah, a Rohingya born in Pakistan who had moved with his family to Saudi

Arabia at a young age. With funding from the Rohingya diaspora, he and other exiles infiltrated Northern Arakan and organized independent cells in the region. Fatwas issued by influential imams and mullahs supporting the group's struggle convinced many people to join.

According to an investigation by Agence France-Presse conducted in Pakistan, while organizing Al-Yakin in 2012, Ata Ullah had sought the support of people linked to the Afghan and Pakistani Taliban and Kashmiri separatist groups such as Lashkar-e-Taiba – organizations that had publicly expressed support for the Rohingya and condemned the Burmese government.[14] He had reportedly given some of them huge amounts of money, but had been snubbed and even cheated by jihadis, who took his money but never delivered the promised weapons. He left Pakistan resenting those jihadist organizations that had refused to offer tangible support, and later on he in turn he refused the support such organizations offered when Al-Yakin/ARSA became prominent after its attacks against the Burmese security forces.

By all accounts, Ata Ullah and Al-Yakin/ARSA were committed to an ethno-nationalist struggle for their people. The early overtures to transnational jihadist networks seen to have been purely instrumental – made in order to secure weapons and training. The renaming of the organization from Al-Yakin to ARSA seems to have been an attempt to project a secular image to an international audience that might identify a religiously inflected name with international jihadism.

After meeting Tin Maung Shwe and interviewing several displaced Buddhists, I visited once again the camps where Muslims had been confined since 2012. In the aftermath of the attacks, security had been beefed up, but otherwise not much seemed to have changed. Nevertheless, there was a palpable sense of foreboding everywhere in the camps. Nobody expressed it more eloquently than my old friend Kyaw Hla Aung, the lawyer and politician I had met many times in previous years.

'I have condemned the attacks from the beginning. We have tried to appeal peacefully to the international community, and these attacks are a huge mistake. Other ethnic groups in Myanmar can do that, but we can't', he told me in his rickety house in the village of Tet Kal Pyin. 'We have told repeatedly our Rohingya youth not to engage in violence because we don't like it and it would make things worse for our people, but we cannot control them in this situation.' He also criticized the government for its double standards: 'Why [did the government not] take action against the Rakhine terrorists who set fire [to] Muslim houses in Sittwe four years ago? Now they accuse us of encouraging terrorism, but the government encourages terrorism against us.'

Any possible hope he might have harboured about Suu Kyi's government had faded away completely. 'She can't do anything – she can't even set foot in Rakhine State, and she doesn't know what is happening here', he told me. When I asked him whether he thought that this very sense of hopelessness might have led some young people to take weapons, he answered sadly and somewhat cryptically: 'We are asphyxiated.'

A few months later, in March 2017, I was granted a rare permit to visit northern Arakan. Ever since the emergence of Al-Yakin/ARSA, the government had organized a few tightly controlled tours for selected foreign media, in which there was no freedom to talk with eyewitnesses and local Rohingya without the surveillance of officials. People interviewed during those media tours were harassed by the local authorities for denouncing atrocities committed by the security forces, while others were probably later killed by the insurgents for denying them. But I was able to travel on my own, accompanied by a photographer and my own translator, so we could conduct our interviews without any government official present.

We visited the first village attacked by the security forces after the Al-Yakin/ARSA attacks on 9 October. Myo Thu Gyi, four kilometres away from Maungdaw town, the home of about 1,000 Rohingya people. It was split into two sections, about 500 metres apart, separated by the paddy fields that are the sole source of livelihood for many of its inhabitants.

The first person we interviewed was a man I shall call Hussein Muhammad. Hussein was quite old, probably older than seventy; but, like many people in Northern Arakan, he did not know his real age. An extremely thin man, he sported a white beard that half-covered a face crossed with deep wrinkles. He and his extended family of sixteen people lived in a small compound with two bamboo houses, two latrines and a sink with a couple of taps. On 10 October, at around six in the morning, he was suddenly awakened by the noise of people surrounding his house. More than a dozen armed men, members of the army and the BGP, had invaded the family's compound.

'They asked us if there was any terrorist in our house', Hussein recounted. 'Then they dragged out two of my grandsons and told me they were taking them to talk to their superior. I tried to stop them and gave them my family list to show them they were my grandsons, but they beat me up and threatened me with their weapons.' Hussein could not contain his tears when he recalled how his grandsons were snatched from him. Their names were Ali Muhammed and Ali Ayaz, and they were twenty and thirteen years old. Hussein could not see with his own eyes what had happened next, as he was not allowed to leave the compound. As he begged soldiers and policemen to spare his grandsons, the boys were dragged along with another man to a small forest around one hundred metres away. Ahmed Mahmood, a farmer in his late twenties, was hiding in a hut nearby and could see what happened next: 'Four members of the Border Guard Police made them sit down on the ground with their hands under their legs. One of the policemen executed them while the others were looking around. He kicked them first in their backs and then put a bullet in their heads, one by one. He shot the youngest one twice, once in his back and once in his head.'

'My grandsons had nothing to do with the insurgency. They were here in our house when the insurgents attacked the Border Guard Police. They just sold betel nut, worked, and tried to study. They never got into trouble', Hussein told me while unsuccessfully trying to contain his tears. They had been picked up by the soldiers for the only reason that they were seen peeking through the bamboo fence surrounding the family's compound when the security forces invaded the village.

Around the same time that the grandsons of Hussein Muhammad were executed in the betel nut garden, two military men stormed into a small mud house in the other section of the village. 'They beat up my husband in front of me and my seven children. We cried and pleaded with them, but they didn't listen to us. They kept beating him, and I passed out. When I regained consciousness, he wasn't there', recalled Noor Begum, a fragile woman in her forties who was in the house that day.

The previous afternoon, her husband, Tayoub Ali, a man in his early fifties who made a living doing odd jobs in town, had told his family to stay in their house. He foresaw trouble. He had learned of the insurgent attacks, and had returned home immediately to warn his family. A few hours later, Ali was dragged by the soldiers to a spot near the cemetery.

He was executed there with a shot in the head. His brother had been dragged from his house, but soldiers and border policemen had beaten him so brutally that he was unable to walk, so he was shot halfway to the execution ground, near a vegetable garden on the edge of that section of the village. Fatima, a woman in her twenties whose house was not far from the spot, saw the killings unfold: 'The area was full of soldiers and Border Guard Police; I couldn't distinguish who was which because all of them were wearing dark green raincoats. They were dragging that man, but he could not walk, so they just shot him right there, in front of me.'

A total of seven men were assassinated in Myo Thu Gyi on that fateful day. Several hundred soldiers and members of the Border Guard Police took part in the operation. They returned a couple of hours after the assault to take away the bodies, including those of Muhammad's grandsons. Relatives and neighbours had time to hide three other corpses, including that of Tayoub Ali, in order to give them a proper Muslim burial the next day. My findings were confirmed by Amnesty International, whose researchers had conducted interviews with witnesses who had fled to Bangladesh, and Chris Lewa, director of the organization Arakan Project, who had also conducted interviews with eyewitnesses.

The executions were cruel and completely random, as if the security forces just wanted to take their revenge for the insurgents' attacks without caring whether those they executed were guilty or innocent. The seven men killed were not armed, and they did not attack the security forces; in one case, one man just ran away when he saw the soldiers approaching, and was shot in the back. Only a few hours passed between the attacks by ARSA and the assault on Myo Thu Gyi, and it was impossible that the security forces could have conducted a proper investigation to ascertain whether there were insurgents in the village.

The assault on Myo Thu Gyi was a straightforward case of collective punishment. Similar incidents had happened in several villages throughout Northern Arakan.

A few hours after visiting Myo Thu Gyi, that very same night, we could see things from the other side in Maungdaw town. In an unexpected show of openness, the police allowed us to accompany them for a few hours as they patrolled the town under curfew. The commanders in charge showed a surprising willingness to talk to us.

Maungdaw is a dusty, decaying town that lies along the Naf river, which marks the border with Bangladesh. Only a few of its streets are properly paved, and most of the houses are rickety wooden structures. Most of its inhabitants are Rohingya, but there is a sizeable Rakhine population. The two communities live mostly in segregated quarters, often across the road from one another, but the central market is dominated by Muslims, for whom it is easier to conduct trade across the border. The two communities meet there on a daily basis, but not much elsewhere. An apparent normality reigned during the day, but things were different at night. As we patrolled, the contrast between the Rohingya and the Rakhine quarters was revealed in all its starkness. In the Rakhine quarters, lights were on, and it was not uncommon to see people watching television through open windows or sitting in their courtyards. By contrast, the Rohingya quarters were completely deserted: windows were closed, no light came from any house, and no human presence was visible.

At that time, 600 Rohingya had been arrested, but no leader had been caught and the police were on alert. At one point we stopped and left the vehicle for a cigarette. Kyaw Aye Hlaing, the police captain, remarked: 'They must be hiding somewhere. We know their faces and their names, but for us all these Bengalis look the same, so it's difficult to recognise them. The government has offered them National Verification Cards, but many refused to accept them. That makes our task of identifying people very difficult. I think they refused the NVC cards so they can join the insurgency more easily.' He was apparently unable to recognize the fact that such cards do not offer proof of citizenship, and are seen by many Rohingya as a trap designed to perpetuate their statelessness. As I had seen many times before, any behaviour by the Rohingya was seen in the worst possible light. That was also a consequence of ignorance. Kyaw Aye Hlaing admitted to me that the police had almost no trustworthy Rohingya informants, and virtually no policemen or soldiers spoke their language.

A deeply ingrained contempt for the Rohingya dominated the way the police dealt with them. 'The Bengalis don't belong here. They are illegal immigrants, and they can't possibly integrate because they are uneducated. For instance, [they] don't respect women's rights', Kyaw Aye Hlaing told me in one of our smoking breaks. We somehow engaged in an argument about the way Muslims treated women, and he insisted on giving me a real-life example to prove his point. He called over the Rohingya translator who accompanied the patrol. The man approached with trepidation, visibly intimidated. 'Do you allow your wife to leave your house?' the captain asked him. The translator was cowed, almost trembling, and smiled nervously. He hesitated for a few seconds, possibly pondering what answer would save him from a beating, and he replied with a tentative and barely audible 'No'. Turning to us, Kyaw Aye Hlaing said triumphantly: 'You see? They don't respect women's rights!' Then he dismissed the translator with a brusque gesture, and the man left as quickly as he had approached us.

Assuming that what the translator had said was true, he could have had good reasons for preventing his wife from leaving her home. A month before, the Office of the United Nations High Commissioner for Human Rights had released a report on abuses in Arakan during the 'clearance operations', gathered from hundreds of interviews with refugees in Bangladesh. Fifty-two of the 101 women interviewed reported having suffered rape or sexual violence at the hands of the security forces.[15] The standard argument from Rakhine nationalists and state officials to refute such accusations is that Rohingya women are so ugly and dirty that no Burmese soldier would rape them.

At the end of our tour with the Maungdaw police, we stopped at a bridge that marked the limit of their jurisdiction. I asked Kyaw Aye Hlaing what lay beyond, even though I already knew. One kilometre away, in the darkness and under the jurisdiction of the BGP, was Myo Thu Gyi, the village we had visited without the knowledge of those policemen. When I asked the captain why the security forces had decided to raid that particular village after Al-Yakin/ARSA's attacks, he said: 'We have known for years that this village is full of extremists. It was a very troublesome village during the violence in 2012, so the army and the BGP decided to go there first.' His reply confirmed that no serious investigation had been carried out, and that the raid had been nothing but revenge.

For all their brutality, the 'clearance operations' carried out by the Tatmadaw after October 2016 paled in comparison with what came next. In the early hours of 25 August 2017, ARSA attacked again, this time mobilizing a larger number of villagers in new coordinated attacks at around thirty security forces' positions in Northern Arakan. The attacks came a couple of weeks after the military had increased its presence in the region by sending hundreds of troops there.[16] The move was a reaction to a spate of killings of both Muslim and Buddhist villagers that the government attributed to the insurgents, and was accompanied by the arrests of dozens of alleged militants. Some Rohingya villages in Rathedaung had been blockaded for weeks by the security forces and by their Buddhist neighbours, in what was an increasingly tense environment.[17]

ARSA launched its attacks just hours after the Commission on Arakan State, chaired by Kofi Annan, released its final report and recommendations. In a statement issued the day of the attacks, ARSA blamed the military, accusing it of 'ramping up' its presence in the state 'in order to derail' the work of the Commission.[18] 'We have been taking our defensive actions against the Burmese marauding forces in more than 25 different places across the region', it explained through its Twitter account, arguing that its goal was 'to drive the Burmese colonizing forces away'.[19]

But the arguments deployed by the militant group were scarcely convincing. The attacks may well have been a reaction to previous aggression by the military, but they could hardly be described as defensive. And ARSA, unlike older and much better-established armed insurgent groups elsewhere in the country, lacked any capacity to defend the people it claimed to be protecting, let alone drive away an infinitely more powerful army. The attacks provided the Tatmadaw with an excuse to attack the Rohingya population in northern Arakan in its entirety with a ferocity that was unprecedented.

The new 'clearance operations' launched by the Tatmadaw brought the 'Four Cuts' strategy to its extremes of brutality. And they provided the chance to do something far more drastic than neutralizing a group of ragtag militants. 'The Bengali problem was a long-standing one which has become an unfinished job', were the ominous words of Senior General Min Aung Hlaing, the commander-in-chief of the armed forces, in early September, suggesting a plan to get rid of the Rohingya once and for all. The job was done mostly by two elite light-infantry divisions, the 33rd and the 99th, well-known for their ruthlessness.[20] Their ferocity was enhanced by their hatred towards 'Bengali immigrants'. 'If they're Bengali, they'll be killed', a soldier posted on his Facebook account before heading to northern Arakan. The troops were aided by the local

Border Guard Police, and by some Rakhine villagers who were invited to take part in the orgy of violence.

The brutality of the operations was even visible from space. Two months later, Human Rights Watch released satellite images that showed that 288 Rohingya villages, mostly in Maungdaw township, had been totally or partially destroyed by fire.[21] The government accused the Rohingya of torching their own villages – a style of denial that had become customary since the pogroms in 1978. In the next months, more than 700,000 Rohingya fled to Bangladesh seeking refuge, in what was the biggest and swiftest exodus since the aftermath of the genocide in Rwanda in the mid 1990s. It was also the biggest and swiftest exodus in Burma's history, even dwarfing the exodus of half a million Indians at the beginning of World War II. Around 380,000 of the refugees were children, many of them unaccompanied.[22]

As northern Arakan has been closed to independent researchers since late August 2017, the full scale of the carnage remains unknown. Estimates of the number of Rohingya killed range from 6,700, including 730 children below the age of five, 'in the most conservative estimations' carried out by MSF,[23] to 24,800 deaths and around 18,500 raped, according to a report made by a consortium of international researchers.[24] Some Rohingya refugees worked on elaborating a full list of victims, including their names and villages, and compiled a total of more than 10,000 killed during 'clearance operations' during 2016 and 2017.[25]

Abdullah, a skinny man in his forties, witnessed one of the cruellest massacres. Traumatized and overwhelmed by grief, he told me his story in one of the sprawling refugee camps in Bangladesh two months after the fact. He was a mullah in the religious school of Tula Toli, a village of almost 800 Rohingya households in northern Maungdaw. According to him, relations with Rakhine neighbours from nearby villages had always been peaceful. That peace was broken on 30 August 2016. In the early morning, Aung Kyaw Sein, the Rakhine headman of the whole village, phoned Rohingya leaders in the village to tell them that there were soldiers in a Rakhine village in the north, and that they would later move on to Tula Toli. 'He told us that we didn't have to worry, that nothing would happen to us provided we stayed in our houses, but that they could shoot anybody they saw in the street', Abdullah recounted. Most people seemed to trust the headman, and locked themselves in their houses.

Despite the headman's promises, when around 150 soldiers arrived from the north, they set fire to a house with a rocket launcher, and the flames immediately spread throughout the village to the south, jumping easily from one wood-and-bamboo building to the next. People left their houses, trying to escape from the fire, and many were shot on sight. Some tried to flee to a forest nearby, but a mob of Rakhine villagers armed with machetes and spikes was waiting for them. In this way, the villagers were pushed to the bank of the river marking the southern limit of the village.

Hundreds of them attempted to cross the river while the soldiers shot at them from a hilltop. 'Many people were killed by the bullets as they crossed the river; I managed to escape with other fifteen people', Abdullah told me. Near the cemetery, hidden in the bush, he witnessed the atrocities that unfolded next. 'The military gathered all the people in the same place, and then put them in different groups: one for men, another for old women, another for girls and another for children. Then, a group of soldiers shot the group of men, for about ten minutes, laughing and shouting savagely in Burmese.' Once they had finished, the soldiers walked in the midst of the bodies and finished off the survivors, hacking them with machetes. 'People, men and women, were crying for help, but there was nobody to help them. A group of Rakhine villagers stood nearby, but they did nothing.' The operation was repeated with the older women, after which the soldiers made a big pile out of the bodies, poured petrol on it and set it on fire. 'After that, they threw the small children to the fire – they burned them alive', Abdullah said.

In the meantime, some soldiers had tied the young women to trees nearby. When they finished off the other groups, they untied them and took them to a group of houses that had not been burned by the fires. 'Groups of three or four soldiers entered the houses, taking turns of about half an hour. I couldn't see what was going on inside, but I could imagine. One of my daughters was possibly in one of them', Abdullah recalled, bursting into tears. For three hours, Abdullah watched the soldiers entering and leaving the houses. He remembered that everything was in silence, and he was unable to move, as if possessed by the sheer horror of what he was witnessing.

'When the soldiers finished, they torched the houses one by one. I could hear some of the girls screaming. They didn't even give them the mercy of a quick death – they burned them alive.' Some girls were shot when they escaped from the houses, and a few managed to escape and tell of the rapes they had suffered after reaching Bangladesh. 'After all that, the soldiers left. Some of the people hiding with me went back to the village to see if there was anybody alive, but I just couldn't do it. The idea of discovering the corpses of my wife and my children terrified me', Abdullah recounted. He eventually arrived in Bangladesh, where he was now living with his oldest daughter, who had not been killed in Tula Toli because she was living in another village. 'What happened was the will of God', he concluded, with his face still drenched in pain. It was evident that the thought provided no consolation. A shattered man, Abdullah left the house where we had conducted our interview and was soon lost in the camps.

Tula Toli was a genocidal massacre that has been amply documented by human rights groups, researchers and journalists.[26] The figures of how many Rohingya were killed there, and how many girls were raped before being burned alive, remain a mystery, as only the local authorities have household lists to compare with the number of survivors. Five hundred is probably a conservative estimate, and more than 1,000 most likely. But Tula Toli is not an isolated case. Several genocidal massacres, of varying intensity and scope but similar nature, took place in northern Arakan.[27]

Not all the refugees in Bangladesh had fled from direct violence. Many, particularly those who had been the most recent arrivals two months after the exodus, told me that they had escaped out of fear, as they knew they might be next, and because life there had become unbearable. With their villages surrounded by security forces and mobs of Rakhine villagers, many were not able to farm their lands or go to work anymore. To escape, many had to make gruesome journeys on foot, which often took up to a week, before paying huge sums of money to Bangladeshi boatmen to cross the Naf river, which separates Burma from Bangladesh. Some spent days or even weeks in the no-man's-land separating the two countries. The Burmese government had long ago built a fence on its side, a few metres away from the shore.

In October 2017, when I visited Bangladesh to cover the crisis, a group of up to 5,000 waited under a scorching sun on a beach between the fence and the river. I managed to talk on the phone with one of them, who told me how people were starting to become sick as a consequence of the heat and the scarcity of food. The BGP often observed them from the other side of the fence, not quite telling them to go, but their mere presence reminding them that they were not welcome back in their own country. By then, broken boats lay on the Bangladeshi side of the river, as the local authorities had cracked down on the boatmen who ferried the Rohingya to safety and destroyed many of their boats. The chance of crossing safely had thus diminished, at least at those points in the river that were not narrow enough to swim or walk across. But, two months after the clearance operations, there was still a constant stream of refugees who somehow managed to find a way out of Arakan and cross to what had already become the biggest refugee camp in the world.

By 19 September, less than three weeks after ARSA's attacks and the beginning of the 'clearance operations', around 430,000 Rohingya had already fled to Bangladesh – roughly half the population of northern Arakan. That day, Aung San Suu Kyi gave a speech in Naypyidaw to foreign diplomats and media. She made some extraordinary claims. She assured her listeners that security forces had ceased their 'clearance operations' on 5 September – but that was clearly false, and was contradicted by satellite images showing dozens of villages that had been burned after that date. Ignoring the already numerous reports of atrocities committed against the Rohingya, she said: 'We want to know why this exodus is happening.' She also tried to deflect attention towards the 'positive' side of the story:

> More than 50 per cent of the villages of Muslims are intact. They are as they were before the attacks took place. We would like to know why. This is what I think we have to work towards. Not just looking at the problems, but also looking at the areas where there are no problems. Why have we been able to avoid these problems in certain areas? For this reason, we would like to invite the members of our diplomatic community to join us in our endeavour to learn more from the Muslims who have integrated successfully into the Rakhine State.[28]

The implication was clear: the Rohingya who had fled had done so because they had not 'integrated successfully' – a convoluted argument that amounted to victim-blaming in its purest form. Of course, the number of refugees would almost double over the next few months.

Suu Kyi was not directly responsible for the 'clearance operations' overseen by the commander-in-chief, Min Aung Hlaing, but she tried hard to cover up the atrocities committed by the Tatmadaw. In one instance, responding to allegations of sexual violence against Rohingya women, her official Facebook page called them as instances of 'Fake Rape', in big letters.[29] The Facebook page is probably not personally managed by her. But this woman, who in 2011 had denounced the Tatmadaw for using sexual violence as a weapon of war in the country's border areas, did not comment on the post, and has always expressed scepticism towards any such allegations.[30] Meanwhile, the Karen Women's Organization, a group that has nothing to gain from defending the Rohingya, issued a statement in solidarity with the women who had been raped by Burmese soldiers in northern Arakan.[31]

Suu Kyi was playing the convenient role of a shield for the military, whose public appearances were much rarer. Her public declarations were devoid of shrill racist rhetoric against the Rohingya, but the subtext was clear. It is difficult to know whether she truly believed what she said, but her denials and distortions of the real situation on the ground amounted to vain attempts to hide the ongoing ethnic cleansing of the Rohingya, justifying it or making it palatable to foreign audiences. It had become evident that Aung San Suu Kyi was fully on board with the generals in carrying out once and for all the 'unfinished job' in Arakan, despite some speculation about tensions between the military and civilian wings of government, which she dispelled by saying that relations were 'not that bad', and that the generals in her cabinet were 'all rather sweet'.[32]

Meanwhile, evidence of atrocities was piling up, and the reaction of the authorities was to silence the few Burmese who dared to reveal them. That was the case of two local journalists working for Reuters, Wa Lone and Kyaw Soe Oo, who investigated the massacre of ten Rohingya men in the village of Inn Dinn. Their investigation included chilling interviews with some of the perpetrators themselves, as well as with Rakhine witnesses, and the government was forced to admit the facts – though it claimed that the ten men killed had been 'terrorists', who had to be executed because the ongoing conflict in the area made it difficult to arrest them.[33]

Nonetheless, the young journalists had been arrested by the police and charged with breaking the colonial-era Official Secrets Act. They had been set up by the police, who summoned them, ostensibly to give them some documents, and then arrested them. A policeman even acknowledged that in court, only to be expelled from the police, arrested by his colleagues and jailed. Despite a trial full of irregularities, the journalists were eventually sentenced to seven years in jail. When Aung San Suu Kyi was asked about the sentence in September 2018, she said that the defendants 'were not jailed for being journalists' but for breaking the law. 'I wonder whether very many people have actually read the summary of the judgment which had nothing to do with freedom of expression at all, it had to do with an Official Secrets Act', she added. After repeating her mantra of 'rule of law', she said that it meant 'they have every right to appeal the judgment and to point out why the judgment was wrong'.[34]

The investigation carried out by Wa Lone and Kyaw Soe Oo pushed the Tatmadaw to recognize the killings that its soldiers had perpetrated in Inn Dinn, with another similar massacre the only atrocity committed during the 'clearance operations' in Arakan ever officially acknowledged by the military or the government, even though the authorities claimed that the ten Rohingya villagers assassinated were 'terrorists'. Seven soldiers were arrested and condemned to ten years in jail for their actions. Meanwhile, the reporters appealed their own sentences, but to no avail. Finally, after the Supreme Court upheld their sentences, they were released under a presidential pardon on 7 May 2019, after spending more than 500 days behind bars.[35] Shortly after, it was uncovered that the soldiers who had perpetrated the massacre had been quietly released by the military in November 2018.[36] All in all, the soldiers who killed ten unarmed Rohingya men had spent less time in jail than the journalists who uncovered the massacre.

In the meantime, international criticism had been steadily growing, despite Suu Kyi's increasingly unconvincing attempts to whitewash the situation. One week before her speech in Naypyidaw, Zeid Ra'ad Al Hussein, the United Nations High Commissioner for Human Rights, in Geneva, described the situation as 'a textbook example of ethnic cleansing'.[37] One year later, the Fact Finding Mission appointed by the UN Human Rights Council doubled down on the accusation, concluding its report by saying there was 'sufficient information to warrant the investigation and prosecution of senior officials in the Tatmadaw chain of command, so that a competent court can determine their liability for genocide in relation to the situation in Rakhine State'.[38]

Moreover, the International Criminal Court ruled in September 2018 that it could exercise its jurisdiction on crimes committed against the Rohingya. Burma is not a signatory of the ICC's Rome Statute, but Bangladesh is, and had been affected by the crime of forced deportation when the hundreds of thousands of Rohingya refugees fleeing Arakan flooded Cox's Bazar, on the border with Burma.[39]

It is doubtful that Min Aung Hlaing and his generals will ever face any punishment for their actions beyond seeing their Facebook accounts deleted,[40] but the ruling definitely shattered any illusions about Burma's fabled 'transition to democracy'. China and Russia hold veto power in the UN Security Council, and are likely to use it to block any possible indictment against the Burmese generals. As a consequence, the rapprochement between Burma and Western countries is probably over, and Burma is likely to move closer to China once again. The crisis in Arakan has made Western companies reluctant to invest in Burma and, by the admission of state officials, has already had a negative impact on the country's economy.[41] But the possibility that any of this will push the government to change its policies towards the Rohingya is extremely remote. It is far more likely that the Burmese state will return to some form of isolationism, in order to continue its project of exclusionary nation-building without foreign interference.

The ethnic cleansing of the Rohingya seems to have popular support inside the country. Both the military and the civilian wings of government have justified the military campaign as a fight against terrorism to protect national sovereignty, and ARSA was duly declared a terrorist organization almost immediately after the attacks on 25 August 2017. This was a narrative echoed by most Burmese media, including some outlets formerly in exile that had been highly critical of the military regime. This narrative exaggerates the threat posed by a ragtag group like ARSA, but it has boosted the popular legitimacy of the Tatmadaw to unprecedented levels.

Even one of the most respected religious leaders in Burma supported the military in its fight against 'Bengali terrorists'. The Buddhist monk Sitagu Sayadaw, widely known for his preaching and charity works, gave a sermon to military officers in October 2017 in which he claimed: 'We have learnt and read about that in history books. Buddhist monks and Burmese soldiers are inseparable', before invoking the principle of unity: 'There must be unity between the King (leadership) and its people as well as the unity between the Army and the Sangha (the Monks). The

Four of them also have to be united. It's like the four legs of a chair. They all have to support the country.'[42]

But the most striking passage of the sermon was its apparent endorsement of genocidal violence. Sitagu Sayadaw told an ancient story about a Buddhist king in Sri Lanka who had defeated an army of Hindu Tamils in the fifth century. The king was overwhelmed by remorse after slaughtering 'millions' of Tamil soldiers, and was unable to sleep. A group of eight Arahants (Buddhist monks counselling the monarch) became aware of the king's worries and went to visit him. They tried to reassure him by telling him: 'Do not be worried at all, Your Majesty. It was only a tiny bit of unwholesome action that you have committed'. In the words of Sitagu Sayadaw, they explained their reasoning in the following manner:

> Even though millions of beings had been destroyed, there [were] only one and a half human beings who [were] genuine being[s]. There were only one and a half beings who can be regarded as a human being. Out of these Tamil invaders, there was only one who had adopted the five precepts, and one who had adopted the five precepts and taken the three refuges in the Buddha, the Dhamma and the Sangha. Therefore, there were only one and a half human beings.[43]

After telling this story, Sitagu Sayadaw seemed to distance himself from its message, saying, 'We did not say it, who said it?' and answering himself, 'The Arahants said it.' But the implication of his sermon, in the context of the 'clearance operations' against the Rohingya, was clear. In order to defend Buddhism and the nation, it was allowed to kill men who could not be 'regarded as human beings'.[44]

17

After the Ethnic Cleansing

The military operations against the Rohingya effectively 'cleansed' the three northernmost townships in Arakan, Maungdaw, Buthidaung and Rathedaung of the overwhelming majority of their Muslim population. From those areas, 90 per cent of Rohingya are now in Bangladesh, with somewhere between 400,000 and 600,000 Rohingya remaining in the whole of Arakan State. Many are confined in internment camps and their villages; all are frightened of the authorities, their Buddhist neighbours and a future that appears more dangerous than ever.[1] The government, alleging security concerns, has intermittently blocked the aid agencies on which those communities had relied for years from travelling to northern Arakan, and restricted their access to villages and camps in central Arakan, compounding the misery and fears of the remaining Rohingya.

For some Rakhine nationalists, this situation provided an opportunity to recover what they regard as their land. 'They are not refugees and they have not been expelled from their land – they have returned to their country', Than Tun, a mathematics teacher and well-known civil society leader told me in December 2017, commenting on the exodus. A chubby and short-tempered man in his early fifties, he scolded me harshly whenever I used the word Rohingya, and retorted angrily when I told him that I wanted to tell both sides of the story that 'there is only one true side, ours – those Bengalis are just liars'.

I was interviewing him as the secretary-general of the Ancillary Committee for the Reconstruction of Rakhine National Territory in the

Western Frontier (better known by its more manageable acronym, CRR). The Committee had been created only one week after the ARSA attacks in August that year, with the aim of resettling Rakhine people in the hitherto Muslim-majority areas of northern Arakan. Presided over by Aye Chan, a strongly nationalistic Rakhine historian based in Rangoon, CRR was one of two Rakhine civil society organizations devoted to this project.[2] Its stated goal was to 'recover the demographic balance that existed before the Second World War in Northern Arakan.'[3] To this end, it offered houses to impoverished Rakhine from the slums of Sittwe and other places, paying their expenses for the relocation and to begin their livelihoods. Relying on private donations, CRR had managed to relocate forty families when I interviewed Than Tun, in a project with strong echoes of the Na Ta La villages programme started by the government in the 1990s. Meanwhile, the local authorities had been quietly inviting Buddhists from Bangladesh to settle in northern Arakan as well.[4]

But these projects have been low-key so far. Given that they would lend credence to the accusations of ethnic cleansing the government has so forcefully denied, no mass social engineering project to make northern Arakan a region with a renewed population of 'national races' has yet taken place.

Meanwhile, the military was busy bulldozing dozens of Rohingya villages ravaged by the 'clearance operations', in what seemed an attempt to erase evidence of atrocities committed there. If impartial researchers ever have the chance to visit those sites in the future, it will be extremely difficult for them to find mass graves or signs of the violence perpetrated by the security forces.[5] The government duly denied that it was destroying evidence, alleging that the bulldozing was being done 'to ensure that the buildings for the people that return can be easily built' – an unconvincing explanation that implicitly assumed that the repatriation would happen anytime soon.[6] In any case, those who might want to go back, provided they were allowed to return to their old villages, would have to live in close proximity to the same military personnel who had expelled them in the first place, as the Tatmadaw began building new military bases in many of the emptied villages as part of its further securitization of the region.[7]

As part of the 'unfinished job' of ethnically cleansing Northern Arakan, the government reclaimed the land of abandoned villages in the name of development. One month after the military operations, the minister for social development, relief and resettlement announced that burned villages would become 'government-managed land', applying a law about reconstruction in areas damaged in natural disasters, including fires.[8] Moreover, when the 'clearance operations' were raging, the local government had announced that it would establish an economic zone in Maungdaw dedicated to fostering trade and industry in the area.[9] The government also created the Union Enterprise for Humanitarian Assistance, Resettlement and Development in Rakhine, which has channelled and coordinated efforts to rebuild northern Arakan, mostly through investments by the wealthy 'cronies' that Suu Kyi has done so much to bring to her side.[10] The enterprise is portrayed as a 'patriotic duty', and includes the reinforcement of the fence separating Arakan from Bangladesh to prevent 'illegal immigration'.

Some analysts have argued that the driver of the crisis in Arakan is land-grabbing, as opposed to intercommunal tension or narrow ethno-nationalism. But such explanations reduce a highly complex conflict to a crude materialism that ignores the forces at play in Arakan and Burma.[11] Land-grabbing for development projects is more a consequence of the ethnic cleansing of the Rohingya than a primary cause of it. Some wealthy businessmen will likely benefit from it, but the ethnic cleansing is primarily the consequence of the state's project of nation-building, not of a capitalistic greed that has merely grabbed a good opportunity.

The 'unity' and 'national reconciliation' so long advocated by Aung San Suu Kyi and other politicians seemed at last to have arrived in the aftermath of the ethnic cleansing – at least for the Burman majority. There was a consensus among virtually all Burmans who had a voice in the country's public sphere – politicians, journalists, activists, monks – about closing ranks around the military and the civilian government when it came to the Rohingya, either by denying the brutality or by offering justifications of it. It was often implied that the 'Bengalis' had got what they had deserved for decades. Even pro-democracy activists who knew well how brutal the Tatmadaw could be, either through their own experiences or those of their comrades, and had denounced it for years, chose to keep silent or denied the atrocities; some even joined in cheering its campaign to defend 'national sovereignty'.

Nobody can say for sure how many Burmese share these views, but it is safe to assume that many follow what seems to be the national consensus. In any case, speaking out in favour of the Rohingya inside Burma is potentially dangerous.

Meanwhile, international condemnation has been met with defensiveness bordering on xenophobia. The reaction to criticisms of the military or of Suu Kyi has been to portray them as 'bullying' from more powerful countries, and many have taken refuge in anticolonial rhetoric to fend off what they see as aggressive interference in national affairs, while conspiracy theories abound about Muslims worldwide plotting against Burma and controlling the UN. It appears as if the whole country were complicit in the brutal ethnic cleansing of the Rohingya, and such complicity is doing more than anything to reinforce an increasingly paranoid Burmese nationalism.

Nevertheless, there are limits to such unity, and they largely coincide with ethnic boundaries. Rakhine nationalists may join forces with the military and the government when it comes to dealing with the Rohingya, but their resentment towards Burman domination is never too far from the surface. Thus, in January 2018, Rakhine nationalists made plans to organize an event commemorating the 233rd anniversary of the fall of the Arakanese kingdom to the Burmese in Mrauk-U, the ancient royal capital of Arakan. The authorities cancelled the event and thousands of protestors took the streets. The demonstration became rowdy and, when the police intervened, eight demonstrators were shot dead.[12] The incident happened a few days after a prominent Rakhine writer and Aye Maung, chairman of the Arakan National Party, were arrested by the police for giving speeches in Sittwe that were highly critical of the government. Both would be prosecuted for the crimes of high treason and defamation of the state.[13]

Meanwhile, the Arakan Army (AA) continued to operate both in northern Burma, where it is part of the Northern Alliance, and in some areas in central Arakan, on the border with Chin State. Then, on 4 January 2019, the anniversary of Burma's independence, the AA launched its most ambitious operation to date inside Arakanese territory, attacking four police posts in the township of Buthidaung, killing thirteen policemen and injuring nine.[14] The date was not chosen randomly, as on that day a six-month ceasefire began that had been unilaterally declared by the Tatmadaw in the north of the country and that excluded the territory of Arakan, in the same way as the AA, duly declared a terrorist organization, was excluded from the peace process between the Burmese army and other ethnic armed organizations.

Thus began a major escalation of the ongoing conflict between the Rakhine guerrillas and the Tatmadaw, in which the AA has steadily reinforced its fighting strength as well as its popular support, and the military has ramped up its presence in the state. The conflict has affected even urban centres like the town of Mrauk-U, and the Army has deployed helicopters and heavy artillery to fight the guerrillas.[15] Information from the ground is difficult to come by, as the Tatmadaw has closed the area to external observers and even blocked internet access in the regions affected by the conflict for more than one month in the summer of 2019, which has had the side effect of making it extremely difficult to deliver humanitarian aid. As of July 2019, it is calculated that more than 55,000 people have been displaced from their villages to makeshift camps in several townships.[16] By all accounts and my personal observations, the AA enjoys wide support among the Rakhine population and Arakan will probably turn into the theatre of another protracted war in a way not too dissimilar to Kachin state.[17] The Burmese government, the Tatmadaw and Rakhine ethno-nationalists may have largely resolved the 'unfinished business' of expelling most of the Rohingya population, but that has not brought peace to Arakan, and the old conflict between Rakhine nationalists and the Burman-dominated government, which seemed to be somewhat dormant as long as they faced the common enemy of the 'Bengali intruders' has returned with a vengeance.

Meanwhile, on the other side of the border, the Bangladeshi authorities insisted that the refugees should return to their country as quickly as possible. This suited the Burmese government; Suu Kyi said from early on that Burma was 'prepared to start the verification process at any time' for those refugees who wished to return to Burma. It is doubtful that her government and the Tatmadaw had any sincere intention of receiving the refugees, but they needed to show they were willing to do so in order to deflect accusations of ethnic cleansing and genocide. Three months after the beginning of the exodus, when many Rohingya were still crossing the border to the neighbouring country, Burma and Bangladesh signed a repatriation agreement that was essentially based on the one they had signed in 1993.[18]

A few months later, in May 2018, the United Nations signed a Memorandum of Understanding with the Burmese government for the repatriation.[19] The terms of the MoU were kept secret at first at the insistence of the Burmese, and the refugees themselves were not consulted in its drafting. As we have seen in the cases of previous exoduses in 1978 and 1992, the UN scarcely has an honourable record in dealing with Rohingya refugees. Not bothering to hear their voices, and negotiating behind their backs with the very same government that has tortured, expelled and killed them is part of an unedifying tradition.

I talked with many refugees in the camps who expressed their wish to return to their land, but were too afraid to return under the prevailing conditions. Almost invariably, they voiced the same demands: that the government restore full citizenship to them, that their rights be respected, that their properties be returned to them, that justice be done for the atrocities they had suffered, and that they be provided with adequate protection. Neither the agreement that Burma signed with Bangladesh nor the MoU that it agreed with the UN, which was leaked a few weeks later, made any reference to citizenship or freedom of movement.[20] The refugees were aware that the Burmese government would not be willing to meet their demands anytime soon, and they knew all too well that returning would mean delivering themselves into the hands of an army that had massacred so many of their community.

The Burmese government declared that the repatriation could be completed within two years – but the two reception centres it had set up could only process 300 returnees per day.[21] At that rate, it would take ten years to take back into Burma all the refugees from Bangladesh.[22] Moreover, the Burmese government has never guaranteed that it will allow them to return to their villages, or help restore the property of their lands and rebuild their houses. It has even prepared some 'processing centres' that, given Arakan's recent history, might easily turn into permanent concentration camps.[23] As a consequence, the offers of repatriation have had virtually no takers so far. And the few who have accepted have suffered torture at the hands of the police during long periods of detention.[24]

The refugees live in extremely precarious camps, where sanitation, health and education services are sorely lacking. In late August 2018, the

UN had attained less than 34 per cent of the funding deemed necessary for the camps.[25] The refugees are not legally allowed to work, or even to leave the camps, and monsoon rains provoke landslides, contributing to the spread of disease. Yet, despite the harsh conditions, many of them told me: 'At least we are safe here.'

The camps are built in a government forest reserve, and have had a negative impact on the environment. The initial hospitality with which the host community in Cox's Bazar and Teknaf received the Rohingya is not inexhaustible. Hostility among the local population grew after a few months, as food prices increased and salaries decreased due to the large pool of desperate people willing to work in exchange for little money.[26] The refugee crisis has also contributed to a reduction in the price of drugs, as many desperate Rohingya in the camps have fallen prey to criminal networks trafficking methamphetamine (known as *yaba* in Burma), produced in Shan State and smuggled to Bangladesh.[27]

There is little doubt that almost one million Rohingya, including the 700,000 who arrived in the 2017 exodus and those who had fled before, will remain in those camps for the foreseeable future; but everybody responsible for making decisions on their fate seems unable to acknowledge that fact, and act accordingly. The Bangladeshi government has already made clear that it does not want them in the long term. 'We are not thinking of assimilating them in Bangladesh. They belong to Myanmar', the Bangladeshi foreign secretary said in September 2018.[28]

The Burmese government needs to pretend it is ready to accept them, for reasons already explained. The UN agencies are trapped by the inertia involved in dealing with refugees by confining them in camps, which has a long history.[29] Integrating them into the host community – an idea that has worked in other contexts[30] – is not something that seems to have been contemplated, as it would be an admission of the fact that nobody wants to confront but is increasingly inescapable: a million Rohingya are in Bangladesh for the long haul. The only possible preparation for a long-term presence of the refugees has tentatively been made by Bangladesh: dumping at least 100,000 of them on an island in the Bay of Bengal, which is barely liveable for so many people and is badly exposed to typhoons and other natural disasters.[31]

Deprived of their legal status at home, and not recognized as citizens in Burma or anywhere else, almost one million Rohingya refugees are effectively treated as a burden to bear, or a problem to tackle, rather than

as human beings. They are thus condemned to a life of passive accept-
ance of their fate, decided by others who have paid little attention to
their voices. Their plight in Burma, Bangladesh and elsewhere poign-
antly illustrates what Hannah Arendt wrote in *The Origins of
Totalitarianism*:

> The fundamental deprivation of human rights is manifested first and
> above all in the deprivation of a place in the world which makes opin-
> ions significant and actions effective. Something much more funda-
> mental than freedom and justice, which are rights of citizens, is at
> stake when belonging to the community into which one is born is no
> longer a matter of course and not belonging no longer a matter of
> choice, or when one is placed in a situation where, unless he commits
> a crime, his treatment by others does not depend on what he does or
> does not do. This extremity, and nothing else, is the situation of people
> deprived of human rights. They are deprived, not of the right of free-
> dom, but of the right of action; not of the right to think whatever they
> please, but of the right to opinion.[32]

We have seen in previous chapters how the Rohingya were stripped over
the years of their 'right to action' and their 'right to opinion' within
Burma. Outside Burma, as refugees in Bangladesh, at least they are not
killed or tortured en masse; but, like many other refugees in the world,
they are deprived of 'a place in the world', and rendered equally power-
less – deprived of their rights to both action and opinion.

Al-Yakin/ARSA disappeared from view once again after the second
wave of 'clearance operations' in 2017. Two weeks after its wave of
attacks in late August, it declared a one-month 'unilateral ceasefire' in
order to allow humanitarian access to the affected areas.[33] Nevertheless,
nothing happened after that month; indeed, at the time of writing, it has
not launched any further attack. It is difficult to know whether its inac-
tivity in Burma is due to a lack of resources or unwillingness to carry on
a struggle that backfired disastrously, but the group seems to be dormant,
and the whereabouts of its leader Attah Ullah are unknown.

Nevertheless, it is common knowledge that ARSA can rely on a
network of militants in the refugee camps in Bangladesh. In the first
year after the beginning of the exodus, about two dozen refugees, mostly

community leaders, were savagely murdered in mysterious circumstances.[34] Some of them had publicly criticized the insurgent group, blaming it for their people's plight, and that has prompted accusations that ARSA members might be behind the killings, though the group has forcefully denied the accusations, claiming that other unspecified armed groups have used its name to tarnish its image. These cases may well never be solved, and the Bangladeshi authorities have declared that they are the consequence of criminal activities and personal feuds that some refugees have pursued from Burma.[35]

In any case, ARSA is not above killing civilians. As we have seen, in all likelihood militants killed dozens of Rohingya informants and suspected collaborators, as well as villagers of other ethnicities, but there may be more. On May 2018, Amnesty International accused the group of perpetrating a massacre of up to ninety-nine Hindu villagers during its attacks in August the previous year.[36] They would also have kidnapped several Hindu women and, after forcibly converting them to Islam, taken them to Bangladesh. Amnesty International concluded that the perpetrators had been members of ARSA, but did not specify whether the killings were ordered by the leadership or were committed by rogue elements within the group. The report does not answer all the questions about the massacre, but it casts strong suspicion on the militants.

ARSA denied the allegations, and many Rohingya and pro-Rohingya activists condemned Amnesty International in the strongest terms. Ironically, the reaction by many of them mirrored the usual response to allegations of atrocities by the Tatmadaw from Burmese and Rakhine nationalists. Just as the latter often peddle conspiracy theories about international human rights organizations being on the payroll of Muslim countries, now some Rohingya activists made use of social media to accuse Amnesty International of having been bribed by the Burmese government. Also ironic, but not entirely unsurprising, was the reaction of the Burmese state media, which used Amnesty International's report to denounce ARSA when it had in the past invariably dismissed the findings of the organization when it pointed to the far more extensive and systematic atrocities committed by the military. The controversy brought to light the clash of irreconcilable narratives that is simultaneously a cause and a consequence of the conflict in Arakan.

We may never know for sure who was behind the massacre of Hindus in northern Arakan, as the blockage by the government makes any investigation on the ground impossible. In any case, if ARSA has damaged anyone, it is undeniably the Rohingya community itself, by provoking an entirely predictable response from the Burmese military. It is true that ARSA had its supporters among the Rohingya. In one of the camps in Bangladesh, a woman told me: 'They are our people and they are fighting for our Rohingya homeland and our rights. We are ready to die in the fight for our future generations.' But many others blamed ARSA for their fate, some of whom were themselves disillusioned members of the group.

One of them was a twenty-one-year-old man I shall call Rasheed Ali, who I interviewed in a safe house in the Bangladeshi camps in October 2017. He used to live in a village in southern Maungdaw, where he worked as a farmer. In June 2017, as he was walking to his house after praying in the local mosque, the mullah who had taught him to recite the Koran when he was a child approached him with an offer he could not refuse. 'He told me that I had to join ARSA to defend our religion, which is under attack in our country, and that ARSA was also fighting for our rights so we could recover our citizenship', Rasheed Ali told me. When he showed some hesitation, the mullah insisted: 'He told me I would be branded as a traitor if I refused to join, that he would make sure that the community would shun me and that I could even be killed.' The young recruit claimed that he did not receive any training, and was kept in the dark about ARSA's wider strategy. He only knew seven other members from his village, and he received orders solely from the mullah, without having any knowledge of the organization's hierarchy beyond him. His only task was to watch the movements of four local informants and periodically report on them. 'You have to do it for God', the mullah told him.

The case of Rasheed Ali is not unique. The human rights organization Fortify Rights has documented the use of coercion and threats to recruit reluctant militants in several villages.[37] But many other young men, frustrated and hopeless, joined voluntarily. Others still were deceived into doing so.

One month before Rasheed Ali was coerced into joining the militants, a man in another village volunteered to do so. 'People of Al-Yakin came to our village and asked us to join them. We liked them because they assured us that they would get citizenship and rights for us. Some village elders knew people in the group and told us to join. A famous mullah in the village also told us that it was the right group to join, because they keep religious practices and follow the Prophet', said Ahmad Jarmal (not his real name), a twenty-five-year-old shopkeeper, in the same safe house in Bangladesh. He estimated that around a hundred people had signed up in his village, many of them his friends. He asked his recruiter when they would receive weapons to fight the military. 'They told us we didn't have to worry, so we thought we would receive weapons at some point. But we never got them', he told me. Like Rasheed Ali, Ahmad Jarmal did not receive any training, and was in touch with only a few other members and his immediate superior – a man he was told received his orders from the organization's commanders. 'When I joined, one of my tasks was to be a sentry in the village, to warn people if the BGP or the military approached the village. Another task was to make sure people fulfilled their religious duties, so we would tell them to go to the mosque before prayers if we saw them walking in the street.'

Rasheed Ali's experiences with ARSA suggest that religion plays a bigger role in the group than its public statements reveal, but this does not necessarily imply an al-Qaeda or ISIS-style jihadist ideology. In general, Rohingya society is profoundly religious and conservative, and any movement that wants to mobilize its members would have to appeal to religion. Nevertheless, it is unknown how extensive the practice was of using its members as the sort of 'religious police' that he described, though it probably depended on the leaders in each village.

Both Rasheed Ali and Ahmad Jarmal were adamant that they had no prior knowledge of the attacks on 25 August 2017. They only learned of them later, when the military and BGP attacked their villages in retaliation. Ahmad Jarmal recalled, 'The day after the attacks, the BGP came to our village and some Rakhine people joined them. We wanted to fight them, but we only had sticks and knives. We couldn't defend ourselves, and we ran. My brother was shot by the BGP and I carried him, but he died when we reached the border. I saw four people shot by the BGP. All the people in the village fled, and the BGP and the Rakhine torched our houses.' Burmese security forces attacked the village of Rasheed Ali in the early hours of 26 August, and he was forced to flee alone. He found his family a day later, hiding in a nearby pond, and they subsequently travelled together to Bangladesh. Finally, after their gruelling journeys, both men and their surviving family members reached the border with Bangladesh, and were taken to the camps.

Both ARSA members were deeply embittered at the group's leadership, and by not having been informed about its plans for the attacks. 'If I could talk with the leaders I would ask them, "Why did you do this? You knew we couldn't win and that the Tatmadaw and the BGP would massacre us. Why didn't you just kill us directly?"', Rasheed Ali said. Furthermore, he believed that ARSA 'provoked the military deliberately' to trigger a reaction against its own people that they were hardly equipped to counter or resist. Ahmad Jarmal also felt betrayed. He told me he no longer regarded himself as a member of the group, even though he could not sign off without risking his life, and still had to pretend he was part of it. When I asked about his desire to fight back against Myanmar's military, he replied: 'I would join the struggle if we got weapons, wherever they come from.'

The strategy of ARSA is difficult to comprehend, and its public utterances, with their hollow claims of protecting its own people, provide few clues. The group clearly lacked the weapons, capacity and numbers to protect anybody against the immensely more powerful Tatmadaw, and by its actions provoked retaliation from the security forces that had made life much worse for the people it purported to be defending. Even the words of Atta Ullah, the leader of the organization, seemed to contradict claims that ARSA was defending its own people. In an interview he gave to Reuters, he said, 'If we don't get our rights, if 1 million, 1.5 million, all Rohingya need to die, we will die. We will take our rights. We will fight with the cruel military government.'[38] Abu Abdul Wahed, another leader of the organization, said to the *Dhaka Tribune*: 'How long must we remain silent? For over 70 years, the Burmese have been oppressing us. Until we fight back, this culture of oppression will not end. We will keep fighting till the global community forces Myanmar to ensure our civil and human rights.' He added grimly: 'To gain something, you have to lose something. We have been dying for 70 years. At least now the world is taking notice of our deaths!'[39]

These statements show that the leaders of the insurgent group were well aware of the consequences of their actions for their people, but were apparently willing to risk those consequences, perhaps because they expected a strong international reaction against the Burmese government. In the process, their plans unleashed the killings of thousands, possibly tens of thousands, of Rohingya, and the biggest mass displacement in Burma's history. Erecting themselves as representatives of the Rohingya, they took a gamble in which they put at stake the lives of countless others. Once again, most Rohingya were stripped of their power to decide their fate – only this time they were stripped of that power by people of their own ethnicity, who were doing so in the name of their freedom and their rights.

The twisted logic that seemed to underlie the actions of ARSA's leadership, in which clearly offensive actions like the attacks in October 2016 and August 2017 are described as 'defensive', and decisions that surely lead one's own civilians to almost certain death are justified as 'protective', is only possible in the context of a genocide – a crime that ARSA has attributed to the Burmese government. Sacrificing the lives of thousands of innocents in the name of saving the community only makes sense if those lives are seen as doomed in any case – that is, if the community is *already* suffering the 'crime of crimes'.

The accusation of genocide had become widespread among pro-Rohingya activists since 2012. As we have seen, some have argued that a 'slow-burning genocide' began in the late 1970s, when the regime of General Ne Win began to ramp up its discriminatory policies against the Rohingya. The notion is almost a contradiction in terms, and does not bear any serious scrutiny, as it implies a genocidal *intent*, stretching for decades, that is willingly slowed down for some reason by successive governments. Equally, it fails to take into account how erratic and unsystematic policies aimed at containing the alleged 'Bengali demographic threat' have been.

But the word has been used as a political weapon by activists, rather than as an analytical tool, and has taken root. This is not to deny the seriousness of the crimes committed by the Burmese state for four decades, but only to point out that the sum of such crimes did not amount to genocide – at least until 2016 or 2017. The Burmese government's policies were animated by an ideology of exclusion that was potentially genocidal, and contributed to creating the conditions in which genocide, or at last ethnic cleansing, was possible, provided there was a trigger that the military could use to depict the Rohingya as an urgent existential threat to Burma.

ARSA may well have provided such a trigger. What has befallen the Rohingya since the emergence of the insurgent group can be more credibly described as genocide than anything that had happened to them before – at the very least, it is an example of very brutal ethnic cleansing, and the difference between the two is not clear-cut. To the extent that the actions of ARSA contributed to provoking it, and may have been conducted on the assumption that a 'slow-burning genocide' was taking place, the catastrophe that has befallen the Rohingya since 2016 can be read as a self-fulfilling prophecy.

But these considerations should not make us lose sight of the real identity of the primary and ultimate culprits for the tragedy of the Rohingya: the generals who ordered the successive waves of 'clearance operations' in 2016 and 2017; a pro-democracy opposition that played a large role in spreading and consolidating racial prejudices against them; a civilian government, led by the saint-patron of that former opposition, that defended the military, legitimized hate speech, and failed to take any action to integrate the Rohingya into Burmese society. It was they who perpetrated or supported the atrocities against the Rohingya, exaggerating the threat represented by ARSA; but it was also they who created the conditions in which a group like ARSA could find fertile ground in the first place.

By disenfranchising the Rohingya – stripping them of citizenship, political representation and any hope that their future would be different to the misery they had known – they opened the door to violence as the only imaginable means for them to regain their rights and their dignity. There is another self-fulfilling prophecy here. For years, the Rohingya have been accused of terrorism, while in fact they had not engaged in any form of armed struggle for decades. At the same time, those very policies of disenfranchisement, partially based on the baseless accusation of terrorism, in fact pushed them to embrace an organization that many Burmese could credibly see as terrorist, thus justifying the final crackdown on the Rohingya.

In short, ARSA provided the Tatmadaw with an excuse for completing what Senior General Min Aung Hlaing had described as its 'unfinished job'. By all indications, when ARSA struck in August 2017, the military was well prepared to carry out those plans, having already sent several battle-hardened divisions to northern Arakan; but without the insurgents' attacks in October 2016, and the expectation that they would strike again, those plans would probably have not been laid.

There was little hope for the Rohingya before 2016, as it is doubtful that the government would have implemented the sensible recommendations made by the Kofi Annan Commission; but today there is even less hope. Anti-Rohingya sentiment has probably never been higher in Burma, and it is very unlikely that international sympathy for its victims will be translated in any meaningful action to restore their rights. In any case, the solution to their plight has to come from within their own country; their tragedy will continue as long as they are rejected as a strange, malignant 'influx virus' in Burmese, with no legitimate right to speak with their own voice and no place in the nation.[40] And there are no indications that this is going to change in the foreseeable future.

Conclusion: The Failure of Burmese Nationalism

The brutal 'clearance operations' that pushed out more than half of the Rohingya population in 2017 were the culmination of the gradual process of expulsion from Burmese social and political life initiated by the Ne Win regime in the late 1970s. This process should not be read as an intentional plan devised by Ne Win and carried out by his regime and its heirs over the years, with extermination as its deliberate ultimate goal, as the 'slow-burning genocide' thesis claims. Criminal and gravely harmful to the Rohingya though his policies were, there is no reason to believe that Ne Win had in mind the final eradication of the Rohingya when he ordered Operation Naga Min in 1978, or introduced a new Citizenship Law in 1982. The Burmese state has implemented many policies of exclusion and apartheid against the Rohingya ever since, but, far from coherent or systematic, they have been mostly ad hoc, and have occasionally even appeared to go against this general trend of exclusion, as when the Rohingya were allowed to vote in the referendum for the Constitution in 2008 and the general election in 2010.

There have been two changes of regime since 1978, and it is very difficult to believe that all the leaders in Burma were following a long-term plan carefully drawn in the middle of the Ne Win era. The 'Rohingya problem' only gradually acquired over the years the central role as the legitimizing tool for the regime that it plays now, and it seems that the military has for many years had two fundamental goals: its own survival, and maintaining national unity. It has struggled on both fronts. The

Tatmadaw has managed to maintain its power, but national unity remains elusive. I have argued, on the one hand, that the military is the most powerful institution in the country and, on the other, that it was never strong enough to impose anything close to a 'totalitarian' state, as its control over the population and territory of Burma has always been far from complete. The two statements are not incompatible. The fact that the military is the strongest and most enduring force in the country's politics does not mean it wields absolute power. In these circumstances, its policies against the Rohingya were far from coherent and systematic.

That does not exculpate the various people making decisions on the Rohingya over the years from pursuing the specific policies they have implemented; but they are not fully responsible for a final outcome that they did not necessarily either foresee or intend – as far as we know, given the extraordinarily opaque nature of the regime. The fact that there are strong reasons to suspect, for instance, that Ne Win might not have lamented the final outcome is not relevant to the apportioning of responsibility for what he did, at least from a legal point of view. The record shows that what Ne Win wanted to accomplish was the containment of a population that he and many others erroneously perceived as foreign, and to block the entrance of massive waves of 'illegal immigrants' that only existed in their imagination – not that his policies were aimed at obliterating the Rohingya. Whatever the criminal nature of his policies – and there is no dispute that they were indeed criminal – they were not necessarily genocidal in themselves.

Something similar could be argued about the policies implemented by the SLORC/SPDC through the 1990s. In a sense, those policies backfired spectacularly by their own standards: if their goal was to contain the demographic growth of the Rohingya population, we have seen that the result was the opposite from the late 1970s and early 1980s – a period in which the growth rate among the Rohingya population was higher than over the previous part of the post-independence era. The Tatmadaw managed only to contain them geographically, while making life for most of them utterly miserable.

There are two interconnected qualifications to make here, both of which cut to the bone of the tragedy of the Rohingya. The policies implemented by the Burmese state between the late 1970s and the emergence of ARSA in 2016 may not have been genocidal, but they were the key factor in creating the conditions in which a genocide, or a very brutal ethnic cleansing, became increasingly likely. Secondly, such policies were primarily motivated by a series of assumptions – what I have called the 'national races ideology' – that are potentially genocidal, insofar as they violently excluded the Rohingya. In short, the Burmese leaders have framed the Rohingya as a 'problem to be solved', and this framing has pushed them to adopt increasingly radical and murderous 'solutions', culminating, in 2017, in the extremely violent expulsion of hundreds of thousands and the massacre of perhaps tens of thousands of people.

The 'national races ideology' is more a worldview, a conceptual framework within which people are categorized, than a coherent doctrine – a system of ordering rather than a programme. And it is not only adhered to by the Tatmadaw. As has become increasingly clear in the period of political opening that began in 2011, it is shared by the most influential figures of the old pro-democracy camp, and possibly the majority of Burmese. That does not mean that every single person in Burma believes in the 'national races ideology' – a claim that is impossible to substantiate. But there is little doubt that it is a hegemonic idea that very few challenge inside the country, and that determines irrevocably who is seen as belonging in Burma.

In this context, it is not surprising that Rohingya activists and intellectuals should articulate their claim to citizenship mostly on the basis that they are a 'national race' whose roots in Burma are as deep as those of any other indigenous ethnic group – and even deeper than those of the Rakhine – often downplaying or altogether denying the fact that many are descendants of Chittagonian migrants who entered Burma during colonial times.[1] It may be argued that these Rohingya activists are legitimizing the very same worldview that underpins their exclusion; but they are Burmese too, and it is no surprise that they should share a conceptual framework so deeply ingrained in Burmese political and social life.

Some observers have asserted that it would be easier for the Rohingya to regain their citizenship by arguing that most of them arrived before independence, avoiding claims to a distinct ethnicity that apparently only serve to antagonize Rakhine nationalists, and the Burmese government and public at large.[2] But that assumes a good faith on the part of the Burmese government, as well as respect for its own laws, that has been entirely lacking for decades. The Rohingya are seen as outsiders no matter what, so it is only natural that they should emphasize their indigenousness over strictly legalistic arguments. Those are the rules of the game in Burma, where rights are allocated collectively on the basis of ethnicity, rather than individually. As a result, some Rohingya may at times distort their own history to gain citizenship; but that only mirrors the historical distortions made by those who have deprived them of their rights.

It is true that the Rohingya as an ethnic group fit uneasily within the classification system of the national races – which, as we have seen, determines that those groups that were in Burma before the colonial period are the only ones that qualify as such. Many of the ancestors of present-day Rohingya date their presence in Arakan back several centuries before the arrival of the British, though many others arrived during the colonial period. The numbers of those who arrived after independence are negligible; but since the group as such is regarded as foreign, past colonial migration from Bengal is transposed to the present era. The problem is not whether or not the Rohingya fit within the classification system; the problem is the system itself.

The national races ideology anachronistically presupposes that rigid borders between nation-states and ethnic groups that only exist today as social realities were already in place before the arrival of the British. As we have seen, Arakan had for centuries been a frontier area between Burma and Bengal in which the two cultural worlds mixed indistinguishably. Consequently, the hard border between Rohingya and Rakhine ethnicities that came into being later simply did not exist until the colonial period. The two groups emerged as separate entities in opposition to each other after the arrival of the British, with their penchant for imposing rigid ethnic classifications, with corresponding geographical territories.

The various peoples inhabiting Burma were thrown during the colonial period into the world of modern nation-states that was imposed upon them, as it was on most of the colonized world, in a deeply traumatic manner. As Étienne Balibar has pointed out, 'In a sense, every modern nation is a product of colonization: it has always been to some degree colonized or colonizing, and sometimes both at the same time.'[3] Such was the case in Burma, and the Burmans had been alternately colonized and colonizers. Such was the modern world of nations in which those groups emerged as political actors that would contend for power in the Burmese nation-state after independence: the Burmans, the Kachin, the Rakhine, the Rohingya, and so on. This is the most enduring legacy of the colonial period – not so much the specific classifications of ethnic groups the British contributed so much in solidifying, but the world-view itself that divides different human groups into watertight boxes called 'nations'. Nonetheless, the members of such groups were not mere passive recipients of classifications imposed from above; they also contributed to cementing such classifications by turning their own groups into political actors in whose name their leaders made their demands and expressed their grievances. These are the origins of the 'national races ideology', from which the Rohingya were excluded early on, as the British made a clear-cut and artificial distinction between Arakan, which was seen as part of the Burmese world, and Bengal, which was not.

There were constant debates on strategy and ideology between the various nationalist movements that emerged during the colonial period. They also debated what groups belonged to the future Burmese inde-pendent nation – though most nationalists seemed to accept the ethnic distinctions introduced by the British. Aung San favoured accepting the Indian immigrants who wished to remain in the country after inde-pendence, and wanted to create a unified nation that would include disparate groups that had never before existed under the same political authority. But from early on, Burmese nationalism contained two assumptions that were two sides of the same coin: national unity among different 'national races', and an implicit exclusion of those who do not belong to them.

Those two assumptions served as the ideological underpinnings of the wars in the borderlands, and ultimately of the ethnic cleansing of the Rohingya. They were already part of the 1947 Constitution and the 1948 Citizenship Laws. The concept of 'national races' figured as one of the criteria of belonging within the new nation, albeit not the primary one. The Indians were viewed with deep suspicion in the first years after independence, and the Rohingya were at the time seen by many as Indians rather than Burmese – though there were signs that the government was willing to accept them as one of the 'national races'. Meanwhile, the central government and the Tatmadaw began to be dominated by leaders hailing from the Burman majority from a very early stage, and were bent on imposing a unitary model of the state that paid little attention to demands for self-determination of the ethnic minorities in the borderlands, distrusting them as collaborators of the colonial power.

In the first years after independence, Burma was an extremely fragile and weak state besieged on virtually every front, with Communists and ethno-nationalist insurgencies and the Kuomintang incursions in the north threatening its aspirations of national unity and sovereignty. The Tatmadaw, built by Ne Win, emerged during the first years of independence as the strongest single force, and the dictator assigned himself the mission of 'giv[ing] the Burmese people back their country' and preserving national unity. In the process, rather than giving the country to the Burmese, he gave it to the military for many years to come.

With his dictatorship, Burmese nationalism, which had been a tool of liberation from British domination, was turned into a tool of oppression; but its ideological underpinnings changed little. Ne Win was a product of his time, and he believed in ideas of what Burma should be that were shared by many Burmese. The military dictatorships of Ne Win and the SLORC/SPDC did not create the inter-ethnic and inter-communal divisions that have plagued the country, but they contributed to deepening them.

There is no reason to think those leaders were not believers in notions of national unity and belonging that were widespread even among the pro-democracy opposition, and pre-dated their dictatorship. But they reinforced them by stifling any but the most controlled political involvement by the citizenry. As a consequence, any possible debate on national identity in the country was blocked for decades. Meanwhile, the Tatmadaw only managed to reinforce ethno-nationalist movements among the minorities through their heavy-handed military approach, which repeatedly confirmed their fears of Burman domination.

The pro-democracy opposition led by Aung San Suu Kyi's NLD and the 88 Generation has proved not to be an alternative to prevalent ideas of what Burma should or could be. Suu Kyi famously said in her speech at the Shwedagon Pagoda in 1988 that the popular uprising and the fight for independence constituted a 'second struggle for national independence' – and Burma has indeed seen several false starts since its independence in 1948. But that 'second struggle' failed to offer a new vision for Burma. Moreover, Suu Kyi, with her charisma and unchallenged power in the 'democratic camp', has contributed to further depoliticizing Burma's society. Her moralistic approach to politics has contributed to the prevention of any meaningful political debate on national identity or the structures of power prevalent in Burma beyond the hegemony of the Tatmadaw.

The transition to a 'discipline-flourishing democracy' reflected a rapprochement between the Tatmadaw and the pro-democracy opposition which allowed them to throw their hitherto isolated country into the neoliberal world order. As the transition was basically a pact between those two elites, it has left little room for participatory politics, which has been only marginally less repressed by the new regime than by the military dictatorship. Many Burmese have only been allowed to engage in nationalistic politics – and that has served to cement further the 'national races' worldview as the hegemonic ideology in the country, in spite of the opposition of a small and brave minority of activists who otherwise lack any significant platform to voice their opposition to the treatment of the Rohingya or to the wars in the borderlands. It has been a lost opportunity for the pro-democracy opposition, a great part of which has proved to be as chauvinistic as the Tatmadaw.

Suu Kyi, some of the leaders of her party and a few other pro-democracy politicians enjoy significant moral authority, and have a public more willing to listen to them than to the hated military. They have failed to use their platform to challenge the very 'national races ideology' that serves to exclude the Rohingya, or to defend their status within the confines of that ideology. They have also failed to introduce a meaningful debate on federalism and the aspirations of the ethnic minorities. Ultimately, the Tatmadaw is primarily responsible for the 'clearance operations' against the Rohingya; but Suu Kyi and the main figures in the pro-democracy camp are as responsible as the generals, if not more so, for the climate of public opinion that has made such operations acceptable to so many Burmese.

There was nothing inevitable about the ethnic cleansing of the Rohingya, but it became increasingly inexorable as both ARSA and the diarchic government of the Tatmadaw and the NLD painted themselves – through their own actions as well as their inaction, and through their delusions – into an increasingly constricted corner, in which the options they were able to contemplate were gradually reduced. Tragically, it has proved easier for the Burmese to expel (most of) the Rohingya than to change their erroneous assumptions about belonging in the country that have led them to perceive the Rohingya presence there as a 'problem'.

From the very beginning of Burma's experience as a modern nation-state, there has been a contradiction at the ideological heart of mainstream Burmese nationalism. It was predicated on restoring the nation to the state of power and independence that preceded the disruptive colonial encounter, which interrupted the putative 'natural development' of the nation. But that past has been seen through a colonial lens, which largely defined the membership of the national community according to the same mode of classification introduced by the colonial power against which the newly independent nation had struggled, and saw the Burman core as the seat of a civilization to which the groups in the periphery should be subordinated. In this way, a great part of Burmese anticolonial nationalism was ideologically infected by colonialism from the start. With the military dictatorship, this form of colonial nationalism became predominant, and the democratic transition has only shown how deeply embedded it is in Burmese society. Burma seems to be overwhelmed by the weight of history, seeking to recover a national past that never was. The neuroses about the 'Rohingya problem' and the incapacity to reach a political settlement in the borderlands emerge from a nexus of power structures in which the Tatmadaw is the only strong institution, and the pro-democracy opposition ultimately lacks the capacity, or perhaps the will, to offer any new vision for the country. Ultimately, all these conflicts have also been the consequence of a failed project of nation-building that needs to be fundamentally overhauled.

It is impossible to foretell the shape that such a project will take, and that is precisely the point; the outcome should not be preordained. But to create a fresh and viable project for Burma's future it is necessary to demolish the myths in which the existing failed Burmese nationalism has been based for decades. The starting point should be a critical scrutiny of the pervasive notion of a unity of 'national races' that had lived in harmony up until the colonial encounter disrupted their peaceful coexistence by sowing discord among them and introducing extraneous elements such as the so-called 'Bengali invaders' or other immigrants from the Indian subcontinent.

The extremes of delusion to which such myths might lead are shown in an exchange I had a few years ago with Ko Ko Gyi, one of the main student leaders of the 1988 revolt against the Ne Win regime and a prominent figure in the 'pro-democracy camp' ever since. It was the year 2012, and we met for an interview in Rangoon only a few weeks after the first wave of sectarian violence between the Rohingya and Rakhine communities in Arakan. By then, he had already made clear his position on the issue, going as far as to declare publicly that he was willing to take up arms alongside the military to fight against the Rohingya 'foreign invaders'. At some point in our conversation he made the astonishing claim that there are 'not any outstanding disputes among each other', referring to the 'national races'. I reminded him that war was raging in Kachin state and other places, involving groups regarded as indigenous to Burma, to which he retorted that the military regime was to blame for those conflicts. 'Then why did the war with the Karen or the Kachin conflicts begin before the military dictatorship?' I asked him. 'Because of the non-Federal system', he replied. We did not go further than that, but if we had done it, probably we would have realized that there was never a long period in history when all 'national races' had been at peace.

As my exchange with Ko Ko Gyi shows, in order to maintain the fiction of that solidarity between the different groups forming the putative 'Burmese family' it is necessary to invent a common threat extraneous to it, and at an ideological level the 'othering' of the Rohingya serves just that purpose. But when that 'other' is removed from the picture – as happened in the aftermath of the brutal ethnic cleansing of the Rohingya in 2017 that left in Arakan only a fraction of its Muslim population, confined in ghettos and concentration camps – the conflict between the 'national races' remains. Ever since, a new front has been opened in Arakan, with the increasingly brutal war between the Tatmadaw and the Arakan Army, demonstrating that, under the present circumstances, any solidarity between Rakhine and Burman ethno-nationalists is only possible *against* the Rohingya common enemy.

A look at both the tumultuous past and present of Burma as I have attempted in this book shows that there has never been a Burmese nation of which all its members might feel they belong to, despite such official trappings as the recognition of Burma after independence by international institutions or the issuing of passports and ID cards by the state.[4] Nevertheless, the peoples that fall under the modern Burmese nation-state share a common history and are part of a relatively self-enclosed community. But such a historic community is far from being the 'big family' whose peaceful coexistence was broken by the British conquerors.

To understand what type of community Burma has historically been and still is, we can find an adequate model in the description of Europe made by the Spanish philosopher Gustavo Bueno: 'The unity of the really existing Europe is the unity of a community, but provided we take the term in the sense that it takes in biological ecology, as the equivalent of the term "biocenosis",[5] that is, 'a society constituted by organisms from different species, animal or vegetal . . . but to such degree of mutual interaction and interdependence that it might be referred to as a supra-organic unity, established in a habitat and "self-sustained". In Burma, as in Europe, those 'species' would be the different kingdoms, states, communities, tribes and nations that, from antiquity to the modern era, have lived in its territory. But, as Bueno pointed out, we have to keep in mind that 'the harmony that allows the self-sustaining of a given biocenosis is not so much the harmony of love and peace . . . as the harmony of the struggle for survival among the members of such biocenosis'.[6] Thus, the historical unity of Burma is to be found not so much 'in a unity of common solidarity', but in the 'unity of a battlefield'.[7] The groups striving for survival in the Burmese 'battlefield' have evolved enormously over the centuries, arguably solidifying into several modern ethno-nationalist movements fighting each other and the dominant Burmans as a consequence of the violent and traumatic changes brought by the colonial encounter, but the British did not sow discord in a land of peace and harmony. They may have worsened the situation, but the territory corresponding to the contemporary nation-state of Burma had already been a battlefield for most of its history before their arrival.

Such is the all too present legacy that the diverse peoples of Burma have to confront if they wish to find a modus vivendi acceptable to all. If the country is to have a chance of moving forward from its state of 'biocenosis' into a future where *all* of its peoples might have a chance to live in peace and freedom, it is at the very least necessary to take as the starting point a full reckoning of its real history of perpetual conflict and war, rather than an entirely fictional past of peace and harmony, in the name of which all types of crimes have been perpetrated against the Burmese population – and are still being perpetrated.

Acknowledgments

The act of writing is a solitary endeavour, but a book of this kind relies on the collaboration of many people. I could not have written this book about the labyrinthine history, conflicts and politics of Burma without the help of innumerable people who accompanied me through the years in my work in the country as a journalist, or simply contributed to improving my understanding of what I was covering. Among the people with whom I have had the privilege to work over the years as fixers and translators, or who have helped me to meet people and generously provided their insights, I would like to express my heartfelt gratitude to Saw Nang Lwin, Bo Bo Kyaw, Saed, Sai Latt, Peace Muhammad, Kaung San Hla, Khaing Mra, John Sanlinn, 'Fisherman', Van Biak, U Hla Min, Gambira and U Kyaw Hla Aung, many of whom have become dear friends. I prefer to keep the names of others anonymous for their own safety, but I am equally thankful to them. In Aceh, I had the opportunity to work with Liliane Fan, Hermanto Hasan and the wonderful people of Yayasan Geutanyoe, with whom I have forged a lasting friendship that goes beyond the professional sphere. Sona and Rasheed were of invaluable help to me in navigating the ocean of misery that are the refugee camps in Cox's Bazar.

Some people have been kind enough to read various parts of the book, helping me to make it more readable, or saving me from various errors. They are, in no particular order, Mary Callahan, Michael Charney, Taylor O'Connor, Laur Kiik, Kevin McLeod, Ma Htike,

Vincenzo Floramo, Alberto Pérez Centella and Antolín Avezuela Aristu. This book would have been much worse than it is without their input. It goes without saying that none of them is responsible for whatever mistakes may remain.

Over the years, I have had a few partners in crime while working in Burma. Working with the photographers Vincenzo Floramo, Antolín Avezuela, Borja Sánchez Trillo, Enric Catalá, Eduardo de Francisco and Arturo Rodríguez taught me a great deal – not only about photography. Their company made it less distressing to witness some of the tragedies we covered together. My closest collaborators in Burma included Veronica Pedrosa, Ma Htike, Lilianne Fan, Chris Lewa, and the friend in Rangoon – the best comrades one can imagine, with whom I have tested many of the ideas contained in this book. Others with whom I have had long conversations and/or worked pleasantly are Kayleigh Long, Alex Bookbinder, Wolfgang Trost, Sai Wansai, the heathen Emanuel Stoakes, Closay Saw, Elliott Prasse-Freeman, Kirt Mausert, Sai Latt, David Mathieson, Francis Wade, Raúl Gallego Abellán, Roger Arnold and Paul Greening. I would also like to mention Marwaan Macan-Markar, who years ago helped this Spanish guy he had never heard of to publish his first story in English, after I approached him at the Foreign Correspondents Club of Thailand.

Thanks are due to my editors at Verso, who have much improved the text by correcting my occasionally clumsy English and helping to clarify some passages. Leo Hollis was particularly helpful in taking me through the whole process, and the copyeditors Duncan Ranslem and Charles Peyton have very much helped to polish the final text. Perry Anderson was instrumental in getting this project started by putting me in touch with the editors at Verso.

There are four people who apparently had little direct role in the writing of this book, but without whom I doubt I would have been able to write it. This book is dedicated to them. The first two are my parents, Dori and Felipe, to whom I simply owe everything. Their unflinching support and understanding have always meant everything to me, and I will never be able to thank them enough for being who they are. The late Ben Anderson passed away before I even thought of writing this book, but he has been a huge influence in how I see Southeast Asia in general, and Burma in particular. Both a friend and a mentor, with his gentle Socratic questioning he taught me to see this region more clearly during our endless conversations. I still miss him terribly. Piyarat Nisangkard, the woman I love, put up with me in the inevitable moments of crisis that come with writing a book, and gave me more support than she probably imagines, often saving me from going insane just by being there and reminding me that there are other things in life than Burma and its many conflicts.

Notes

1. The Transition

1 National League for Democracy, *NLD Statement: A Message to the People of Burma*, Rangoon, 6 April 2010. Available online at burmacampaign.org.uk.

2 See Transnational Institute, *Unlevel Playing Field: Burma's Election Landscape*, TNI–BCN Burma Policy Briefing No. 3, 30 September 2010. Available online at tni.org.

3 *Constitution of the Republic of the Union of Myanmar*, Printing and Publishing Enterprise, Ministry of Information, Myanmar, September 2008, Art. 436 (a), pp. 173–4. Available online at burmalibrary.org.

4 Ibid., Art. 232, pp. 85–6.

5 See Kyi Pyar Chit Saw and Matthew Arnold, *Administering the State in Myanmar: An Overview of the General Administration Department*, Asia Foundation, Discussion Paper No. 6, October 2014. Available online at asiafoundation.org.

6 *Constitution of the Republic of the Union of Myanmar*, Art. 59 (f), pp. 19–20.

7 Ibid., Art. 261, pp. 103–4.

8 Seth Mydans, 'Myanmar Refugees Flee to Thailand', *New York Times*, 8 November 2010.

9 *The Irrawaddy*, 'Rohingya Party Prevented from Campaigning', 22 October 2010. Available online at irrawaddy.com.

10 See Bertil Lintner, 'Burma Delivers Its First Rebuff to China', Yale Global Online, 3 October 2011. Available online at yaleglobal.yale.edu.

11 See Mary Callahan, 'The Generals Loosen Their Grip', *Journal of Democracy*, 23: 4 (October 2012).

12 See Andrew Selth, 'Why Myanmar's Military Is Not Planning a Coup', *Nikkei Asian Review*, 8 May 2017. Available online at asia.nikkei.com.

13 Francis Wade, *Myanmar's Enemy Within: Buddhist Violence and the Making of a Muslim 'Other'* (London: Zed, 2017), p. 13.

14 Tomas Fuller, 'Myanmar Jarred by Peace Laureate at Military Parade', *New York Times*, 27 March 2013.

15 Aung San Suu Kyi, 'Speech to a Mass Rally at the Shwedagon Pagoda', in *Freedom from Fear and Other Writings* (London: Viking, 1991).

16 See Amnesty International, *Myanmar: Open for Business? Corporate Crime and Abuses at Myanmar Copper Mine*, 10 February 2015. Available online at amnesty. org.

17 Thomas Fuller, 'Burmese Laureate Heckled Over Backing Copper Mine', *New York Times*, 14 March 2013.

18 Democratic Voice of Burma, 'Suu Kyi Stands by Commission's Report During Monywa Visit', 13 March 2013. Available online at english.dvb.no.

19 Democratic Voice of Burma, 'Suu Kyi Squares Off with Protestors for Second Day', 14 March 2013. Available online at english.dvb.no.

20 See Renaud Egreteau, *Caretaking Democratization: The Military and Political Change in Myanmar* (London: Hurst, 2016), pp. 27–37.

21 Htet Naing Zaw, 'Are Burma's Opposition MPs Too Quiet? Critics and Lawmakers Weigh In', *Irrawaddy*, 15 July 2013. Available online at irrawaddy.com.

22 Htet Naing Zaw, 'Aung San Suu Kyi Woos Tycoons in Naypyidaw Meet-up', *Irrawaddy*, 24 October 2016. Available online at irrawaddy.com.

23 See Supalak Ganjanakhundee, 'Suu Kyi's Call for Multi-ethnic Conference Sparks Hope', *Nation*, 16 November 2010. Available online at mysinchew.com.

2. The War in the 'Green Hell'

1 Aung Hla Tun, 'Myanmar Leader Urges Kachin Peace, Rules Out Independence', Reuters, 1 March 2012. Available online at reuters.com.

2 Steve Tickner, 'The Battle for Laiza', *Irrawaddy*, 7 October 2013. Available online at irrawaddy.com.

3 The best analysis of the Myitsone controversy, on which I rely heavily in the following paragraphs, is probably Laur Kiik, 'Nationalism and Anti-Ethno-Politics: Why "Chinese Development" Failed at Myanmar's Myitsone Dam', *Eurasian Geography and Economics* 57: 3 (2016). Available online at academia.edu.

4 See Thomas Maung Shwe, 'KIO Warns China: Myitsone Dam Could Spark "Civil War"', *Mizzima News*, 20 May 2011. Available online: burmariversnetwork.org.

5 Thomas Fuller, 'Myanmar Backs Down, Suspending Dam Project', *New York Times*, 30 September 2011.

6 Yimou Lee and Shoon Naing, 'Exclusive – China in Talks to Sell Electricity to Myanmar Amid Warming Ties', Reuters, 4 August 2017. Available online at uk.reuters.com.

7 Martin Smith, 'Reflections on the Kachin Ceasefires: A Cycle of Hope and Disappointment', in Mandy Sadan, ed., *War and Peace in the Borderlands of Myanmar: The Kachin Ceasefire, 1994–2011* (Copenhagen: NIAS Press, 2016), p. 85.

8 See Transnational Institute, *A Changing Ethnic Landscape: Analysis of Burma's 2010 Polls*, TNI-BCN Burma Policy Briefing Nr 4, 14 December 2010. Available online at tni.org.

9   See Human Rights Watch, 'Untold Miseries': Wartime Abuses and Forced Displacement in Burma's Kachin State, Washington DC, 20 March 2012. Available online at hrw.org.

10 The best study on the Kachin and the emergence of Kachin nationalism to date, from which I have drawn most of my knowledge on Kachin history, is Mandy Sadan, Being and Becoming Kachin: Histories Beyond the State in the Borderworlds of Burma (Oxford: Oxford University Press, 2013).

11 See Hkanhpa Tu Sadan, 'Kachin Student Life at Yangon University in the Mid-1990s', in Sadan, War and Peace, p. 323.

12 See Laur Kiik, 'Conspiracy, God's Plan and National Emergency: Kachin Popular Analyses of the Ceasefire Era and Its Resources Grabs', in Sadan, War and Peace, pp. 214–18.

13 Thanks to Laur Kiik for bringing this point to my attention.

14 See Kiik, 'Conspiracy, God's Plan and National Emergency'.

15 See Tom Kramer, The United Wa State Party: Narco-Army or Ethnic Nationalist Party?, East-West Center, Policy Studies 38 (Southeast Asia), Washington, DC, 2007.

16 See Bertil Lintner, 'The Core Issues Not Addressed', Irrawaddy, 5 May 2015. Available online at irrawaddy.com.

17 Global Witness, Jade: Myanmar's 'Biggest Secret', London, 23 October 2015. Available online at globalwitness.org.

18 United Nations Office on Drugs and Crime, Myanmar Opium Survey 2017, Geneva, December 2017. Available online at unodc.org.

19 See Kiik, 'Conspiracy, God's Plan and National Emergency'.

20 See Smith, 'Reflections on the Kachin Ceasefires', p. 81.

21 Min Zin, 'One Year of the Kachin War', Foreign Policy, 8 June 2012. Available online at foreignpolicy.com.

22 Nan Htin Htwe, 'Funeral Society Donates to Kachin Displaced', Myanmar Times, 6 August 2012. Available online at mmtimes.com.

23 See Thinn Thinn, 'A Journey to the North', Tea Circle Oxford, 15 January 2018. Available online at teacircleoxford.com.

24 See Matthew J. Walton, 'The "Wages of Burman-ness": Ethnicity and Burman Privilege in Contemporary Myanmar', Journal of Contemporary Asia 43: 1, 2013.

25 Lawi Weng, 'Kachin Silence to Avoid Worsening Crisis: Suu Kyi', Irrawaddy, 24 September 2012. Available online at irrawaddy.com.

26 Agence France-Presse, 'Suu Kyi Says Kachin Peace "Up to Government"', 6 January 2013. Available online at dailystar.com.lb.

3. Days of Fury in Arakan

1   See Human Rights Watch, 'The Government Could Have Stopped This': Sectarian Violence and Ensuing Abuses in Burma's Arakan State, Washington, DC, 31 July 2012. Available online at hrw.org.

2   See Penny Green, Thomas MacManus and Alicia de la Cour Venning, Countdown to Annihilation: Genocide in Myanmar, International State Crime Initiative (ISCI), School of Law, Queen Mary, University of London, 2015. Available online at state-crime.org.

3 San Lin, 'Seminar Held to Protest Misuse of the Term "Arakan"', *Mizzima News*, 6 September 2011. Available online at e-archive.bnionline.net.

4 Narinjara News, 'Mass Protest Around Misuse of the Term "Arakan" Arises in Arakan State', 1 November 2011. Available online at kyaukphru.blogspot.com. See also Francis Wade, *Myanmar's Enemy Within: Buddhist Violence and the Making of a Muslim 'Other'* (London: Zed, 2017), p. 98.

5 Radio Free Asia, 'Call to Put Rohingya in Refugee Camps', 12 July 2012. Available online at rfa.org.

6 Lawi Weng, '"Trauma Will Last Long Time": Ko Ko Gyi', *Irrawaddy*, 16 July 2012. Available online at irrawaddy.com.

7 For an example of this kind of argument, see Ronan Lee, 'A Politician, Not an Icon: Aung San Suu Kyi's Silence on Myanmar's Muslim Rohingya', *Islam and Christian-Muslim Relations* 25: 3 (2014).

8 Democratic Voice of Burma, 'Suu Kyi: I started as a Politician Not a Human Rights Defender', 29 October 2013. Available online at english.dvb.no.

9 Nirupama Subramanian, '"Let's Not Be Over-Optimistic about Burma": Interview with Aung San Suu Kyi', *Hindu*, 13 November 2012. Available online at thehindu.com.

10 See Human Rights Watch, *'All You Can Do is Pray': Crimes Against Humanity and Ethnic Cleansing of Rohingya Muslims in Burma's Arakan State*, Washington, DC, 22 April 2013. Available online at hrw.org.

11 Francis Wade, 'Photos Emerge of Anti-Muslim Witch Hunt in Burma', *Asian Correspondent*, 4 December 2012. Available online at asiancorrespondent.com.

12 Agence France-Presse, 'Thein Sein Accuses Politicians, Monks of Inciting Ethnic Hatred', 27 August 2012. Available online at english.dvb.no.

13 See Joseph Allchin, 'The Rohingya, Myths and Misinformation', *Democratic Voice of Burma*, 22 June 2012. Available online at english.dvb.no.

14 Hillary Clinton, 'Statement from Hillary Clinton on the Burmese Election', *American Presidency Project*, 11 November 2015. Available online at presidency.ucsb.edu. See also Catherine A. Traywick and John Hudson, 'Hillary's Burma Problem', *Foreign Policy*, 27 March 2014.

15 Barack Obama, *Remarks by President Obama at the University of Yangon*, White House, Office of the Press Secretary, 19 November 2012. Available online at obamawhitehouse.archives.gov.

16 Human Rights Watch, *'All You Can Do is Pray'*.

17 Jason Szep and Andrew R. C. Marshall, 'Special Report: Witnesses Tell of Organized Killings of Myanmar Muslims', Reuters, 12 November 2012. Available online at reuters.com.

18 Human Rights Watch, 'Burma: New Violence in Arakan State; Satellite Imagery Shows Widespread Destruction of Rohingya Homes, Property', 26 October 2012. Available online at hrw.org.

4. 'We Will Build a Fence With Our Bones if Necessary'

1 See Democratic Voice of Burma, '11 Dead, 14 Injured in Religious Riots in Kyaukse', 22 October 2003. Available online at burmatoday.net. See also Agence France-Presse, 'Muslim Minority Attacked in Myanmar', 3 November 2003. Available online at aljazeera.com.

2 Moe Myint, 'Concerns Surface over U Wirathu's Visit to Arakan State', *Irrawaddy*, 4 May 2017. Available online at irrawaddy.com. For a portrait of Ashin Wirathu which, despite its shortcomings on the historical background of anti-Muslim violence, provides good insights on the man himself, and includes images of his visit to Maungdaw in 2012 never seen before, see the documentary by Barbet Schroeder, *The Venerable W.*, Les Films du Losange, France–Switzerland, 2017.

3 *Irrawaddy*/Associated Press, 'Mandalay Monks Hold Anti-Rohingya Protests', 3 September 2012. Available online at irrawaddy.com.

4 Human Rights Watch, 'Burma: Peaceful Protest Organizers Charged', 1 October 2012. Available online at hrw.org.

5 Nyein Nyein, 'President Yields to Protesters, Says No to OIC Office', *Irrawaddy*, 15 October 2012. Available online at irrawaddy.com.

6 Andrew R. C. Marshall, 'Special Report: Myanmar Gives Official Blessing to Anti-Muslim Monks', Reuters, 27 June 2013. Available online at reuters.com.

7 With the exception of 'associate citizens' and 'naturalized citizens', as Burmese citizenship law has three layers of citizenship. This discussion refers fundamentally to full citizens.

8 Sai Latt, 'Alienation and Ethnocide in Burma', *Asia Sentinel*, 25 June 2013. Available online at asiasentinel.com.

9 Mya Maung, 'On the Road to Mandalay: A Case Study of the Sinonization of Upper Burma', *Asian Survey* 34: 5 (May 1994).

10 See 'Anti Muslim Monk Wirathu Instigates People Before Meiktila (Burmese) Riot'. Video available online at youtube.com/watch?v=3GE7BI4f0VE.

11 See Burma Campaign UK, 'Examples of Anti-Muslim Propaganda', *Burma Briefing* 21 (March 2013). Available online at burmacampaign.org.uk.

12 Jason Szep, 'Special Report: Buddhist Monks Incite Muslim Killings in Myanmar', Reuters, 8 April 2013. Available online at reuters.com.

13 See Richard Sollom and Holly Atkinson, *Massacre in Central Burma: Muslim Students Terrorized and Killed in Meiktila*, Physicians for Human Rights, Washington, DC, May 2013. Available online at physiciansforhumanrights.org.

14 Kyaw Phone Kyaw, 'The Healing of Meiktila', *Frontier Myanmar*, 21 April 2016. Available online at frontiermyanmar.net.

15 Aye Nai, 'Taunggyi Wedding Party Sentenced on Terrorism Charges', Democratic Voice of Burma, 13 January 2015. Available online at images.dvb.no.

16 Carlos Sardiña Galache and Veronica Pedrosa, 'Myanmar, Muslims Arrested for Joining Terror Group that Doesn't Exist', *Intercept*, 25 May 2015. Available online at theintercept.com.

17 Carlos Sardiña Galache, 'Prison for Supposed Members of Dubious "Myanmar Muslim Army"', Democratic Voice of Burma, 10 December 2015. Available online at images.dvb.no.

18 Hannah Beech, 'The Face of Buddhist Terror', *Time*, 1 July 2013.

19 Personal communication, August 2013.

20 Hanna Hindstrom, 'Burma President Backs Anti-Muslim "Hate Preacher" Wirathu', Democratic Voice of Burma, 24 June 2013. Available online at english.dvb.no.

21 See Justice Trust, *Hidden Hands Behind Communal Violence in Myanmar: Case Study of the Mandalay Riots*, Justice Trust Policy Report, March 2015. Available online at burmalibrary.org.

22 Matthew J. Walton and Susan Hayward, *Contesting Buddhist Narratives: Democratization, Nationalism, and Communal Violence in Myanmar*, East–West Center, Policy Studies 71, Washington, DC, 2014. Available online at eastwestcenter.org.

23 See Matthew J. Walton, 'What are Myanmar's Buddhist Sunday Schools Teaching?', East Asia Forum, 16 December 2014. Available online at eastasiaforum.org.

24 Shameema Rahman and Wendy Zeldin, 'Burma: Four "Race and Religion Protection Laws" Adopted', *Global Legal Monitor*, Law Library of Congress, 14 September 2015. Available online at loc.gov.

25 Shwe Aung and Feliz Solomon, 'Battle Lines Drawn on Interfaith Marriage Proposal', *Democratic Voice of Burma*, 16 May 2014. Available online at images.dvb.no.

26 Nyein Nyein, 'Nationalist Monks call NGOs "Traitors" for Opposing Interfaith Marriage Bill', *Irrawaddy*, 12 May 2014. Available online at irrawaddy.com.

27 See Matthew J. Walton, Melyn McKay and Ma Khin Mar Mar Kyi, 'Why Are Women Supporting Myanmar's "Religious Protection Laws"?', East Asia Forum, 9 September 2015. Available online at eastasiaforum.org.

28 See 'Timeline of Student Protests Against Education Law', *Irrawaddy*, 10 March 2015. Available online at irrawaddy.com.

29 Win Naung Toe, Wai Mar Htun and Khin Khin Ei, 'Aung San Suu Kyi Calls on Student Protestors to Negotiate with Myanmar Government', Radio Free Asia, 27 January 2015. Available online at rfa.org.

5. The Counted and the Excluded

1 'National Bus Tour Hits the Road to Rally Participation for Myanmar Census', *United Nations Population Fund News*, undated. Available online at asiapacific. unfpa.org.

2 The next three paragraphs rely heavily on Mary P. Callahan, 'Distorted, Dangerous Data? Lumyo in the 2014 Myanmar Population and Housing Census', *Journal of Social Issues in Southeast Asia* 32: 2 (July 2017).

3 Yen Saning, 'No Census for Rebel-Controlled Parts of Kachin State', *Irrawaddy*, 6 March 2014. Available online at irrawaddy.com.

4 See International Crisis Group, 'Myanmar Conflict Alert: A Risky Census', 12 February 2014. Available online at crisisgroup.org.

5 Yen Saning, 'Chin Group Says Burma Census Ethnicity Question Caused Confusion', *Irrawaddy*, 9 May 2014. Available online at irrawaddy.com.

6 Yen Saning, 'Ethnic Groups Voice Concern Over Census Classification System', *Irrawaddy*, 10 January 2014. Available online at irrawaddy.com.

7 Fiona MacGregor, 'Census Ethnicity Data Release Delayed Until After Election', *Myanmar Times*, 4 August 2014. Available online at mmtimes.com.

8 Ministry of Labour, Immigration and Population of the Union of Myanmar, Department of Population, *The 2014 Myanmar Population and Housing Census. The Union Report: Religion. Census Report Volume 2-C*, July 2016. Available online at drive.google.com/file/d/0B067GBtstE5TSl9FNElRRGtvMUk.

9 Most of those in the Kachin in KIO-controlled areas, where the census was not conducted, were in all likelihood Christians, but there may also be many Buddhists in the townships in Karen State, where the census was not conducted. In any case,

the total number of the non-enumerated population in those areas was around 100,000, so it would not change the totals significantly.

10 Ko Htwe, 'Burmese Census Will Offer Ethnicity of Choice', *Democratic Voice of Burma*, 27 January 2014. Available online at english.dvb.no.

11 International Crisis Group, *Counting the Costs: Myanmar's Problematic Census*, Asia Briefing No. 144, Yangon/Brussels, 15 May 2014, p. 12. Available online at crisisgroup.org.

12 BBC News, 'Medecins Sans Frontieres' Shock at Myanmar Suspension', 28 February 2014. Available online at bbc.com.

13 The 'Buddhist flag' is composed by the five colours of the Buddhist halo. The flag is not indigenous to Burma or Arakan, nor is it an ancient symbol of Buddhism. It was designed in the late nineteenth century by the American Henry Steel Olcott, the co-founder of the Teosophical Society with Helena Petrovna Blavatsky, but it has come to be widely used in Theravada Buddhist countries today. See Richard F. Gombrich, *Theravada Buddhism: A Social History from Ancient Benares to Modern Colombo*, 2nd edition (London: Routledge, 2006), p. 184.

14 See Carlos Sardiña Galache, 'Myanmar's Rohingya Face a Humanitarian Crisis', *Al Jazeera English*, 19 April 2014. Available online at aljazeera.com.

15 Min Thein Aung, 'Aid Groups in Rakhine State Required to Report Activities in Advance', *Radio Free Asia*, 23 April 2014. Available online at rfa.org.

16 Ministry of Labour, Immigration and Population of the Union of Myanmar, Department of Population, *The 2014 Myanmar Population and Housing Census. The Union Report: Census Report Volume 2*, May 2015. Copy in possession of the author.

17 United Nations High Commissioner for Refugees, Regional Office for South-East Asia, *Mixed Movements in South-East Asia: 2016*, April 2017. Available online at reporting.unhcr.org.

18 Jason Szep and Andrew R. C. Marshall, 'Special Report: Thailand Secretly Supplies Myanmar Refugees to Trafficking Rings', Reuters, 5 December 2013. Available online at reuters.com.

19 Associated Press, 'Rohingya Trafficking: Thai Army Officer Held in First Military Arrest Over Disaster', *Guardian*, 3 June 2015.

20 Kate Hodal, Chris Kelly and Felicity Lawrence, 'Revealed: Asian Slave Labour Producing Prawns for Supermarkets in US, UK', *Guardian*, 10 June 2014.

21 Emanuel Stoakes, Chris Kelly and Annie Kelly, 'Revealed: How the Thai Fishing Industry Traffics, Imprisons and Enslaves', *Guardian*, 20 July 2015.

22 See Eric Petchanet Pratruangkrai, 'EU Warning to Thai Fishery', *Nation*, 22 April 2015. See also Felicity Lawrence and Kate Hodal, 'Thai Government Condemned in Annual US Human Trafficking Report', *Guardian*, 20 June 2014.

23 Amy Sawitta Lefevre, 'Thai Mass Grave Held Bodies of 26 Suspected Trafficking Victims', Reuters, 2 May 2015. Available online at reuters.com.

24 Amy Sawitta Lefevre and Aubrey Belford, 'Thai Police Arrest Rohingya Man Suspected of Running Deadly Jungle Camp', Reuters, 4 May 2015. Available online at reuters.com.

25 Gabriel Domínguez, 'Myanmar's Rohingya Stripped of Right to Vote in Referendum', *Deutsche Welle English*, 12 February 2015. Available online at dw.com.

26 Guy Dinmore, 'Uncertain Future for Hundreds of Thousands as White Cards are Revoked', *Myanmar Times*, 1 April 2015. Available online at mmtimes.com.

27 See Kayleigh E. Long, '"Mafia-Run" Camps Adding to the Misery of Myanmar's Rohingya People', ABC News, 20 June 2016. Available online at abc.net.au.

6. The Burmese Cage

1 See Elliott Prasse-Freeman and Phyo Win Latt, 'Class and Inequality', in Adam Simpson, Nicholas Farrelly and Ian Holliday, eds, *Routledge Handbook of Contemporary Myanmar* (London: Routledge, 2018).

2 See Elliott Prasse-Freeman, 'Burma's Revolution from Below', *Foreign Policy*, 20 April 2015.

3 See Matthew J. Walton, 'The Disciplining Discourse of Unity in Burmese Politics', *Journal of Burma Studies*, 19: 1 (June 2015).

4 See Anthony D. Marx, *Making Race and Nation: A Comparison of the United States, South Africa and Brazil* (Cambridge: Cambridge University Press, 1998).

5 See Richard Potter, 'Myanmar: New Front in an Old War', *Diplomat*, 22 July 2015.

6 See the classic introduction by Fredrik Barth in Fredrik Barth, ed., *Ethnic Groups and Boundaries: The Social Organization of Cultural Life* (Boston, MA: Little Brown, 1969).

7 Clifford Geertz, 'The Integrative Revolution: Primordial Sentiments and Civil Politics in the New States', in Clifford Geertz, *The Interpretation of Cultures: Selected Essays by Clifford Geertz* (New York: Basic Books, 2000 [1973]), p. 259.

8 Orlando Patterson, 'Implications of Ethnic Identification', in C. Fried, ed., *Minorities: Community and Identity* (Berlin: Springer, 1983), pp. 28–9. Quoted in Eric Hobsbawm, 'Identity Politics and the Left', *New Left Review* I: 217 (May–June 1996).

9 Donald L. Horowitz, 'Ethnic Identity', in Nathan Glazer and Daniel P. Moynihan, eds, *Ethnicity: Theory and Experience* (Cambridge, MA: Harvard University Press, 1975), p. 114.

10 David Keen, 'War and Peace: What's the Difference?' *International Peacekeeping* 7: 4 (2000).

11 Shibani Mahtani, 'Separatist Voices Dominate Myanmar Conference', *Wall Street Journal*, 30 April 2014.

12 See Esther Htusan, 'Lack of Health Care Deadly for Burma's Rohingya', Associated Press, 8 May 2014.

13 As one example among many, this is the way the *New Yorker* explained the violence in Arakan in a long and congratulatory feature on the democratic transition and the role the United States had supposedly played in it: 'The risk that withdrawing the military from Burma's politics could lead to flashes of unrest became vivid in June, when sectarian clashes exploded near the border with Bangladesh, between a Muslim ethnic group, the Rohingya, and local Buddhists. The President declared a state of emergency in the region – his first exercise of that power since taking office – and by the time calm had been restored more than two dozen people were dead and thirty thousand had been displaced. This did not bode well for ethnic harmony. On Burma's newly uncensored Internet forums, bloggers poured rage on the Rohingya – a stateless people who are persecuted in Asia, much like the Roma in Europe – calling them terrorists, bandits, and dogs.' Evan Osnos, 'The Burmese Spring', *New Yorker*, 6 August 2012.

14 One example is to be found in Zarni and Cowley, 'The Slow Burning Genocide of Myanmar's Rohingya', *Pacific Rim and Policy Journal*, 23:3 (2014).

15 Rogers Brubaker, *Ethnicity without Groups* (Cambridge, MA: Harvard University Press, 2004), p. 8.

16 For a general critique of the notion of ethnic conflicts as stemming from 'ancient animosities', see Susanne Hoeber Rudolph and Lloyd I. Rudolph, 'Modern Hate: How Ancient Animosities Get Invented', *New Republic*, 22 March 1993.

17 For a profile of Sai Han Htike and his activities aiding the Rohingya, see Carlos Sardiña Galache, 'Building Bridges in Sittwe', *Democratic Voice of Burma*, 17 November 2015. Available online at images.dvb.no.

18 Thin Lei Win, 'Monogamy Law Takes Aim at New Target', *The Myanmar Times*, 11 December 2015. Available online at mmtimes.com.

19 Michael Mann, *The Sources of Social Power, Volume 2: The Rise of Classes and Nation States, 1760–1914* (Cambridge: Cambridge University Press, 1993), p. 251.

20 Michael Mann, *The Dark Side of Democracy: Explaining Ethnic Cleansing* (Cambridge: Cambridge University Press, 2005), p. 5.

21 SPDC, 2002, Information Sheet, Yangon, Myanmar. C-2103 (1), 30 January. Quoted in Martin Smith, *State of Strife: The Dynamics of Ethnic Conflict in Burma*, Policy Studies 36 (Washington, DC: East-West Center, 2007).

22 Eric J. Hobsbawm, *Nations and Nationalism Since 1780: Programme, Myth, reality* (Cambridge: Cambridge University Press, 1990), p. 12.

23 Anthony D. Smith, *Myths and Memories of the Nation* (Oxford: Oxford University Press, 1999), p. 85.

24 Ernest Gellner, *Nations and Nationalism*, 2nd edn (Oxford: Blackwell, 2006), p. 1.

25 Ibid., p. 120.

26 Patrick Wolfe, *Traces of History: Elementary Structures of Race* (London: Verso, 2016), p. 7.

7. The Worlds of Precolonial 'Burma'

1 Victor Lieberman, *Strange Parallels: Southeast Asia in Global Context, c. 800–1830, Volume 1: Integration on the Mainland* (Cambridge: Cambridge University Press, 2003), pp. 88–9.

2 D. G. E. Hall, *A History of South-East Asia*, 4th edn (New York: Palgrave Macmillan, 1981), pp. 151–6.

3 See Michael Aung-Thwin, *Pagan: The Origins of Modern Burma* (Honolulu: University of Hawaii Press, 1985), pp. 22–3.

4 Ibid., p. 99.

5 Lieberman, *Strange Parallels*, p. 112.

6 Ibid., p. 92.

7 Stanley J. Tambiah, *World Conqueror and World Renouncer: A Study of Buddhism and Polity in Thailand against a Historical Background* (Cambridge: Cambridge University Press, 1976), p. 112.

8 See Thongchai Winichakul, *Siam Mapped: A History of the Geo-Body of a Nation* (Honolulu: University of Hawaii Press, 1994), Chapter 1. This highly influential book in Southeast Asia studies deals with Thailand, but its arguments can be extended to neighbouring Burma or any other Southeast Asian country.

9 Edmund R. Leach, 'The Frontiers of "Burma"', *Comparative Studies in Society and History* 3: 1 (October 1960).

10 See E. Michael Mendelson, *Sangha and State in Burma: A Study of Monastic Sectarianism and Leadership* (Ithaca, NY: Cornell University Press, 1975), pp. 39–42.

11 See Richard F. Gombrich, *Theravada Buddhism: A Social History from Ancient Benares to Modern Colombo*, 2nd edn (London: Routledge, 2006), Chapter 3.

12 On this distinction, see Melford E. Spiro, *Buddhism and Society: A Great Tradition and Its Burmese Vicissitudes*, 2nd edn (Berkeley, CA: University of California Press, 1982), Chapters 2 and 3.

13 Thanks to Michael W. Charney for bringing this point to my attention.

14 On the *nat* cult and its relations with Buddhism, see Melford E. Spiro, *Burmese Supernaturalism: A Study in the Explanation and Reduction of Suffering* (Englewood Hills: Prentice-Hall, 1967).

15 Donald Eugene Smith, *Religion and Politics in Burma* (Princeton, NJ: Princeton University Press, 1965), p. 14.

16 Spiro, *Burmese Supernaturalism*, p. 52.

17 Personal observation of *nat* festivals in the suburbs of Mandalay during the summer of 2013, attended by Buddhists, Muslims and Christians.

18 On Asoka's model of political authority, I rely heavily on Tambiah, *World Conqueror and World Renouncer*, Chapter 5.

19 Ibid., p. 64.

20 See Aung-Thwin, *Pagan*, p. 65ff.

21 Ibid., pp. 149–50.

22 Mendelson, *Sangha and State in Burma*, p. 64.

23 Lieberman, *Strange Parallels*, p. 120.

24 Aung-Thwin, *Pagan*, p. 142.

25 Victor Lieberman, 'Reinterpreting Burmese History', *Comparative Studies in Society and History* 29: 1 (January 1987).

26 Lieberman, *Strange Parallels*, pp. 151–2.

27 Ibid, p. 156.

28 Victor Lieberman, *Burmese Administrative Cycles: Anarchy and Conquest, c. 1580–1760* (Princeton, NJ: Princeton University Press, 1984), p. 56.

29 See Thant Myint-U, *The Making of Modern Burma* (Cambridge: Cambridge University Press, 2001), pp. 88ff.

30 Chie Ikeya, *Refiguring Women, Colonialism, and Modernity in Burma* (Chiang Mai: Silkworm, 2012), p. 25.

31 Lieberman, *Strange Parallels*, pp. 167–73.

32 Ibid., pp. 174–5.

33 See Thant Myint-U, *Making of Modern Burma*, pp. 27–34.

34 This paragraph draws heavily from Victor B. Lieberman, 'Ethnic Politics in Eighteenth-Century Burma', *Modern Asian Studies* 12: 3 (1978).

35 See Moshe Yegar, *The Muslims of Burma: A Study of a Minority Group* (Wiesbaden: Otto Harrassowitz, 1972), pp. 2–17.

36 Ibid., p. 15.

37 For an in-depth, if somewhat controversial, study of Zomia, see James C. Scott, *The Art of Not Being Governed: An Anarchist History of Southeast Asia* (New Haven, CT: Yale University Press, 2009). The name and concept of Zomia was put in circulation by Willem van Schendel, 'Geographies of Knowing, Geographies of Ignorance: Jumping Scale in Southeast Asia', *Environment and Planning D: Society and Space* 20 (2002). But the intention of van Schendel's paper was not so much to inaugurate a new field of studies, but to call attention to the limitations of traditional 'area studies'.

38 Scott, *Art of Not Being Governed*, p. 330.
39 Edmund R. Leach, *Political Systems of Highland Burma: A Study of Kachin Social Structure* (London: Athlone/University of London, 1970 [1954]), p. 41.
40 Ibid., p. 1.
41 Ibid., pp. 2–3.
42 F. K. Lehman, 'Ethnic Categories in Burma and the Theory of Social Systems', in Peter Kunstadter, ed., *Southeast Asian Tribes: Minorities and Nations* (Princeton, NJ: Princeton University Press, 1967), p. 106–7.
43 Ibid., p. 108.
44 Leach, *Political Systems of Highland Burma*, p. 39.
45 Mandy Sadan, *Being and Becoming Kachin: Histories Beyond the Borderworlds of Burma* (Oxford: Oxford University Press, 2013), p. 33.
46 Leach, 'Frontiers of "Burma"'.
47 Pamela Gutman, 'Ancient Arakan, with Special Reference to Its Cultural History between the 5th and 11th Centuries', PhD thesis, Australian National University, 1976, p. 9. Available online at openresearch-repository.anu.edu.au.
48 Hall, *History of South-East Asia*, pp. 36–7.
49 Gutman, 'Ancient Arakan', pp. 24ff.
50 Ibid., p. 325.
51 Ibid., p. 16.
52 For this argument, see Azeem Ibrahim, *The Rohingyas: Inside Myanmar's Hidden Genocide* (London: Hurst, 2016), pp. 20–1.
53 Gutman, 'Ancient Arakan', p. 17.
54 See G. E. Harvey, *History of Burma: From the Earliest Times to 10 March 1824, the Beginning of the English Conquest* (London: Frank Cass, 1967 [1925]), p. 140.
55 See, for example, Ibrahim, *Rohingyas*, p. 24.
56 See Harvey, *History of Burma*, p. 139.
57 Ibid., pp. 137–49.
58 Michael W. Charney, 'Where Jambudipa and Islamdom Converged: Religious Change and the Emergence of Buddhist Communalism in Early Modem Arakan (Fifteenth to Nineteenth Centuries)', PhD thesis, University of Michigan, 1999, p. 5. Available online at eprints.soas.ac.uk.
59 Ibid., pp. 164–5.
60 Ibid., p. 171.
61 Harvey, *History of Burma*, pp. 146–9.
62 See Jacques P. Leider, 'Forging Buddhist Credentials as a Tool of Legitimacy and Ethnic Identity: A Study of Arakan's Subjection in Nineteenth-Century Burma', *Journal of the Economic and Social History of the Orient* 51: 3 (2008), p. 413.
63 Hall, *History of South-East Asia*, p. 626.
64 Charney, 'Where Jambudipa and Islamdom Converged', p. 260.
65 See Harvey, *History of Burma*, p. 282. Harvey estimates that 50,000 people fled to Bengal. The estimate of one-quarter of the population comes from Michael W. Charney, personal communication, April 2018.
66 Francis Buchanan, 'A Comparative Vocabulary of Some of the Languages Spoken in the Burma Empire," *Asiatic Researches* 5 (1799). Available online at eprints.soas.ac.uk.
67 Michael W. Charney, '"Theories and Historiography of the Religious Basis of Ethnonyms in Rakhaing (Arakan), Myanmar (Burma)', paper submitted at Arakan History Conference, Bangkok, 2005. Available online at eprints.soas.ac.uk.

68 G. P. Ramachandra, 'Captain Hiram Cox's Mission to Burma, 1796–1798: A Case of Irrational Behaviour in Diplomacy', *Journal of Southeast Asian Studies* 12: 2 (September 1981).

69 For the full text of the letter, see Harvey, *History of Burma*, pp. 291–2.

70 See Ramachandra, 'Captain Hiram Cox's Mission to Burma'.

71 For the period between the Burmese conquest of Arakan and the First Anglo-Burmese war, see Hall, *History of South-East Asia*, pp. 625–41.

8. Burma Under the British

1 John F. Cady, *A History of Modern Burma* (Ithaca, NY: Cornell University Press, 1958), p. 74.

2 See San Shwe San Bu, 'The Arakan Mug Battalion', *Journal of the Burma Research Society* 13 (1923).

3 Cady, *History of Modern Burma*, p. 85.

4 Charles Paton, 'A Short Report on Arakan', 26 April 1826. Available online at scribd. com.

5 Cady, *History of Modern Burma*, p. 86.

6 Jacques P. Leider, 'Forging Buddhist Credentials as a Tool of Legitimacy and Ethnic Identity: A Study of Arakan's Subjection in Nineteenth-Century Burma', *Journal of the Economic and Social History of the Orient* 51: 3 (2008), p. 423.

7 See John Ogilvy Hay, *Arakan: Past, Present, Future* (London: William Blackwood, 1892), p. 7. Hay was a former magistrate in Akyab who wrote a series of letters to the government and several newspapers advocating for the development in Arakan. His petitions were largely unheeded.

8 See Thant Myint-U, *The Making of Modern Burma* (Cambridge: Cambridge University Press, 2001), pp. 106–7.

9 On King Mindon's reign and his reforms, see ibid., Chapter 5.

10 See . G. E. Hall, *A History of South-East Asia*, 4th edn (New York: Palgrave Macmillan, 1981), pp. 664–5.

11 Donald Eugene Smith, *Religion and Politics in Burma* (Princeton, NJ: Princeton University Press, 1965), p. 26.

12 Cady, *A History of Modern Burma*, pp. 116–7.

13 Ibid., pp. 128–9.

14 See Michael Aung-Thwin, 'The British "Pacification" of Burma: Order without Meaning', *Journal of Southeast Asian Studies* 16: 2 (September 1985).

15 Cady, *History of Modern Burma*, p. 134.

16 Thant Myint-U, *Making of Modern Burma*, p. 200.

17 J. S. Furnivall, *Colonial Policy and Practice: A Comparative Study of Burma and Netherlands India* (Cambridge: Cambridge University Press, 1948), pp. 74–6.

18 See Andrew Huxley, 'Positivists and Buddhists: The Rise and Fall of Anglo-Burmese Ecclesiastical Law', *Law & Social Inquiry* 26: 1 (2001).

19 See Smith, *Religion and Politics in Burma*, pp. 39–42.

20 Ibid., pp. 46–7.

21 See Alicia Turner, *Saving Buddhism: The Impermanence of Religion in Colonial Burma* (Honolulu: University of Hawaii Press, 2014), pp. 53–9.

22 Michael Adas, *The Burma Delta: Economic Development and Social Change on an Asian Rice Frontier, 1852–1941* (Madison, WI: University of Wisconsin Press, 1974), p. 58.

23 Ibid., p. 29.

24 Furnivall, *Colonial Policy and Practice*, p. 89.

25 Ibid., p. 119.

26 See James Baxter, *Report on Indian Immigration* (Rangoon: Government Printing & Stationary, Burma, 1941), p. 15. Available online at networkmyanmar.org.

27 For the year 1925 and for Hindu Indians; the rate for Muslim Indians was slightly lower. See Nalini Ranjan Chakravarti, *The Indian Minority in Burma: The Rise and Decline of an Immigrant Community* (London: Oxford University Press, 1971), p. 49.

28 Ibid., Chapter 4.

29 Furnivall, *Colonial Policy and Practice*, pp. 117–18.

30 Ibid., p. 122.

31 Ibid., p. 119.

32 On *chettiars'* operations and their impact on the Burmese economy, see Sean Turnell, *Fiery Dragons: Banks, Moneylenders and Microfinance in Burma* (Copenhagen: NIAS, 2009), Chapter 2.

33 Ibid., p. 37.

34 Furnivall, *Colonial Policy and Practice*, p. 123.

35 According to the 1872 Burma census, the population density at that time was 451 people per square mile in Chittagong, and of 33.84 people per square mile in Arakan.

36 See Baxter, *Report on Indian Immigration*, p. 16.

37 See relevant tables in 'Census of Burma', 1931. Available online at burmalibrary.org.

38 See R. B. Smart, comp., *Burma Gazetteer: Akyab District, Volume A* (Rangoon: Government Printing, Burma, 1917), p. 90. Available online at networkmyanmar. org.

39 For an instance of this kind of argument, see Derek Tonkin, 'The "Rohingya" Identity: British Experience in Arakan 1826–1948', 9 April 2014. Available online at archive.org.

40 See Erin L. McAuliffe, 'Caste and the Quest for Racial Hierarchy in British Burma: An Analysis of Census Classifications from 1872–1931', unpublished MA thesis, University of Washington, 2017.

41 Mandy Sadan, *Being and Becoming Kachin: Histories Beyond the Borderworlds of Burma* (Oxford: Oxford University Press, 2013), p. 158.

42 Martin Smith, *Burma: Insurgency and the Politics of Ethnicity*, 2nd edn (London: Zed, 1999), p. 40.

43 See Joseph Silverstein, *Burmese Politics: The Dilemma of National Unity* (New Brunswick, NJ: Rutgers University Press, 1980), pp. 29–32. See also Smith, *Burma*, pp. 42–3.

44 Mahmood Mamdani, *Citizen and Subject: Contemporary Africa and the Legacy of Late Colonialism* (Princeton, NJ: Princeton University Press, 1996), p. 18.

45 See James C. Scott, *The Art of Not Being Governed: An Anarchist History of Southeast Asia* (New Haven, CT: Yale University Press, 2009), pp. 238–40.

46 See Edmund R. Leach, *Political Systems of Highland Burma: A Study of Kachin Social Structure* (London: Athlone/University of London, 1970 [1954]), pp. 43–9.

47 Ibid., p. 244.

48 See Mary P. Callahan, *Making Enemies: War and State Building in Burma* (Ithaca, NY: Cornell University Press, 2003), pp. 34–7.

49 Donald L. Horowitz, *Ethnic Groups in Conflict* (Los Angeles: California University Press, 2000), p. 164.

9. The Emergence of Nationalisms

1   Benedict Anderson, *Imagined Communities: Reflections on the Origins and Spread of Nationalism*, rev. edn (London: Verso, 2006), pp. 118–23.

2   This paragraph relies heavily on Alicia Turner, *Saving Buddhism: The Impermanence of Religion in Colonial Burma* (Honolulu: University of Hawaii Press, 2014), Chapter 4.

3   See Anderson, *Imagined Communities*, Chapter 3.

4   See Jacques P. Leider, 'Forging Buddhist Credentials as a Tool of Legitimacy and Ethnic Identity: A Study of Arakan's Subjection in Nineteenth-Century Burma', *Journal of the Economic and Social History of the Orient* 51: 3 (2008).

5   U Maung Maung, *From Sangha to Laity: Nationalist Movements of Burma, 1920–1940* (Columbia, MO: South Asia Books, 1980), p. 3.

6   Donald Eugene Smith, *Religion and Politics in Burma* (Princeton, NJ: Princeton University Press, 1965), pp. 87–92.

7   Ibid., p. 96.

8   For a brief biography of U Ottama, see E. Michael Mendelson, *Sangha and State in Burma: A Study of Monastic Sectarianism and Leadership* (Ithaca, NY: Cornell University Press, 1975), pp. 199–206.

9   Smith, *Religion and Politics in Burma*, pp. 97–8.

10 See Maitrii Aung-Thwin, *The Return of the Galon King: History, Law, and Rebellion in Colonial Burma* (Athens, OH: Ohio University Press, 2011), pp. 1ff.

11 See Michael Adas, *The Burma Delta: Economic Development and Social Change on an Asian Rice Frontier, 1852–1941* (Madison, WI: University of Wisconsin Press, 1974), pp. 201ff.

12 For a history of the Dobama Asiayone, see Khin Yi, *The Dobama Movement in Burma (1930–1938)* (Ithaca, NY: Cornell University Southeast Asia Program, 1988).

13 See Kei Nemoto, 'The Concepts of Dobama ("Our Burma") and Thudo-Bama ("Their Burma") in Burmese Nationalism, 1930–1948', *Journal of Burma Studies* 5 (2000).

14 See Martin Smith, *Burma: Insurgency and the Politics of Ethnicity*, 2nd edn (London: Zed, 1999), p. 53.

15 See Chie Ikeya, *Refiguring Women, Colonialism, and Modernity in Burma* (Chiang Mai: Silkworm, 2012), pp. 143–6.

16 Ibid., pp. 129–40.

17 Ibid. pp. 156–62.

18 See Mary P. Callahan, *Making Enemies: War and State Building in Burma* (Ithaca, NY: Cornell University Press, 2003), pp. 36–40.

19 See John F. Cady, *A History of Modern Burma* (Ithaca, NY: Cornell University Press, 1958), Chapter XI.

20 See extracts from the official Committee of Enquiry on the riots in E. J. L. Andrew, *Indian Labour in Rangoon* (Oxford: Oxford University Press, 1933), Appendix X, pp.

278–92. See also Nalini Ranjan Chakravarti, *The Indian Minority in Burma: The Rise and Decline of an Immigrant Community* (London: Oxford University Press, 1971), pp. 132–4.

21 For a good account of the riots and their context, see Moshe Yegar, *The Muslims of Burma: A Study of a Minority Group* (Wiesbaden: Otto Harrassowitz, 1972), pp. 29–39.

22 See Nemoto, 'Concepts of Dobama'.

23 See Adas, *Burma Delta*, pp. 192–6.

24 See Chakravarti, *Indian Minority in Burma*, p. 111.

25 See Thein Pe, 'The Indo-Burman Conflict', originally published in Burmese by Nagani Book Club, Rangoon, 1938. English translation originally published in Tin Htway, 'The Emergence and Development of Political Writing in Burmese Literature, 1914–1942, with Special Reference to U Lun', MPhil thesis, SOAS, London. Available online at phil.uni-passau.de.

26 See Bertil Lintner, *The Rise and Fall of the Communist Party of Burma (CPB)* (Ithaca, NY: Cornell University Southeast Asia Program, 1990), p. 3.

27 See Smith, *Burma*, pp. 56–7.

28 Ibid., p. 55.

29 See Cady, *History of Modern Burma*, pp. 137–40.

30 Ibid., pp. 368–73.

31 Mandy Sadan, *Being and Becoming Kachin: Histories Beyond the State in the Borderworlds of Burma* (Oxford: Oxford University Press, 2013), p. 252.

32 Ibid., p. 234.

33 Ibid., pp. 228–9.

34 Ibid., pp. 242ff.

10. World War II and the Road to Independence

1 For a biography of Aung San, see Angelene Naw, *Aung San and the Struggle for Burmese Independence* (Chang Mai: Silkworm, 2001).

2 See Martin Smith, *Burma: Insurgency and the Politics of Ethnicity*, 2nd edn (London: Zed, 1999), pp. 57–9.

3 See Andrew Selth, 'Race and Resistance in Burma, 1942–1945', *Modern Asian Studies* 20: 3 (1986).

4 Smith, *Burma*, p. 60.

5 Naw, *Aung San*, p. 124.

6 Smith, *Burma*, p. 60.

7 See Mandy Sadan, *Being and Becoming Kachin: Histories Beyond the State in the Borderworlds of Burma* (Oxford: Oxford University Press, 2013), pp. 257–65.

8 See Selth, 'Race and Resistance in Burma'.

9 Smith, *Burma*, p. 62.

10 Ibid., p. 64.

11 Moshe Yegar, *The Muslims of Burma: A Study of a Minority Group* (Wiesbaden: Otto Harrassowitz, 1972), pp. 95–6.

12 See Christopher Bayly and Tim Harper, *Forgotten Armies: Britain's Asian Empire and the War with Japan* (London: Penguin, 2005), pp. 272–6.

13 For a detailed account of the Indian exodus, see Hugh Tinker, 'A Forgotten Long March: The Indian Exodus from Burma, 1942', *Journal of Southeast Asian Studies* 6: 1 (1975). Nalini Ranjan Chakravarti, *The Indian Minority in Burma: The Rise and Decline of an Immigrant Community* (London: Oxford University Press, 1971), p. 170.

14 Bayly and Harper, *Forgotten Armies*, p. 167.

15 Ibid., p. 171.

16 See Christopher Bayly and Tim Harper, *Forgotten Wars: The End of Britain's Asian Empire* (London: Allen Lane, 2007), pp. 231–2.

17 Smith, *Burma*, p. 66.

18 See Hugh Tinker, *The Union of Burma: A Study of the First Years of Independence* (Oxford: Oxford University Press, 1959), pp. 20–2.

19 Smith, *Burma*, pp. 77–8.

20 For a compilation of Aung San's writings and speeches, see Josef Silverstein, ed., *The Political Legacy of Aung San* (Ithaca, NY: Cornell Southeast Asia Program, 1993).

21 Ibid. p. 153.

22 Ibid., pp. 93–112.

23 Ibid., pp. 151–1.

24 See Matthew Walton, 'The Disciplining Discourse of Unity in Burmese Politics', *Journal of Burmese Studies* 19: 1 (June 2015).

25 For an excellent analysis of the strengths and shortcomings of the Panglong Agreement, in which the following two paragraphs rely heavily, see Matthew J. Walton, 'Ethnicity, Conflict and History in Burma: The Myths of Panglong', *Asian Survey* 48: 6 (2008).

26 Thanks to Mary Callahan for bringing this point to my attention.

27 See Lian H. Sakhong, *In Search of Chin Identity: A Study in Religion, Politics and Ethnic Identity in Burma* (Copenhagen: NIAS, 2003), pp. 210–14

28 Smith, *Burma*, p. 82.

29 Ibid., pp. 80–1.

30 See Yegar, *Muslims of Burma*, pp. 96–7.

31 Ibid.

32 For an analysis of the 1947 Constitution, see Josef Silverstein, *Burmese Politics: The Dilemma of National Unity* (New Brunswick, NJ: Rutgers University Press, 1980), pp. 185–205.

33 Frank N. Trager, *Burma from Kingdom to Republic: A Historical and Political Analysis* (New York: Frederick A. Prager, 1966), pp. 88ff.

34 Ibid., p. 91.

11. An Embattled Democracy

1 Quoted in Frank N. Trager, *Burma from Kingdom to Republic: A Historical and Political Analysis* (New York: Frederick A. Prager, 1966), p. 98.

2 See John F. Cady, *A History of Modern Burma* (Ithaca, NY: Cornell University Press, 1958), p. 568.

3 Martin Smith, *Burma: Insurgency and the Politics of Ethnicity*, 2nd edn (London: Zed, 1999), p. 109.

4 See Cady, *History of Modern Burma*, pp. 590–2.

5 See Smith, *Burma*, pp. 110–12.

6 See Mary P. Callahan, *Making Enemies: War and State Building in Burma* (Ithaca, NY: Cornell University Press, 2003), pp. 127–9.

7 Ibid., pp. 132–4.

8 Mandy Sadan, *Being and Becoming Kachin: Histories Beyond the State in the Borderworlds of Burma* (Oxford: Oxford University Press, 2013), p. 267.

9 Bertil Lintner, *Burma in Revolt: Opium and Insurgency since 1948* (Chang Mai: Silkworm, 1999), p. 96.

10 Ibid., pp. 98–9.

11 See table with the increase of KMT troops from January 1950 to February 1952 in Callahan, *Making Enemies*, p. 155.

12 For a good overview of the 'secret war' of the KMT on Communist China from northern Burma, see Lintner, *Burma in Revolt*, pp. 110–62.

13 See ibid., p. 148. See also Callahan, *Making Enemies*, p. 158.

14 See Alfred W. McCoy, *The Politics of Heroin: CIA Complicity in the Global Drug Trade* (Chicago: Lawrence Hill, 2001), pp. 162–78.

15 Callahan, *Making Enemies*, p. 159.

16 Ibid., pp. 159–71.

17 See Mary P. Callahan, 'On Time Warps and Warped Time: Lessons from Burma's Democratic Era', in Robert I. Rotberg, ed., *Burma: Prospects for a Democratic Future* (Washington, DC: Brookings Institution, 1998).

18 See Manning Nash, 'Party Building in Upper Burma', *Asian Survey* 3: 4 (April 1963).

19 See Callahan, *Making Enemies*, pp. 176–9.

20 Ibid., pp. 183–4.

21 See Smith, *Burma*, pp. 168–74.

22 See ibid., pp. 175–9.

23 See Callahan, *Making Enemies*, pp. 184–8.

24 Ibid., p. 193.

25 Ibid., p. 189.

26 See Donald Eugene Smith, *Religion and Politics in Burma* (Princeton, NJ: Princeton University Press, 1965), pp. 157–65.

27 See Fred von der Mehden, 'Burma's Religious Campaign against Communism', *Pacific Affairs* 33: 3 (September 1960).

28 Smith, *Religion and Politics in Burma*, p. 253.

29 Ibid., pp. 269–80.

30 Moshe Yegar, *The Muslims of Burma: A Study of a Minority Group* (Wiesbaden: Otto Harrassowitz, 1972), p. 98.

31 Smith, *Burma*, p. 87.

32 Yegar, *Muslims of Burma*, p. 97.

33 Ibid. p. 100.

34 See 'Pakistan Warns Burma: Says Influx of Arakan Moslems May Cause Disturbances', *New York Times*, 20 December 1951.

35 See 'Supreme Court Quashes Expulsion Orders against Arakanese Muslims', *Guardian* (Rangoon), 27 October 1960.

36 Smith, *Burma*, p. 182.

37 Ibid., pp. 103–5.

38 For a transcription of the speech in Burmese and an English translation, see 'Official Transcript of the Address Delivered by Brigadier General Aung Gyi, Vice Chief of

Staff of the Union of Burma Armed Forces to Mujahid Insurgents' Surrender Ceremony', Maungdaw Town, Burma, 4 July 1961. Available online at freerohingya-coalition.org.

39 For an example of this kind of argument, see Khin Maung Saw, *Behind the Mask: The Truth Behind the Name 'Rohingya'* (Rangoon: Taunggyi, 2016). For a critique of this book and the theses it defends, see Carlos Sardiña Galache, 'Arakan Divided', *New Left Review* II/104 (March–April 2017).

40 See Jacques Leider, 'Rohingya: The Name, the Movement, the Quest for Identity', in *Nation Building in Myanmar* (Rangoon: Myanmar Egress/Myanmar Peace Center, 2013). Available online at academia.edu.

41 See Nay San Lwin, 'Making Rohingya Statelessness', *New Mandala*, 29 October 2012. Available online at newmandala.org.

42 See Smith, *Burma*, pp. 190–5.

43 For the next two paragraphs, I rely on Sadan, *Being and Becoming Kachin*, Chapter 6.

44 See also Seamus Martov, 'A Lifetime of War, with No Peace in Sight', *Irrawaddy*, 11 August 2014. Available online at irrawaddy.com.

45 See Smith, *Burma*, p. 196.

46 See Callahan, *Making Enemies*, pp. 202–4.

47 See Lintner, *Burma in Revolt*, p. 210.

12. The Burmese Way to Socialism

1   See Bertil Lintner, *Burma in Revolt: Opium and Insurgency since 1948* (Chang Mai: Silkworm, 1999), pp. 213–14.

2   See Robert H. Taylor, *The State in Burma* (London: Hurst, 1987), pp. 300–1.

3   The English translations of both documents are available online: 'The Burmese Way to Socialism' at burmalibrary.org.

4   See Robert Taylor, *General Ne Win: A Political Biography* (Singapore: ISEAS, 2015), p. 463.

5   See Taylor, *State in Burma*, pp. 292–5.

6   Taylor, *General Ne Win*, p. 346.

7   Mary P. Callahan, *Making Enemies: War and State Building in Burma* (Ithaca, NY: Cornell University Press, 2003), p. 209.

8   Ibid., p. 258, n. 2.

9   Taylor, *General Ne Win*, p. 341.

10 See Nalini Ranjan Chakravarti, *The Indian Minority in Burma: The Rise and Decline of an Immigrant Community* (London: Oxford University Press, 1971), p. 181.

11 Ibid., p. 186.

12 The full text of 'The Blueprint for Burma' is included in Josef Silverstein, ed., *The Political Legacy of Aung San* (Ithaca, NY: Cornell Southeast Asia Program, 1993).

13 See Gustaaf Houtman, 'Aung San's *Lan-Zin*, the Blue Print and the Japanese Occupation of Burma', in Kei Nemoto, ed., *Reconsidering the Japanese Military Occupation in Burma (1942–45)* (Tokyo: Research Institute for Languages and Cultures of Asia and Africa, Tokyo University of Foreign Studies, 2007).

14 See Donald Eugene Smith, *Religion and Politics in Burma* (Princeton, NJ: Princeton University Press, 1965), pp. 281ff.

15 See Tin Maung Maung Than, 'The "Sangha" and "Sasana" in Socialist Burma', *Journal of Social Issues in Southeast Asia* 3: 1 (February 1988).

16 See Taylor, *General Ne Win*, p. 236.

17 Ibid., p. 439.

18 See Tin Maung Maung Than, 'The "Sangha" and "Sasana"', pp. 38ff.

19 See Yoshihiro Nakanishi, *Strong Soldiers, Failed Revolution: The State and Military in Burma, 1962–1988* (Singapore: NIAS, 2013), pp. 112ff.

20 Ibid., pp. 137–41.

21 Martin Smith, *Burma: Insurgency and the Politics of Ethnicity*, 2nd edn (London: Zed, 1999), pp. 208ff.

22 Ibid., pp. 258ff.

23 Ibid., p. 219.

24 Ibid. p. 244.

25 See Bertil Lintner, *The Rise and Fall of the Communist Party of Burma (CPB)* (Ithaca, NY: Cornell University Southeast Asia Program, 1990), pp. 19–21.

26 See Hongwei Fan, 'The 1967 Anti-Chinese Riots in Burma and Sino–Burmese Relations', *Journal of Southeast Asian Studies* 43: 2 (2012).

27 See Lintner, *Rise and Fall of the Communist Party*, pp. 25ff.

28 Ibid., p. 29.

29 Ibid., p. 23.

30 See Smith, *Burma*, p. 269.

31 See Lintner, *Rise and Fall of the Communist Party*, p. 30.

32 See Mandy Sadan, *Being and Becoming Kachin: Histories Beyond the State in the Borderworlds of Burma* (Oxford: Oxford University Press, 2013), pp. 333ff.

33 Ibid., p. 346.

34 Ibid., p. 380.

35 Ibid., pp. 338–9.

36 See Lintner, *Rise and Fall of the Communist Party*, p. 25.

37 Ibid.

38 Ibid., p. 331.

39 See Nick Cheesman, 'How in Myanmar "National Races" Came to Surpass Citizenship and Exclude Rohingya', *Journal of Contemporary Asia* 47: 3 (2017).

40 See David I. Steinberg, 'Burma in 1982: Incomplete Transitions', *Asian Survey* 23: 2 (February 1983).

41 See Henry Kamm, 'Proposed Law to Create 2 Kinds of Burmese Citizenship Worries Millions', *New York Times*, 13 August 1980.

42 See Taylor, *General Ne Win*, pp. 483–5.

43 See 'Meeting Held in the Central Meeting Hall, President House, Ahlone Road, on 8 October 1982', full speech translated into English in *Working People's Daily*, 9 October 1982. My emphasis. Available online at burmalibrary.org.

44 Taylor, *General Ne Win*, p. 484.

45 See Tun Tun Aung, 'An Introduction to Citizenship Card under Myanmar Citizenship Law', *Journal of the Study of Modern Society and Culture* 38 (2007).

46 See Cheesman, 'How in Myanmar 'National Races' Came to Surpass Citizenship and Exclude Rohingya'.

47 See Moshe Yegar, *Between Integration and Secession: The Muslim Communities of the Southern Philippines, Southern Thailand, and Western Burma/Myanmar* (Oxford: Lexington, 2002), p. 54.

48   Ibid., p. 55.

49   Smith, *Burma*, p. 241.

50   See Nyi Nyi Kyaw, 'Unpacking the Presumed Statelessness of Rohingyas', *Journal of Immigrant and Refugee Studies* 15: 3 (2017), p. 275.

51   See Alan C. Lindquist, 'Report on the 1978–79 Bangladesh Refugee Relief Operation', June 1979. Available online at ibiblio.org.

52   Ibid.

53   Yegar, *Between Integration and Secession*, p. 58.

54   Quoted in Lintner, *Burma in Revolt*, p. 317.

55   See Willem van Schendel, *The Bengal Borderland: Beyond State and Nation in South Asia* (London: Anthem, 2005), esp. Chapters 7, 8 and 9.

56   For an argument on 'illegal immigration' that takes ample liberties with the data, see Kyaw Lat, 'Buddha's Teaching and the Problems in Rakhine State', *Irrawaddy*, 25 June 2018. Available online at irrawaddy.com.

57   See Carlos Sardiña Galache, ' "Illegal Migration" in Arakan: Myths and Numbers', *New Mandala*, 16 August 2018. Available online at newmandala.org.

58   See Robert H. Taylor, 'The Legal Status of Indians in Contemporary Burma', in A. Mani Kernial and Singh Sandhu, eds., *Indian Communities in Southeast Asia* (Singapore: ISEAS, 2006), p. 674.

59   See Timothy McLaughlin and Andrew R. C. Marshall, 'Suu Kyi Says She Will Be above President in New Government', Reuters, 5 November 2015. Available online at irrawaddy.com.

60   See Caroline Brothers, 'Perceptions of Migration Clash with Reality, Report Finds', *New York Times*, 5 December 2011.

61   I borrow the phrase 'self-imposed "Rohingya problem" ' from the felicitous description of Nazi policies towards the Jewish population in Europe as responding to a 'self-imposed Jewish problem' offered by the historian Christopher Browning in *The Origins of the Final Solution: The Evolution of Nazi Jewish Policy, September 1939– March 1942* (Lincoln, NE: University of Nebraska Press, 2007).

62   See Bertil Lintner, *Outrage: Burma's Struggle for Democracy* (Hong Kong: Review, 1989), pp. 94–6.

13. A Long 'Caretaker Government'

1   See Bertil Lintner, *Outrage: Burma's Struggle for Democracy* (Hong Kong: Review, 1989), Chapter 1.

2   See Robert Taylor, *General Ne Win: A Political Biography* (Singapore: ISEAS, 2015), pp. 522–9.

3   See Christina Fink, *Living Silence in Burma: Surviving under Military Rule*, 2nd edn (London: Zed, 2009), pp. 54ff.

4   Several biographies of Aung San Suu Kyi have been published over the years. I have mostly relied on the most recent, Hans-Bernd Zöllner and Rodion Ebbighausen, *The Daughter: A Political Biography of Aung San Suu Kyi* (Chang Mai: Silkworm, 2018).

5   See Lintner, *Outrage*, pp. 164ff.

6   For a full transcript of the speech, see Khin Nyunt, *Burma Communist Party's Conspiracy to take over State Power*, Special Press Conference held on 5th August 1989 in Rangoon. Available online at ibiblio.org.

7 See Aung Zaw, 'Secrets of Commune 4828', *The Irrawaddy*, August 2008. Available online at irrawaddy.com.

8 Lintner, *Outrage*, pp. 203–4.

9 Martin Smith, 'Waving a White Flag? Problems of Burma's CP', *Inside Asia*, February–March 1986. Available online at burmalibrary.org.

10 Bertil Lintner, *The Rise and Fall of the Communist Party of Burma (CPB)* (Ithaca, NY: Cornell University Southeast Asia Program, 1990), p. 46.

11 For the view that it was already known by election day that the purpose was to elect a constituent assembly, see Derek Tonkin, 'The 1990 Elections in Myanmar: Broken Promises or a Failure of Communication?', *Contemporary Southeast Asia* 29: 1 (April 2007). For the opposite argument, see Bertil Lintner, 'The 1990 Election: Sorting Fact from Fiction', *Irrawaddy*, 20 October 2015. Available online at irrawaddy.com.

12 See Thein Tun, 'Experiences of Myanmar Privatisation Programme', in proceedings of *NAM Reform: Privatisation and Public-Private Partnership*, Brunei Darussalam, December 2002. Available online at csstc.org.

13 See Michele Ford, Michael Gillan and Htwe Htwe Thein, 'From Cronyism to Oligarchy? Privatisation and Business Elites in Myanmar', *Journal of Contemporary Asia* 46: 1 (2016).

14 See Burma Campaign UK, *TOTAL Oil: Fuelling the Oppression in Burma*, February 2005. Available online at burmacampaign.org.uk.

15 Amitav Ghosh, *Incendiary Circumstances: A Chronicle of the Turmoil of Our Times* (Boston, MA: Houghton Mifflin Harcourt, 2005), p. 183.

16 See Toshihiro Kudo, 'The Impact of US Sanctions on the Myanmar Garment Industry', *Asian Survey* 48: 6 (November 2008).

17 For a cogent and critical assessment of sanctions in Burma, see Lee Jones, *Societies Under Siege: Exploring How International Sanction (Do Not) Work* (Oxford: Oxford University Press, 2015), Chapter 3.

18 Ibid., p. 109.

19 See Andrew Selth, *Burma's Armed Forces: Power Without Glory* (Norwalk, CT: EastBridge, 2002), pp. 78–9.

20 Ibid., pp. 137–8.

21 Fink, *Living Silence in Burma*, p. 88.

22 Ibid., p. 123.

23 The full text of the speech appears in Aung San Suu Kyi, *Freedom from Fear and Other Writings*, ed. Michael Aris (London: Penguin, 1995).

24 Ibid., p. 141.

25 Quoted in Gustaaf Houtman, *Mental Culture in Burmese Crisis Politics: Aung San Suu Kyi and the National League for Democracy* (Tokyo: Tokyo University of Foreign Studies, 1999), p. 216.

26 Quoted in Zöllner and Ebbighausen, *The Daughter*, p. 119.

27 See Matthew J. Walton, *Buddhism, Politics and Political Thought in Myanmar* (Cambridge: Cambridge University Press, 2017).

28 'Suu Kyi: I Started as a Politician Not a Human Rights Defender', Democratic Voice of Burma, 29 October 2013. Available online at equalitymyanmar.org.

29 See Houtman, *Mental Culture in Burmese Crisis Politics*, Chapter 1.

30 Myanmar Ministry of Education, *History Textbook: Grade 6*, 2006. Quoted in Nicolas Salem-Gervais and Rosalie Metro, 'A Textbook Case of Nation-Building:

The Evolution of History Curricula in Myanmar', *Journal of Burma Studies* 16: 1 (June 2012).

31 See Houtman, *Mental Culture in Burmese Crisis Politics*, pp. 43–53.

32 Fink, *Living Silence in Burma*, p. 97.

33 Michael Aung-Thwin, 'From Rangoon to Pyinmana', *Bangkok Post*, 25 November 2005.

34 See above, Chapter 8, pp. 127–38.

35 Houtman, *Mental Culture in Burmese Crisis Politics*, pp. 88–9.

36 Ibid., p. 122.

37 See Bruce Matthews, 'Buddhism under a Military Regime: The Iron Heel in Burma', *Asian Survey* 33: 4 (April 1993).

38 Houtman, *Mental Culture in Burmese Crisis Politics*, p. 124.

39 See Chin Human Rights Organization, 'Threats to Our Existence': Persecution of Ethnic Chin Christians in Burma*, September 2012. Available online at burmacampaign.org.uk.

40 See the Department for the Promotion and Propagation of the Sanana's website: mora.gov.mm.

41 See Human Rights Watch, *Crackdown on Burmese Muslims*, Washington DC, July 2002. Available online at hrw.org.

42 See Andrew Selth, *Burma's Muslims: Terrorists or Terrorised?*, Canberra Papers on Strategy and Defence No. 150, Strategic and Defence Studies Centre, Australian National University, Canberra, 2003.

43 See 'Arakan Rohingya National Organization contacts with Al Qaeda and Burmese Insurgent Groups on the Thai Border', Confidential Cable 02RANGOON1310_a, 10 October 2002. Available online at wikileaks.org.

44 For a general overview, see Mary P. Callahan, *Political Authority in Burma's Ethnic Minority States: Devolution, Occupation and Coexistence*, Policy Studies 31 (Southeast Asia) (Washington, DC: East-West Center, 2007).

45 See Tom Kramer, *The United Wa State Party: Narco-Army or Ethnic Nationalist Party?* Policy Studies 38 (Southeast Asia) (Washington, DC: East-West Center, 2007).

46 See Kevin Woods, 'Ceasefire Capitalism: Military-Private Partnerships, Resource Concessions and Military-State Building in the Burma–China Borderlands', *Journal of Peasant Studies* 38: 4 (October 2011).

47 Selth, *Burma's Armed Forces*, p. 136.

48 Martin Smith, 'Reflections on the Kachin Ceasefire: A Cycle of Hope and Disappointment', in Mandy Sadan, ed., *War and Peace in the Borderlands of Myanmar: The Kachin Ceasefire, 1994–2011* (Copenhagen: NIAS, 2016), p. 65.

49 See ibid., pp. 64–9.

50 See Cheesman, 'How in Myanmar "National Races" Came to Surpass Citizenship and Exclude Rohingya'.

51 See Nyi Nyi Kyaw, 'Unpacking the Presumed Statelessness of Rohingyas', *Journal of Immigrant and Refugee Studies* 15: 3 (2017); and Cheesman, 'How in Myanmar "National Races" Came to Surpass Citizenship and Exclude Rohingya'.

52 See above, Chapter 6, pp. 91–104.

53 'Foreign Ministry Statement on Rohingya Muslims', BK2102154192, Rangoon Radio Burma in Burmese, 21 February 1992. Copy of English translation in the author's possession. My emphases. The statement also appears, with slight

differences in translation, in Amnesty International, *The Rohingya Minority: Fundamental Rights Denied*, May 2004, p. 3. Available online at amnesty.org.

54 See Radio Free Asia, 'Call to Put Rohingya in Refugee Camps', 12 July 2012. Available online at rfa.org.

55 Moshe Yegar, *Between Integration and Secession: The Muslim Communities of the Southern Philippines, Southern Thailand, and Western Burma/Myanmar* (Oxford: Lexington, 2002), p. 63.

56 See International Federation of Human Rights Leagues, *Burma: Repression, Discrimination and Ethnic Cleansing in Arakan*, April 2000. Available online at fidh.org.

57 Irish Centre for Human Rights, *Crimes against Humanity in Western Burma: The Situation of the Rohingyas* (Galway: National University of Ireland, 2010), p. 26. Available online at burmaactionireland.org.

58 UN Human Rights Council, 'Progress Report of the Special Rapporteur on the Situation of Human Rights in Myanmar, Tomás Ojea Quintana', 10 March 2010, p. 17. Available online at ohchr.org.

59 Arakan Project, *Issues to Be Raised Concerning the Situation of Stateless Rohingya Women in Myanmar (Burma)*, submission to the Committee on the Elimination of Discrimination Against Women, October 2008, p. 11. Available online at burmalibrary.org.

60 For this argument, see Maung Zarni and Alice Cowley, 'The Slow-Burning Genocide of Myanmar's Rohingya', *Pacific Rim Law & Policy Journal* 23: 3 (2014). Available online at digital.lib.washington.edu.

61 I visited some of those villages in Buthidaung in early 2016. For a useful description of the Na Ta La villages, with the caveat that it somewhat exaggerates the size and impact of the programme, see Francis Wade, *Myanmar's Enemy Within: Buddhist Violence and the Making of a Muslim 'Other'* (London: Zed, 2017), Chapter 5.

62 See Min Min and Moe Aung, 'The Welcome Migrants from Bangladesh', *Frontier Myanmar*, 23 September 2015. Available online at frontiermyanmar.net.

63 See Amnesty International, *'Caged Without a Roof': Apartheid in Myanmar's Rakhine State*, London, November 2017, p. 75. Available online at amnesty.org.

64 See David Dapice and Nguyen Xuan Thanh, *Creating a Future: Using Natural Resources for New Federalism and Unity*, Harvard Kennedy School, July 2013 – esp. 'Appendix A: Muslim Population Growth and Migration from Bangladesh into Rakhine State: What Do We Know?' Available online at ash.harvard.edu.

65 For a good analysis predicting this low growth before the census was conducted, see Thomas Spoorenberg, 'Demographic Changes in Myanmar since 1983: An Examination of Official Data', *Population and Development Review* 39: 2 (June 2013).

66 For a full analysis comparing the demographic growth of the Rohingya with that of other communities during the period, see Carlos Sardiña Galache, '"Illegal Migration" in Arakan: Myths and Numbers', *New Mandala*, 16 August 2018. Available online at newmandala.org.

67 See Su Phyo Win, 'Rakhine Migration Drains Residents of hope', *Myanmar Times*, 7 January 2016. Available online at mmtimes.com.

68 See, for example, University of Missouri-Columbia, 'Economics Influence Fertility Rates More than Other Factors', *ScienceDaily*, 30 April 2013. Available online at sciencedaily.com.

69 See Associated Press, 'Burmese Muslims Given Two-Child Limit', *Guardian*, 25 May 2013.

70 See Mary P. Callahan, 'Myanmar's Perpetual Junta', *New Left Review* II/60 (November–December 2009).
71 See Human Rights Watch, *Crackdown: Repression of the 2007 Popular Protests in Burma*, Washington, DC, 6 December 2007. Available online at hrw.org.
72 BBC News, 'Burma Toll At Least 31, UN Says', 7 December 2007. Available online at news.bbc.co.uk.

14. The Election

1 Clare Hammond, 'Revealed: NLD's Economic Plan', *Myanmar Times*, 18 August 2015. Available online at mmtimes.com.
2 Andrew R. C. Marshall and Timothy McLaughlin, 'Myanmar's Suu Kyi Says Will Be Above President in New Government', *Reuters*, 5 November 2015. Available online at reuters.com.
3 *Constitution of the Republic of the Union of Myanmar*, Printing and Publishing Enterprise, Ministry of Information, Myanmar, September 2008, Article 58, p. 19. Available online at burmalibrary.org.
4 See above, Chapter 1.
5 Thomas Fuller and Wai Moe, 'Woman Killed While Protesting Chinese Copper Mine in Myanmar', *New York Times*, 22 December 2014.
6 For a profile of Kaung San Hla, see Kayleigh E. Long, 'A Man of Many Letters', *Myanmar Times*, 25 November 2015. Available online at mmtimes.com.
7 'NLD Cofounder Tin Oo Plays to Rakhine Fears', *Frontier Myanmar*, 3 November 2015. Available online at frontiermyanmar.net.
8 Personal communication with Cheery Zahau, Rangoon, December 2015. See also Charlotte England, 'Female Candidates Face Fierce, Unfair Fight in Myanmar's Elections', *Guardian*, 5 November 2015; and Oliver Slow, 'Cheery Zahau: "I Grew Up with a Very Strong Sense that Something Was Wrong for the Chin People"', *Frontier Myanmar*. Available online at frontiermyanmar.net.
9 Ye Mon, 'UEC Cancels Voting in Two More Shan Townships', *Myanmar Times*, 28 October 2015. Available online at mmtimes.com.
10 See Enlightened Myanmar Research, *Important Data of 2015 General Election Myanmar*, October 2015. Available online at themimu.info.
11 For a profile of Ja Seng Hkawn, see Thin Lei Win, 'A Kachin Leader's Legacy Lives on through His Daughter', *Myanmar Now*, 25 January 2016. Available online at mizzima.com.
12 Only 75 per cent of the seats are contested, as the Constitution reserves 25 per cent of the seats in each house of parliament for soldiers appointed by the military.
13 Oliver Holmes, 'Final Myanmar Results Show Aung San Suu Kyi's Party Won 77% of Seats', *Guardian*, 23 November 2015.
14 See Ardeth Thawnghmung, 'The Myanmar Elections 2015: Why the National League for Democracy Won a Landslide Victory', *Critical Asian Studies* 48: 1 (2016).

15. 'The Lady' in Power

1 Htoo Thant, '"State Counsellor" Bill Approved Despite Military Voting Boycott', *Myanmar Times*, 5 April 2016. Available online at mmtimes.com.

2 Aung Hla Tung and Hnin Yadana Zaw, 'Myanmar's Ex-Dictator Sees Suu Kyi as Country's "Future Leader": Relative', *Reuters*, 5 December 2015. Available online at reuters.com.

3 Gardiner Harris, 'Obama Lifts Some Sanctions against Myanmar', *New York Times*, 2 December 2016.

4 See Lun Min Mang, Aung Shin, Thomas Kean and Laignee Barron, 'Who's Who: Myanmar's New Cabinet', *Myanmar Times*, 23 March 2016. Available online at mmtimes.com.

5 See Hnin Yadana Zaw and Antoni Slodkowski, 'Myanmar Military Chooses Hardliner to Work with Suu Kyi's Proxy President', *Reuters*, 11 March 2016. Available online at reuters.com.

6 See Htet Naing Zaw, 'Aung San Suu Kyi Woos Tycoons in Naypyidaw Meet-up', *Irrawaddy*, 24 October 2016. Available online at irrawaddy.com.

7 See 'Exclusive: Success Is Determined by How Dispensable I Can Make Myself, Says Suu Kyi', Channel News Asia, 8 December 2016. Available online at channelnewsasia.com.

8 See Su Myat Mon and Nyan Hlaing Lynn, '"Strong and Decisive": Meet Myanmar's New President', Frontier Myanmar, 28 March 2018. Available online at frontiermyanmar.net.

9 See Ei Ei Toe Lwin, 'NLD "Iron Rules" Stifle New Parliamentarians', *Myanmar Times*, 25 April 2016. Available online at mmtimes.com.

10 See Poppy McPherson, 'Aung San Suu Kyi: Myanmar's Great Hope Fails to Live Up to Expectations', *Guardian*, 31 March 2017.

11 See Zoltan Barany, 'Burma: Suu Kyi's Missteps', *Journal of Democracy* 29: 1 (January 2018).

12 See Elliott Prasse-Freeman, 'The New Burma Is Starting to Look Too Much Like the Old Burma', *Foreign Policy*, 28 June 2016.

13 Antoni Slodkowski, 'New Myanmar Government Proposes Keeping Some Junta Curbs on Protests', *Reuters*, 13 May 2016. Available online at reuters.com.

14 On the Aung San Suu Kyi administration's earlier peace efforts, see Transnational Institute, *Beyond Panglong: Myanmar's National Peace and Reform Dilemma*, TNI–BCN Burma Policy Briefing No. 21, 19 September 2017, pp. 26ff. Available online at tni.org.

15 Shwe Yee Saw Myint and Antoni Slodkowski, 'Myanmar's Suu Kyi Kicks Off Peace Conference with Appeal for Unity', *Reuters*, 31 August 2016. Available online at reuters.com.

16 Ei Ei Toe Lwin and Pyae Thet Phyo, 'UWSA Pulls Out of Panglong', *Myanmar Times*, 1 September 2016. Available online at mmtimes.com.

17 Hannah Beech, 'Aung San Suu Kyi Seeks Elusive Peace in Burma with Panglong Summit', *Time*, 31 August 2016.

18 Not counting the Arakan Rohingya Salvation Army, whose emergence I will discuss in the Chapter 16.

19 See Bobby Anderson, 'Stalemate and Suspicion: An Appraisal of the Myanmar Peace Process', *Tea Circle Oxford*, 6 June 2018. Available online at teacircleoxford.com.

20 See Amnesty International, *Myanmar: 'All the Civilians Suffer': Conflict, Displacement, and Abuse in Northern Myanmar*, 14 June 2017. Available online at amnesty.org.

21 See 'Skirmish Breaks out in KNU Brigade 5 Area amid 21st Century Panglong Conference', *Karen News*. Available online at karennews.org.

22 See Matthew J. Walton, 'Has the NLD Learned Nothing about Ethnic Concerns?', *Tea Circle Oxford*, 29 March 2017. Available online at teacircleoxford.com.

23 See Nan Lwin Hnin Pwint, 'Karenni Halt Protests against General Aung San Statue', *Irrawaddy*, 25 July 2018. Available online at irrawaddy.com. See also Zarni Mann, 'Naga Youth Oppose Aung San Statue in Sagaing', *Irrawaddy*, 13 July 2018. Available online at irrawaddy.com.

24 See Matthew J. Walton, 'What the State Sangha Committee Actually Said about Ma Ba Tha', *Tea Circle Oxford*, 29 July 2016. Available online at teacircleoxford.com.

25 See International Crisis Group, *Buddhism and State Power in Myanmar*, Asia Report No. 290, Yangon/Brussels, 5 September 2017, pp. 16–17. Available online at crisis-group.org.

26 See Burma Human Rights Network, 'BHRN Publishes Research Revealing State-Led Persecution of Burma's Muslim Minority', 5 September 2017. Available online at bhrn.org.uk.

27 Wai Moe, 'U Ko Ni, a Prominent Muslim Lawyer in Myanmar, Is Fatally Shot', *New York Times*, 29 January 2017.

28 See Melissa Crouch, 'A Personal Tribute to U Ko Ni', *New Mandala*, 31 January 2017. Available online at newmandala.org.

29 See Wai Moe, Mike Ives and Saw Nang, 'Brazen Killing of Myanmar Lawyer Came after He Sparred with Military', *New York Times*, 2 February 2017.

30 See 'U Wirathu Takes to Social Media to Thank Suspects in U Ko Ni's Murder', *Irrawaddy*, 1 March 2017. Available online at irrawaddy.com.

31 See Roseanne Gerin, 'Myanmar Journalist Charged with Defamation Refuses to Apologize to Firebrand Monk', Radio Free Asia, 13 February 2018. Available online at rfa.org.

16. 'An Unfinished Job'

1 See Austin Ramzy, 'After Myanmar Election, Few Signs of a Better Life for Muslims', *New York Times*, 18 November 2015.

2 See Brooks Boliek, 'Death Toll Rises in Myanmar Boat Accident', *Radio Free Asia*, 20 April 2016. Available online at rfa.org.

3 See Richard C. Paddock, 'Aung San Suu Kyi Asks US Not to Refer to "Rohingya"', *New York Times*, 6 May 2016.

4 Swe Win, 'Nationalist Buddhists Protest at US Embassy against Its Use of Word "Rohingya"', *Myanmar Now*, 29 April 2016. Available online at mizzima.com.

5 Lesley Wroughton, 'Suu Kyi Calls for "Space" to Address Myanmar's Rohingya Issue as Kerry Visits', Reuters, 22 May 2016. Available online at reuters.com.

6 See 'Myanmar Bans Officials from Saying "Rohingya"', *Agence France-Presse*, 22 June 2016. Available online at aljazeera.com.

7 See Poppy McPherson, 'Inside the "Glaringly Dysfunctional" UN Mission in Myanmar', IRIN News, 17 July 2017. Available online at irinnews.org.

8   See official announcement in 'Govt Forms Committee to Implement Peace, Stability, Development in Rakhine State', President's Office of the Republic of the Union of Myanmar, Naypyidaw, 31 May 2016. Available online at president-office.gov.mm.

9   See official announcement in 'Establishment of the Advisory Commission on Rakhine State', Ministry of the Office of the State Counsellor, Naypyidaw, 23 August 2016. Available online at statecounsellor.gov.mm.

10 For an excerpt of the speech, see 'Daw Aung San Suu Kyi, State Counsellor: Viewpoint', Oxford Business Group, September 2016. Available online at oxford-businessgroup.com.

11 See Richard Horsey, 'Myanmar Border Attacks Fuel Tensions with Rohingya Muslim Minority', International Crisis Group, 12 October 2016. Available online at crisis-group.org.

12 See, for example, 'Press Release Regarding the Attacks on the Border Guard Police Posts in Maungdaw Township, 13 October 2016, English Translation', Myanmar President's Office, 14 October 2016. Available online at facebook.com/myanmar-presidentoffice.gov.mm/posts/1113520795362322.

13 See, for example, 'Pakistan, ISIS Allegedly behind Rakhine Imbroglio', Mizzima News, 5 September 2016. Available online at mizzima.com.

14 See 'Friend or Foe? Ata Ullah, the Man Behind Myanmar's Deadly Rohingya Insurgency', Agence France-Presse, 24 September 2017. Available online at japantimes.co.jp.

15 See United Nations Office of the High Commissioner for Human Rights, Flash Report of OHCHR mission to Bangladesh: Interviews with Rohingyas Fleeing from Myanmar since 9 October 2016, 3 February 2017. Available online at ohchr.org.

16 See Wa Lone, 'Myanmar Sends Hundreds of Troops to Rakhine as Tension Rises: Sources', Reuters, 11 August 2017. Available online at reuters.com.

17 See Shoon Naing, 'Exclusive: Rohingya Villagers Blockaded amid Fresh Tensions in Myanmar's Rakhine – Residents', Reuters, 22 August 2017. Available online at reuters.com.

18 See ARSA statement released on Twitter on 25 August 2017, 'Statement 2: Current Unrest Triggerred [sic] by Burmese Military to Derail @KofiAnnan Commission Report on Arakan State'. Available online at twitter.com/ARSA_Official/status/900904120076435457.

19 See ARSA statement released on Twitter on 25 August 2017, 'Urgent Statement: #Arakan State Situation'. Available online at twitter.com/ARSA_Official/status/900877804425932800.

20 See Simon Lewis, Zeba Siddiqui, Clare Baldwin and Andrew R. C. Marshall, 'Tip of the Spear: The Shock Troops Who Expelled the Rohingya from Myanmar', Reuters, 26 June 2018. Available online at reuters.com.

21 See Human Rights Watch, 'Burma: New Satellite Images Confirm Mass Destruction', 17 October 2017. Available online at hrw.org.

22 See Jared Ferrie and Annie Banerji, ' "Lost Generation" Looms for Rohingya Refugee Children without Education', Reuters, 23 August 2018. Available online at reuters.com.

23 See Médecins Sans Frontières, 'MSF Surveys Estimate that at Least 6,700 Rohingya Were Killed During the Attacks in Myanmar', 12 December 2017. Available online at msf.org.

24 See Mohshin Hamid, Christine A. Jubb, Salahuddin Ahmad and Masudur Rahman, *Forced Migration of Rohingya: The Untold Experience*, Ontario International Development Agency, Ottawa, August 2018. Available online at researchgate.net.

25 See Clare Baldwin, 'The Rohingya Lists: Refugees Compile Their Own Record of Those Killed in Myanmar', Reuters, 17 August 2018. Available online at reuters. com.

26 For the massacre in Tula Toli, see Human Rights Watch, *Massacre by the River: Burmese Army Crimes against Humanity in Tula Toli*, Washington, DC, 19 December 2017. Available online at hrw.org. Among the reports on human rights violations and crimes against humanity committed during the clearance operations in August and September 2017, see Amnesty International, *'We Will Destroy Everything': Military Responsibility for Crimes Against Humanity in Rakhine State, Myanmar*, London, June 2018. Available online at amnesty.org. See also Fortify Rights, *'They Gave Them Long Swords': Preparations for Genocide and Crimes Against Humanity Against Rohingya Muslims in Rakhine State, Myanmar*, 19 July 2018. Available online at fortifyrights.org.

27 For the concept of 'genocidal massacre', see Leo Kuper, *Genocide: Its Political Use in the Twentieth Century* (London: Penguin, 1981), p. 32.

28 For a full transcription of the speech, see 'Speech Delivered by Her Excellency Daw Aung San Suu Kyi, State Counsellor of the Republic of the Union of Myanmar on Government's Efforts with Regard to National Reconciliation and Peace', Naypyidaw, 19 September 2017. Available online at myanmarembassydhaka.com.

29 See Jonah Fisher, 'Hounded and Ridiculed for Complaining of Rape', BBC News, 11 March 2017. Available online at bbc.com.

30 She condemned sexual violence at the hands of the Tatmadaw in a video message sent to 'Women Forging a New Security: Ending Sexual Violence in Conflict', a conference held in Canada in May 2011. The video is available on YouTube, at youtube.com/watch?v=SOHEosj-M5U.

31 See Karen Women Organization, 'KWO Message: On-Going Use of Rape by Burma Army', 5 December 2015. Available online at karenwomen.org.

32 See John Geddie and Fathin Ungku, 'Myanmar's Suu Kyi Says Relations with Military "Not That Bad"', Reuters, 21 August 2018. Available online at reuters.com.

33 See Wa Lone, Kyaw Soe Oo, Simon Lewis and Antoni Slodkowski, 'Massacre in Myanmar: How Myanmar Forces Burned, Looted and Killed in a Remote Village', Reuters, 8 February 2018. Available online at reuters.com.

34 See Hannah Ellis-Petersen, 'Aung San Suu Kyi on Reuters Jailing: Show Me the Miscarriage of Justice', *Guardian*, 13 September 2018.

35 See Simon Lewis and Shoon Naing, 'Two Reuters Reporters Freed in Myanmar After More than 500 Days in Jail', Reuters, 7 May 2019. Available online at reuters. com.

36 See Shoon Naing and Simon Lewis, 'Exclusive: Myanmar Soldiers Jailed for Rohingya Killings Freed After Less than a Year', Reuters, 27 May 2019. Available online at reuters.com.

37 See Stephanie Nebehay, 'UN Sees "Textbook Example of Ethnic Cleansing" in Myanmar', Reuters, 11 September 2017. Available online at reuters.com.

38 See United Nations Human Rights Council, *Report of the Independent International Fact-Finding Mission on Myanmar*, Geneva, 27 August 2018. Available online at ap.ohchr.org.

39 See Pre-Trial Chamber of the International Criminal Court, *Decision on the 'Prosecution's Request for a Ruling on Jurisdiction under Article 19(3) of the Statute'*, ICC-RoC46(3)-01/18-37, Geneva, 6 September 2018. Available online at icc-cpi.int.

40 See 'Facebook Ban on Army Chief Silences Myanmar's Military Mouthpiece', Reuters, 27 August 2018. Available online at reuters.com.

41 See John Geddie, 'Myanmar Official Says "Totally Underestimated" Economic Impact of Rohingya Crisis', Reuters, 5 September 2018. Available online at reuters.com.

42 For a full translation of the sermon, see Paul Fuller, 'Sitagu Sayadaw's Mahavamsa Sermon', 11 August 2018. Available online at paulfullerbuddhiststudies.wordpress.com.

43 Ibid.

44 See Paul Fuller, 'Sitagu Sayadaw and Justifiable Evils in Buddhism', New Mandala, 13 November 2017. Available online at newmandala.org.

17. After the Ethnic Cleansing

1   See Moe Myint, 'Ninety Per Cent of Rohingya Population Ejected from Rakhine', *Irrawaddy*, 23 February 2018. Available online at irrawaddy.com.

2   See Htun Khaing, 'Resettling Rakhine "In Their Native Land"', Frontier Myanmar, 25 April 2018. Available online at frontiermyanmar.net.

3   See Moe Myint, 'Settling Scores in Northern Rakhine', *Irrawaddy*, 14 December 2017. Available online at irrawaddy.com.

4   See Agence France-Presse, 'Buddhists "Lured" to Settle on Rohingya Land', 2 April 2018. Available online at aljazeera.com.

5   See Human Rights Watch, 'Burma: Scores of Rohingya Villages Bulldozed', 23 February 2018. Available online at hrw.org.

6   See Shoon Naing, 'Bulldozing Rohingya Villages Was Not "Demolition of Evidence", Myanmar Official Says', Reuters, 26 February 2018. Available online at reuters.com.

7   See Amnesty International, 'Myanmar: Military Land Grab as Security Forces Build Bases on Torched Rohingya Villages', 12 March 2018. Available online at amnesty. org.

8   See Simon Lewis, 'Government Will Take Over Burned Myanmar Land: Minister', Reuters, 27 September 2017. Available online at reuters.com.

9   See Chan Mya Htwe, 'Rakhine to Construct Maungdaw Economic Zone', *Myanmar Times*, 1 September 2017. Available online at mmtimes.com.

10 See Ben Dunant, 'Tycoons on the Frontline of Rakhine Reconstruction', Voice of America, 23 January 2018. Available online at voanews.com.

11 For an instance of this kind of argument, see Saskia Sassen, 'Is Rohingya Persecution Caused by Business Interests Rather than Religion?', *Guardian*, 4 January 2017. For a well-argued critique of this approach, see Lee Jones, 'A Better Political Economy of the Rohingya Crisis', New Mandala, 26 September 2017. Available online at newmandala.org.

12 See Mratt Kyaw Thu, 'At Least Eight Killed in Mrauk U Clashes', Frontier Myanmar, 17 January 2018. Available online at frontiermyanmar.net.

13 See Min Aung Khine, 'Rakhine Political Leader Faces High Treason, Defamation Charges', *Irrawaddy*, 10 September 2018. Available online at irrawaddy.com.

14 See '13 Policemen Die in Rakhine Rebel Attacks,' *The Straits Times*, 5 January 2019. Available online at straitstimes.com.

15 See Kyaw Lwin Oo and Khin Khin, 'Myanmar Army Helicopter, Artillery Strikes Force Hundreds to Flee in Rakhine State,' 21 June 2019, Radio Free Asia. Available online at rfa.org.

16 See 'End of mission statement mission to Thailand and Malaysia,' United Nations Special Rapporteur on the situation of human rights in Myanmar, Kuala Lumpur, 18 July 2019. Available online at ohchr.org.

17 See Anthony Davis, 'Why Myanmar is Losing the Rakhine War,' Asia Times, 3 July 2019. Available online at asiatimes.com.

18 See Oliver Holmes, 'Myanmar Signs Pact with Bangladesh over Rohingya Repatriation', *Guardian*, 23 November 2017.

19 See 'UN and Myanmar Agree Outline of Rohingya Return Deal, No Details', Reuters, 31 May 2018. Available online at reuters.com.

20 See Poppy McPherson and Zeba Siddiqui, 'Secret UN–Myanmar Deal on Rohingya Offers No Guarantees on Citizenship', Reuters, 30 June 2018. Available online at reuters.com.

21 See Ministry of Foreign Affairs of Bangladesh, 'Physical Arrangement for Rohingya Return Finalized', Relief Web, 16 January 2018. Available online at reliefweb.int.

22 See United Nations Human Rights Council, *Oral Update of the High Commissioner for Human Rights on Situation of Human Rights of Rohingya People*, Geneva, 3 July 2018. Available online at ohchr.org.

23 See Min Thein Aung, 'Myanmar Officials Show Refugee Processing Centers to Ambassadors, UN Agencies', Radio Free Asia, 15 February 2018. Available online at rfa.org.

24 See Mark Inkey, 'The Nightmare Awaiting Rohingya Returnees', *Diplomat*, 19 September 2018.

25 See United Nations Office for the Coordination of Humanitarian Affairs website on the 'Rohingya Crisis', at unocha.org.

26 See Clare Baldwin and Andrew R. C. Marshall, 'Rohingya Refugees Test Bangladeshi Welcome as Prices Rise and Repatriation Stalls', Reuters, 28 February 2018. Available online at reuters.com.

27 See Ahmar Shahbazi, 'Bangladesh Drugs Gangs Exploit Rohingya Refugees', *Nikkei Asian Review*, 5 May 2018.

28 See 'Bangladesh Says It Won't Assimilate Rohingya Muslims', Reuters, 12 September 2018. Available online at uk.reuters.com.

29 For an analysis of UNHCR policies and culture, see Guglielmo Verdirame and Barbara Harrell-Bond, *Rights in Exile: Janus-Faced Humanitarianism* (London: Berghahn, 2005).

30 Ibid.

31 See Ruma Paul, Clare Baldwin and Andrew R. C. Marshall, 'Floating Island: New Home for Rohingya Refugees Emerges in Bay of Bengal', Reuters, 22 February 2018. Available online at reuters.com.

32 See Hannah Arendt, *The Origins of Totalitarianism* (New York: Harcourt Books, 1976), p. 296.

33 See ARSA Press release on Twitter, dated 10 September 2017, at twitter.com/ARSA_Official/status/906570961985658880.

34 See Zeba Siddiqui and Ruma Paul, 'Killings Sow Fear Inside Rohingya Refugee Camps in Bangladesh', Reuters, 4 July 2018. Available online at reuters.com.

35 See Radio Free Asia, 'At Least 22 Rohingya Slain in Refugee Camps in 11 Months: Bangladeshi Police', Radio Free Asia, 16 July 2018. Available online at rfa.org.

36 See Amnesty International, 'Myanmar: New Evidence Reveals Rohingya Armed Group Massacred Scores in Rakhine State', 22 May 2018. Available online at amnesty. org.

37 See Fortify Rights, '*They Gave Them Long Swords*', pp. 76–80.

38 See Antoni Slodkowski, 'Exclusive: Rohingya Rebel Leader Challenges Myanmar's Suu Kyi, Vows to Fight On', Reuters, 31 March 2017. Available online at reuters.com.

39 See Adil Sakhawat, 'Exclusive: ARSA Open to Surrender, but Only Under UN Supervision', *Dhaka Tribune*, 21 October 2017. Available online at dhakatribune. com.

40 'Influx virus' is taken from the title of an anti-Rohingya screed coauthored by the prominent Rakhine historian Aye Chan. See U Shw Zan and Dr. Aye Chan, *Influx Viruses: The Illegal Muslims in Arakan* (New York: Arakanese in United States, 2005).

Conclusion: The Failure of Burmese Nationalism

1 See, for example, Kyaw Min, 'Why Not Rohingya an Antiquity? [Part 2]: An Assessment on Rohingyas' Genuineness', Rohingya Blogger, 30 April 2014. Available online at rohingyagenocide.net.

2 One of the most conspicuous defenders of this line of argument is the retired British diplomat Derek Tonkin. See, for example, his 'Exploring the Issue of Citizenship in Rakhine State', in Ashley South and Mary Lall, eds, *Citizenship in Myanmar: Ways of Being in and from Burma*, (Chiang Mai: ISEAS Singapore and Chiang Mai University Press, 2017).

3 See Étienne Balibar and Immanuel Wallerstein, *Race, Nation, Class: Ambiguous Identities* (London: Verso, 1991), p. 89.

4 Here is worthy reminding that, according to the 2014 census, 27 per cent of the population above ten years of age lack any legal document. See ch. 5, pp. 75–90.

5 See Gustavo Bueno, *España frente a Europa*, (Bercelona: Alba Editorial, 1999), p. 405. Here, as in subsequent citations, the translation from the original Spanish is mine.

6 Ibid, p. 406.

7 Ibid, p. 408.

Index